10/3/11
#94.00

Aboriginal Title
and Indigenous Peoples

Law and Society Series
W. Wesley Pue, General Editor

The Law and Society Series explores law as a socially embedded phenomenon. It is premised on the understanding that the conventional division of law from society creates false dichotomies in thinking, scholarship, educational practice, and social life. Books in the series treat law and society as mutually constitutive and seek to bridge scholarship emerging from interdisciplinary engagement of law with disciplines such as politics, social theory, history, political economy, and gender studies.

A list of the titles in this series appears at the end of this book.

Edited by Louis A. Knafla and Haijo Westra

Aboriginal Title and Indigenous Peoples: Canada, Australia, and New Zealand

UBCPress · Vancouver · Toronto

20 19 18 17 16 15 14 13 12 11 10   5 4 3 2 1

Printed in Canada on FSC-certified ancient-forest-free paper (100% post-consumer
recycled) that is processed chlorine- and acid-free.

Library and Archives Canada Cataloguing in Publication .

   Aboriginal title and indigenous peoples : Canada, Australia, and New Zealand /
edited by Louis A. Knafla and Haijo Westra.

(Law and society, ISSN 1496-4953)
Includes bibliographical references and index.
ISBN 978-0-7748-1560-4

   1. Aboriginal title – Canada. 2. Native title (Australia). 3. Maori (New Zealand
people) – Land tenure. 4. Native peoples – Legal status, laws, etc. – Canada.
5. Indigenous peoples – Legal status, laws, etc. – Australia. 6. Maori (New Zealand
people) – Legal status, laws, etc. I. Knafla, Louis A., 1935- II. Westra, Haijo Jan,
1947- III. Series: Law and society series (Vancouver, B.C.)

KE7739.L3A265 2010   346.7104'3208997   C2010-900142-7
KF8224.L2A265 2010

Canadä

UBC Press gratefully acknowledges the financial support for our publishing program
of the Government of Canada (through the Canada Book Fund), the Canada Council
for the Arts, and the British Columbia Arts Council.

This book has been published with the help of a grant from the Canadian Federation
for the Humanities and Social Sciences, through the Aid to Scholarly Publications
Programme, using funds provided by the Social Sciences and Humanities Research
Council of Canada.

UBC Press
The University of British Columbia
2029 West Mall
Vancouver, BC V6T 1Z2
www.ubcpress.ca

Contents

Aboriginal Title
and Indigenous Peoples

"This Is Our Land": Aboriginal Title at Customary and Common Law in Comparative Contexts

Louis A. Knafla

The history of Aboriginal (Native) title is one of the most significant topics of legal-historical scholarship. The commonality of the chapters that comprise this book is that they explore the issues of Aboriginal title in relatively similar time frames and under comparable common law regimes.[1] Conflict over land between indigenous peoples and colonizers took place in the second half of the nineteenth century in all three regions: the western half of Canada, Australia, and New Zealand. Although each region developed differently, the issues remained the same to the end of the twentieth century and beyond as Aboriginals faced mass immigration and institutional and ideological intolerance. These issues included how the land was settled, what use could be made of it by whom, what rights Aboriginals had at customary and common law, how their voices were made known by word and action, how their title was expropriated and extinguished, who spoke for whom in this process, and the consequences of the legal disputes and settlements that emerged. From the 1760s on, an era of confrontation over Native rights and title has been in play in all three countries. Promoting special relationships, shared power, and self-determination, Aboriginals have become proactive in regaining their status as distinct peoples. Although they have gained citizenship since the 1970s, their political rights are still fragile and subordinate to the crown.

As noted Aboriginal rights lawyer Peter Hutchins has explained, in Canada Native-state conflicts over rights and interests in land are fought in the courts, where history and state power often come into conflict and where there is a notion that the crown can do no wrong.[2] The role of the crown, however, has not been consistent. It has acted both as protector and as destroyer of Aboriginal rights; it has treated with some indigenous peoples and not with others; and it has used natural and international law, as well as common law, to serve its political interests of the moment.[3] Prime Minister Pierre Trudeau stated in 1969 that there was neither Aboriginal title nor rights; indigenous or non-indigenous, we are all Canadians.[4] In the *Calder* case, which Hutchins suggests was the beginning of our "Thirty Years War" in 1973, the Supreme Court of Canada (SCC) held that Aboriginal peoples have rights, but half of the judges stated that they had been extinguished.[5] Later, in the 1990s, the crown recognized that not all of those rights had been extinguished and that it had an obligation to negotiate Aboriginal land claims in good faith.[6] Negotiations, however, have been troublesome, and litigation has been hugely time consuming and expensive. Problems of recognizing national and provincial borders, interpreting old proclamations and treaties, and accepting oral history as proof have complicated the litigation process. The congested and costly cases that have ensued, with long lists of witnesses and expert witnesses, have placed the burden of change in the hands of courts not wholly adept at dealing with such issues.

The chapters in this book contribute to the analysis, dialogue, and understanding of Aboriginal title in these three British regimes within a comparative context that has been developed in major studies of the past decade,[7] in the volumes of essays on indigenous peoples' rights edited by Paul Havemann in 1999[8] and by Benjamin Richardson, Shin Imai, and Kent McNeil in 2009,[9] and in the major detailed history of Aboriginal sovereignty and status in British settler colonies by Paul McHugh in 2004.[10] This introductory chapter simply prepares the reader for the issues that are discussed by the authors in the following chapters and introduces the major themes that each author brings to the study of Aboriginal title in Australia, Canada, and New Zealand, with reference to those issues in the United States.

This introduction is organized as follows. First, it defines the history of Aboriginal title at customary and common law, from pre- to postcontact eras, including major cases in all three countries. Second, it summarizes the major themes in each of the chapters, which are divided into two parts: "Sovereignty, Extinguishment, and Expropriation of Aboriginal Title" and "Aboriginal Land, Litigation, and Indigenous Rights." Third, it brings those themes together in their comparative contexts and concludes with the voices of the indigenous peoples who are at the centre of the battleground in these legal contests and whose lives have the most to gain or lose from the outcomes.

Australia

The term *"terra nullius"* ("land without owners"), at the centre of concepts of imperial sovereignty that denied Native title in the nineteenth century, was not actually part of Australian legal discourse until the twentieth century, but that in fact was how the continent was treated.[11] Some would argue that this treatment was part of a historical accident. When Captain James Cook sailed up the east coast of Australia in 1770 with Sir Joseph Banks, Banks thought that the few Aborigines he saw had no economic enterprise and that most of the continent was uninhabited. But when Cook considered a settlement at Nootka Sound on the west coast of what is now British

Columbia in 1790, he saw commercial possibilities and said that he must have agreements with the Natives.[12]

The *Mabo* and *Delgamuukw* cases have set the framework for litigating Aboriginal title in Australia, Canada, and New Zealand.[13] In *Mabo v. Queensland (No. 2)*, decided in the High Court of Australia (HCA) in 1992 after a decade of litigation, Eddie Koiki Mabo was a Torres Strait Islander who fought for the premise that the Meriam people in the Murray Islands had a system of land ownership before European colonization.[14] European settlers saw Melanesian fishers and gardeners as hunters rather than occupiers. Although Queensland enacted legislation that purported to extinguish the land rights of Torres Strait Islanders, that legislation was held invalid in *Mabo (No. 1)* in 1988 because it conflicted with the *Racial Discrimination Act* (1975) as well as Australia's ratification of the *United Nations Convention on the Elimination of Racial Discrimination*.[15] Although Mabo died just before the court's verdict, no compensation was awarded. The order of the court by Chief Justice Brennan (who gave one of five opinions) was that the Meriam people are entitled to possession, occupation, and use against the whole world – which established a new template for Aboriginal land rights.

According to Henry Reynolds, the noted scholar who discussed the history of the islanders with Eddie Mabo from the late 1970s on, the decision was a legal revolution.[16] It was tempered, however, by the court's opinion that, although the Meriam people had the authority to possess and use the islands, Queensland had the right to extinguish their title as long as the state adhered to the laws of the Australian Commonwealth.[17] It is interesting to note that the *Mabo* case was influenced by Canada's *Calder* case of 1973. Lawyers from the two countries exchanged views and arguments. Justice Blackburn cited the Court of Appeal decision in the *Calder* case in denying title in *Milirrpum v. Nabalco Pty. Ltd.*,[18] but the HCA cited the SCC in overruling Blackburn's judgment as "wholly wrong" in *Mabo (No. 2)*. Conversely, when the SCC decided the *Delgamuukw* case on appeal, it cited *Mabo (No. 2)*.[19]

In the nineteenth century, as Aborigines continued to be denied rights to real property in Australia, British colonial officials such as James Stephen were able to secure their right to testify in criminal cases as British subjects even if they had to disallow state legislation to the contrary.[20] This small window of opportunity – recognizing Aboriginals as "persons," as British subjects and not indigenous peoples with their own sovereignty and full equality – lasted only a few decades throughout the British Empire from the 1820s to the 1850s.[21] But even here the evangelical Aborigines Protection Society was unable to see Aborigines as indigenous peoples. Thus, settlers, under the cloak of law and order in the second half of the century, decimated the Aborigines and enclosed the survivors in "stations" across the continent under the guise of "protection."[22] Between 1897 and 1910, the various states brought in protection legislation in the belief that Aborigines would soon die. By the late 1930s, it was clear that they would not, and thus a policy of assimilation was adopted that became state policy until the political resistance of the late 1960s.

The state's legal recognition of Aboriginal title in Australia, post-*Mabo*, depends on proving traditional laws and customs. This proof, however, as Kent McNeil explains, is onerous: one must prove use, laws, and customs continuously, and customs have to be translated into rights in law. There is also no room for expanding those rights for commercial purposes (as in mining or the discovery of oil and gas) or for self-government. The *Mabo* decision was followed by the *Native Title Act* of 1993 that validated previous land grants and authorized the states to do the same. It also established a National Native Title Tribunal to mediate application by Aborigines to recognize their title and an Indigenous Land Fund to provide compensation where their title had been extinguished. The crown, however, remains supreme as it can over-rule decisions of the tribunal.[23]

In *Wik Peoples v. Queensland* (1996), the HCA held that Aboriginal title was not necessarily extinguished by pastoral leases.[24] Afterward, the federal government's Ten Point Plan of 1998 provided for the coexistence of Native title and pastoral leases with processes for settling Native title claims in the states.[25] But in *Western Australia v. Ward and Others* (2002), the High Court held that the *Native Title Act* mandated partial and permanent extinguishments of Aboriginal title.[26] Given over 500 communities and 170 language groups (Aborigines comprise some 2 percent of the population),[27] Native title law remains central to Australia's recent legal history.[28]

Many other issues involving Aboriginal title, however, have remained unresolved. Some of these issues have been litigated in cases after *Mabo* and *Wik*. For example, in *Fejo v. Northern Territory* in 1998, the High Court held that Native title had been extinguished totally and forever by grants of freehold title.[29] In *Yanner v. Eaton* (HCA 1999), the right of Aborigines to control their resources, as in hunting, was upheld as part of their property rights even though it was regulated by the state.[30] In *Commonwealth v. Yarmirr* (HCA 2001), called the "*Mabo* of the seas," Native title rights to the seabed out to twelve nautical miles was confirmed but not to the extent of exclusive possession and use, which would conflict with the sovereignty of the state.[31] In *Western Australia v. Ward* (HCA 2002), the process for adjudicating interests in land that extinguish partially or fully Native title under the *Native Title Act* was clarified.[32] Holding that indigenous and non-indigenous interests could coexist, and pleading for negotiated settlements to resolve such issues, the court also reversed earlier rights won by the Miriuwung Gajerrong and allowed the extinguishment of title rights considered "inconsistent" with traditional rights created by crown grant.[33] Unlike in Canada and New Zealand, Aboriginal customs in Australia were superseded in part by the expansion of public commercial rights.[34]

This situation set the stage that year for the *Yorta Yorta* decision, which has been thoroughly explored by Bruce Rigsby, in which the HCA held that an interruption or discrepancy in the history of an Aboriginal group's law or custom could be fatal to its title. The extent to which a group had the continuity necessary for a successful claim was addressed by the Federal Court of Australia (FCA) in *De Rose v. South Australia (No. 2)* in 2005, in which a short absence coupled with intimidation did not extinguish non-exclusive rights.[35] This case was influenced by *Neowarra v. Western Australia* (FCA 2003-4), in which the court upheld a mixture of exclusive and coexisting rights of several indigenous groups over 7,226 square kilometres from a wide range of anthropological, archaeological, genealogical, and historical evidence supporting the existence of a normative system for a broadly constructed group.[36]

Following *Mabo*, the government of Australia created an Aboriginal land fund to enable Aborigines to buy back their land, funded Native litigation, and created land use agreements between Aborigines and settlers. As Nicolas Peterson explains in this volume, the courts have become more useful as forums where Aborigines can tell their stories and influence government policies through the public arena. The *Mabo* case brought the courts into the mainstream of developing Native title law by recognizing that Native title had always existed when identified by a group who could prove their uninterrupted use of the land through laws and customs. Numerous cases after *Mabo* explored those parameters. But the *Native Title Act* of 1993, which allowed the Commonwealth to enact legislation affecting Native title, brought statutory law into conflict with common law just as it had in early modern England before the rise of parliamentary sovereignty. The act and its amendments gave legislative validation to the dispossession of Aborigines and restricted the meaning and value of their title. The results, however, have been mixed. As Lisa Strelein has found, from 2002 to 2005 more than fifteen court decisions in Australia have confirmed Aboriginal title.[37] This situation bears testimony for the need to resolve outstanding claims.

Canada

The pre-Confederation treaties in Canada were mainly "pacts,"[38] emanating from a century of relatively symbiotic relations and recognizing Native customs of peaceful coexistence. Confederation brought First Nations under the control of the dominion.[39] The second generation of treaty-making in the 1870s was due largely to conflict, in particular the Riel Resistance of 1870. The resistance led to the *Manitoba Act* and Métis scrip policy. Natives took the initiative for negotiating the treaties. Framed in narrow terms, with much that was said left unwritten, the eleven numbered treaties of 1871-1921 were first for peace and settlement in western regions and later for resource development in the north.[40] They were honoured by a policy of neglect that complemented John A. Macdonald's "National Policy." Most Natives, however, did not know that title to their lands was being expropriated.[41] After the *Constitution Act* of 1867, they were reduced to subjects and wards of the state. In *St Catherine's Milling and Lumber Co. v. The Queen* (1888), the Judicial Committee of the Privy Council (JCPC) held that Aboriginal title came only at the pleasure of the crown and indeed could be taken away at any time.[42]

By the end of the nineteenth century, all Native affairs were under settler-state control in the guise of protection and assimilation.[43] Settler demands for land, coupled with the rise of nationalism, compromised Aboriginal rights across British North America and Australasia as settler-states sought to turn communal and collective rights into individual ones pertaining to subjects of federal states. As First Nations in Canada were reduced to "bands," and limited to reserves, their title became dependent on federal legislation. The comprehensive *Indian Act* of 1876 – as amended from time to time – excluded the Inuit, Métis, and non-status Indians, criminalized many Aboriginal customs, eroded reserve lands, and precluded self-government. In 1927, an amendment even prohibited raising money and paying legal counsel to pursue Aboriginal land claims.[44] The repeal of this restriction in the 1951 revised act enabled suits for Native title, resulting in *Calder v. Attorney-General of British Columbia,* which concluded in 1973 with the SCC holding that Aboriginal title existed in Canadian law whether or not it had ever been granted. As McNeil has argued, Canadian courts avoided specifying the precise origins of Aboriginal title, agreeing on its existence based on historical occupation and possession.[45] This right was enshrined in section 35(1) of the *Constitution Act* of 1982 as a territorial right of exclusive collective control[46] and advanced in the 1996 report of the Royal Commission on Aboriginal Rights that recommended a new royal proclamation promoting treaties with Aboriginals as First Nations, legislation to facilitate land claims settlements, and recognition of their governments.[47]

The *Calder* case allows the courts to consider First Nations as political groups with their own legal systems and the right to seek remedies from the crown for failure to perform its obligations. It led to the Quebec agreement with the Cree for the development of the James Bay hydro complex in 1974 and formed the genesis of the dominion's comprehensive claims policy.[48]

In British Columbia, there was no attempt by the Colonial Office to control First Nations. Governor James Douglas recognized Aboriginal title in the 1850s. But later governors and commissioners happily removed Natives from their land, a situation that was not improved in the terms of union.[49] After entering the dominion in 1873, Natives in British Columbia were brought under state control as in the rest of North America and Australasia. In *Delgamuukw v. British Columbia,* the SCC held that practices precede customs and traditions, that British sovereignty was limited by Aboriginal title, and that this title was in a special class and vested in the community. The appellant, Delgamuukw, known as Earl Muldoe, was joined by members and representatives of the Gitksan and Wet'suwet'en "houses." They represented some 7,000 Natives over portions of 58,000 square kilometres in the Hazelton area from before c. 2000 BC who were appealing the Supreme Court of British Columbia's (SCBC) denial of their Aboriginal title.

The decision, given on 11 December 1997, concluded a decade of litigation by accepting much of the oral history of the Gitksan and Wet'suwet'en people that was corroborated by expert witnesses.[50] These witnesses were crucial to the court, and for legal context Chief Justice Antonio Lamer made repeated references to McNeil's *Common Law Aboriginal Title*. The role of experts, such as some of those who have written chapters for this book, was acidly noted by opponents of the decision: the court "was swayed by the sophistry of the Royal Commission on Aboriginal Peoples and its coterie of like-minded academics."[51]

The SCC reviewed the legal history of the region from the Royal Proclamation of 1763 to the *Constitution Act* of 1982, superior court cases from *Calder v. Attorney-General of British Columbia* (1973) that explored the nature and scope of the constitutional protection for common law Aboriginal title, and the original and interim cases before the BC courts. Thus, SCBC Justice Allan MacEachen's view in 1991 that Aboriginal rights exist at the pleasure of the crown, and can be extinguished whenever the crown wishes, was struck down in a case that cost $25,000,000 – a small sum today.[52] The special oral histories that the court gave credence to for proving uninterrupted usage were the *adaawk* and *kungax* stories to which MacEachen gave no independent weight. Chief Justice Lamer wrote that Aboriginal title is not limited to traditional uses, although there is an inherent limit that prevents land from being used in ways that are incompatible with its original usages, which predate the British crown's declaration of sovereignty in the *Oregon Boundary Treaty* of 1846. Those rights, however, may be infringed by provincial and federal governments when justified by general economic development, protection of the environment, infrastructure, and settlement. Such infringements, however, must receive compensation because of the economic element contained in Aboriginal title.

The *Delgamuukw* decision left indigenous groups in Canada in a similar situation as those in Australia. Justice Lamer, by holding that Aboriginal title was present in both English common law and Native custom, placed the onus of proof on Natives who never assented to the view that the underlying title to their land resides in the crown. The proof of Aboriginal title had to be made in British terms, had to be reconciled with an alien crown sovereignty, and even then was subject to the economic and social needs of the state.[53]

Faced with the "inconvenient truths" of a foreign legal system and sovereign power that litigate and legislate on their behalf, first peoples in both countries must become more aggressive and vigilant to assert their customary rights. There has been progress, however, as witnessed in the successful litigation of the Haida Nation, where the SCC in a unanimous decision on 18 December 2004 held that the crown must recognize the potential existence of Aboriginal title to the lands and waters of Haida Gwaii, must not make unilateral decisions on land transfers, and must consult on Aboriginal rights even if title has not been proved.[54] On the same day, the SCC upheld similarly on appeal for the Taku River Tlingit First Nation, where the duty to consult was met.[55] In both cases, the governments of Canada and various provinces had intervener status on behalf of British Columbia.

The situation of Aboriginal title in Canada today, however, is still problematic as First Nations struggle both to secure it and to benefit from its alleged attributes. With some forty politically autonomous and eleven language groups, they comprise – including Indians, Inuit, and Métis – approximately 3 percent of the population.[56] On the western shores of British Columbia, for example, south of where *Delgamuukw* arose, the Musqueam Nation, at the mouth of the Fraser River, has gained land holdings in Vancouver from land claims settlements that make it one of the wealthiest Aboriginal groups in the country, yet its people are among the poorest Natives in the province and locked in internal conflict. South of Vancouver, the treaty signed by the Tsawwassen Nation that was ratified by Parliament in June 2008 will allow the provincial government to construct a megaport as part of the Pacific agenda for Asian trade. The port is opposed by "resident" Natives of that nation and by the president of the BC Indian Chiefs, and annual cash payments to band members – most of whom live outside the reserve across North America – will result in the majority of the proceeds being sent out from the reserve. The plan has also led to suits filed by municipalities, which claim that their land has been expropriated without their consent.[57] Thus, for some participants, the benefits of economic development rights and political self-government appear to be illusionary. Although court decisions have broadened the concept of Aboriginal rights that has spurred land claims agreements, the problems that gave rise to those suits continue. But as Peter Hutchins has observed, it may be through court supervised mediation that Native claims in Canada may find the most amicable forum for resolution.

New Zealand
New Zealand was founded as a colony under the *Treaty of Waitangi* in 1840, and the Māori ceded suzerainty (*kawanatanga*) to the British crown, while their chiefs retained local authority. The British interpreted their authority as sovereignty, which was not how the Māori understood it. English law was

applied selectively in the middle decades of that century, allowing local custom to prevail. This discretion was upheld in *R. v. Symonds* (1847) and confirmed by the *Constitution Act* of 1852 that followed British colonial practice in the Australian and Canadian colonies. The act provided for crown sovereignty in the face of *de facto* tribal authority and allowed the crown to extinguish Aboriginal title.[58] The wars of the 1860s, however, necessitated some resolution of Māori land claims. A Land Court was created in 1865 to individualize their land holdings with a moral obligation to protect their rights, but the *Native Land Act* of 1873 furthered the process of fragmenting them.[59] Finally, in the *Wi Parata* case of 1877, the Supreme Court considered Aboriginals incapable of making treaties. The JCPC disapproved of the decision, which disapproval the New Zealand courts ignored.[60] As a result, the *Native Land Act* of 1909 stated that customary title existed only at the pleasure of the crown.

Since then, the Māori have the Waitangi Tribunal to act on their behalf in ruling on treaty rights – protected ostensibly by the Māori Land Court. When enhanced powers were given to the tribunal in 1975, and the High Court held in *Te Weehi v. Regional Fisheries Officer* (1986) that customary rights below the high-water mark were not extinguished, the *Calder* case was considered influential.[61] Citing US, Australian, and especially Canadian cases, President Robin Cooke, later Lord Cooke of Thorndon, held in the Court of Appeal for *Te Runanga o Muriwhenua* that the rights of the Māori are not "less respected than the rights of Aboriginal peoples ... in North America."[62] Since then, the courts have focused more on recognizing the laws of separate societies under New Zealand common law, leaving the exercise of customary rights to face-to-face negotiations.[63] Thus, although the Waitangi Tribunal became a permanent commission under the *Te Ture Whenua Māori Act* of 1993, the government has tried to bring closure to the era of Aboriginal claims.[64] Customary entitlements are customary rights that now must be negotiated along the lines of comprehensive settlements in Canada, although more recently the New Zealand Parliament has extinguished some Māori rights to the foreshore and seabed.[65]

The Māori are a significant people in New Zealand, being with the Pākehā one of the two founding Aboriginal cultures, traditional and modern, in New Zealand. Māori is one of the two official languages, and the people comprise thirty-six to forty-three tribal groups and almost 13 percent of the country's population.[66]

Since New Zealand was one of the last temperate coastlands colonized by the British in the 1840s, the recent experiences of imperial authority as seen in Westminster were more persuasive in recognizing Aboriginal rights in New Zealand than in British Columbia. Both the *Mabo* and the *Delgamuukw* decisions on Aboriginal title to land factored in New Zealand's Court of Appeal decision on Aboriginal title to the seabed. The Māori, like numerous indigenous groups in Australia and Canada, depend on the sea for their material and spiritual welfare. But the courts until 2003 held that Aboriginal title to the seabed had been extinguished by the assertion of crown sovereignty in 1840. Thus, when the Court of Appeal in *Ngati Apa v. Attorney-General* (2003) allowed the Hapu group to prove their customary ownership of the foreshore and seabed (going back to an earlier precedent set in 1847), Chief Justice Dame Sian Elias cited recent Australian and Canadian decisions. If there were customary indigenous property interests at the outset, then those interests are part of New Zealand's common law, and "there is no room for a contrary presumption derived from English common law."[67]

Ngati Apa forced the New Zealand government to renounce the court's decision and set in motion a classic English legal battle between common and statute law: the courts versus the legislature. The legislation in 2004 that curtailed Māori title has had a significant effect.[68] When, in the Northern Territory of Australia, Aboriginal title to the sea was restricted in *Commonwealth v. Yarmirr* (2001), this decision was endorsed in Queensland in the *Lardil* case of 2004, which did not reference *Ngati Apa*.[69] Therefore, this partial extinguishment of Aboriginal title to the sea in Australia and New Zealand raises an issue that may well be a critical one in Canada, where numerous indigenous groups such as the Haida have similar material and spiritual connections with the sea. Amid growing demands to exploit the seabed for minerals, oil, and gas, Aboriginal title claims to the sea may lead to similar battles where title to fisheries has been in dispute.[70]

The United States

Since Aboriginal (Indian) title in the United States is referred to frequently in the following chapters, a short introduction to its history will provide context for the reader. Indian title was based on prior occupation. Many land transfers from Indian nations to settler governments from the early seventeenth century on were legal transfers. At first, these transfers were beneficial to Indians, but then other lands were appropriated. The commerce clause of the US Constitution considered Indian tribes as "other" sovereigns, but they were never defined. The Cherokee Nation and the Iroquois Confederacy were promised statehood in the late eighteenth century, and the *Northwest Ordinance* of 1787 spoke of honouring the lands of first peoples. After the 1780s, their lands were taken indiscriminately by settlers. An important point, often lost, is that Chief Justice John Marshall's "discovery doctrine" in *Johnson v. McIntosh* (1823) unintentionally allowed settlers in the southern states to use that doctrine to claim lands of indigenous peoples, a device that they continued to use even after Marshall reversed himself in *Worcester v. Georgia* (1832).[71] Marshall had rejected British policy for the "residual sovereignty" of the founding fathers of the Constitution.

The *General Allotment Act* of 1887 (the *Dawes Severalty Act*) changed the landscape for Indians. Designed to extinguish tribal sovereignty, and erase the reservation boundaries by allotting communal land to families and promoting assimilation, it led to large divestitures of indigenous land and increased poverty and was repealed in 1934. The thirst for land in manifest destiny drove Indians west in diminishing numbers and with deleterious effects.[72] Thus, treaties were framed in broad terms to destroy their culture, force their adoption of settler culture, and transform them into Christian "yeoman farmers." The plains Indians, equestrians with a good supply of firearms, emboldened their opposition to making the red man white, and the resulting Indian wars devastated them.[73]

A turning point did not come until the *Indian Reorganization Act* of 1934 (*IRA*), which empowered first peoples by endorsing self-government. Although the goals of the *IRA* were curtailed with the Hoover Commission report of 1949, which recommended full assimilation, President Lyndon Johnson reversed this policy in 1968 to sponsor indigenous self-determination as "First Americans."[74] Later legislation enabled terminated treaties to be restored and allotments reversed. In 2000, Indian tribes were granted rights of self-government, but Congress retained the right to expropriate their lands without compensation unless their title is recognized.[75] Recent decisions of the US Supreme Court (USSC) have made dependency on the federal government "more devastating than colonialism."[76]

Since land rights are connected to sovereignty, Indian tribes are drawn into the legislative sphere. Thus, when an Alabama case arose in 1951 after the first expiration of an Indian Land Claims Commission five-year statute of 1946, the tribes went to Congress, which passed an act to extend the statute that enabled Indians to prove in court possession of sovereignty and title that had not been extinguished before 1845. They ended up with 2.4 million acres.[77] However, given that the USSC holds that Natives comprise "quasi-sovereign" domestic dependent nation-states, what is needed, according to Rebecca Tsosie, is for Natives to assert control over their own stories and present themselves to the courts as sovereign peoples.[78] A prime example is William Lewis Paul of Fort Simpson, British Columbia, who, while the Nisga'a were fighting for their title, fought for the *Tee-Hit-Ton Indians v. United States* in the USSC, which held that Indian title in Alaska had not been extinguished by the *Alaska Purchase Treaty* of 1867.[79]

There are two remaining problems, however. The first problem is jurisdiction. Of the 560 Native tribes and villages in the fifty states, some are not recognized federally or by the state, some have "Indian" identity but no legal standing, and there are no consistent models of self-government. The second problem is process. Although the interests of Indians are recognized, the means of promoting those interests are slow, burdensome, legalistic, and underfunded.[80] Indians in the United States are in a very contested space.[81]

Common Law and Aboriginal Custom

Aboriginal title was discussed formally by European canon lawyers in the sixteenth century. In the great debate between Bartolomé de Las Casas and Juan Ginés de Sepúlveda at Valladolid in 1550-51, the latter won the debate for the Spanish policy of conquest over Native sovereignty. As a result, over a million Aboriginals were slain on the Caribbean Islands, and by the end of the nineteenth century over 94 percent of all Aboriginals in the Americas had died as a result of war or disease.[82] Many English writers in the seventeenth century saw indigenous societies of the Americas as civilizations having economic systems, political organization, and military power.[83] As local inhabitants, Aboriginals also had status at English law. In England, though one could sue at Westminster Hall in the central courts of both common law (Common Pleas, Exchequer, and King's Bench) and equity (Chancery and Admiralty), it was in the customary and statutory local courts in towns, ports, boroughs, and counties where most litigation took place.[84] This amalgam of legal traditions was a separate sphere, called customary or municipal law, and was understood by the phrase "the custom [or course] of the common law."[85] Comprising sublegal cultures, customary law gave a quintessential pluralistic basis to English law[86] and was not dissimilar from the local law practised in the colonial courts of England's colonies. Colonial judges in the communities knew of Sir Edward Coke and William Blackstone and may have read some of their works. But in court, they often recited, as did their English contemporaries, from personal copies of Richard Burns's *Justice of the Peace,* in which municipal law and its formularies were prevalent.[87]

European states enforced their will on indigenous peoples on the basis of the international law of conquest.[88] The classic argument was posed in the early seventeenth century by the author of modern international law, Hugo Grotius, in his "just war" theory. According to Grotius, a conquest replaced the former political state with that of the conqueror, making previous rights extinct. Monarchs must have absolute power, and the rights of the conqueror must be unlimited.[89] This concept was a reiteration of the Spanish concept of a "holy war" derived from the medieval Crusades and used to justify the conquest of Mexico in the sixteenth century. Conquest, colonization, and confiscation were based on natural and divine law.[90] Later a revisionist argument was made by Samuel Pufendorf, who held that, though states must accept the results of war, they were not bound by "unjust wars."[91] His position was based on the earlier writings of Francisco de Vitoria, who argued that Amerindians had princes, rights, and duties that could not be abrogated without careful scrutiny.[92] Pufendorf's position was expanded in the Enlightenment by Jean-Jacques Rousseau, who argued in his *Social Contract* that unjust treaties or wars did not settle questions of rightful possession. Wars were between states.[93]

The major writer of the Enlightenment on this question was Emmerich de Vattel. Agreeing with Rousseau on the limitations of conquest, he went on to discuss how positive law did not distinguish between just and unjust wars. The laws of war protected the rights of individuals as well as the rights of states, and he accepted the law of prescription (title held uninterrupted for a long time) as well as that of conquest. Since international law demanded stability, the results of wars had to be observed. Thus, the victors had to enter into treaties with those who were defeated, and the terms of treaties were indisputable facts that had the force of law.[94] This practice led to a Eurocentric positivist school of international law in the nineteenth century, justifying the dispossession of all indigenous peoples.[95]

According to Sidney Harring, "in tribal society, culture, law and politics are an indivisible part of the whole life of a people."[96] As European society's relationship with tribal society was colonial and imperial, Europeans influenced the institutions of indigenous peoples. Tribal law became more centralized, moving from the level of the community to that of the tribe or tribal nation. Sovereignty became critical for their own protection and for their negotiations with neo-European bodies. As Harring explains, their legal culture became deeply entwined with tribal sovereignty, and notions of law and legality became more deeply engrained in their culture.[97]

The key to British acceptance of indigenous law was proof of its continuity over time: the peoples' identities, territorial foundations, and judicial precedents. In the imperial (presettlement) period, local municipal laws were accepted as an early concept of legal pluralism. Coke said that England and its possessions were governed by their municipal (internal) laws.[98] The legal rules governing their interactions were derived from the "law in dominions," later called the law of empire or imperial law.[99] Since most of the law's principles were from custom and judicial precedent, not statutes or prerogative law, it was an "imperial common law."[100] In countries uninhabited by Europeans, settlers had their municipal laws by "birthright," parallel to the local customs of indigenous peoples.[101] This arrangement led to the common law doctrine of Aboriginal rights.[102] But in inhabited countries taken by conquest, the Eurocentric school of legal thought applied, and local law was in force only until altered or abrogated by the crown.[103]

The first test of indigenous law in what would become the Canadian colonies was Rupert's Land, an immense territory drained by waters flowing into Hudson Bay that was granted to the Hudson's Bay Company (HBC) by a royal charter of 1670. According to the charter, the law of this land was the law of England insofar as it applied to those people who did not live under the authority of other previously established nations in the region.[104] In practice, the company accepted the rule of Aboriginal law for the domestic concerns of Native people.[105] In fact, the economic and diplomatic protocols established by the HBC and First Nations were carried over into the numbered treaties of western Canada. Such usage was confirmed much later when the Court of Queen's Bench of Quebec upheld Native customs as they applied to actions of HBC employees.[106] This usage was also upheld later by the Supreme Court of the North-West Territories.[107]

Meanwhile, in the United States, the conquest theory prevailed and was found in Chief Justice Marshall's judgment that Indian title could be extinguished by conquest.[108] Marshall, citing Vitoria and buttressed by the European concept of discovery that was diminishing the sovereignty and land rights of Indian nations, held that Indian tribes had minimal sovereignty as "domestic dependent nations" that had been incorporated into the United States and thus allowed the federal government to extinguish their title.[109] This view became legal orthodoxy in the famous Cherokee Nation's cases of 1831-32.[110] "Civilizing" the "barbarians" was a European doctrine that became part of the American concept of "manifest destiny" in subsequent decades that stretched across the Great Plains to the California and Oregon Trails.[111] The extension of federal power over Amerindian culture, law, and land, and congressional allowance of acts to override treaties, marked the republic's "new colonialism" in the second half of the nineteenth century.[112]

What, then, is indigenous law or Aboriginal jurisprudence? It is often based on knowledge derived from Aboriginals' Creator or "Life-Giver," found only in their original language, and handed down through the generations by oral tradition. Derived from the family and the community, indigenous law states that there is no sovereign or political state but "a normative vision, a product of shared thoughts and consciousness, of a community's beliefs and imagination."[113] First peoples are bound by covenants with the Creator for their land and its uses and have a harmonious relationship with their environment, which, with its life forms, is seen as interrelated sacred spirits comprising the essence of all life. Thus, "laws" are coincidental, expressed in circles by those who can remember and perform them in speech and music. Sound, sight, smell, and touch are the candles of illumination of the law.[114] And those candles still flicker in areas of indigenous communal life such as marriage, adoption, wrongdoing, trespass, hunting, and fishing.

Aboriginal customary law has many similarities with English common law. Both originated with laws made by "folk" lawmakers, communal courts as lawgivers, oral testimony, and judges telling stories of the past as guidelines for their decisions.[115] In both Australia and Canada, if not in New Zealand, several contemporary common law judges have concluded that their recognition of Aboriginal customs and laws is a "golden thread" that runs through their history of Euro-Aboriginal relations. Ambiguous as this may be,[116] Lord Ellesmere's declaration in *Calvin's Case* (1608) that all local laws and customs of peoples who came under English sovereignty were recognized as part of the common law when that sovereignty was claimed has not been reversed.[117] This view represents the extent to which "law ways" (the hearing and resolution of disputes) in modern civil and common law societies denote the legal pluralism that accepts diverse legal institutions.[118] It also reflects a revival of indigenous legal traditions in the courtrooms of postcolonial societies.[119] This is the kind of juridical context that allowed Justice Brennan in *Mabo (No. 2),* and Chief Justice Lamer in *Van der Peet,* to hold that Aboriginal title did not require executive or legislative recognition as long as it existed prior to contact.

Sovereignty, Extinguishment, and Expropriation of Native Title

Arthur Ray's chapter in this volume, "From the US Indian Claims Commission Cases to *Delgamuukw*: Facts, Theories, and Evidence in North American Land Claims," posits the view that establishment of the Indian Claims Commission (ICC) by the US Congress in 1946 marked the beginning of the modern Aboriginal and treaty rights claims era. The commission acted as a catalyst for the development of a multi-sourced and interdisciplinary approach to Native history in North America that became known as "ethnohistory." From the early 1950s on, the development of ethnohistory has been strongly influenced by research undertaken for land claims purposes, where land tenure systems, politics, and economics rather than "primitive cultures" were critical factors. In turn, this applied field has had an impact on the development of case law and adjudication procedures. Ray, who studied under one of the prominent historical geographers, shows how research undertaken for early ICC land claims shaped the subsequent development of ethnohistory and, as a result, strongly influenced the evidence and interpretations that experts presented in the *Delgamuukw* trial in Canada over thirty years later – a case in which Ray was a critical expert witness.

Prior to the ICC era, anthropologists assumed that indigenous cultures were static until European contact. The federal research funding provided by the ICC enabled detailed local research to identify and define tribal boundaries and to explore how they had changed over the postcontact era. In Canada, where claims research began a quarter century after the ICC, research in the United States had a fundamental influence as many tribes in Canada had close contact with those south of the border. Thus, a historical approach took root in Canada in the early 1970s, the results of which can be seen in the trials of Aboriginal title claims from *Calder* in 1973 to *Baker Lake* in 1980 and *Delgamuukw* in 1987-97. The ethnohistorical research model explores features of Native life that are unique to each group. Such studies demonstrate that the issues and problems faced in court today are similar to what they were sixty years ago. As Ray has observed, researchers "hold fundamentally different views about the impact that contact had on the core features of Aboriginal societies and cultures," bringing a debate of continuity versus change in the early contact era to the study of Native peoples across western Canada.

Bruce Rigsby's chapter, "Social Theory, Expert Evidence, and the *Yorta Yorta* Rights Appeal Decision," spans a wide range of topics and issues. Rigsby provides a short history of the recognition of Aboriginal land rights in Australia, the evidential parameters for title litigation established in the High Court of Australia's 2002 *Yorta Yorta* appeal decision, the crucial terms and concepts that anthropologists and lawyers must understand to analyze Aboriginal property rights ethnographically, and an assessment of which of those terms and concepts have been settled, simply acknowledged, or contested. *Yorta Yorta*, heard from 1994 to 2002, rehearsed the unrest of the nineteenth and twentieth centuries over Aboriginal lands in southern Australia and elaborated the evidential requirements mandated by the *Native Title Act* of 1993 (amended in 1998). This decision, which held that the Yorta Yorta had "lost its character as a traditional community," disappointed many people, who saw more potential in the *Mabo (No. 2)* decision for the recognition of Aboriginal title rights and interests. Rigsby discusses the new evidential requirements and places them in the context of the history of anthropological and sociological theory in common law countries.

Critical to this discussion, Rigsby argues, are crucial terms such as "social norms," "rights in general," and "rights in particular." Their proper understanding and use affect the standards and quality of Native title research and expert witnessing. Thus, social, philosophical, and legal theories are essential in deciding rights, and their enforcement, in interests in land. Equally essential is the study of people's behaviour and action. Proposing a rights-based approach to Native title, Rigsby says that there is too much emphasis on "the spiritual aspect of Aboriginal traditional ownership of land to the disregard and perhaps devaluation of its social and material functions." Thus, there is an irony in appreciating that the classical method of participant observation in anthropology offers strong evidence yet may not be practised freely in the highly charged social and political situations of land claims. Since Australia never accepted the doctrine of communal title until the legislation of the 1970s and 1990s, claims litigation has hinged on statutory interpretation without the courts' acceptance of the common law precedents that have held sway in other Commonwealth countries. This situation leaves Australia in the midst of a "history" war in which Aboriginal groups in settled areas try to recover rights that have been extinguished due to their "historical" but not "traditional" status as Aborigines, and expert witnesses, legal counsel, and judges seem to be relatively uninformed on the traditions, norms, and rights that lay at the centre of Aboriginal title.

David Yarrow's chapter, "Law's Infidelity to Its Past: The Failure to Recognize Indigenous Jurisdiction in Australia and Canada," suggests that, though Aboriginal rights have been recognized in land, they have not been accommodated with jurisdiction. Since English law recognizes public and private property, and as indigenous property is a form of communal custom that was accepted as part of public law into nineteenth-century Britain, it is not surprising that in the United States Aboriginals gained status as "domestic dependent nations" with the recognition of having limited jurisdiction of their affairs. However, in colonial Canada and Australia, though there were early hints of recognizing legal diversity, by the mid-nineteenth century Aboriginal jurisdiction took a back seat to perceived indigenous life in a "state of nature" and an unsuitability to operate any institutions of justice. Presenting deprecating portrayals of indigenous social organization, and intent on separating title from possession, the courts had little knowledge of Aboriginal law in denying its jurisdiction.

Although contemporary Native title jurisprudence in Australia and Canada has departed significantly from colonial norms and premises in their treatment of indigenous property interests, the same cannot be said for the recognition of indigenous jurisdiction. In Australia, Yarrow argues, the court in *Mabo* left the door open for indigenous jurisdiction. This door was quickly closed in *Walker v. New South Wales* in 1994. In Canada, though *Delgamuukw* did not address Native jurisdiction on Aboriginal land, in *R. v. Pamajewon* the SCC denied it. More interesting was *Campbell v. British Columbia* in 2000, where the BC Supreme Court held that the *Nisga'a Final Agreement* included the limited power of jurisdiction and self-government. The long civil law tradition in Quebec has demonstrated, although with some difficulties, that legal systems can coexist. What is needed, Yarrow concludes, is the legal education of lawyers and judges on the indigenous legal norms in Australia and Canada.

As Yarrow notes, "the terms 'Aboriginal title' and 'Native title' are highly evocative" and "immediately presumed to be related," yet, as in public (government) and private (citizens) law, the boundaries are demarcated conceptually but not always clearly. In the eighteenth and nineteenth centuries, colonial legal and judicial authorities did not see indigenous legal systems within the context of English local institutions, where there was a wide diversity of local custom and administration and little separation of public and private law. The conquering Normans accepted the folk rights of the people whom they conquered as the municipal law of the realm as long as they met the test of continuity.[120] Although there was conflicting case law in both Australia and Canada, by the mid-nineteenth century indigenous jurisdiction and legal pluralism were displaced by British sovereignty. Thus, both *Mabo* and *Delgamuukw* should be placed within the context of this legal-historical background to reveal the persistence of colonial understandings of the nature of indigenous jurisdiction. History has shown that common law can exist side by side with indigenous law, and our courts and societies must learn to respect indigenous legal norms.

Haijo Westra's chapter, "The Defence of Native Title and Dominion in Sixteenth-Century Mexico Compared with *Delgamuukw*," examines a little-known and only recently rediscovered neo-Latin treatise, *De dominio infidelium et justo bello*, by the Spanish Augustinian and first professor of the University of Mexico, Alonso de la Vera Cruz. This work, from a series of lectures given at the university in 1533-34, provides a defence of Native sovereignty and ownership of the land by a close observer only decades after the conquest. Alonso applied the principles of natural and international law – the *jus gentium* – to defend the Native community's dominion against the conquistadores. Basically, their lands had been unjustly acquired, and the Natives were owed full restitution; sovereignty resided in the Native community. The passage of time and the length of illegal occupation do not alleviate the original injustice: rightful property is inalienable.

Alonso's arguments on behalf of the *populus novi mundi* were repeated in the early seventeenth century when Jesuits in the colony of Maryland were given land by Natives for a mission that was seized by Lord Baltimore in 1641. The Jesuits argued, as European civilians had before them, not only that the indigenous people were the true lords and owners but also that they held title in both private and public law. Earlier Roger Williams had argued against the charter of the Massachusetts Bay Company, holding that the crown did not have title to Native land and had confiscated it without compensation. A comparison with the common law principles in *Delgamuukw* demonstrates that the concepts of full and just dominion and the inalienability of rightful ownership are essential to Aboriginal title and self-government. As argued by Yarrow, title (jurisdiction) and self-government are as inseparable in the twenty-first century as Alonso argued them to be in the sixteenth century. The crown must protect Natives as it does all its peoples. Westra argues that the recognition of First Nations' sovereignty would be our way of restitution. Hence, common law principles are not necessarily incompatible with those of natural law.

Brian Ballantyne's chapter, "Beyond Aboriginal Title in the Yukon: First Nations Land Registries," assesses the evidence that has been derived from visiting nine First Nations in the Yukon and three Inuit communities in Nunavut in 2002-4 and eight territorial and federal administrations. These visits, in conjunction with the collection and examination of documentary and oral evidence, have revealed that land claims agreements are a necessary but not stand-alone condition to ensure that Native title has some meaning in northern Canada. The study of the resulting land registries, which are presented here, demonstrates that negotiated agreements must include capacity building among local communities as well as the development of mechanisms – such as rudimentary yet appropriate systems of registering rights in land – that allow First Nations and the Inuit to benefit from such rights. For Aboriginals in the Yukon, land is not a commodity but the heritage of their community. As with the Māori in New Zealand, land is inseparable from the water that nourishes it.

Given the decision in the *Powley* case in 2003, that Métis have the legal right to hunt as a historical Aboriginal people, Ballantyne states that mechanisms have been created to register rights in land throughout the country. In the Yukon, there were no treaties until the *Umbrella Final Agreement* of 1993, in which First Nations were given the right to establish a system to record their land interests. This means that First Nations would lose their original title if they registered under the *Yukon Land Title Act*. Since land title registration is growing expeditiously in the region, there is a necessity to create an Aboriginal central registry. The problems of accomplishing this are many, including which principles should be followed, having entire or partial interests, which interests take precedence, who determines and handles the liabilities, and appropriation of the duties and obligations of the crown, Aboriginals, and settlers. Concluding with a prototype, Ballantyne observes that, "without rights in land, registration is not simply unnecessary but impossible."

Native Land, Litigation, and Indigenous Rights
Paul Chartrand's chapter, "The 'Race' for Recognition: Toward a Policy of Recognition of Aboriginal Peoples in Canada," holds that Canada, built on the lands of historical First Nations, has long had an "Indian policy" that has dismantled them, causing the disintegration of their social and political institutions. First peoples lobbied for changes in a process of national constitutional reform that led to a constitutional amendment in section 35 of the *Constitution Act* of 1982. This provision recognizes and affirms the rights of "the Aboriginal peoples of Canada" and expressly includes the Indian, Inuit, and Métis peoples. Although all these peoples are now "recognized," Chartrand argues for a "re-cognition" in negotiated legislation that makes Aboriginal and treaty rights effective to all members of these groups, for whom the common denominator was belonging to a collective rights-bearing community. This recognition is especially important in a country where there is a large increase in persons reporting Aboriginal identity and where the "third generation" of collective human rights has been enshrined in the UN *Declaration on the Rights of Indigenous Peoples* of September 2007.

.Who are these peoples? For Natives ("Indians"), blood was not mixed or unmixed; identity came from the community. This identity was recognized clearly by early British explorers, who accepted Aboriginals as a distinct society, original peoples who later saw their historical nations dismantled by colonial governments and many of their brethren disenfranchised from their historical communities. In Canada, after treaties, the federal government ignored the implications of legal recognition, while in the United States Natives were recognized legally as "domestic dependent nations" with sovereign authority to govern themselves at least in principle. Since there has been no "rational legislated policy" in Canada, many Natives were left out of the membership code in the *Indian Act,* according to which daughters who marry outside their reserve lose their status, Métis are excluded, and bands can make their own codes that produce "bandless" Natives. Chartrand assesses the problems of recognition of Natives, Inuit, and Métis, emphasizing their historical "descendant communities," and the types of rights to which various groups and subgroups should be entitled. A member of the Royal Commission on Aboriginal Peoples, 1991-95, he emphasizes the need to end "the rhetoric of race" and "make clear the distinction between citizenship and Aboriginal rights" for these three distinct Canadian indigenous peoples. Comparatively, while the problem is still elusive in the United States and Australia, it is better informed in New Zealand, where the Māori have a legislated "belonging" to their collective rights and the ability to identify themselves formally or informally without reference to their bloodlines.

Kent McNeil's chapter, "The Sources and Content of Indigenous Land Rights in Australia and Canada: A Critical Comparison," states that there can be no doubt that the content of indigenous land rights is heavily influenced, if not determined, by the source of those rights. This has been confirmed by the significant decisions on such land rights delivered by the SCC and the HCA over the past twenty years. The chapter critically assesses the divergent approaches to indigenous land rights taken by the two courts of final appeal. It suggests that the Australian approach after the *Native Title Act* of 1993, which requires proof of uninterrupted continuity, imposes an overly onerous burden of proof on indigenous peoples, places judges in the difficult position of having to decide which rights arise from systems of law that are outside their cultural experience, and produces unjust results. The Canadian approach of exclusive occupation, though deficient in some ways, is preferable because it is broader, makes it easier to prove Aboriginal title as a proprietary interest, and does not limit its content to traditional land uses.

Three sources of indigenous land rights are examined in this chapter: indigenous legal systems (the doctrine of continuity), evidence of exclusive occupation (the doctrine of common law title), and (more recently from the SCC) traditional rights that are integral to the distinctive culture of the group. These sources are examined with regard to their efficacy and limitations in light of the case law that has evolved in each country: from Justice Brennan in *Mabo v. Queensland (No. 2)* to subsequent restrictive decisions in *Yorta Yorta, Commonwealth v. Yarmirr* (2001), and *Western Australia v. Ward* (2002) in Australia, and from Chief Justice Lamer in *Delgamuukw* and subsequent decisions in cases such as *R. v. Powley* (2003) in Canada. McNeil concludes with a comparative analysis of those sources of land rights in the two countries. He contends that, whatever approach to rights gains precedence, those rights should not be frozen in time but be "dynamic in that they could be changed through the exercise of the decision-making authority vested in the community" through the exercise of self-government.

Nicolas Peterson's chapter, "Common Law, Statutory Law, and the Political Economy of the Recognition of Indigenous Australian Rights in Land," explains that the Australian Commonwealth recognizes Aboriginal rights only within a narrow range. Aboriginal rights were disregarded until 1966, when statutory land rights started to be granted. However, since 1992, there has been the possibility of holding land under "original" Native title where those rights have been "continuously activated" since British sovereignty in 1788 and not extinguished by legislation. Although Aboriginal land title was won by Aboriginals in Alaska due to the initiative of commercial interests to bring on stream the Prudhoe Bay oil pipeline in 1971, and won by Aboriginals in Quebec to enable construction of the James Bay hydroelectric project in 1975, a similar attempt to win land title provoked by a bauxite mine in the Australian Northern Territories failed in the *Milirrpum* case of 1971 even though Aborigines constituted 27 percent of the population.

The major problem for indigenous people in Australia is that the land claims of the 72 percent who live in urban, settled areas, many of whom are of mixed descent, are "historical" claims for people who have moved, or been moved, from their original lands. These claims are not as readily accepted by the public as those of Aborigines who live in remote areas. Examining the *Mabo, Wik,* and *Yorta Yorta* decisions, Peterson suggests that few of these groups will have their Aboriginal title recognized. The adversarial process, coupled with the dozens of Aboriginal witnesses disadvantaged in cross-examination, is not a promising one for recognition of their rights. But given the possibility for negotiated indigenous land use agreements made possible by the *Native Title Act,* the Indigenous Land Commission, and the government's social justice package, there are opportunities for redress. Thus, the current emphasis on mediation and negotiation has at least brought progress in land use agreements, even though the results have been in "shreds and patches." With some 511 applications for the recognition of Native title in process, there still may be many cases coming to the Federal Court in the future.

Jacinta Ruru's chapter, "Claiming Native Title in the Foreshore and Seabed," focuses on New Zealand and the groundbreaking 2003 Court of Appeal decision in *Ngati Apa*. It indicated, to the horror of the government and the public majority, that Māori should be allowed the opportunity to prove customary ownership of the foreshore and seabed. Described as a "tsunami," the decision polarized the country. The government, in its attempt to find a win-win solution, announced and implemented legislation to ensure that the Māori would never hold exclusive title to the foreshore and seabed. Facing an inevitable redefinition of Aboriginal title, this decision of the Court of Appeal, the government's reaction to it, and the aftermath in the legislature and the courts are analyzed in this chapter within a comparative *Delgamuukw* and *Mabo* context.

The Māori believe that all things, material and immaterial, are interrelated, and they embrace a culture that ensures a natural balance. Dependent on the resources of the sea, both economically and spiritually, they regard land and water as indivisible. The British colonists viewed the seabed and foreshore as public ownership, and a series of court cases and government actions, which are examined from 1840 to 2003, went back and forth on the question of Māori title. Although the high court held for the Hapu people in 2003, the government vowed to turn back the clock regardless of opposition from a UN committee on racial discrimination and the Waitangi Tribunal. In a close reading of these recent events, Ruru assesses *The Foreshore and Seabed Act* of 2004 and the extent to which it has changed the landscape of Māori rights and interests. Given the difficulty of proving uninterrupted usage since 1840, and as in Australia protecting only usufructuary rights, these actions have used legal fictions and presumptions to limit Aboriginal rights to traditional precolonial uses, thus closing the door to a sustainable society and economy in the twenty-first century.

Kenichi Matsui's chapter, "Waterpower Developments and Native Water Rights Struggles in the North American West in the Early Twentieth Century: A View from Three Stoney Nakoda Cases," examines the effect of hydroelectric dams on Native communities in late-nineteenth-century and twentieth-century North America in light of recent scholarship that largely has centred on Indian land rights and cultural damages and paid scant attention to Aboriginal water rights issues. Matsui, focusing on the construction of three hydroelectric dams on the Stoney Reserve in southwestern Alberta from 1907 to 1930, and how they influenced later construction of dams in western Canada, argues that Aboriginal water rights became highly contentious political and economic issues among federal and provincial officials, entrepreneurs, and indigenous peoples. Comparing these developments with those in British Columbia and the western United States, we can then examine how Native leaders refined their bargaining strategy and gained political recognition of their rights to water, waterpower, and waterbeds.

The Stoney Nakoda were able to negotiate their way through the land-mines of federal and provincial jurisdictions for the Horseshoe Falls, Kananaskis Falls, and Ghost River dam and hydroelectric sites. They drew from experiences in the western American states and in British Columbia, where the provincial government had opposed such Native water rights beyond supply for domestic and irrigation purposes. On the Canadian Prairies, Native water rights were not specified in either dominion or territorial legislation, while in the United States the Supreme Court had recognized Native water rights in the Montana *Winters* case of 1908. There was no federal or state legislation that recognized Native water rights in the United States either, and there were few other Native water rights cases in the American west. The Department of Indian Affairs (DIA) tried to negotiate for the Stoney Nakoda for hydroelectric dams on the Bow River from 1903 on, but they were resolute over price and terms. Finally, after much stiff bargaining, they agreed with the newly formed Calgary Power Company to construct the three dams over the period of 1907-30, reserving their rights to waterpower and the riverbed. After the *Natural Resources Transfer Agreements* of 1930, the western provinces attempted to gain control of Native water rights under provincial jurisdiction. But Matsui demonstrates how the Stoney Nakoda gained the recognition of their rights to the water, waterpower, and waterbed in Alberta in the absence of federal legislation, thereby gaining "recognition" of their control of interests in water as well as land. Readers should note the relationship of land and water to Native title interests in both Canada and New Zealand. Given the current problem of water resources in Australia, it is becoming an issue there as well.

Conclusions

Contemporary Aboriginal problems were born in the early colonial era, from the Royal Proclamation of 1763 and the War of 1812 onwards. Among the ideas that clashed in this conflict in British North America were two very different notions about the status of indigenous peoples and Aboriginal title in the ordering of international relations. The makers of the United States opposed the military might of the British Empire and Tecumseh's Indian Confederacy in order to push aside imperial and Aboriginal obstacles to western expansion. Providing land for settlers was also a prime mover of colonial rulers in Australia and New Zealand. In so doing, these leaders set patterns and precedents for a range of issues that is again becoming prominent in modern global geopolitics as countries address the status to be afforded to indigenous peoples around the world.

In the colonial arena, however, both the Roman and the common law of property were used to extinguish indigenous title in a discriminatory manner. Through the decolonization process, the Roman law concept of *uti possidetis, ita possideatis* (as you possess, thus you may possess) and the common law concept of customary law (protection of communal property rights) took hold, providing collective rights to title that were derived from use and occupation *sui generis* (particular to itself). This view was held throughout the early colonial period. In the late eighteenth century, Friedrich Karl von Savigny held, with reference to nomadic people, that absence did not bar title to land.[121]

Bringing the past into the future, it was, after all, the British authors of the Royal Proclamation of 1763 who recognized indigenous groups as "nations" and acknowledged the duty of the crown to negotiate with them, nation to nation, to determine the nature of Native rights.[122] A major problem is that although custom was always a strong element of the common law in England, a pluralistic concept of law did not ride in all the ships that sailed across the Pacific or Atlantic Ocean in the early years of colonization. When those colonists came to North America, unlike Australia, they needed Native allies against continental European imperial rivals. Thus, they needed to accommodate indigenous people, as the HBC did in the 1680s-90s. In this light, the Royal Proclamation anticipated troubles with British colonists, as perhaps did the later *Treaty of Waitangi*. As Yarrow has suggested, the common law that left the shores of England landed in other worlds "as a starched white sheet."[123] Thus, it remains curious to this day how Australian settlers and legal officials were able to claim the land as uninhabited when there were over half a million Aborigines in peaceful possession of their lands.[124]

The British began using treaties to dissolve "tribalism" and gain sovereignty over First Nations from the mid-nineteenth century. Treaties signed with First Nations in the Pacific islands and Africa in the second half of the century acknowledged clearly that the British government recognized Aboriginal sovereignty and was willing to negotiate and conclude treaties of cession, whether the Aboriginal group was considered to hold its possession either *de facto* or *de jure*. The legal theory was that, even in a *de facto* state, Aboriginal customary law and governance had a continuity that gave it the force of a sovereign authority.[125] Although in practice this theory was not always coherent, deference was nonetheless given to the contractual ability of Aboriginals. After all, the earliest practitioners of law were indigenous peoples, and many of the more than 500 treaties made with Europeans followed indigenous law.[126] By the end of the nineteenth century, physical control of Aboriginals succeeded jurisdiction with more aggressive intervention, creating an "Empire of Uniformity."[127]

Since World War II, international law has had an increasing influence in settler-state authority over Aboriginal peoples. Recognition and accommodation of Aboriginal rights to land and self-government in international forums have encouraged Aboriginals, especially in the past decade, to articulate a conception of their unique collective rights and to negotiate them as state to state, people to people. Rejecting the terms "primitive" and "tribal" that have been accorded to them, they have tried to escape those conceptual academic classifications.[128] As international law remains entrenched in a Western approach to proprietary rights, a growing recognition of collective ownership in sustaining the social, cultural, and spiritual aspects of indigenous life may lead to a wider acceptance of Aboriginal title in postcolonial states.[129] In Central America, this recognition was confirmed by the Inter-American Court of Human Rights when it held for the Awas Tingni Nation's title to customary lands and resources against the state of Nicaragua in 2001.[130] This growing recognition can be seen in the rise of truth commissions and in the creation of a Truth and Reconciliation Commission at the Fifth World Park Congress in 2003 to investigate and resolve cases of Aboriginal dispossession in national parks.[131]

Under the UN *Declaration on the Rights of Indigenous Peoples* in June 2006 (the result of the 2004 Decade of the World's Indigenous Peoples),[132] first peoples are attributed to have the rights of self-determination and self-government, control or ownership of ancestral lands, and freedom of culture without assimilation. Since the principle of an internationally accepted criterion of self-government has been rejected by the United States and several other countries, including Canada,[133] the concept of Native title has considerable roadblocks in front of it. An example is South Africa, where the Constitutional Court refuted the reasoning in *Mabo (No. 2)* and held that the customary law of its indigenous peoples was actually part of the law of the state.[134] The ruling of that court, however, is simply symbolic, as the Richtersveld community must file claims with the Land Claims Court or negotiate with the government to attain its rights.[135] More recently, in Botswana, most of the Bushmen of the vast Kalahari Desert – the oldest indigenous group in Sub-Saharan Africa who date back c. 30,000 years – were "relocated" from 1985 on, pushed out with "signs" that were not in their own language. When the remaining 1,000 were evicted in 2002, a group of 200 led by Chief Maiteela Segwaba sued in 2004 for the occupation of their ancestral lands. Heard by a judicial panel of three in the remote desert enclave of New Xade, they won on 13 December in a two-to-one vote, and on 18 December 2006 the government declared that it would abide by the decision.[136]

In Canada, the federal government instituted a comprehensive claims policy in 1981 – *In All Fairness: A Native Claims Policy* – that, with subsequent modifications, guides all treaty negotiations with First Nations.[137] Designed to obtain consensual extinguishments of Aboriginal title from First Nations, this policy holds that there are inherent Aboriginal rights, but not actual title to the land and its resources, and gives provincial governments a veto over distribution of land, resources, and revenues. It acknowledges, however, that title held continuously since time immemorial cannot be extinguished without consent, and it allows for municipal self-government.[138]

The SCC established in *Delgamuukw* some basic principles and standards for identifying Aboriginal title, a process for reconciliation, and negotiations for its resolution. But some federal officials still maintain that declarations of title must be established in the courts. This stipulation makes treaty making difficult because it is the non-Aboriginal governments who define the parameters of negotiations, and their economic and political interests – tied to assimilation in a global marketplace – are at odds with Aboriginal needs for recognition, regaining rights and lands lost, and self-government. The progress to date has been due largely to the political agency of First Nations, but their efforts have been hampered by having to deal with multiple levels of government.[139]

The problems of litigating Aboriginal title are many. A major one concerns the words *Aboriginal* and *Native*. Whom do they represent? As Chartrand has explained, the term "mixed bloods" is racist and unhelpful. Historically, there was no difference between "mixed" and "unmixed" bloods. What defined "blood" was the community and its links to place and time. Native stories depict material objects as containing the spirits of their people. The Haida, for example, believe that the trees in the old-growth forests contain the spirits of their ancestors, and thus cannot be cut down, and that they as original people have descended from creatures of the sea and therefore have rights to the seabed.[140] If the purpose of the state is to protect people, their lands, and their interests, then why do groups such as the Métis have to go back hundreds of years to prove their ancestral rights when those rights were part of their community?[141] There are no common law rules to resolve this problem. Only recently have Canadian courts hinted at including Aboriginal custom in the common law, a fundamental issue that also concerns Australia, New Zealand, and the United States.[142]

Another problem is the voice of indigenous peoples. A major contribution of *Delgamuukw* for future cases was the pronouncement that Native voices can be accepted as evidence. As Ray explains, whether it is accepted as "proof" is still problematic. In the recent *Powley* case, the elders gave evidence before the court, but the judges cited the documentary evidence in holding for the Métis land claims.[143] Whether judges can move past this point is a question that only time will tell. As in Australia, much oral evidence is given now in Canada, but often it is not recognized by the bench. The situation is similar in New Zealand with the Waitangi Tribunal, despite more openness to oral evidence. An essential problem here, as both Ray and Rigsby have raised, is that judges, unlike anthropologists, are not trained in how to read people and often view Native oral history as precarious. But leaving aside the question of how judges handle it, we should note that the challenging process of gathering and testing evidence of Native custom has enabled Aboriginals to acquire, document, and publicize their history in ways that would never have been possible otherwise. Critical to this process is the preservation of indigenous languages.[144]

There is also the role of expert witnesses to document the past of first peoples. In some cases, these witnesses themselves become a battleground, as in the *Samson Cree* case, in which twenty experts were examined and cross-examined. The Gitksan had anthropologists live with them for three years so that they could document accurately the social economy of the tribe. But their evidence was not admissible in court because they had worked with the Gitksan. The court deemed that expert witnesses, in that case, must be "outsiders."[145] This leaves the fate of many cases in the hands of such expert witnesses – anthropologists, archaeologists, linguists, historians, and lawyers – who must produce a body of evidence that fills the gaps and silences in the white man's written record.[146]

A further problem is cost. Up to and including *Calder,* most cases concerning Native title were short, heard within a week. But since then, the crown no longer concedes Native evidence and contests as many facts and issues as it can even if not critical to the case. Given the adversarial nature of "black letter" common law, in which artificial positions are framed that often do not reflect reality, arguments are made and allegedly proven that completely validate one position and invalidate another. This result of "winners" and "losers" obtained at great cost is not conducive to the resolution of issues that lie deep in the human psyche. Appointing experts to chart the way forward has been equally costly. Although Canadian taxpayers paid $56 million for a royal commission that recommended face-to-face negotiations, dual citizenship, and abandonment of extinguishment, their governments must face up to those recommendations "before any just future can begin to be built."[147] In addition, there is the massive problem of Aboriginal compensation, as either part of negotiating rights and title or resolving them in court.[148]

Although Aboriginal title doctrine has become part of the common law, legislatures strive to provide for the recognition and protection of that title in ways that are not always beneficial. Recognizing changing customs is not an easy practice at common law, where "custom" (and the strength of custom) were viewed originally as unchanging. In Australia, however, Justice Merkel has done just that in holding for the FCA the principle "that *traditional* laws and customs are not fixed and unchanging."[149] Indeed, customary law at common law assumes change over time and resides at the heart of the common and civil law systems. Westra, for example, brings us back to the sixteenth and seventeenth centuries for European views of customary rights and how they might pertain to Aboriginals, views that are deeply rooted in the past. It was Thomas Aquinas who argued that custom was central to the theology of law and provided the basis for a "just" legal system.

Law that does not stem from the customs of the populace alienates those to whom it belongs.[150] It was this concept of custom that attracted Coke and early modern lawyers in search of a legal concept that would predate the crown's exercise of sovereignty in Parliament. Although common lawyers searched for an "ancient constitution," their arguments for ancient custom as the bedrock of common law won the day in Britain and the colonies, especially in western Canada.[151]

In general, competing sovereignties of Native versus crown, and settlements of Aboriginal title made in the context of the interests of the crown, prejudice Aboriginal title jurisprudence.[152] What is badly needed, as John Borrows writes so eloquently, is the judiciary's acceptance of indigenous laws and their stories and its willingness to receive and apply them to Aboriginal issues litigated before the courts.[153] In Canada, for example, from *St. Catherines Milling* in 1888 to *Sparrow* in 1990 and beyond, Aboriginal law continues to be an inferior source to legal rights that emanate from the crown,[154] even though the courts have accepted that Aboriginal rights are *sui generis,* arising from ancient customs and serving as the fountain of Aboriginal law.[155] As Ray argues, indigenous people would be better served by a forum other than law courts. This forum would allow, as Hutchins and Rigsby have argued, more input from social scientists to frame the issues for lawgivers to adjudicate.[156]

Natives themselves, however, are not necessarily pleased with these public "white" activities. As Edward George of the Peigan has explained, many Natives wish to be left alone to deal with the immediate problems of alcohol, drugs, violence, and unemployment and to care for their families. Questions of "title" are theoretical and not practical. Since the 1980s, they have become greatly overrepresented in jails and prisons. In his view, established society (those with power) has little interest in them here or anywhere else. They are at the mercy of a four-corner blanket, a quilt patched with corporations, contracts, legislation, and policies of assimilation.[157]

Alongside this pessimism among first peoples is pessimism among a number of academic commentators. Some of them argue that demands for Aboriginal rights and title obscure deeper problems within indigenous societies. The litigation process strengthens the role of their leaders, which leads to greater authoritarian rule in their societies. Aboriginal practices have included aspects of brutality – from the law of blood feud to fighting and domestic violence – that should be abandoned; state-sponsored solutions to Aboriginal problems should be abandoned too so that indigenous people (especially the younger generation) can choose their own lifestyles.[158] These problems and possible solutions are difficult to resolve, however, when Aboriginals have little power to control their lives, must work both within and against the state, and live in a space where there are no governing structures to accommodate diverse forms of rights and governance.[159] Although it is too simple to critique judicial decisions that have brought advances to Aboriginal title across the common law world in recent decades, we must not forget the invigorating debates that those cases have brought to the tables of government as well as to the public mind.[160] In the end, society itself must set the parameters for lawgivers and lawmakers.

Interestingly, the early modern concept of custom would have accommodated the case for Aboriginal rights and title and would have given heart to contemporary Native leaders such as Chief Crowchild of the Tsuu T'ina Nation. As he stated, "why do we ever have to buy back our own land?"[161] As Hutchins has put it, the process of cession, release, and surrender of land by indigenous peoples "is a juridical oxymoron."[162] Living in a pluralistic society, all parties must resolve the land question so that indigenous communities can be empowered to handle the problems that they face in a modern, industrial world. Perhaps recent events, such as the formal apology by Prime Minister Kevin Rudd of Australia to the stolen generations of Aboriginal and Torres Strait Islanders for being removed from their families and communities, and Prime Minister Stephen Harper's apology to former students of Native residential schools for their forceful removal from their homes, will herald a more optimistic future of Aboriginal-settler relations.[163]

Notes

1 Since Aboriginal peoples have different nomenclatures in English that stem from outsiders, I am using the term generically, and the name of Aborigines for those in Australia, Natives and First Nations for Canada, Māori for New Zealand, and Indians for the United States, with the term "indigenous" for all original peoples.

2 Peter W. Hutchins, "The Thirty Years War: A Practitioners' Guide to Aboriginal Litigation since Calder," paper presented at the conference on *Delgamuukw, Mabo,* and *Ysleta,* University of Calgary, 18 September 2003.

3 For a defence of prior Native against non-Native sovereignty, see Macklem, "Distributing Sovereignty," 1316-23, 1345-50.

4 The Trudeau quotations are in Foster, Raven, and Webber, eds., *Let Right Be Done,* at 46 and 247, with discussions at 3-6, 47-49, 57, 101, 219, and 222.

5 *Calder v. A.G.B.C.* (1973), 34 D.L.R. (3rd) 145 (S.C.C.).

6 The crown in right of Canada acknowledged this in the mid-1970s when it created its comprehensive claims policy, but British Columbia did not acknowledge it until the early 1990s. I wish to thank Kent McNeil for this comment.

7 See, for example, the collection of essays on cases and legislation for Australia, Canada, New Zealand, and South Africa in Keon-Cohen, ed., *Native Title in the New Millennium*; the outline discussion of Native rights and title in those countries and the United States in Dorsett and Godden, *Guide to Overseas Precedents*; and the documentary collection of Odawi, *Sovereignty, Colonialism, and the Indigenous Nations.*

8 Havemann, ed., *Indigenous Peoples' Rights.*

9 Richardson et al., eds., *Indigenous Peoples and the Law.*

10 McHugh, *Aboriginal Societies and the Common Law.*

11 Connor, *Invention of Terra Nullius.*

12 Nettheim, "The Influence of Canadian and International Law," 177-79.

13 The name Delgamuukw is spelled without the apostrophe throughout the chapter and the book for consistency.

14 For the history of Australian law with regard to Aborigines, and of the court cases that preceded *Mabo,* see Russell, *Recognizing Aboriginal Title,* chaps. 5-7.

15 *Mabo v. Queensland (No. 1)* (1988), 166 C.L.R. 186.
16 Reynolds, *The Law of the Land*, 2nd ed., postscript.
17 *Mabo v. Queensland (No. 2)*, [1992] 175 C.L.R. 1. For the decision and commentary, see Butt, Eagleson, and Lane, *Mabo, Wik, and Native Title*.
18 *Milirrpum v. Nabalco Pty. Ltd.* (1971), 17 F.L.R. 141.
19 Nettheim, "Influence of Canadian and International Law," 183-84.
20 Smandych, "Contemplating the Testimony of 'Others,'" 282-83.
21 This theme runs through the essays in Daunton and Halpern, eds., *Empire and Others*.
22 See, for example, the in-depth studies of Attwood and Foster, eds., *Frontier Conflict*; Foster, Hosking, and Nettelbeck, *Fatal Collisions*; and Nettelbeck and Foster, *In the Name of the Law*.
23 Bartlett, "Native Title in Australia," 420-27.
24 *Wik Peoples v. Queensland*, [1996] 187 C.L.R. 1.
25 See the discussion in Brennan, *The Wik Debate*, 80-90.
26 Stoeckel, "Case Note," 155.
27 Havemann, *Indigenous Peoples' Rights*, 6.
28 See, in addition to the works above, the commentaries on agreements, cases, legislation, and institutions in Perry and Lloyd, *Australian Native Title Law*.
29 *Fejo v. Northern Territory*, [1998] 195 C.L.R. 96.
30 *Yanner v. Eaton*, [1999] 201 C.L.R. 351.
31 *Commonwealth v. Yarmirr*, [2001] 208 C.L.R. 1.
32 *Western Australia v. Ward*, [2002] 213 C.L.R. 1.
33 Toussaint, ed., *Crossing Boundaries*, chs. 14-17.
34 See the discussion in Nettheim, "Influence of Canadian and International Law," 190-95.
35 *De Rose v. South Australia (No. 2)*, [2005] 145 F.C.R. 290. See also *Bodney v. Bennell*, [2008] F.C.A.F.C. 63, for a different view. I thank Kent McNeil for this reference.
36 *Neowarra v. Western Australia*, [2003] F.C.A. 1402, [2004] F.C.A. 1092.
37 Strelein, *Compromised Jurisprudence*, 118, 164n29.
38 This is a theme in Miller, *Skyscrapers Hide the Heavens*, 25-110 passim.
39 The *Act for the Gradual Enfranchisement of Indians and the Better Management of Indian Affairs*, c. 6, provided for the election of all chiefs, with local bylaws subject to crown approval. These measures were consolidated in the *Indian Act* of 1876, which brought in "resident" government agents to control most affairs. See Bartlett, *The Indian Act of Canada*.
40 Miller, *Skyscrapers Hide the Heavens*, 148-73, 204-24, 396-402. Miller suggests that after the 1870s the dominion lacked interest in the enterprise. See Miller, *Compact, Contract, Covenant*, 34-35.
41 Foster, "Indian Administration from the Royal Proclamation of 1763 to Constitutionally Entrenched Aboriginal Rights," in Havemann, *Indigenous Peoples' Rights*, 354-61.
42 In David Elliott, ed., *Law and Aboriginal Peoples in Canada*, Vol. 3, 10.
43 See, in general, McHugh, *Aboriginal Societies and the Common Law*, 173-78.
44 For this and its subsequent revisions, see Bartlett, *Indian Act of Canada*. The act was part of federal policy to take Native peoples out of their Aboriginal status; see Miller, *Compact, Contract, Covenant*, 36.
45 McNeil, "Meaning in Aboriginal Title." In *R. v. Guerin*, [1984] 2 S.C.R. 335, it was called an "independent legal right."
46 See Otis, "Territoriality," 147-48.
47 Foster, "Indian Administration," 364-66.
48 Gérard V. La Forest, "Reminiscences of Aboriginal Rights," 58.
49 The "charge" of "Indians" was assumed by the dominion government with "a policy as liberal as that hitherto pursued by the British Columbia Government." Term 13 of the *British Columbia Terms of Union*, at http://www.solon.org/.
50 Persky, ed., *Delgamuukw*.
51 Ibid., Melvin Smith quoted at 5.
52 *Buffalo v. The Queen* cost over $100 million prior to appeal and as of May 2008 is ongoing for a claim of over $1.4 billion. http://www.samsoncree.org. See the decision in *Ermineskin Indian Band and Nation v. Canada*, [2009] S.C.C. 9.

53 Borrows, "'Because It Does Not Make Sense,'" in Kirkby and Coleborne, *Law, History, Colonialism*, 198-204.
54 *Haida Nation v. British Columbia (Minister of Forests)*, [2004] 3 S.C.R. 511.
55 *Taku River Tlingit First Nation v. British Columbia (Project Assessment Director)*, [2004] 3 S.C.R. 550.
56 Havemann, *Indigenous Peoples' Rights*, 6.
57 See the "Ministry of Aboriginal Relations and Reconciliation" (2007), at http://www.gov. bc.ca/arr/, and subsequent news stories in the Vancouver *Province*.
58 See, in general, McHugh, *Aboriginal Societies and the Common Law*, 166-73, 185-89.
59 Kirkby and Coleborne, eds., *Law, History, Colonialism*, 84-88.
60 See, for this period, Parsonson, "The Fate of Maori Land Rights," in Kirkby and Coleborne, eds., *Law, History, Colonialism*, 173-89.
61 See Erueti and Charters, eds., *Māori Property Rights*; and Williams, "Customary Rights and Crown Claims," 162-65.
62 Williams, "Customary Rights and Crown Claims," quotation at 165. He also spoke highly of Canadian decisions in the *Te Runanga* case of 1993.
63 This is the conclusion of Godlewski and Webber, "The *Calder* Decision."
64 This is the thesis of McHugh, "From Sovereignty Talk to Settlement."
65 See Erueti and Charters, *Māori Property Rights*.
66 Havemann, *Indigenous Peoples' Rights*, 6.
67 *Attorney-General v. Ngati Apa and Others*, [2003] 3 N.Z.L.R. 643 (C.A.) para. 86.
68 *The Foreshore and Seabed Act 2004* (N.Z.), 2004/93. The *Māori Commercial Aquaculture Claims Settlement Act* of 2004 provided for a limited growth (20 percent of new space) of its marine farming industry without the risk of litigation under treaty grievances.
69 *Lardil Peoples v. State of Queensland*, [2004] F.C.A. 298. I thank Kent McNeil for this reference.
70 See, for example, Harris, *Fish, Law, and Colonialism*.
71 Robertson, *Conquest by Law*, 95-116. For a useful survey, see Pevar, *Rights of Indians and Tribes*, 3-14.
72 Banner, *How the Indians Lost Their Land*.
73 Jill St. Germain, *Indian Treaty-Making Policy*, 158-65, quotation at 162.
74 Pevar, *Rights of Indians and Tribes*, 12.
75 *Tee-Hit-Ton Indians v. United States*, [1955] 348 U.S. 272 and 965, 75 S.C.R. 313 and 521.
76 Howard, *Indigenous Peoples and the State*, 65.
77 Rebecca Tsosie, "Native Claims in the United States: Reparative Justice or Extinguishment of Liability?," paper presented at the *Delgamuukw, Mabo,* and *Ysleta* conference, University of Calgary, 19 September 2003. The act ran for thirty years.
78 Tsosie, "Introduction: Symposium on Cultural Sovereignty," 14.
79 Haycox, "Then Fight for It," 85-93.
80 Miller, *Forgotten Tribes*, 256-61.
81 Wilkins and Lomawaima, eds., *Uneven Ground*, 5-9.
82 Howard, *Indigenous Peoples and the State*, 39-40.
83 This is a theme in Kupperman, *Indians and English*.
84 Over 90 percent took place in London. The role of the central courts declined further from the mid-seventeenth century to the mid-eighteenth century; this is the thesis of Christopher W. Brooks, *Lawyers, Litigation, and English Society since 1450* (London: Hambledon Press, 1998).
85 Louis A. Knafla, "Common Law and Custom in Tudor England: Or, 'The Best State of a Commonwealth,'" in *Law, Literature, and the Settlement of Regimes*, ed. Gordon J. Schochet (Washington, DC: Folger Shakespeare Library, 1990), 171-86 at 176-80. The clearest contemporary explanation was made by Sir John Davies, *Le primer report des cases in les courts del roy* (Dublin: J. Franckton, 1615), sigs. iii-v.
86 Coke's view of common law as *jus scriptum* (written law), published in his *Reports* for *Calvin's Case*, was not the majority view as expressed by Chancellor Ellesmere, who published a separate report of the case with a much wider interpretation. Louis A. Knafla, *Law and*

Politics in Jacobean England: The Tracts of Lord Chancellor Ellesmere (Cambridge, UK: Cambridge University Press, 1977), 216-24.

87 Richard Burn, *The Justice of the Peace and Parish Officer,* 30th ed. (London: Sweet, Maxwell, and Son, 1869). For the role of the justice of the peace in the legal system of the Canadian North-West, see David Carey, ed., *Carey's Manitoba Reports* (Calgary: Carswell, 1918), i-ix.

88 See, in general, the thoughtful work of Sharon Korman, *The Right of Conquest: The Acquisition of Territory by Force in International Law and Practice* (Oxford: Clarendon Press, 1996).

89 Hugo Grotius, *De jure belli ac pacis* [1625], trans. Francis W. Kelsey (Oxford: Clarendon Press, 1925), Book 3, ch. 6.

90 Robert A. Williams Jr., "The Medieval Discourse of Crusade," in *Native American Law and Colonialism, before 1776 to 1903,* ed. John R. Wunder (New York: Garland Publishing, 1996), 77-122. Grotius assumed a world of independent states, a natural society of territorial nations that had the right to conquer non-territorial ones.

91 Samuel Pufendorf, *De jure naturae et gentium* [1688], trans. C.H. Oldfather and W.A. Oldfather (Oxford: Clarendon Press, 1934), Book 3, ch. 8, s. 1.

92 Francisco de Vitoria, *De Indis et de jure belli relectiones* [1540], trans. J.P. Bate (Washington, DC: Carnegie Institution of Washington, 1917), Book 1, ch. 9. Vitoria acknowledged the right of conquest but only if Natives resisted "benign influences."

93 Jean-Jacques Rousseau, *The Social Contract and Discourses* [1762], trans. G.D.H. Cole (London: Dent, 1973), Book 1, Chapter 3.

94 Vattel, *The Law of Nations* [1758], Book 3, Chapter 13.

95 See, in general, Tully, "Aboriginal Property," 153-80.

96 Harring, "Crazy Snake and the Creek Struggle for Sovereignty," 365.

97 Ibid., 365-80. See, more generally, Harring, "'There Seemed to Be No Recognized Law.'"

98 *Calvin's Case,* 7 *Coke's Reports,* 1a at 19b.

99 *Campbell v. Hall,* 20 *State Trials,* 239 at 264.

100 Nigol, "Private Law."

101 Blackstone, *Commentaries on the Laws of England,* 1: 106-7.

102 See Lester, *Inuit Territorial Rights;* Slattery, *Ancestral Lands, Alien Laws,* 10-15; and Walters, "*Mohegan Indians v. Connecticut* (1705-1773)," 785-92.

103 *Calvin's Case,* 17v.

104 A copy of the original charter is in Oliver, ed., *The Canadian North-West,* vol. 1, 135-53.

105 Nigol, "Private Law."

106 *Connolly v. Woolrich* (1867), *Lower Canada Jurist,* 11 (1866), 197-265, by Monk J; and the appeal in *La revue legale* (1869), 253-400. These reports contain a mine of valuable historical documentary evidence.

107 *R. v. Nan-E-Quis-A-Ka* (1889), 1 T.L.R. 211 (C.A.), by Wetmore J.

108 *Johnson and Graham's Lessee v. McIntosh* (1832), 21 U.S. [8 *Wheaton*] 543.

109 See Vine Deloria Jr. and Clifford M. Lytle, "American Indians in Historical Perspective," in Wunder, *Native American Law,* 128-30.

110 Joseph C. Burke, "The Cherokee Cases: A Study in Law, Politics, and Morality," in Wunder, *Native American Law,* 136-67.

111 See Parkman, *The California and Oregon Trail;* and, more generally, Howard, *The Lessons of History.*

112 Wunder, *Native American Law,* Preface.

113 Henderson, *First Nations Jurisprudence,* 122.

114 Ibid. For an illuminating and wide-ranging discussion, see Havemann, *Indigenous Peoples' Rights,* 116-67.

115 See Borrows, *Recovering Canada,* for a fuller discussion.

116 Walters, "Towards a 'Taxonomy' for the Common Law," 125-27.

117 Knafla, *Law and Politics,* 202-53 at 237.

118 Knafla and Binnie, eds., *Law, Society, and the State,* 10-13.

119 See Lajoie, "Introduction: Which Way out of Colonialism?," 3-10.

120 Knafla, "Introduction: Laws and Societies," 6-18.

121 For background to my phraseology here and Von Savigny's discussion of the theme, see Von Savigny, *Treatise on Possession*, 35-40, 83-84.
122 Borrows, "Wampum at Niagara," in Asch, *Aboriginal and Treaty Rights in Canada*, 155-72.
123 Yarrow, Chapter 3 this volume.
124 A useful survey of the evolution of English explorers, settlers, and legal commentators on this problem is Reynolds, *Law of the Land*.
125 See, in general, McHugh, *Aboriginal Societies and the Common Law*, 202-6; and his discussion of territorial sovereignty and extraterritorial jurisdiction at 206-13.
126 Law Commission of Canada, *Justice Within*, 4-6.
127 This is a theme in McHugh, *Aboriginal Societies and the Common Law*, 117-30.
128 Howard, *Indigenous Peoples and the State*, 3.
129 McNeil, "The Inalienability of Aboriginal Title," 486.
130 Anaya and Grossman, "The Case of Awas Tingni."
131 Gilbert, *Indigenous Peoples' Land Rights*, 192-94.
132 Odawi, *Sovereignty*, 693-704, for the draft text, the final being Human Rights Council Resolution 2006/2 (29 June 2006).
133 Ibid., 716-21.
134 *Alexkor Ltd and Another v. Richtersveld Community and Others*, [2003] Case C.C.T. 19/03.
135 Fairweather, *A Common Hunger*, 105-14.
136 http://www.news.bbc.co.uk/.
137 For a recent example of the processes, see Woolford, *Between Justice and Certainty*, 98-120.
138 Asch, "From Calder to Van der Peet," 428-40.
139 See Miller, *Compact, Contract, Covenant*, 38-40.
140 Ray, "History Speaks."
141 In *R. v. Van der Peet*, [1996] 2 S.C.R. 507, the court modified the elements of the precontact test to reflect the ethnogenesis of the Métis and differences between Native and Métis claims.
142 See also Chartrand, ed., *Who Are Canada's Aboriginal Peoples?*
143 *R. v. Powley*, [2003] S.C.C. 43 (online version).
144 Rigsby, "Indigenous Language."
145 Ray, "History Speaks.
146 See, for example, Choo, "Historians and Native Title"; and the essays in Toussaint, *Crossing Boundaries*.
147 Culhane, *The Pleasure of the Crown*, 355.
148 For a study of this problem, see Mainville, *Overview of Aboriginal and Treaty Rights*.
149 *Clarke on Behalf of the Wotjobaluk, Jaadwa, Jadawadjali, Wergaia, and Jupagulk Peoples v. Victoria*, [2005] F.C.A. 1795, [11], cited in Strelein, *Compromised Jurisprudence*, 133.
150 This is the thesis of Van Drunen, *Law and Custom*.
151 Knafla and Swainger, eds., *Laws and Societies*, 5-7, 30-32.
152 For a discussion, see Strelein, *Compromised Jurisprudence*, 120-42.
153 Borrows, *Recovering Canada*, 5, 23-28. For the larger issue of protecting the intellectual property of the indigenous, see Battiste and Henderson, *Protecting Indigenous Knowledge and Heritage*.
154 *St. Catherines Milling and Lumber Co. v. The Queen* (1888), 14 A.C. 46; *R. v. Sparrow*, [1990] 1 S.C.R. 1075.
155 See the discussion in *R. v. Guerin*, [1984] 2 S.C.R. 335, and its context in Borrows, *Recovering Canada*, 6-12. In Canada, both levels of government accepted the ancient legal code of the Nisga'a in their final agreement.
156 Commentary on Rigsby's paper at the conference. See, more specifically, Hutchins, "The Marriage of History and Law."
157 As noted by Edward George at the end of the wrap-up conference panel.
158 See the essayists in Johns, ed., *Waking Up to Dreamtime*. Examples of how Aboriginal communities can create their own structures are offered in Proulx, *Reclaiming Aboriginal Justice, Identity, and Community*.
159 Havemann, *Indigenous Peoples' Rights*, 470-74.

160   Dick, "Comprehending 'the Genius of the Common Law,'" 79.
161   Chief Crowchild, speaking at the conclusion of the *Delgamuukw, Mabo,* and *Ysleta* conference, University of Calgary, 20 September 2003.
162   This is the thesis of Hutchins, "Cede, Release, and Surrender."
163   Addresses delivered to the respective House of Commons: Prime Minister Rudd on 13 February 2008 at http://www.dfat.gov.au/indigenous_background/rudd_speech.html; and Prime Minister Harper on 11 June 2008 at http://www.pm.gov.au/media/speech/2008.

Part 1:
Sovereignty, Extinguishment, and Expropriation of Aboriginal Title

1

From the US Indian Claims Commission Cases to *Delgamuukw*: Facts, Theories, and Evidence in North American Land Claims

Arthur Ray

> The greatest challenge of the litigation cases lies in the fact
> that anthropology and law have difficulties in finding common
> ground in the use of basic concepts and terms. Legal concepts and
> principles, although derived from the Anglo-American cultural
> tradition, must be applied to Indian societies no matter how
> different they may be. Anthropologists have met this difficulty
> by taking positions that are often conflicting and that lack
> self-consistency.
>
> – Julian Steward, "Theory and Practice in Social Science"

When anthropologist Julian Steward made this comment in 1955, he and many of his colleagues were divided into two warring camps – those who appeared before the US Indian Claims Commission (USICC) as experts in support of Indian claimants and those who appeared on behalf of the federal government (the defendant). Optimistically, Congress had created the commission in 1946 to settle the historical grievances that Indian tribes held against the federal government. Most of the claims that the tribes brought before the commission concerned dispossession and therefore raised questions about traditional land tenure. Steward correctly identified a fundamental problem that the *Indian Claims Commission Act* of 1946 and extant case law had created. Anthropological experts had to address their evidence to a specific model of tenure. This meant that they had to apply or develop theoretical frameworks and collect historical data that addressed this model in ways that advanced their clients' objectives.

This quest, which continues to the present day, has had a significant impact on the development of the interdisciplinary approach to Native history known as ethnohistory, although it has not received much scholarly attention until recently.[1] That quest is my concern here. I will pay particular attention to the implications that research undertaken for the USICC cases has had for ethnohistorical research in Canada and for the use of this line of evidence in Canadian Aboriginal land rights litigation. I will focus on the landmark *Delgamuukw v. British Columbia* (1997) case in which the battle of experts echoed the skirmishes that had taken place many years earlier before the USICC.

Development of American Anthropology before the USICC Era

Prior to creation of the USICC, Indian history was largely the domain of anthropologists, who focused on cultural dimensions. It is well known that, from the late nineteenth century until the middle of the twentieth, salvage ethnology and cultural element distribution surveys dominated American anthropology. This work was driven by two underlying and interrelated ideas: the notion that Indian cultures were primitive vis-à-vis those of Europeans, and the belief that these cultures would soon disappear. Accordingly, anthropologists and archaeologists undertook extensive field surveys to collect vestiges of Indian cultures that researchers believed were characteristic of precontact life. They focused their attention on remote areas, where they thought that the impact of European culture had been less destructive. They presumed that retreating into the bush was equivalent to retreating in cultural time.[2]

Two important assumptions informed this salvage research: the belief that Native cultures had been largely static in precontact times, and the idea that European culture had been the main catalyst for change after contact. The popularity of the latter idea meant that acculturation and assimilation viewpoints dominated anthropological studies of Aboriginal cultural change.[3] These ideas and perspectives lingered well into the late twentieth century. Significantly, salvage ethnologists did not devote equal attention to all aspects of Native cultures. Rather, they emphasized material culture, Aboriginal mythology, religion, and language. They devoted relatively little attention to in-depth analyses of land tenure, political, or economic systems – topics that would be the focus of claims research.

In the 1930s, anthropologists began to synthesize the data that they had been collecting. In keeping with Boasian historical particularism, which dominated American anthropology until mid-century, most anthropologists shunned theorizing about Aboriginal cultural development in terms of evolutionary and other untested general theoretical models. Rather, they emphasized local circumstances. They did so by employing two common synthetic methods. One involved writing ethnographies of specific groups; the other sought to explore culture-environment relationships by applying the cultural area approach, a scheme that anthropologists, notably Clark Wissler, initially had developed to organize and display museum artifact collections and infer chronological information from patterns of distribution.[4]

The cultural area approach had come to dominate American anthropology on the eve of the establishment of the Indian Claims Commission. A.L. Kroeber, one of the leading figures of American anthropology at the middle of the twentieth century, and a key expert for the plaintiffs in the California Indian claims of the 1950s, had championed this perspective and had authored two great classics: *Handbook of the Indians of California* (1925) and *The Cultural and Natural Areas of Native North America* (1939).[5]

This approach to ecological anthropology had significant limitations, however. Most notably, anthropologists worked on a macroscale in terms of cultures and environments. Also, they treated the relationships between cultures and environments largely in static terms, seeking mostly to explain distributions of different cultures in terms of key features of the physical environment (notably climate and vegetation) or historical processes such as diffusion and population migration. To circumvent these problems, in the 1930s a small number of anthropologists began promoting an alternative perspective that came to be known as cultural ecology, ecological anthropology, or ethnogeography. It tended to be an economic-deterministic approach that focused on the dynamic interrelationships between technology, economy, and environment (or habitat, economy, and society).[6] Steward, one of Kroeber's most influential students, pioneered this approach in the United States.[7] It was in its infancy on the eve of the USICC era (1946-78). Subsequently, Steward did some of his most important theoretical writing on the subject while he was engaged as an expert witness for the government in USICC cases in the American southwest and California.[8]

These aspects of the early development of American anthropology meant that the anthropological experts who appeared before the USICC drew heavily on the vast cultural element survey database that they and their predecessors had built up over the preceding half-century. The USICC process also forced them to turn to unconventional anthropological sources, notably documentary records. There were three primary reasons for this. First, and of particular importance, the USICC process focused on the postcontact dispossession of American Indians. Second, as noted earlier, claims raised questions about Indian land tenure, economies, and political organization that had received scant attention in the earlier surveys. In many cases, informants were no longer available who could answer questions about these facets of traditional life. Third, the lawyers and commissioners were more familiar and comfortable with documentary evidence than they were with oral and archaeological data. Thus, anthropological experts began combing American archives for ethnographic evidence. They used their disciplinary concepts and perspectives to identify and interpret relevant facts.[9]

Creation of the USICC proved to be a major catalyst for the development of ethnohistory in the United States by making substantial research funding available for the first time. For example, the federal Department of Justice funded the largest ethnohistorical research project to date. It was the Great Lakes and Ohio Valley Ethnohistorical Survey project located at Indiana University. The project had an annual budget in excess of $35,000. Anthropologist Erminie Wheeler-Voegelin served as director from 1956 to 1969.[10] The Department of Justice expected her and her team members to provide the reports and expertise that it needed to defend the US government against claims that Indian tribes brought before the commission in the midwest and west.[11] The *American Journal of Ethnohistory,* founded in 1955, initially was housed in the project's offices, and Wheeler-Voegelin served as its first editor (for volumes 1-11, 1955-66). One of her proteges, Harold Hickerson, followed her as an editor (for volumes 13-15, 1966-68).[12] Hickerson financed his graduate education as a project research associate. This position required him to appear as a government expert in USICC cases.

Land Tenure Models and the Battle of Ethnohistorical Experts before the USICC

The *Indian Claims Commission Act* and American case law set important parameters for researchers. The act specified that Indian tribes were entitled to financial compensation for lost lands if they could prove that their ancestors had lived as an identifiable group holding a communal title to a specific territory, which they had exclusively used and occupied at the time of dispossession. They also had to demonstrate that the latter event had not been the consequence of an equitable treaty or conquest. These terms meant that anthropological experts who supported Indian plaintiffs generally argued that all of North America had been divided into well-defined and defended tribal territories before Euro-American contact.[13] This perspective was called the "contiguous boundary theory." Experts who supported the government defendant countered with the proposition that only the cores of tribal territories had been exclusively used and occupied. This was the "nuclear territory theory." According to this perception, boundaries often were poorly defined because land use intensity decreased outward from the centre, territories often overlapped, and "no-man's-lands" sometimes existed between tribal areas.

The USICC model also raised the vexed question about how long a group had to have occupied a region prior to dispossession for it to hold a valid claim. Ralph Barney, who headed the Department of Justice's USICC claims section, and his staff concluded that Indian tribal groups did not have to prove that their ancestors had "Aboriginal occupancy" or "immemorial possession" to make valid claims. Rather, Barney and his colleagues concluded that claimants merely had to prove that their ancestors had been in exclusive possession of a definable area of land at the time of cession (or acquisition) and had held this territory for a long time prior to that event.[14] The USICC adopted this perspective.[15] It required experts for claimants and the federal defendant to consider the ways in which traditional tenure systems had changed from the time of initial European contact to the time of dispossession. Pursuit of this question forced experts to consider a series of related issues, notably the impacts of epidemics, warfare, migration, economic intercourse with Euro-Americans, and expansion of the colonial settlement frontier. These topics had long been of interest to scholars. The anthropologists who appeared for the plaintiffs searched for documentary evidence to support the supposition that basic cultural elements, such as the land tenure practices, had persisted despite a myriad of postcontact pressures. When government experts claimed that there was no evidence for the existence of distinctive tribal boundaries in a given area, plaintiffs' experts sometimes responded with the argument that Indians had developed various strategies to obscure their tribal boundaries in the hope of protecting their homelands from land-hungry white settlers.[16]

The government's experts, on the other hand, commonly contended that postcontact stresses had led to increases in the numbers and sizes of areas of overlap and no-man's lands. One of these experts, Hickerson, speculated that the latter had served an important ecological role by creating *de facto* game reserves because no tribe could safely hunt in these places.[17] When they confronted solid evidence for the existence of bounded and defended territories, sometimes government experts argued that they had resulted from economic intercourse with Euro-American newcomers and/or through conflicts with these intruders and other Indian groups.[18] This was Steward's perspective. In other words, claimants' experts tended to emphasize the continuity and persistence of "core" customs and practices and tribal boundaries. The defendants' experts, on the other hand, stressed change – particularly in the economic sphere of life. Some, notably Steward, promoted the idea that most Indian notions of property were products of Euro-American contact. In these ways, USICC claims served to intensify a long-standing clash of perspectives about postcontact Indian cultural history.[19] They also accentuated debates about which customs and practices made a culture distinctive.[20]

USICC Claims and Aboriginal and Treaty Rights Claims Research in Canada

Claims research began in Canada slightly more than twenty-five years after creation of the USICC. In the intervening period, the ethnohistorical research undertaken for USICC purposes had a direct impact on developing Canadian scholarship primarily for three reasons.

First, a number of Indian groups who lived along the Canadian border, notably the Assiniboine, Cree, Sioux, and Ojibwa, had filed claims. The ancestors of many of these people had lived in Canada in the precontact and early contact eras, and/or they had close relatives who had lived there.

Second, from the outset, American claims researchers published their findings in scholarly journals, especially in *Ethnohistory*, and in monographs. Regarding the latter, in 1974, Garland Publishing Company published the written reports that experts had submitted to the USICC.[21] Most of these published works had been prepared for the government's defence. Most of the Indians' experts made oral submissions to the USICC before 1965. It was not until after that year that the USICC required both parties to make written submissions. At least twenty of the Garland monographs dealt with borderland tribes in the midwestern and plains areas (see Appendix 1). Thus, a substantial portion of the early ethnohistorical literature of direct relevance to Canada had been generated for claims purposes or was an outgrowth of that work.

Third, the pioneering Canadian ethnohistory studies by Charles A. Bishop and me had direct links to USICC research and the experts who had taken part in it. Bishop, for example, was a protege of Hickerson, who, as noted above, had begun his career as a government expert in the upper Great Lakes Ojibwa cases. Hickerson applied a historical cultural ecology methodology and focused his attention on Ojibwa migrations and their changing postcontact social organization. He emphasized the atomistic impact that European contact had had on Ojibwa society. Bishop followed in Hickerson's footsteps, but he shifted his focus northward to the Ojibwa who lived in central Canada. Eventually, Bishop appeared as a government expert in *Bear Island Foundation and Gary Potts v. Regina* (1991). This case concerned some of the Anishnabay (Ojibwa) that he had included in his landmark study, *The Northern Ojibwa and the Fur Trade: An Historical and Ecological Study*, published in 1974.[22] In fundamental respects, Bishop's line of argumentation echoed those that his mentor had presented to the USICC in the northern Minnesota Chippewa cases.[23]

At the University of Wisconsin, I was a student of historical geographer Andrew H. Clark, who had received his doctorate from the Department of Geography of the University of California Berkeley, where he had studied with Carl Sauer and A.L. Kroeber. One member of my doctoral supervisory committee, archaeologist David Baerreis, had served as a government expert in the midwestern USICC cases, though I was unaware of this when I was a student.[24] He had used fur trade company account books to document postcontact economic change among the Delaware. Baerreis' work, published in *Ethnohistory* in 1961, stimulated my interest in applying a similar historical approach to Canadian groups.[25] As a student of the geography and anthropology departments at the University of Wisconsin, I also became very interested in employing the cultural ecological approach, particularly Steward's, to gain insights into the processes that facilitated the rapid migration of western Canadian First Nations across major environmental and cultural boundaries during the postcontact era. Subsequently, beginning in the early 1980s, I too became involved in First Nations and Métis treaty rights cases in Alberta (two cases), British Columbia (two), Manitoba (one), and Ontario (four).[26] I will now focus on the Gitksan and Wet'suwet'en claim (*Delgamuukw*).

Delgamuukw

Canada lagged far behind the United States in using ethnohistorical data in Indian claims litigation. Before the 1973 *Calder* ruling, Canadian land claims had centred on interpretations of the law.[27] After this ruling, it became clear that ethnohistorical information about First Nations cultural history, particularly land use and more general livelihood issues, would be central. It remained uncertain, however, which kinds of legal models this evidence would have to address. In his 1980 ruling concerning *Baker Lake v. Minister of Indian Affairs and Northern Development,* Justice J. Mahoney of the Federal Court of Canada, Trial Division, adopted a historical tenure model strikingly similar to the one that the USICC had used. He decided that, to be successful, Aboriginal plaintiffs had to demonstrate that their ancestors had been members of an organized society that had occupied a specific tract of territory to the exclusion of other groups. He stipulated further that the claimants' ancestors' occupation had to have been an established fact at the time that Britain had asserted its sovereignty. Although *Baker Lake* was never appealed to higher courts, Mahoney's test became a standard in Canada, though the Supreme Court modified it in its *Delgamuukw* ruling (1997) to allow for overlapping territories, something that the USICC had also done in later years.[28] The Mahoney model strongly influenced the presentation of ethnohistorical evidence at trial (1987-90) in *Delgamuukw,* the first major land claim after *Calder* to be appealed to the Supreme Court.

The "frozen rights doctrine" also weighed heavily on the minds of lawyers and experts during the *Delgamuukw* trial. This legal theory held that Aboriginal rights only encompassed traditions in place when Europeans had asserted sovereignty – the mythical "time immemorial" of Canadian law. According to this outlook, cultural practices were considered to be ineligible for legal protection if they had been extensively modified or created as a consequence of interactions with the newcomers. This presumption held sway until 1990, when the Supreme Court rejected this notion in its *Regina v. Sparrow* judgment. The court ruled that traditional rights could exist in modern forms.[29] By this time, however, the *Delgamuukw* trial was in its final phase, and most of the ethnohistorical evidence had been presented and examined. Significantly, the frozen rights theory had different implications for researchers who supported the plaintiffs versus those who supported the defendants. Also, it had the effect of once again bringing the long-standing academic debate about continuity versus change into the courtroom, as the discussion below will highlight.

The Mahoney test and the frozen rights doctrine were additionally problematic for the ethnohistorical experts who appeared in *Delgamuukw* because the courts had not determined when the British had established effective sovereignty over the disputed territory. The operating assumption during the trial was that British sovereignty had occurred sometime between the arrival of Captain James Cook in 1778 and the creation of the colony of British Columbia in 1858 (or possibly even later in more remote areas). This ambiguity precluded ethnohistorical experts from targeting their research to a specific year, as had been the case in most USICC claims, which usually had addressed historical treaties.[30]

Given these circumstances, the Gitksan and Wet'suwet'en believed that, to be safe, they had to demonstrate at trial that their ancestors' way of life met the Mahoney test throughout the period from the eve of Cook's visit until at least the end of the nineteenth century. This demonstration involved gathering evidence to show that their people had traditionally lived in villages, each of which had been comprised of a number of land-owning lineages (houses) headed by hereditary chiefs. It was essential for them to demonstrate that house territories had been clearly defined, that lineage heads had effectively managed these territories on behalf of the house, and that customary laws – the *Adaawk* of the Gitksan and the *Kungax* of the Wet'suwet'en – had underpinned the system. In other words, organized societies had controlled bounded territories. Finally, the Gitksan and Wet'suwet'en thought that they needed to prove their house-territory system was neither a product of the European fur trade nor had been transformed significantly by it during the early contact period.

When the Gitksan and Wet'suwet'en began preparing for their claim in the early 1980s, a massive archaeological and ethnographic literature already existed that dealt with the northwest coast cultural area.[31] Salvage ethnology and cultural element distribution surveys dominated this early scholarship. This literature posed several problems for the Gitksan and Wet'suwet'en claimants, however. Few ethnographers had studied their ancestors. Rather, most scholars had focused their research on the Tshimshian coastal neighbours of the Gitksan and Wet'suwet'en. And, as with other regions, ethnographers had paid little regard to local land tenure systems. Another problem for the plaintiffs was that, in northern British Columbia, ethnohistorical research had lagged far behind that in other areas of the country. Consequently, on the eve of the *Delgamuukw* claim, there were no published ethnohistories of the Gitksan's and Wet'suwet'en's participation in the Pacific slope fur trade (or that of their neighbours) comparable to those that focused on the Assiniboine, Cree, Huron, and Ojibwa involvement in the French and Hudson's Bay Company (HBC) fur trades of central Canada.[32]

Most worrisome of all, the limited ethnographic literature that did address local land tenure practices suggested that those of the Wet'suwet'en were a postcontact invention. In 1932, ethnologist Diamond Jenness planted the seeds for this idea when he suggested that western Carrier groups had borrowed many cultural elements from their Tshimshian neighbours.[33] Nine years later Irving Goldman explored this idea with respect to the Alkatcho Carrier, who lived to the south of the Wet'suwet'en, and the Stuart Lake Carrier. Goldman argued that the European fur trade had provided the key stimulus for the cultural borrowing that Jenness had postulated.[34]

At about the same time, Julian Steward also became interested in western Carrier land tenure practices, particularly those of Stuart Lake. This was because his theories about cultural ecology postulated that common cultural patterns normally emerged when environmental settings, technologies, and the economic orientations of groups were broadly similar. This was the case throughout most of the Athapascan-speaking area. The western Carrier people were a marked exception. Their house-territory scheme differed from those of most other Athapascan groups. He undertook fieldwork in the Stuart Lake area in 1939-40 to search for an explanation of this apparent anomaly. Steward published a field report in 1940 and a short article a year later. He did not write about these people again until 1955 and 1961.[35] By this time, his USICC claims work had encouraged him to theorize about the interrelationships between levels of sociopolitical organization and tenure systems and to consider the impact that European contact had had on those relationships. As noted, he believed that contact with Euro-Americans had led many groups to adopt more elaborate sociopolitical and land tenure systems. These had been central issues in the northern Shoshone case, in which he had argued that before Euro-American contact these Indians' cultures had not evolved sufficiently for them to have developed a property system.[36]

Given his perspective on this issue, it is not surprising that the Jenness-Goldman diffusionist explanation for the western Carrier house-territory system appealed to Steward. When elaborating on their ideas, he too embraced the European fur trade as the catalyst. He thought that the local environment facilitated adoption of the Tshimshian-like tenure system because the region abounded in salmon and had limited populations of large game. According to Steward, these factors favoured settled village life over the nomadic hunting ways common to most other Athapascans.[37] Steward also argued that the fur trade had led the western Carrier to develop a regulatory scheme that protected local beaver populations. The fundamental problem with his theorizing was that he did not test his ideas against data that he could have obtained by combing the published and unpublished accounts of the North West Company fur traders who had been in the area before 1821.

To challenge the Jenness-Goldman-Steward perspective and obtain the ethnographic data that they needed to fill in the gaps in the extant literature, the Gitksan and Wet'suwet'en enlisted the help of anthropologists to undertake a massive oral history project with the objective of mapping the various house territories, recording their histories, and articulating how their tenure system operated. They also retained two historical geographers, Robert Galois and me, to provide documentary histories of the regional economy during the postcontact era. They asked me to focus on the fur trade history of the region and pay particular attention to their ancestors' involvement in the European fur trade from the time of initial local contact until the mid-nineteenth century. Galois looked at the later period.

My research in the HBC archives revealed that, in the early 1820s, one of the company's senior officers, William Brown, wrote a series of district reports and post journals that provided detailed accounts of the Gitksan and Wet'suwet'en (particularly the latter) house-territory and feast system. Apparently, he dwelt on this topic because he was new to the area and their tenure system seriously interfered with his efforts to expand the company's beaver returns from the upper Skeena River area. Of particular importance for the plaintiffs' claim, Brown noted that each village included "nobles or men of property" who controlled access to the resources of their house's territory.[38] In other words, his description provided independent corroboration for the oral evidence that the elders presented.

The accounts also provided important clues about the antiquity of the land tenure practices that Brown observed. Of crucial importance, he made it abundantly clear that the Wet'suwet'en and their eastern relatives, the Babine, carefully managed their beaver stocks in order to assure themselves of a supply of beaver meat, a very important ceremonial food. This meant that their conservation effort was not aimed at hoarding beaver pelts for trading purposes, as Steward supposed.[39] This fact suggested the probability that the beaver conservation measures, and the house-territory system that made them possible, originated in the precontact period. Rather than being the genesis of the conservation system, as Goldman and Steward proposed, the fur trade likely provided the Babine and Wet'suwet'en with an additional reason to perpetuate it. This is what I argued at trial. Understandably, crown counsel vigorously challenged my interpretation using several lines of attack. They noted that my previous research about the impact of the early fur trade on the Assiniboine, Cree, and Ojibwa of central Canada had emphasized cultural change rather than stability. They asked me why Brown had only mentioned beaver if the chiefs had husbanded all the resources of their territories. Finally, drawing on archival records, they cited many instances of interhouse and intervillage conflicts (mostly from the late nineteenth century) to suggest that the chiefs had no real authority and that the Gitksan and Wet'suwet'en lived in a Hobbesian world of chaos until British Columbia and Canada brought the gift of civilization and established order in the region.[40]

I replied to these propositions and questions as follows. With regard to the impact of the fur trade, I took a particularistic stance and emphasized the importance of doing detailed empirical research that focused on the local area. I stressed that the cultural and environmental circumstances in which the European-oriented fur trade unfolded in Skeena River country were radically different from those of the Sub-Arctic and Plains cultural areas. For these reasons, I contended that it was unsound to assume that the post-contact histories of groups from these very dissimilar regions were parallel. I observed that Brown's own experience made this point. Brown had gained his trading experience east of the Rocky Mountains among the band societies of the Cree, Ojibwa, and Dene. His accounts reveal that he found it difficult to deal with the Gitksan and Wet'suwet'en, who were very different. Most notably, they were led by hereditary chiefs who wielded considerable influence and power and had their own agendas.

Concerning Brown's focus on beaver conservation practices to the exclusion of similar discussions about the management of other resources, I pointed out that his primary goal was to increase beaver returns. Other resources, except salmon, were not of interest to Brown, which likely explains why he did not discuss the chiefs' supervision of them. His reports for the districts that he managed before moving to Gitksan and Wet'suwet'en territory in 1821 support this explanation. In these other documents, he wrote at length about the issues most relevant to his performance as a fur trader. Mostly, he dwelt on the actions of opposing traders. Of particular relevance in his earlier reports, he did not provide detailed descriptions of Aboriginal tenure systems.

The report and testimony of historical geographer Sheila Robinson comprised the centrepiece of the crown's defence. She argued that there was "no conclusive evidence that suggests that, prior to the advent of European influence in the claim area, the Gitksan and Wet-suet'en lineages and families identified ownership rights to large and precisely defined tracts of hunting territories." Elaborating on her theory, Robinson continued:

> Speaking generally, one may expect that some form of organized control would have been exercised over access to the fisheries and other resources which were necessary for survival and over the local trails and bridges which facilitated prehistoric trade networks. But prior to the intensification of pressure on interior fur resources sparked by European demands for furs there would appear to have been no need of a sophisticated and elaborate body of rules governing access to resources or for extensive and defined areas of land for the exploitation. In the absence of competition over scarce resources, there is no reason for the rules to exist.[41]

Robinson concluded by speculating that, before the advent of the European fur trade, Native territorial holdings "were in all likelihood more limited in size, to include mainly the area surrounding villages."[42] In other words, she was advancing a theoretical model reminiscent of the one that the government's experts had often advanced in USICC cases.[43] Her "model" was much cruder than that of her predecessors, however. For example, she made no effort to calculate land use intensity and relate it to effective occupancy, as the government's experts had done thirty years earlier in the California Indian claims. Rather, Robinson offered a "lines and nodes" perspective that recognized usage only in terms of cultural modifications of the physical landscape (villages, trails, developed fishing sites, etc.). This was an outlook that echoed Lockean notions about property rights and was in keeping with the perspectives of successive colonial and provincial governments.[44]

At the outset of her report, and in her testimony, Robinson admitted that she had not carried out any fieldwork among the Gitksan and Wet'suwet'en, nor had she done any archival work to test her theory of Aboriginal land tenure. Instead, she mostly relied on Goldman and Steward and on more recent elaborations of their work in the late 1970s by anthropologists Vernon Kobrinski and Charles A. Bishop (1979).[45] These anthropologists, as was the case with Steward, explicitly stated that they were being speculative. Of particular importance, neither Bishop nor Kobrinski had examined HBC trader Brown's records, which had been available since the late 1960s, when the HBC archives were opened to scholars. In other words, in *Delgamuukw*, Robinson was perpetuating the speculative approach to the cultural history of the western Carrier that had become an anthropological tradition. Reiterating what her secondary sources had claimed, particularly Steward, she argued that the immediate postcontact fur trade must have brought about major transformations of Wet'suwet'en land tenure systems because the enterprise had had such impacts elsewhere in North America. When making this historical/ethnographic analogy, she did not inform the court that ethnohistorians have been debating the impact that the fur trade had on Algonquian tenure systems in eastern Canada since the beginning of the twentieth century. To date, they have not reached a consensus.[46]

Conclusion

It has been almost sixty years since the Indian claims era began in North America. Many of the issues and problems that arose during the first decade of USICC hearings remain with us today. There are a number of reasons for this. Most notably, ethnohistorical experts are still expected to address their research to the same basic land tenure model that case law and the USICC act mandated, although the courts now allow for overlapping territories.

Also, scholars continue to hold fundamentally different views of the impact that contact had on the core features of Aboriginal societies and cultures, such as land tenure systems. Some emphasize continuity; others stress disruptive change. These contrasting perspectives have great significance in the legal arena, where proving or disproving the continuity of a tradition can lead to recognition or denial of Aboriginal rights.

Appendix 1

List of written reports submitted to the USICC and published by Garland Publishing*

Baerreis, David A., Erminie Wheeler-Voegelin, and Remedios Wycoco-Moore. *Indians of Northeastern Illinois: Anthropological Report on the Chippewa, Ottawa, and Potawatomi Indians.*

Berthrong, Donald J. *Indians of Northern Indiana and Southwestern Michigan: An Historical Report on Indians' Use and Occupancy of Northern Indiana and Southwestern Michigan.*

Ewers, John C. *Ethnological Report on the Chippewa Cree Tribe of the Rocky Boy Reservation and the Little Shell Band of Indians.*

Hickerson, Harold. *Chippewa Indians II: Ethnohistory of Mississippi Bands and Pillager and Winnibigoshish Bands of Chippewa.*

–. *Chippewa Indians III: Ethnohistory of Chippewa of Lake Superior.*

–. *Chippewa Indians IV: Ethnohistory of Chippewa in Central Minnesota.*

–. "The Genesis of a Trading Post Band: The Pembina Chippewa." *Ethnohistory* 3, 4 (1956): 289-345.

–. "The Journal of Charles Jean-Baptiste Chaboillez, 1797-1798." *Ethnohistory* 9 (1962): 265-316, 363-427.

–. *Sioux Indians I: Mdewakanton Band of Sioux Indians.*

Sharrock, Susan, and Floyd Sharrock. *A History of the Cree Indian Territorial Expansion from the Hudson Bay Area to the Interior Saskatchewan and Missouri Plains in Montana, 1640-1916.*

Stout, David B. *Chippewa Indians: Ethnohistorical Report on the Saginaw Chippewa.*

Tanner, Helen. *Chippewa Indians: The Chippewa of Eastern Lower Michigan.*

–. *Indians of Northern Ohio and Southeastern Michigan: The Location of Indian Tribes in Southeastern Michigan and Northern Ohio.*

Wheeler-Voegelin, Erminie. *Anthropological Report on the Ottawa, Chippewa, and Potawatomi Indians, Part 1.*

–. *Chippewa Indians V: Anthropological Report on Indian Land Use and Occupancy of Northern Michigan.*

–. *Indians of Illinois and Northwestern Indiana.*

–. *Indians of Ohio and Indiana Prior to 1795: Ethnohistory of Indian Use and Occupancy in Ohio and Indiana Prior to 1795.*

–. *Indians of Northern Ohio and Southeastern Michigan: An Ethnohistorical Report.*

–. *Indians of Northern Ohio and Southeastern Michigan: Ethnohistorical Report on the Wyandot, Ottawa Munsee, Delaware, Shawnee, and Potawatomi of Royce Areas 53 and 54.*

–. *Indians of Northwestern Ohio: Ethnohistorical Report on the Wyandot, Potawatomi, Ottawa, and Chippewa of Northwestern Ohio.*

Wheeler-Voegelin, Erminie, and Harold Hickerson. *Chippewa Indians I: Red Lake and Pembina Chippewa.*

* *Note*: All works were published by Garland in 1974 unless otherwise noted.

Notes

Epigraph: Steward, "Theory and Practice," 292-93.

1 Initially, experts who took part in the process wrote about their reactions and concerns. One of the most notable publications was the special issue of *Ethnohistory* 4 (1955), in which anthropologists Nancy Lurie, Julian Steward, and A.L. Kroeber all made contributions. Thirty years later Imre Sutton edited an important collection of essays on the USICC, which also included essays by some of the important experts. See Sutton, ed., *Irredeemable America.*

2 This was known as the "space-time equivalency hypothesis." The problem in Canada, of course, is that some of the areas that scholars thought were remote, such as Hudson Bay and James Bay, had some of the longest periods of sustained contact with Euro-Canadians.

3 One of the classic acculturation studies is that of Ralph Linton, *Acculturation.*

4 Barnard, *History and Theory*, 55-56. Chronology was inferred from the notion that cultural elements diffused outward from the centre of a cultural area. Therefore, the oldest artifacts presumably were located at the outer edges of a region. Wissler developed the age-area model because archaeologists had few reliable dating techniques in the early twentieth century.

5 Kroeber finished the handbook in 1919: Kroeber, *Handbook of the Indians of California*, 78; and Kroeber, *Cultural and Natural Areas.*

6 The classic general study of this type is Cyril Daryll Forde, *Habitat, Economy, and Society.*

7 Ralph Linton also made an important contribution in *The Study of Man.*

8 See Clemmer, Meyers, and Rudden, eds., *Julian Steward and the Great Basin*, 170-202.

9 Nancy Lurie, an early participant in ICC claims as an expert, noted that initially the government expected that most of the experts would be historians. Government officials were unaware that historians had, prior to the act, focused little attention on Indian history. Interview with Nancy Lurie, Milwaukee Public Museum, October 2002.

10 Ray, "Anthropology, History, and Aboriginal Rights: Politics and the Rise of Ethnohistory in North America in the 1950s," keynote paper presented at a symposium on Dialogues between the Disciplines: History and Anthropology, Center for Critical Theory and Transnational Studies, University of Oregon, 3-5 April 2003, 9; Ray, "Anthropology, History, and Aboriginal Rights: Politics and the Rise of Ethnohistory in North America in the 1950s," 89-112.

11 On 20 July 1955, Wheeler-Voegelin noted that the Department of Justice had assigned fifty ICC dockets to her project. Of these, she anticipated that forty would be tried before the commission. She anticipated that another sixty reports would be needed. Erminie Wheeler-Voegelin to Ralph A. Barney, 20 August 1955, Indian University Archives, Great Lakes and Ohio Valley Ethnohistorical Survey [GLOVES], box 1.

12 Dorothy Libby served as editor for volume 12 (1965).

13 Ray, "Anthropology, History, and Aboriginal Rights"; and Ray, "Constructing and Reconstructing Native History," 15-38.

14 Ralph Barney, US Department of Justice, to Erminie Wheeler-Voegelin, 29 August 1956, Wheeler-Voegelin Papers, Indiana University, box 1/3.

15 According to Lurie, legal theories advanced by the Department of Justice strongly influenced the thinking of commissioners. Interview with Lurie.

16 For example, Anthony Wallace made this argument in the Iowa claim. Besides deliberately obfuscating boundary information, he contended that Indians created alliances with neighbouring groups so that individual tribes could not surrender their lands without the consent of their allies. See Ray, "Constructing and Reconstructing Native History," 23-25.

17 Hickerson initially developed this idea in print in "The Virginia Deer and Intertribal Buffer Zones," 43-66. This paper was based on research that he had undertaken for USICC claims in central and northern Minnesota. Subsequently, Hickerson elaborated this thesis in his classic work, *The Chippewa and Their Neighbors*, 64-119.

18 Ray, "Constructing and Reconstructing Native History," 21.

19 Studies of cultural "continuity and change" also became popular.
20 There is little doubt that the *R. v. Van der Peet* (1996) decision of the Supreme Court of Canada will renew this outdated debate in Canada. In this decision, the court held that "to be an Aboriginal right an activity must be an element of a practice, custom or tradition integral to the distinctive culture of the Aboriginal group claiming the right ... To be integral, a practice, custom or tradition must be of central significance to the Aboriginal society in question – one of the things which made the culture of the society distinctive." *R. v. Van der Peet,* [1996] 2 S.C.R. 507.
21 Ross, *Index to the Expert Testimony,* vii.
22 In particular, he argued that contact, especially their involvement in the fur trade, led to a breakdown of the clan system. See Bishop, *The Northern Ojibwa and the Fur Trade,* viii-ix.
23 Essentially, Bishop argued that the ancestors of the claimants had immigrated into the claimed area after contact and had emerged as a "trading post band" after the Robinson Treaty of 1850. See Hodgins and Benidickson, *The Temagami Experience,* 268. Hickerson took a similar approach to the Chippewa claims in Minnesota. He developed the idea that bands had formed around trading posts; Hickerson, "Genesis of a Trading Post Band: The Pembina Chippewa," 289-345. This opinion was based on research that he had undertaken for Docket 18-A, Red Lake, Pembina, and White Earth Bands and Minnesota Chippewa Tribe.
24 As an undergraduate, I had also taken courses with him.
25 Baerreis, "The Ethnohistoric Approach and Archaeology," 49-77.
26 Those that went to trial are: *R. v. Horseman,* [1990] 1 S.C.R. 901, *Victor Buffalo et al. v. Regina,* 2002 F.C.T. 1226, *Delgamuukw v. British Columbia, [1997] 3 S.C.R. 1010, Regina v. Spade, Regina v. Wassaykessic* (Ontario Court Provincial Division [unreported], 1992), and *R. v. Powley,* [2003] 2 S.C.R. 207, 2003 S.C.C. 43.
27 *Calder v. Attorney-General of British Columbia,* [1973] S.C.R. 313. Personal communication, Professor Doug Sanders, Faculty of Law, University of British Columbia.
28 *Delgamuukw v. Regina* (s. 196).
29 The court acknowledged that traditional rights could exist in modern forms. *R. v. Sparrow,* [1990] 1 S.C.R. 1075.
30 In his judgment, Chief Justice Allan MacEachen decided that it had taken place between 1803 and 1858. Chief Justice Allan MacEachen, *Reasons for Judgment,* Supreme Court of British Columbia, Smithers Registry 0843, 8 March 1991.
31 Franz Boas had done the pioneering fieldwork in the region in 1886.
32 In 1977, Robin Fisher published *Contact and Conflict,* which contained chapters on the fur trade. Fisher's work did not focus on any single group, however.
33 Jenness, *Indians of Canada,* 365. The eastern Canadian studies included Bishop, *Northern Ojibwa and the Fur Trade* (1974); Heidenreich, *Huronia* (1971); Ray, *Indians in the Fur Trade* (1974); Ray and Freeman, *"Give Us Good Measure"* (1978); and Trigger, *Children of Aataensic* (1976).
34 Goldman, "The Alkatcho Carrier," 396-418.
35 Steward, "Recording Culture," 83-90. In 1955 he devoted Chapter 10 in his *Theory of Culture Change* to the Carrier.
36 Ronaasen et al., 174-76.
37 Steward, "Carrier Acculturation," 732-44.
38 Arthur J. Ray, "The Early Economic History of the Gitksan and Wet'suwet'en-Babine Tribal Territories: 1822-30," unpublished paper (1985).
39 Ray, "Fur Trade History of Gitxzan and Wet'suet'en Territory," *Delgamuukw* Proceedings at Trial, Supreme Court of British Columbia, Smithers Registry No. 0843, 20 March 1989, Exhibit Number 963.
40 Arthur J. Ray, "Creating the Image of the Savage," 13-28.
41 Sheila Robinson, "Protohistoric Developments in Gitksan and Wet-suet'en Territories," unpublished report, 12 May 1987, 5.
42 Ibid., 6.

43 Ray, "Kroeber and the California Claims," 248-74.
44 This is known as the labour theory of property. According to this perspective, rights derive from the modification of the natural environment through the investment of human labour.
45 Kobrinski, "The Tsimshianization of the Carrier Indians," 201-10; Bishop, "Limiting Access to Limited Goods," 148-61.
46 For an excellent discussion of this debate, see Tanner, "The New Hunting Territory Debate: An Introduction to Some Unresolved Issues," *Anthropologica* 28 (1986): 19-36.

2
Social Theory, Expert Evidence, and the *Yorta Yorta* Rights Appeal Decision
Bruce Rigsby

"Legal theory" is the body of systematic thinking about (or bearing closely on) law to which nonlawyers can and do make important contributions, and which lawyers ignore at their peril. My conception of legal theory is broad, sweeping within it matters that might be thought to belong to political or social theory rather than to legal theory. This breadth reflects the broadening of interests that is characteristic of contemporary legal scholarship. We live at a time when economists like Ronald Coase and Gary Becker, philosophers, like John Rawls and Richard Rorty, and literary critics, like Stanley Fish, are real presences in legal scholarship.

– Richard A. Posner, *Overcoming Law*

These are intellectually engaging and exciting times to do Native title anthropology in Australia, even though the litigated outcomes of the cases leave much to be desired. The range of Native title work on offer provides contexts and situations in which we can do ethnographic and historical research that bears critically on some classical topics and questions of social anthropological theory. I have in mind here particularly what I like to call "property theory." It concerns me that many anthropologists have not yet taken seriously that in Native title research we are studying the phenomena of property and property rights.

The late Ken Maddock touched on the point when he asked whether we were advancing anthropology through our land claims work.[1] I am more optimistic than he was in those pre-*Mabo* days. We share a history with comparative law and jurisprudence from the nineteenth century, when forms of property were a common concern.[2] There are also a number of contemporary academic lawyers whose work on property is comparative, such as Susan Bright, John Dewar, James Harris, and James Penner.[3] There cannot be, nor should there be, disparate legal and anthropological theories of property.[4] That said, I would not like to see anthropologists fail to rise to the opportunities and challenges of Native title research for developing our knowledge and theory of property, as Julian Steward and other anthropologists failed to do during land claim research when the Indian Claims Commission operated in America.[5]

This chapter is in several parts. The first provides background on the history of recognition of Aboriginal land rights in Australia. The second reviews the *Yorta Yorta* rights case, in which the High Court of Australia decision has reduced, and sets the evidential parameters for, Native title litigation for some time to come. The third describes the current situation in which anthropologists and lawyers find themselves working. The fourth considers some crucial terms and concepts for analyzing and describing Aboriginal property rights ethnographically and for improving our contribution to Native title work in the post-*Yorta Yorta* period. For some time, I have been concerned about the quality and standard of Native title research, writing (especially of expert reports), and expert witnessing. Thus, this final part reviews some terms and concepts of basic social theory to see what is settled and acknowledged (if not universally accepted) and what remains problematic and contested. If our judges are going to engage in exercises of social theory, then they should not have to rediscover it for themselves.

Historical Background

It is well known that, among English common law countries, legal recognition of the rights and interests that Aboriginal people might have in lands and waters came late in Australia.[6] The *Gove Land Rights Case* ended in Justice Blackburn 1971 decision in *Milirrpum* that "the doctrine of communal native title ... did not form, and ... never formed, part of the law of any part of Australia. Such a doctrine has no place in a settled colony except under express statutory provisions."[7]

That finding signalled an end to attempts to gain common law recognition of Aboriginal real property rights in the courts, and action shifted to the political arena. In February 1973, the Labor federal government established the Aboriginal Land Rights Commission to inquire into the situation and make recommendations.[8] The commission reported in July 1973 and August 1974, making recommendations for legislation. In due course, the new Coalition federal·government enacted the *Aboriginal Land Rights (Northern Territory) Act (ALRA)* of 1976, and a regime was put in place that enabled Aboriginal groups to claim certain lands and to gain legal titles to them.

Aboriginal claimants had to demonstrate to a tribunal headed by the Aboriginal land commissioner that they were the *traditional Aboriginal owners* – that is, that they were a *local descent group* "having common spiritual affiliations to a site on the land, being affiliations that place the group under a primary spiritual responsibility for that site and the land; and are entitled by Aboriginal tradition to forage as of right over the land."[9] The titles that they gained under *ALRA* were creations of statute. Although based on the successful group's evidence of its relations to specific land, the titles were rooted in an act of the Commonwealth Parliament. They only indirectly acknowledged the *traditional Aboriginal title* of the claimants that was rooted in the creative acts of the dreamings or stories, the ancestral spirit beings, and the consubstantiality of spirit among the ancestral spirit beings, their places of repose and activity on the land and in the water, the spirits of the dead (the Old People) and the living. Nonetheless, *ALRA* titles are safe free-hold titles, and without doubt they offer more scope of action to their holders than determinations of Native title in the current situation.

The years from 1980 to 2000 were a busy period in the Northern Territory, when many land claims were made, heard, and decided. Many anthropologists worked for the Northern and Central Land Councils, which organized and ran the claims, and worked for government and other parties. Outside the territory, the states differed in their positions on land rights, and my own state of Queensland was noted for its antipathy to them.

In 1981, at a conference at James Cook University in Townsville, a small group of lawyers, scholars, and Aboriginal and Torres Strait Islander people discussed the situation and decided on a return to the courts. In May 1982, three Meriam men (Eddie Mabo, David Passi, and James Rice) instigated an action against Queensland in the High Court of Australia. They sought a declaration that the crown's dominion over their Murray Island home was subject to (1) their local custom, (2) their original Native ownership, and (3) their actual possession, use, and enjoyment of the islands. Phrased differently, we might say that they sought common law recognition of their traditional Aboriginal title.[10]

I will not revisit details of the progress of their action through the High Court and the Supreme Court of Queensland, but I clearly recall telling students in my Aboriginal Australia courses during the 1980s to watch the case, that it would likely succeed or "get up," as we say in Australian English. And, indeed, in June 1992 the High Court announced its *Mabo No. 2* decision in the *Murray Island Land Rights Case*. Justice Brennan declared "that the Meriam people are entitled as against the whole world to possession, occupation, use and enjoyment of the island of Mer [Murray Island] except for ... [certain specific tracts under lease or appropriated for administrative use]."[11]

This is a classical formulation of a property right, a right *in rem*. We are inclined to say now that their right is sourced in the intersection of the common law with the traditional Aboriginal title of the Meriam people of Murray Island, but Kent McNeil usefully reminds us that the High Court's order "was based on exclusive occupation of the lands, albeit in accordance with Meriam law and custom, at the time the Crown acquired sovereignty."[12]

The year after *Mabo No. 2*, the Commonwealth Parliament enacted the *Native Title Act* (1993), which established a statutory regime for claimant and non-claimant groups to seek determinations whether Native title exists over particular lands and waters. The act also established a National Native Title Tribunal to register claims, conduct mediation, and perform other tasks and provided for the recognition of representative bodies, including the negotiation and registration of Indigenous Land Use Agreements (ILUAs). There was a general view then that Native title had already been lawfully extinguished for the great majority of contemporary Aboriginal groups, especially in settled (as contrasted with remote or outback) Australia, and that they had no prospects of getting successful Native title claims. Thus, the Indigenous Land Fund was established as part of a social justice package to purchase properties for people who would otherwise remain landless (or nearly so).

A few hundred Native title claims were lodged in the next few years. No one had correctly assessed the deep feelings of many Aboriginal people in settled Australia about the dispossession of their ancestral homelands and their desire for recognition of their status as the traditional owners of particular tracts of land. The successes of a few rogue lawyers in lodging hopeless ambit claims arose from the groundswell of sentiments that people had not expressed so publicly in less propitious circumstances. In 1998, the Commonwealth Parliament passed the *Native Title Amendment Act* (NTA), which generally raised the bar and tightened up the procedures and requirements for registering Native title claims and moving them forward.

By way of example, the 1998 amendments to the *NTA* required the Federal Court to adhere to the customary rules of evidence in hearings "except to the extent the Court otherwise orders," and the new *NTA* permitted the court to "take account of the cultural and customary concerns of Aboriginal peoples and Torres Strait Islanders, but not so as to prejudice unduly any other party to the proceedings."[13] The original act had not bound the court so narrowly. The effect of the amendments has been to ensure that hearings do not differ significantly from conventional adversarial proceedings. The desirability of a less adversarial, more inquisitorial mode of operation has been suggested in a number of venues and at conferences, but the chances of that are remote.[14]

After *Mabo*, a number of significant claims proceeded through the Federal Court, and some reached the High Court on appeal. Thus, the years 1999-2002 saw five cases decided that, observers agree, set the parameters of Native title litigation for the foreseeable future:

- *Yanner v. Eaton* (1999);
- *Commonwealth v. Yarmirr* (2001-2);

- *Western Australia v. Ward* (2002);
- *Wilson v. Anderson* (2002);
- *Members of the Yorta Yorta Aboriginal Community v. Victoria* (2002).

Of them, *Yorta Yorta* is the most important and far reaching.

There is a good deal of unease, even dissatisfaction, with the current situation, and some of the High Court justices have expressed views on it.[15] Basically, there are two informed views. The first view has been most clearly developed by Noel Pearson, an Aboriginal lawyer much influenced by Mc-Neil's work on common law Aboriginal title. Pearson has noted that the High Court has resolutely turned its back on overseas common law decisions and precedents (which I first noticed in its 1998 *Fejo* decision) and opted instead for "essentially an exercise in statutory interpretation."[16] In line with McNeil's reasoning, Pearson believes that the source of Native title is to be found in the common law recognition of prior occupation that gives rise to possession. The specific contents of the law and custom that define and apportion rights and interests in real property among people and groups are matters internal to Aboriginal polities then and now, not matters to be examined and assessed by non-Aboriginal courts and such.

The current majority position is that the Commonwealth Parliament put its wishes into statute when it passed the *Native Title Act* of 1993 and its 1998 amendments. Put bluntly, statute has trumped precedent. Pearson recognizes that reality in his broader assessment and recommendations for change. It won't set things right to find another case like *Mabo*, run it, and hope to reverse recent decisions, and now there is no popular and political support or will to legislate again. I think that Pearson is "punting" on the high transaction costs of the current situation for business and government interests to lead to future reconsideration. We are indeed in the situation that McNeil foreshadowed:

> In the cross-cultural context of native title claims, few judges have the background and training necessary to understand and evaluate Indigenous legal systems. This is not a criticism of judges – it is simply a reality. Judges, who in most instances have little or no previous knowledge or experience of the particular Indigenous society whose rights are in question in a case, should not be placed in the next-to-impossible position of having to determine whether the traditional laws and customs of that society contained concepts of specific rights at the time the Crown acquired sovereignty.[17]

This is not a good situation, and it poses problems for anthropological practice, Aboriginal aspirations, and national reconciliation.

The *Yorta Yorta* Rights Case[18]

The *Yorta Yorta* case attracted considerable attention from its onset in 1994, as any claim in southern settled Australia does.[19] The claim was for "public lands" in an oval-shaped region of about 2,000 square kilometres along the Murray River in north-central Victoria and adjacent New South Wales (NSW), the two oldest Australian states.

The Yorta Yorta are a self-aware ethnic group of 4,000-6,000 Aboriginal people, the descendants of indigenous people who have lived in the region from time immemorial and who occupied it in 1788 when the crown acquired sovereignty and at settlement in the 1840s.[20] They have a long history of speaking up to government about their dispossession, unfair treatment, and so on. Recruitment to the group is by cognatic descent as in-marriage does not give membership.[21] Yorta Yorta people are organized in a variety of formal (e.g., the Yorta Yorta Murray Goulburn Clans Group Inc., housing co-operatives at Shepparton, Echuca, and Mooroopna) and informal social forms. Cognatic descent groups – "families of polity" – are important social groups.[22] They share a relatively small number of surnames, and women head many households. Most Yorta Yorta people live in the towns of the general region, many live and work in Melbourne (but return home regularly), and others are found elsewhere and interstate. They clearly are a group who know where they come from and are here to stay, despite their loss in court.

Another reason that the claim attracted public attention was that Aboriginal people in settled Australia, especially urban ones, are regarded by many other Australians as less authentic or genuine than "full-blood"[23] or "tribal" people in outback places. People such as the Yorta Yorta are also characterized as "acculturated," "assimilated,"[24] "detribalized,"[25] "got no culture," "half-castes," "more white than black," "not traditional Aboriginals," and the like.

Finally, the case attracted interest for offering a societal measure or standard. In popular and some social scientists' thought, there is a distinction between *traditional* and *modern* forms of social organization, and it is seen in crude views such as those discussed in the preceding paragraph.[26] Over recent years, Australianist anthropologists have come to replace that qualitative or typological dichotomy with a temporal-structural one, discriminating *classical* from *postclassical* social forms[27] while recognizing that tradition is a universal social process.[28] If this were not the case, then we could hardly expect our ethnographic research to find contemporary traditional law and custom operating in Native title claimant groups.

Nonetheless, it is obvious that many groups in northern and central Australia are structurally more like their classical antecedents than their southern counterparts. There is an obvious range of postclassical social forms intermediate between, say, the (by and large) successful Miriuwong-Gajerrong claimants of the Kimberley and the unsuccessful Yorta Yorta claimants in Victoria. Thus, people have been watching to see where the courts draw the line between those groups who have Native title and those who do not. One sometimes hears that conservative interest groups such as AgForce say there is no Native title to be found south of Cape York Peninsula in Queensland.

The hearings took place in 1997, and the trial judge was Howard Olney, formerly Aboriginal land commissioner in the Northern Territory and very experienced in Aboriginal land matters. The trial was conducted under the old rules of operation. The applicants called fifty-six Aboriginal witnesses, of whom two were not Yorta Yorta/Bangerang people,[29] and four experts: two anthropologists (Mr. Rod Hagen and Dr. Deborah Rose), an archaeologist (Dr. John Craib), and a linguist (Dr. Heather Bowe).[30]

The applicants tendered thirty written witness statements but did not call all their authors for examination.[31] The judge found the evidence of many witnesses "both credible and compelling," but "two senior members of the claimant group were caught out telling deliberate lies, albeit about a relatively minor matter." He found younger people's evidence "less compelling," describing some of the evidence for oral transmission of tradition as "embellishment" that did not help their case. The judge was impressed especially by older people's genealogical knowledge. Witnesses also recounted what they considered to be the traditional laws and customs of their ancestors as told to them by their "old people."[32] The judge noted that the "cogency" of their evidence was not a matter just of their credibility but also of its assessment in the wider context of other evidence of several kinds. He also referred to the "frequent ... outbursts of ... righteous indignation" of witnesses against their and their ancestors' treatment by government authorities and to the "considerable volume of documentary material" that they tendered, much of it irrelevant to the issues before him.[33]

The non-indigenous parties, the respondents, also tendered a large body of evidence relating especially to particular tracts of land, their tenure status, use (or not) by the claimants, and so on. The judge "was very favourably impressed by the diligence and attention to detail displayed by the witnesses who testified as to the nature of the available records and the processes whereby the required information was extracted and collated."[34] The respondents called six experts: Dr. Marie Fels and Ms. Susan Priestley, historians for Victoria; Ms. Helen Harris, a professional genealogist for Victoria; Professor Kenneth Maddock, anthropologist for New South Wales and Victoria; Dr. Bruce Sommer, linguist for New South Wales; and Dr. Ron Brunton, anthropologist for New South Wales.[35] All of the expert witnesses were examined robustly.

Despite the difficulties in proving facts relating to the past, where oral traditions are "for the most part the only record of events," the judge considered "the inference that indigenous people occupied the claim area in and prior to 1788 [when the crown acquired sovereignty] ... compelling." Summarizing the history of contact and later developments in the claim area, he observed that explorers had visited the area in the 1820s-30s and that settlers had brought stock into or through there from 1836 on.[36]

Two early personalities left records of the Aboriginal people of the claim area. George Augustus Robinson was chief protector of Aborigines of Port Phillip from 1839 to 1849. He made several expeditions into the area and recorded the names and locations of groups with no "serious examination of underlying principles or structures."[37] Edward M. Curr was among the first squatters[38] to take up land in the area, living there from 1841 to 1851 and recounting his experiences in many works.[39] The Aboriginal resistance to settlement was broken by the 1850s and the population greatly reduced through epidemic disease and violence. From the 1860s on, Native affairs policy included missions and reserves (none in the claim area), ration stations, the appointment of local squatters as "guardians," and the removal of children and unmarried young women to stations for "education" away from family.[40]

In 1874, Daniel Matthews opened a school and mission station at Maloga, and the numbers of its residents fluctuated, peaking at about 150 in 1886. An 1886 Victorian act to remove mixed-race people from missions and stations, and move them into the general population and workforce, led to numbers of people crossing the border to live at Maloga in New South Wales. During the 1880s, Matthews' administration became increasingly authoritarian and resented. A new manager, George Bellenger, replaced Matthews in 1887, and the next year Bellenger led some disaffected residents and shifted most of the buildings to a neighbouring reserve block, where they established a new community named Cummeragunja.[41]

Unrest continued at Cummeragunja. Bellenger proved just as unpopular, and over the next four decades there were attempts to farm on allotted blocks. New South Wales enacted legislation, as in Victoria, to force mixed-descent people off the missions and reserves, and much of the land was leased to a neighbouring white farmer. The Depression struck residents hard as funding was cut, no relief was paid, and able-bodied people could not draw rations. The manager's discipline was unpopular, and some residents' houses were pulled down while they were away working. Children could go to third grade on the mission but could not enrol in state schools.[42]

In 1939, the remaining families walked off Cummeragunja and crossed the river to set up camp near earlier expellees living near Barmah in Victoria. Cummeragunja never recovered, and closure of the station was announced in 1953. Only 200 acres remained after the remainder was rented to local white farmers, but a small group stayed on until floods forced them out in 1956, when they crossed to Echuca in Victoria and camped near the tip and on the river flats. The police evicted them and burned their houses the next year. In 1958, a "transitional housing" development on five acres of crown land was established at Rumbalara near Mooroopna, but the houses and land were inadequate for the numbers.[43]

In 1966, the New South Wales government revoked the improperly granted leases at Cummeragunja and made the land available again to residents, who turned off a good crop that year. Rumbalara closed in 1972, and its residents shifted to other towns. Under the *Aboriginal Land Rights Act* (1983, NSW), the Yorta Yorta Local Aboriginal Land Council gained freehold title over the former Cummeragunja reserve in 1984 and later acquired two more blocks nearby. The council is a corporation whose membership is open to all Aboriginal adults living in its area and to others who have an association with it.[44]

The applicants asserted in the amended statement of facts of contentions that their "Yorta Yorta/Bangerang group was comprised of indigenous persons biologically descended from the original occupiers; or adopted into and/or otherwise accepted[45] as part of this group," and they identified eighteen "known ancestors" from one or more of whom they were descended. The judge identified two issues in the applicants' claim that they were the descendants of the indigenous people who had occupied the claim area in or about 1788. He thought that inference might answer the question of whether one or more ancestors were present thereon, but "mere presence" would not prove their rights and interests in lands and waters, nor would the "geographical limits of the land and waters" in which they exercised rights and interests.[46]

Robinson and Curr left records of indigenous groups in the area as they were named, their places of habitual occupation, and their language varieties. The applicants relied on these materials to demonstrate that their ancestors occupied all the claim area, and the respondents used them to lessen its extent. The judge "derived little assistance from the testimony of the ... experts ... because ... much of ... [their] evidence was based upon speculation."[47]

Hagen presented the anthropological and historical evidence for the applicants orally over five days and in a "comprehensive" expert report that dealt "in some detail with the works of Curr and Robinson." He had done five weeks of fieldwork with the applicants to prepare his report, and "in evidence he conceded that his active participation in the conduct of the proceedings indicates a close association with the applicants and perhaps a degree of partisanship." Rose supported Hagen's interpretation, but the judge noted "that she had no prior anthropological experience in the area under consideration, she had not read the ethnographic literature of the region and [she] had relied upon the written witness statements, not all of which were in evidence and some of which were shown to be inaccurate."[48]

There was a problem in connecting any of the eighteen known ancestors to persons holding rights at the time of sovereignty, and this problem was compounded as most of them were born after Robinson and Curr left the area. The experts spent much time trying to clarify the names, locations, boundaries, and social character (clan, local group, etc.) of the many indigenous groups – and categories – that appear in the early records. The judge commented that "in the end it ... proved to be a sterile argument," and their evidence appears not to have aided him to connect the claimant group with the persons in the claim area at sovereignty or to ascertain whether they had Native title there.[49]

Hagen asserted that Robinson's records supported his view that a single "overarching" group, comprising the Pinegerine (Bangerang) and Waveroo "nations," occupied the original lands in the 1840s, but Maddock and Sommer challenged him strongly. The judge was unable to "resolve [the] disputed questions of anthropological interpretation," noting that "no assessment can be made of the credibility of the primary material ... If scholars learned in the relevant discipline are unable to provide an authoritative answer, the Court must have resort to such credible primary evidence as is available and apply the normal processes of analysis and reason."[50]

The boundaries of the current claim area were not reflected in any earlier maps or records, nor were any of the eighteen known ancestors shown to have "any special standing in relation to any particular locality within the claim area." The judge then reviewed all the information available for the eighteen known ancestors from a variety of sources and concluded that, though only the descendants of two of the eighteen "known ancestors" had "been shown to be descended from persons who were in 1788 indigenous inhabitants of part of the claim area," "a significant number of the claimant group" were descended from one or the other of them.[51]

105. As the native title which (in the absence of extinguishment) the common law recognises reflects the entitlement of the indigenous inhabitants, in accordance with their laws and customs, to their traditional lands, (*Mabo No 2 p 15*) *it is necessary to identify the nature of the entitlement which the indigenous inhabitants enjoyed in relation to their traditional lands in accordance with their laws and customs and the extent of the traditional lands [at sovereignty].* (emphasis added)[52]

The judge found Curr's works to be "the most credible source of information concerning the traditional laws and customs of the area from which ... [the two identified ancestors'] early forebears came" because Curr observed a society not yet greatly changed by contact and had "a degree of rapport" with the Aboriginal people with whom he interacted. The judge attended to the oral history evidence of claimants but accorded it less weight in view of the "many generations extending over a period in excess of two hundred years" that it spanned. He found that later writers often did not base their comments on observation. Curr also indulged himself "to a degree of specula-tion ... but his record of his own observations and of what he was told by his Aboriginal informants [in the 1840s] ... must be regarded seriously."[53]

The judge thought that he need only consider the general areas occupied by the two subgroups of the two identified ancestors in trying to identify their "traditional laws and customs in relation to the land," and he rejected extending or generalizing those rights over "the traditional lands of all Bangerang speaking tribes," noting that "Curr's observations ... suggest the contrary." He then reviewed Curr's ethnography, focusing on rights in land (individual and group), the absence of government (i.e., no authority rec-ognized outside the domestic group), unquestioned submission to custom, initiation practices, disputes over women, intergroup relations, gender rela-tions, lack of conservation practices, improvidence with food, and burial practices. He found no evidence from Matthews' time at Maloga of the continuation of the laws and customs that Curr had observed earlier.[54]

In 1881, forty-two Aboriginal people at or connected with the Maloga Mission sent a petition to the governor of New South Wales.[55] The signatories were said to be "members of the Moira and Ulupna tribes," a description not found in Curr's writing. It suggests that the individuals concerned had identi-fied with two main pastoral properties in the region rather than as Bangerang or any of the other subgroups referred to by Curr. No party suggested "that the general thrust of the statements attributed to the petitioners was factually inaccurate or in any way misrepresented their views or their aspirations," and it was the claimants who tendered the petition in their opening address as one in "a long history of efforts to obtain land."[56] Therefore,

> 121. It is clear that by 1881 those through whom the claimant group now seeks to establish native title were no longer in possession of their tribal lands and had, by force of the circumstances in which they found themselves, ceased to observe those laws and customs based on tradition which might otherwise have provided a basis for the present native title claim; and the dispossession of the original inhabitants and their descendants has continued through to the present time. Although many of the claimant group reside within the claim area, many do not. No group or individual has been shown to occupy any part of the land in the sense that the original inhabitants can be said to have occupied it. The claimant group clearly fails Toohey J's test of occupation by a traditional society now and at the time of annexation (*Mabo No 2*, p 192)[,] a state of affairs which has existed for over a century. Notwithstanding the genuine efforts of members of the claimant group to

revive the lost culture of their ancestors, native title rights and interests once lost are not capable of revival. Traditional native title having expired, the Crown's radical title expanded to a full beneficial title.[57]

Contemporary Yorta Yorta activities on the land centre on the protection of sites (scarred trees, oven mounds, and shell middens, not totemic centre sites or places as known over northern Australia) regarded as sacred and on land management practices. As a result, "122. There is no doubt that mounds, middens and scarred trees ... provide evidence of the indigenous occupation and use of the land ... but there is no evidence to suggest that they were of any significance to the original inhabitants other than for their utilitarian value, nor that any traditional law or custom required them to be preserved."[58]

A number of witnesses said that, in accordance with traditional law and custom, they "take from the land and waters only such food as is necessary for immediate consumption": "123. This practice, commendable as it is, is not one which, according to Curr's observations, was adopted by the Aboriginal people with whom he came into contact and cannot be regarded as the continuation of a traditional custom."[59]

From about 1984 on, Yorta Yorta representatives have reburied skeletal remains taken earlier, and more recently repatriated to them, from the claim area: "The modern practices associated with their reburial are not part of the traditional laws and customs handed down from the original inhabitants." Yorta Yorta people have also been much involved "in activities associated with the conservation of the timber and water resources of the area ... But these are issues of relatively recent origin about which the original inhabitants could have had no concern and which cannot be regarded as matters relating to the observance of traditional laws and customs."[60]

One of the visible features of an operating land tenure system relates to whether non-owners have a correlative duty (an obligation) to ask permission to enter and use the resources of another's land. The judge understood the traditional pattern (as described by Curr) to be that, though individuals and families had rights to specific tracts, members of the "tribe" generally were not required to get permission, though outsiders were:

126. The evidence concerning current practices was not entirely consistent from one witness to the next. Many of the senior members of the claimant group gave no evidence of any existing practice concerning the assertion of any rights to exclude others from the claim area and no-one suggested that even the former practices extended to excluding non-Aboriginals. There is overwhelming evidence that Aboriginals and non-Aboriginals alike enter, travel through, live, fish and hunt within the claim area without seeking permission other than such as may be required by State or Commonwealth

law. The tide of history has undoubtedly washed away any traditional rights
that the indigenous people may have previously exercised in relation to
controlling access to their land within the claim area.[61]

The applicants themselves acknowledged that they had long ago stopped
performing initiations and other ceremonies, which elsewhere are signs "of
spiritual attachment to the land." One witness spoke about an area that he
said had been a male initiation ground, but the judge did not consider him
"reliable":

> 129. The facts in this case lead inevitably to the conclusion that before the
> end of the 19th century the ancestors through whom the claimants claim
> title had ceased to occupy their traditional lands in accordance with their
> traditional laws and customs. The tide of history has indeed washed away
> any real acknowledgment of their traditional laws and any real observance
> of their traditional customs. The foundation of the claim to native title in
> relation to the land previously occupied by those ancestors having dis-
> appeared, the native title rights and interests previously enjoyed are not
> capable of revival. This conclusion effectively resolves the application for a
> determination of native title.[62]

The decision was appealed to a full bench of the Federal Court, and in 1999
the majority justices,[63] Branson and Katz, differed from Olney, who clearly
regarded the content of Native title as dependent on the group's traditional
laws and customs at the time of sovereignty, rejecting a "frozen-in-time"
view. The majority took the view that the rights and interests in lands and
waters could change as the laws and customs themselves might undergo
"evolutionary or adaptive change," making the contemporary traditional
laws and customs of a group that provide the content of their Native title.
Nonetheless, they upheld Olney's finding that the group had lost its title,
for there was "more than adequate evidence" that "the relevant indigenous
community [had] lost its character as a traditional community."[64]

After gaining special leave to appeal, the applicants took the case to Canberra in 2001. The High Court handed down its *Yorta Yorta Appeal Decision*
in mid-December 2002. It was expected that the High Court would dismiss
the appeal, and they did.[65] But their focus on the interpretation of the *NTA*
and the specifics of their reasoning led the National Native Title Tribunal,
the Native title branch of the Aboriginal and Torres Strait Islander Commission, various land councils, some lawyers, and anthropologists to take stock
and ask, what must be proved to obtain a successful Native title determination, and what are the new evidential requirements post-*Yorta Yorta*?

Lisa Wright produced a major document in early 2003,[66] and The Aboriginal and Torres Strait Islander Commission's (ATSIC) Technical Advisory

Group held a meeting in Adelaide shortly afterward to discuss the new situation.[67] John Basten QC reviewed the recent High Court decisions and their implications for litigation and mediation. He also spoke of judges' general assumption that they need no anthropologist between them and the Aboriginal witnesses to interpret matters of custom, behaviour, and action, expressing the contrary view and referring to Peter Sutton's important work as very helpful to lawyers.[68] I spoke as an anthropologist and called for dialogue and co-operation between lawyers and anthropologists. I also pointed to the shared history and common intellectual interests of legal theory and anthropology and sought to legitimate our claim to some of the terms and concepts common to social and legal theory (as contrasted with legal practice).[69] *Custom(s), law(s), norms, normative system (system of normative rules)*, and *tradition(s)* are also parts of our intellectual kit; terms such as *rights in rem* and *in personam* and *duties* are also familiar.[70]

The Australian Institute of Aboriginal and Torres Strait Islander Studies held a larger conference on Native title in Alice Springs in early June, and Basten again touched on the topic:

> Lawyers and anthropologists must each have a clear and correct understanding of the relevant legal principles. Secondly, they must work together cooperatively ... One response of lawyers who worry about ... [anthropologists with no legal training taking "statements" from claimants] is to seek to avoid using anthropologists. But that is not a sensible option. A competent anthropologist has training, experience and skills few lawyers could emulate. Nor is it sensible to leave claimants to "speak for themselves" ... Someone needs to address this task.
>
> Anthropologists are not, therefore[,] a disposable luxury, but an essential item of assistance.[71]

I have been more or less constantly involved in land claims work for more than a decade now, and beyond fieldwork and desk research for specific claims I have sought to learn something of property theory and the lawyers' game. I have also lectured and written papers for anthropologist colleagues to help familiarize them with the interface and overlap of legal and social theory.[72]

Following is a partial formulation of our joint task as lawyers and anthropologists in the post-*Yorta Yorta* era. Where it is not established that Native title is completely extinguished, it will be necessary for those asserting Native title to prove, among other things,

- the existence of a *continuously vital society* that, since the time of assertion of *sovereignty* over the area to the present, has had *a system of traditional laws and traditional customs* that constitutes *a body of normative rules or a normative system;*

- that the system has continued to operate without any substantial interruption from the time of assertion of sovereignty by the British crown over the area to the present;
- that *the laws and customs that make up that system* find their origin in *the laws and customs observed and acknowledged* by those who held Native title (better, Aboriginal title) to the area at the time of assertion of sovereignty over the area;
- that *the rights and interests* that they currently possess under that system and that they seek to have recognized as Native title rights and interests also find their origin in *the rights and interests* held by the predecessors at the time of assertion of sovereignty.

They must also show that *the rights and interests are "in relation to lands and waters"* and *that the laws and customs that give rise to them are those laws and customs by which the claimants have a connection to their country.*

Because *Native title is conceptualized* in these judgments *as a bundle of rights, each right in the bundle* must usually be identified with a high degree of particularity. Furthermore, the rights and interests must not be antithetical to the fundamental tenets of the common law and must be capable of being protected by legal and equitable remedies. Finally, they must not have been extinguished. If they have been, then the common law will refuse to recognize them, even where they continue to exist and be exercised as a matter of fact. This is referred to as the withdrawal of common law recognition of Native title.[73]

Since I have discussed matters of *law, custom,* and *tradition* elsewhere,[74] I will now turn to *normative rules* or *norms* and to *rights* and *interests*.[75]

Norms, Rules, Standards, and the Like

Our High Court justices don't realize that the social science concepts of law and custom are inherently normative. They are overly concerned whether patterns of behaviour and action that we observe and infer result from unconscious habit or consciously held norms. That is really not an issue, for it is well known that social patterns are not uniquely accompanied by the same individual psychology or phenomenology.[76] As Margaret Gilbert wrote, "the term 'norm' itself is a relatively recent [i.e., second half of the twentieth century] term in standard social theory usage. The more established terms 'custom,' 'tradition,' 'convention,' 'law,' and so on tend to be used for specific kinds of norms."[77]

Opp recently surveyed the literature and views on "Norms" in the new *International Encyclopedia of the Social and Behavioral Sciences*.[78] He began with

Homans' definition: "A norm is a statement specifying how a person is, or persons of a particular sort are, expected to behave in given circumstances – expected, in the first instance, by the person that utters the norm. What I expect of you is what you ought to do."[79] Opp also identified four semantic features in Homans' definition.

1 *Oughtness*: "A norm is an expectation that some behavior ought to be (or ought not to be) performed."
2 *Conditionality*: "People are expected to behave in a certain way in given circumstances." Thus, norms may be conditional.
3 *Behavioural*: Homans seems to restrict norms to behaviour, but others include beliefs and attitudes as objects of norms.
4 *Actor-centred*: "The *actors* (i.e., the norm-senders) who hold (or utter) a norm are individuals," but other scholars include groups and collectivities as norm holders.

Opp noted the following in addition:

1 Other definitions require that norms be *shared* and *sanctioned*: "An expectation is, by definition, a norm only if the expectation is shared by the members of some group, and if conforming to or deviating from the expectation is sanctioned with some probability." Norms are not preferences: "I may not *like* [it] when you smoke in my company, but I may think that you are *allowed* to smoke; in a similar vein, smoking may be prohibited but I may like your smoking."
2 A second kind of definition is grounded in behaviour, not expectation: "A norm exists if there is a behavioral regularity and if sanctioning occurs with some positive probability in the case of not performing the respective behavior. 'Sanctioning' means that others impose a cost on a person if a behavior is or is not performed ... *Refraining* from a behavior may be a behavioral regularity as well," such as where not smoking is the general case and smoking attracts sanctions.

Opp explained that the behavioural definition does not require any element of *oughtness*, and many of its proponents think that it "allows easier measurement of norms."[80] He also discussed the problems of observing norms. It may not be easy to observe them, the observer's presence may affect the situation, as may a videocamera or such, and a given behaviour may signal different meanings. Opp concluded that "the measurement argument that is often invoked for a behavioral definition is very questionable." Sociologists most often use survey methods to gather observations on norms for measuring norms, but surveys are subject generally to "well-known problems."

Qualitative researchers may in general object that norms are not given but are largely "constructed" in specific situations ... This implies that the measurement of norms is impossible because they do not exist. Survey research does not confirm this view. If norms do not exist[,] the prediction is that factorial surveys [would] yield a large number of missing values[,] which did not turn out to be the case.[81]

Anthropologists have generally been dismissive of survey methods for a host of reasons: they are inappropriate in the small-scale societies in which we work, responses are too sensitive to the ethnic/racial, there are gender and power differences between the interviewer and interviewee(s), and so on. However, there may be some Native title situations in which survey methods can produce the data and evidence we seek on norms, both ideal and real.

The Hartian view of norms and what is normative differs from the conventional view and use of social anthropologists.[82] I believe that they more often distinguish "real" and "ideal," and "statistical" and "expected" norms,[83] and attend to both kinds of phenomena. Social anthropologists need to bear this in mind in analyzing and describing laws and customs because it is not sufficient, for Native title purposes, simply to identify recurring patterns of behaviour and action – that is, the way people do things.[84]

In any case, we want to move beyond claimants' normative statements.[85] We want to learn whether the claimants do (attempt to) exclude others from their land and sea country, whether they do habitually exclude themselves from the land and sea country of others unless invited or licensed, whether they do ask permission of others to go onto their land and sea country to hunt, fish, camp, and so on, whether they do share and exchange the products of their hunting and fishing, and whether the children of women of the group speak for and participate in its affairs on the same basis as the children of its men.

I do not say that we should attend to behaviour and action so that we can highlight or point to discrepancies between the ideal and the real, the normative and the positive.[86] Instead, behavioural and actional data can carry the greater weight in expert evidence. It is the uncovering of both conscious ("public") and unconscious (recall Keesing's earlier distinction) norms or patterns of behaviour and action that we should be doing. We should be looking to see whether people exclude themselves from the lands and waters of others unless they are there by invitation, permission, licence, et cetera. We should attend to how people gain permission from owners to access their lands and waters through ways ranging from explicit direct requests to indirect signalling of one's wish and intent to access another's lands and waters. We should watch to see whether and how people attempt to bail up trespassers, warn, and expel them. Firth wrote that "the anthropologist who has to define native property rights must rely not on verbal usage alone, but on the series of acts in regard to the object which represent immediate and ultimate control over it," and that remains good advice.[87]

Justice Owen wrote eloquently in *Ejai v. Commonwealth* (1993) of the need to attend to the oral evidence of the claimants themselves, evidence that came from "the hearts and minds of the people most intimately connected to Aboriginal culture."[88] With apologies to Owen, the behavioural and actional evidence lets us look into the hearts and minds of people perhaps more clearly than does just listening to them speak about their culture. Here I apply a traditional principle of English-speaking folk epistemology: "Actions speak louder than words."[89]

Rights in General and Rights in Particular

Our High Court justices have pre-Hohfeldian views of rights. They don't realize that Aboriginal people still exercise claim rights, privileges, powers, and immunities among themselves, as they also observe duties, liabilities, and the like.[90] MacLean wrote the entry for "Rights" in the new *International Encyclopedia of the Social and Behavioral Sciences*. He observed that the "concept is ... central to our moral and political thought" but also commented as follows:

> The concept of rights has been debased in recent years, as rights claims have become mere attempts to give rhetorical force to strongly held preferences,[91] but the problem also lies in some deeper puzzles about the nature and justification of rights.[92]
>
> The least controversial rights are those created by laws and the shared norms of our institutions and practices, where rules allow us to coordinate and regulate our activities and to divide fairly the benefits and burdens of social cooperation. Any attempt to understand rights should begin here. If Smith gives tools to Farmer in exchange for a share of the grain Farmer will produce, then Smith has a claim to the grain after the harvest, and Farmer has a duty to turn it over. It seems natural to say that Smith has a right to the grain, and laws will respect and enforce such rights.[93]

MacLean also wrote that some scholars believe that rights are found "in primitive societies and can be inferred from ancient texts," even though these societies may not have had words signifying the concept. "Any society with an institution of property understands the ideas of entitlements to use and claims against infringement, which are part of a theory of law." Others argue that rights did not exist until "the late Middle Ages, when we first find a word to denote the concept." It developed "as the idea that the natural or inherited differences in status could be justified was replaced by a belief in the fundamental moral equality of all people." "Where ancient and medieval philosophers would say that it is right that Smith controls some thing, modern theorists would say that Smith has a right to that thing," so that we now see rights as "something that belongs to individuals" and of which they may be aware.[94]

Anthropologists have long used the notion of rights in their analyses and descriptions. Closer to our time, Ward H. Goodenough wrote that

> Social rules[95] or codes of conduct ... govern how certain categories of persons may act in relation to other categories of persons and things ... Anthropologists know of no human community that is without such rules or whose social relationships cannot be analyzed as an ordered distribution of rights, privileges, and duties among well-defined categories of persons.[96]
>
> *Right, privilege,* and *duty* are ... fundamental concepts for studying the culture of social relationships.[97] They are technically used by anthropologists according to the definition given them by the legal theorist Wesley Hohfeld (1919) ... A system of social rules is basically ... a definition of rights and corresponding duties.

Hohfeld and Rights

Wesley Newcomb Hohfeld remains well known in legal theory for his incisive thought and clarification of "fundamental legal conceptions." His major work (recently reprinted in the Classical Jurisprudence Series)[98] and his thought were given substantial attention and discussion by Hafner and MacLean.[99] Penner, a legal theorist, also confirmed the continuing importance of Hohfeld's work.[100] Hoebel introduced Hohfeld's work to anthropologists, noting that his concepts "fit not only the fundamental legal relations, but also the fundamentals of any complex of imperative social reciprocity."[101] Hallowell also drew attention to Hohfeld's work and used his concepts: "The term 'right' is replete with ambiguity even in the law itself. This has long been recognized by jurists but it was Wesley Newcomb Hohfeld who, in his system of basic legal concepts, forged an analytical tool that has been recognized as of capital importance in clearly distinguishing between rights of various kinds, as well as other *jural* concepts."[102] MacLean again drew attention more recently to the multiple meanings of the term *right*: "Hohfeld categorized legal rights in a way that has profoundly influenced subsequent moral and legal theories. He argued that an assertion of the form 'Smith has a right to P' is ambiguous and could mean any of four things (or some combination of them)."[103]

In keeping with Hohfeld and other legal theorists, I propose to speak of rights in general and rights in particular. My understanding of Hohfeld's thought on these rights is as follows. Hohfeld and MacLean contrasted two sets of basic terms as "*jural* opposites":

right	privilege	power	immunity
no right	duty	disability	liability[104]

and as *"jural* correlatives":

[claim-]right[105]	privilege	power	immunity
duty	no right	liability	disability

In Hohfeld's thought, *jural* relations[106] are dyadic social relationships – they are between two people. When we consider the *jural* correlatives, we see that, if X bears a right, then Y owes a duty; if X has a privilege, then Y has a no right; if X has a power, then Y is under a liability; and if X has an immunity, then Y is under a disability. And with respect to their behavioural and actional content, the table of *jural* opposites shows that a privilege is the opposite of a duty, a power is the opposite of a disability, and so on. Simmonds makes the same point as Hallowell did some sixty years earlier:

> Rights, privileges, powers, and immunities are all of them commonly referred to by lawyers as "rights," but they are quite different in their implications and a more discriminating terminology would distinguish between them rigorously. It will serve the interests of clarity if we adopt a suggestion of Hohfeld's and refer to rights in the strict sense (i.e., "right" as the correlative of "duty") as "claim-rights."[107]

Many scholars substitute the term *liberty* for *privilege*. Simmonds tells us, for example, that

> A Hohfeldian privilege is in fact a liberty, in the sense of the absence of a duty. Thus, if I have a privilege to wear a hat, it follows that I am under no duty not to wear a hat. Since a privilege is a *jural* relation, not a factual one, it does not entail the absence of all obstruction or interference with my action, but merely the absence of a duty not to perform the action. I may have a privilege to wear a hat even if I have no hat to wear, and even if you have credibly threatened me with death should I wear a hat.[108]

Note that privileges entail not correlative duties but "no rights." Duties, instead, are correlative to claim-rights.

A person has a Hohfeldian power when by her act she may alter legal relations. By way of example and admonition, Simmonds writes, "thus one may decide to transfer property to another, or enter into a contract, and in so doing one alters legal relations by assuming duties that one did not previously possess, negating existing duties, acquiring new powers, and so on.

Extreme confusion can be produced when lawyers refer to Hohfeldian powers as 'rights.'"[109]

McCann and Scheingold wrote the entry on "Rights: Legal Aspects" in the new *International Encyclopedia of the Social and Behavioral Sciences* in 2001. We may reasonably interpret their use of the term to be synonymous with a Hohfeldian claim-right, a right in particular. They noted that "the language of rights generally connotes claims of entitlement to certain goods. To assert that 'I have a right ... ' is to articulate a normative claim that certain actions should or should not be performed by other individuals ... [or groups]."[110] They pointed out that "rights are related to, but different from, preferences, interests, and needs." In discourse, as in disputes and arguments, appeals to one's rights typically "trump" other people's assertions or claims of preference and interest – which are subjective – and needs – which "convey an objective status" that others can validate.[111]

The Character of (Claim-)Rights

McCann and Scheingold identified and discussed four features of (claim-) rights:

1 "Because rights constitute relationships between the bearers of rights and other persons or institutions, each person's rights impose correlative duties on others." Duties may be negative, calling for "non-interference or inaction by others," or they may be positive, calling "for action and assistance."
2 Rights "also extend by implication to all other similarly constituted relationships in society and are, thus, inclusive." Like laws, they relate to classes of persons, not just to individual persons.
3 "Similarly, the exercise of rights typically confers responsibilities on the rights-bearer. For example, the person may have a right to drink alcohol and a right to drive, but these rights imply responsibilities for not engaging in both activities at once."
4 "Rights are intrinsically linked to remedies": that is, their infringement requires or occasions some remedy, often specified by custom or tradition.[112]

With respect to the first feature above, the character of the relationship of correlativity between rights and duties has been further noted by several scholars. Hallowell wrote that "in human societies the basis of ownership is the correlative obligations [i.e., duties] others have to allow me to exercise my property rights."[113] And Penner wrote that "it is to Hohfeld that we owe the idea of a strong correlativity thesis. Hohfeld argued that rights formed part of a normative network of *jural* relations composed of pairs. In particular, the existence of a 'claim-right' or a right 'properly so called,' in Hohfeldian terms) necessarily entails the existence of a duty, and *vice-versa*."[114] He also discussed whether duties always entail correlative (claim-) rights and found that they do not.[115] Commenting that philosophers have long sought to understand rights and their normative character, he drew attention to the opposing "interest" and "choice" theories of rights and presented a new argument for the greater strength of the former.[116] In his view, all rights imply correlative duties, but only some duties imply correlative rights: namely, those in the interest of rights holders.

The Enforcement of Rights
With respect to the fourth feature above – that rights are linked to remedies – there is a great difference between societies with state-based organization and those without it. States typically assert and enforce a monopoly on the application of force, and where they do not or cannot, as in Somalia and the Solomon Islands, we speak of "failed states." In contrast, in stateless societies, individuals and groups exercise violence to enforce their rights and redress grievances. Anthropology knows of countless such societies before their encapsulation or incorporation into the social field of a colonial state and/or its successor independent state. Evans-Pritchard's classic monograph *The Nuer* (1940) analyzed and described just such a society as the British were extending *Pax Britannica* through the southern Sudan, bombing and strafing villages.[117] And today the central government of Pakistan observes legal pluralism in its northwestern tribal territories, where individual and group self-help continue to operate without state interference.

In the case of Australia, where Aboriginal people have long been part of the wider local, regional, and national social fields, individuals and small groups cannot lawfully employ self-help, although they may in fact do so. The point is that Aboriginal social groups have not been able to employ force legally against non-indigenous Australians to remedy situations that they might consider such as trespass, wrongful acts, or desecration in their territories since the early contact period.

Smith discussed a recent situation in which a ranger fired and burned nearby areas of a national park when the Queensland Land Tribunal and Ayapathu, Kaanju, and Mungkan claimants were out on a site visit to take evidence on-country.[118] The Aboriginal people, not consulted, were incensed.

However, rather than being voiced as an infringement of their control of the area as "traditional owners," this anger was vocalised in terms of danger presented given the proximity of the fire to the area where the Tribunal was hearing evidence.

This lack of vocalisation of traditional ownership is interesting as, within the local Aboriginal population, the right to burn "*country*" is considered to rest with those owning the area under Aboriginal Law. I believe that for many Aboriginal people in the region, particularly older men and women, the history of relationships with non-Aborigines and government agencies has been such that it would be considered at best useless to vocalise rights based in ownership of *"country"* to them. Whilst such ownership continues as a lived reality and as a basis for social action between Aboriginal people, lived experience and received understanding have engendered it as meaningless in dealings with whites. This has led to a situation in which many Aboriginal people do not appear to consider Aboriginal Law to be relevant in engaging non-Aboriginal agencies despite the sense of injustice that they feel about actions undertaken by these agencies remaining embedded within it.

Does this demonstrate a situation where Aboriginal Law has "all been washed away" by the appearance of non-Aboriginal law and practice? I would suggest not. Rather, the current era has introduced the possibility for Aboriginal people, after many years of radical disempowerment, to realise that they are able to assert more reciprocal relationships with government agencies and the "mainstream" on the basis of their own system of law and custom. However, the repercussions of this fact will take some time to get used to. The confidence and understanding necessary to engage in satisfactory negotiations with outsiders about "country" are still emergent in the case of the Mungkan Kaanju National Park but other examples in the region demonstrate that such emergence is both potential and likely.[119]

Rights and Interests

Section 223(1) of the *Native Title Act* points us to "the rights and interests of Aboriginal peoples or Torres Strait Islanders in relation to land or waters." We have some idea now what rights in general and rights in particular are, but what are "interests" in the Native title context? *Interest* is an English word that has a number of non-technical and technical meanings and/or senses,[120] but in social and legal theory the word *interest* has at least two meanings. The one that we need to know is specific to property theory and property law.[121]

The second meaning that *interest* has in legal theory is shared with philosophy, especially the philosophy of rights and views of practical reason. Penner discussed interests in the second sense.[122] Animal rights advocates such as Peter Singer use the term *interest* in a similar sense when they argue that animals should be recognized as having rights because they can feel pain and are conscious, at least as far as we recognize that they suffer. Singer speaks of animals having interests that should give rise to rights (and correlative duties for humans), but I cannot recall whether he believes that animals critically reflect on values and arrive at their own interests or whether we humans simply attribute interests to them.[123]

Thus, in the Native title situation, interests are best conceived as rights in general of some kind, but they obviously differ in some way from rights in particular. Perhaps we can take Native title interests to be what Peter Sutton calls "contingent rights." These are rights that a person or group acquires contingently or conditionally from the holders of "core rights," and their holders cannot transmit them to others, as can holders of core rights.[124]

Conclusion

Kent McNeil has recently questioned the reasoning of Australian High Court justices on matters such as the unilateral extinguishment of Native title and the relevance of the content of traditional law and custom to determining Native title at common law as well as their inattentiveness to and lack of knowledge of relevant overseas precedent.[125] I have also noted Noel Pearson's similar views. With respect, I think that we might also question the judges' understanding and use of a number of terms and concepts that span legal and social theory, such as *tradition, norm,* and *right.* But I also call on my anthropological colleagues to learn more about their own heritage of property theory and about more recent work by jurists and economists on property theory.

We and our lawyer brethren, I believe, have been too willing to over-emphasize the spiritual aspect of Aboriginal traditional ownership of land,[126] to the disregard and perhaps devaluation of its social and material features.[127] I cannot say whether a rights-based approach in our ethnography and Native title research and writing will produce the determinations that the our clients desire, but I can say that, without a rights-based approach, we are not even in the game anymore.

Acknowledgments
I would like to thank Kent McNeil, Nic Peterson, Skip Ray, Peter Sutton, and David Yarrow for comments and suggestions bearing on this chapter. I would also like to thank the Cape York Land Council, the North Queensland Land Council, the Northern Land Council, and the Office of Litigation, Office of the Australian Government Solicitor, for providing me with opportunities to pursue some of the issues and matters dealt with here. I alone am responsible for the content and arguments of the chapter.

Notes
Epigraph: Richard A. Posner, *Overcoming Law* (Cambridge, MA: Harvard University Press, 1995), vii. Posner is a leading figure in the law and economics movement.
1 Maddock, "Involved Anthropologists," 169-75.
2 de Coulanges, *The Ancient City;* Maine, *Ancient Law;* and Morgan, *Ancient Society.*
3 Bright and Dewar, eds., *Land Law;* Harris, *Property and Justice;* Penner, "Analysis of Rights," and Penner, "Bundle of Rights."
4 Maddock, "Involved Anthropologists," 155-76. He seems not to have known of W.E.H. Stanner, "The Yirrkala Case: Some General Principles of Aboriginal Land-Holding," unpublished briefing paper (1969), prepared for the plaintiffs' lawyers in *Milirrpum* to present the indigenous system of ownership in principles and terms deriving from Roman and common

law traditions. For critical commentary on *Milirrpum*, see McNeil, *Common Law Aboriginal Title*, 290-97. For contemporary anthropological work on property, see Hann, *Property Relations*; Hunt and Gilman, *Property in Economic Context*; Rigsby, "A Survey of Property Theory and Tenure Types," 22-46; and Van Meijl and von Benda-Beckmann, eds., *Property Rights and Economic Development*. For a good overview by an economist, see Demsetz, "Property Rights," 144-55.

Property theory is also important to applied anthropology because it can help us to think more clearly about property regimes that distribute rights and interests in the same lands and waters over a range of owners or parties: that is, regimes in which the rights and interests of multiple owners coexist. It is also not clear whether, over the longer run, Native title forms of property will be adequate to fulfill the needs and aspirations of Aboriginal people and groups in a wider market-based economy where much land is commoditized and if/as their links of shared spirit with the land attenuate, and the land becomes fungible.

5 Steward, *Theory of Culture Change*, 293-94, wrote that "the plain fact is that anthropology has failed to come to grips with this crucially important problem of 'property' in detail and concreteness." Wallace was one of the few anthropologists in the ICC claims who wrote with much knowledge of property matters, and it was no accident that he was a student and colleague of A.I. Hallowell at the University of Pennsylvania. See Anthony F.C. Wallace, "Political Organization and Land Tenure," 301-21. To my mind, Hallowell's paper remains foundational and essential reading for anthropologists; see Hallowell, "The Nature and Function of Property," 236-49. See also my discussion of it, and of Steward's role in the claims cases, in Rigsby, "Anthropologists, Indian Title," 15-45. For Steward, see Ray, "Anthropology, History, and Aboriginal Rights: Politics and the Rise of Ethnohistory in North America in the 1950s," keynote address at the seminar on Dialogues between the Disciplines: History and Anthropology, University of Oregon, 2003; and Ronaasen, Clemmer, and Rudden, "Rethinking Cultural Ecology," 170-202.

6 Simpson, *Land Law and Registration*.

7 *Milirrpum*, 143. *Milirrpum v. Nabalco Pty. Ltd.* (1971), 17 F.L.R. 141.

8 The commissioner was Justice A.E. Woodward, the plaintiffs' barrister in the *Gove Land Rights Case*, and his research officer was Dr. Nicolas Peterson.

9 *Aboriginal Land Rights (Northern Territory) Act* 1976, Part VII, 77A.

10 In Rigsby, "Aboriginal People, Land Tenure," 11-15, I distinguished among traditional Aboriginal title, Native title, and "other forms of title under Australian law, such as freehold and leasehold title," 11. See also Rigsby, "Aboriginal People, Spirituality," 963.

11 Bartlett, *Mabo Decision with Commentary*, 56.

12 McNeil, *Emerging Justice?* 454.

13 *Native Title Act* 1993, including amendments up to Act No. 97 of 1998, ss. 82 (1) and (2).

14 Non-claimant parties with valuable property rights and interests and government bodies with policy and practice interests extending far beyond indigenous affairs will not forgo their rights to their own experts. Forbes preferred "a frankly administrative scheme" to "a complex court and tribunal system." Forbes, "Mabo and the Miners," 64.

15 In *Wilson v. Anderson*, (2002) 190 A.L.R. 313, Kirby J at 126-27, Ward J at 561, and Callinan J at 970. Lisa Wright, a lawyer in the Legal Services Section of the National Native Title Tribunal, observed in a similar vein that "the brief summary given here indicates that resort to the legal process for recognition that is set out in the NTA is unlikely to provide a satisfactory outcome for many Indigenous Australians or, indeed, many others involved in the native title process." Wright, *Themes Emerging from the High Court's Recent Native Title Decisions*, 2. I thank Athol Chase for drawing my attention to the justices' comments.

16 Pearson, "The High Court's Abandonment of 'the Time-Honoured Methodology of the Common Law' in Its Interpretation of Native Title in Mirriuwong Gajerrong and Yorta Yorta," Sir Ninian Stephen Annual Lecture, Law School, University of Newcastle, 17 March 2003, http://www.capeyorkpartnerships.com; Noel Pearson, "Where We've Come from and Where We're at with the Opportunity that Is Koiki Mabo's Legacy to Australia," the 2003 Mabo Lecture, Native Title Representative Bodies Conference, Alice Springs, 3 June 2003, http://www.capeyorkpartnerships.com, 13.

17 McNeil, *Emerging Justice?*, 462-63.
18 In researching this section, I relied mainly on the three decisions, an early draft transcript of the expert evidence, and transcripts of the appeal hearings before the High Court.
19 City dwellers worry needlessly about losing their house blocks and such, despite the inviolable status of freehold land, and some politicians play on their fears.
20 Jenkins, *Social Identity*; Langlois, "Identity Movements," 7163-66; and Sollors, "Ethnic Groups/Ethnicity: Historical Aspects," 4813-17.
21 Sutton, *Native Title and the Descent of Rights*, 85-87, for a summary of Barwick's and Hagen's research findings.
22 Ibid., 55-124.
23 On the concept of race in contemporary anthropology, see Rigsby, "'Race' in Contemporary Anthropology," 57-61.
24 For an informed view of the term and its meaning, see Boyer, "Cultural Assimilation," 3032-35.
25 The term *detribalization* appeared in the title of a collection of essays written about 1960 and published ten years later, but the term has had no currency among Australianist anthropologists for over three decades. It does not appear in the index of Tindale, *Aboriginal Tribes of Australia* or as an entry in Horton, ed., *Encyclopaedia of Aboriginal Australia: Aboriginal and Torres Strait Islander History, Society, and Culture*. See Pilling and Waterman, eds., *Diprotodon to Detribalization*; and Tindale, *Aboriginal Tribes*.
26 See also McNeil, *Emerging Justice?*, 453n185, for a discussion of the same point.
27 Sutton first used the term *classical* in print in his joint introduction to *Dreamings*, 8. Some have mistakenly criticized him for offering an essentialist view of Aboriginal society and culture. His most recent exposition is in *Native Title in Australia*, xvii.
28 Kroeber, *Anthropology*, 411, wrote of "the passing on of culture to the younger generation" and said that "the internal handing on through time is called *tradition*." In this sense, tradition refers to the same phenomena that in other contexts we might call *enculturation*, *socialization*, *learning*, and the like.
29 Bangerang is another name for the group, and some people prefer it.
30 Hagen earned a BA (Honours) in social anthropology and comparative sociology from Macquarie University in the mid-1970s and spent 1975-80 in a senior research position for the Central Land Council in the centre working mainly on ALRA claims. He worked as an anthropological and social research consultant in the Northern Territory, South Australia, and Victoria from 1980 to 1985 and from late 1993 onward. He was on the witness stand for five days, 12-16 May 1997. See his "Lumpers, Splitters, and the Middle Range," 73-84. Rose is a senior anthropologist, well published, with long fieldwork experience in the Northern Territory, including *ALRA* and Native title claims. She was on the stand for three-quarters of the day on 21 May 1997. Craib was on the stand for three-quarters of the day on 19 May 1997. Bowe became interested in linguistics and the Pitjantjatjara language while a teacher in the Pitjantjatjara lands. She earned her MA and PhD in linguistics at the University of Southern California. A few years after her return, she moved into a university position and continued research on Pitjantjatjara. Her "Linguistics and the Yorta Yorta," 101-59, is a thoughtful account of her work on the claim. See also Bowe and Morey, *The Yorta Yorta (Bangerang) Language*. Bowe was on the stand for a day and a half from 19 to 21 May 1997.
31 *The Members of the Yorta Yorta Community v. The State of Victoria and Ors* (1998)], 1606 F.C.A. [cited hereafter as *Yorta Yorta*], 20.
32 Ibid., 20-21. The phrase *old people* is used by Aboriginal people around the country to denote not only those living but also the dead, whether remembered or not.
33 Ibid., 22. It is unclear whether their actions upset the judge. It is true that his task was circumscribed, but it is understandable that people with a history of oppression would look to the courts for recognition and wider relief.
34 *Yorta Yorta*, 23.
35 Fels earned First Class Honours and a PhD in history at Melbourne University in the 1980s. Fels, *Good Men and True*, is based on her doctoral dissertation; Maddock was a senior Australian anthropologist, well known for his books and other publications. He worked for the

Northern Land Council and the Central Land Council in several *ALRA* claims, for the Australian Law Reform Commission 1979-86 in its inquiry into the recognition of Aboriginal customary law, for the Hindmarsh Island Bridge Inquiry, in *Chapman v. Luminis,* and for the Australian government solicitor in *Cubillo and Gunner v. Commonwealth.* He also worked for the relevant state governments in *Yorta Yorta, De Rose,* and *Miriuwong-Gajerrong (Ward's Case).* He was on the witness stand for two and a half days, 5-7 August 1997. See Morton, "I-Witnessing,"; Sommer earned MA and PhD degrees in linguistics from the University of Hawaii in 1968 and 1970 respectively. He also has considerable linguistic and anthropological experience on Cape York Peninsula and the Northern Territory from the late 1960s. During the *Yorta Yorta* hearings, he was enrolled for an MA in anthropology at the Northern Territory University, completing his thesis, "Kunjen: Kinship and Communication," in August 1998. He worked for relevant state governments in *Yorta Yorta, De Rose, Miriuwong-Gajerrong (Ward's Case),* and *Daniel v. WA* and was on the stand for one and a quarter days, 12-13 August 1997; Brunton earned his PhD from Macquarie University, receiving a Centenary Medal in 2003 "for service to Australian society through the advancement of economic, social, and political issues." He was on the stand for a day and a half, 13-14 May 1997.

36 *Yorta Yorta,* 24-31.
37 Ibid., 32.
38 The pastoralist settlers who took up crown lands in areas before they were opened for settlement were called *squatters* because they had no leases or occupation licences. The terms *graziers* and *pastoralists* have greater currency now.
39 Curr, *The Australian Race;* and Curr, *Recollections of Squatting.*
40 *Yorta Yorta,* 36.
41 Ibid., 38-40.
42 Ibid., 41-44.
43 Ibid., 45-46.
44 Ibid., 47-49.
45 Adoption is widely known among historical and contemporary Aboriginal groups, especially the custom of "growing up" children who acquire rights and interests from their fostering-adoptive parent(s). This practice was common on the Queensland missions and government settlements, where children from distant regions and groups were brought in under removal orders and often adopted under Aboriginal law by local traditional owner families.
46 *Yorta Yorta,* 50-52.
47 Ibid., 53-54.
48 Ibid., 55.
49 Ibid., 56, 59.
50 Ibid., 62.
51 Ibid., 63-104.
52 *Yorta Yorta,* 105. See also McNeil, *Emerging Justice?,* 449.
53 *Yorta Yorta,* 106.
54 Ibid., 109-18.
55 Ibid., 119.
56 Ibid., 120.
57 *Mabo v. Queensland [No. 2],* (1992) 175 C.L.R. 1, *Mabo v. Queensland [No. 2],* (1992) 175 C.L.R. 1, per Brennan J at 60.
58 *Yorta Yorta,* 122.
59 Ibid., 123.
60 Ibid., 125.
61 Ibid., 126.
62 Ibid., 127.
63 The two-to-one decision found Black CJ in the minority.
64 *Yorta Yorta,* 201, 125.
65 Pearson, in "Where We've Come From," 17, commented that

> The Yorta Yorta ... proved that a native title burdened the radical title of the Crown at the time of sovereignty. Native title came into existence. They ... proved that these

occupants included two ancestors of the claimants. They had also their descent from these two elders. They had proved their case. So how is it that Olney and the High Court could then presume to cast the Yorta Yorta into an identity wilderness – a *homo nullius,* people who didn't exist as a people anymore? This represents misapplication of the common law – and we cannot accept this.

66   Wright, *Themes Emerging,* is a useful survey that summarizes rather than critiques the decisions.

67   The meeting was attended by ATSIC Native title staff, Land Council officers and lawyers, some invited lawyers, and two invited anthropologists, Dr. Julie Finlayson and me.

68   See, especially, the following works by Sutton: *Aboriginal Country Groups; Kinds of Rights in Country;* and "The Robustness of Aboriginal Land Tenure." A number of his papers appear as revised chapters in his *Native Title in Australia.*

69   Rigsby, "Some Thoughts on Native Title." Paper prepared for the ATSIC Technical Advisory Group Meeting, Adelaide, 7 April 2003.

70   I also suggested that our current difficulties lie not with the judges but primarily with ourselves – anthropologists, lawyers, and claimants. That is only part of the story, as McNeil, *Emerging Justice?,* and Pearson, "High Court's Abandonment" and "Where We've Come From," have told us. Nonetheless, judges can only work with evidence that parties develop in examination and documents submitted. The topic of presenting a claim bears more thought and discussion.

71   Basten, "Beyond *Yorta Yorta.*" Native Title Representative Bodies Conference, Alice Springs, June, 2003.

72   Pearson referred to anthropology as a "B-grade industry" in "Native Title's Days," and expanded on his views more recently in "Where We've Come From."

73   Wright, *Themes Emerging,* 3.

74   Rigsby, "Custom and Tradition"; Rigsby, "Law and Custom," 230-52.

75   I have also drawn extensively on reference works such as Barfield, ed., *Dictionary of Anthropology;* Barnard and Spencer, eds., *Social and Cultural Anthropology;* Newman, ed., *New Palgrave Dictionary;* and Smelser and Baltes, eds., *International Encyclopaedia.* I have also drawn on anthropology textbooks such as Haviland, *Cultural Anthropology;* Keesing, *Cultural Anthropology.* This approach provides a check on unawareness and selectivity.

   Our discipline of anthropology has been infected by postmodernism, and some colleagues regard such terms and concepts as survivals from a discredited positivism and functionalism. I disagree and leave it to them to talk to the courts about *discourses of power, hybridity,* and *indigenous voice.* Just as Dixon's notion of *basic linguistic theory,* first introduced in *The Rise and Fall of Languages,* 128, speaks of that, so too may we identify *basic social theory* and its conventional terms and concepts. Where they are problematic and contested, we expect to make that plain, not try to hide it.

76   See Rigsby, "Custom and Tradition."

77   Gilbert, *On Social Facts,* 425.

78   Opp, "Norms,," 10714-20. See also the papers in Hechter and Opp, eds., *Social Norms.*

79   Homans, *Social Behavior,* 96.

80   Opp, "Norms," 10714.

81   Ibid., 10716.

82   I draw attention to Hart's *The Concept of Law,* because the majority opinion of Gleeson CJ and Gummow and Hayne JJ in *Yorta Yorta (Appeal Decision)* made much use of his thought in their section, "An Intersection of Two Normative Systems," at 39-42. I also note Gummow's comment on transcript during the appeal hearings on 23 May 2002: "Yes, Australians always talk about *traditions* when they mean *habits.* I am talking about Australian Anglo-Saxon culture. They are always talking about *tradition;* [but] they just mean *habits.* When does it become a *tradition* in this expression, '*traditional law*'?" (emphasis added). Transcript of Proceedings, *Members of the Yorta Yorta Aboriginal Community v. Victoria* (High Court, Gummow J, 23 May 2002). Transcript available at http://www.austlii.edu.au/au/other/hca/transcripts/2001/M128/1.html accessed 16 September 2006. As that comment also reflects Hart's

thought closely, I found it revealing to read Hart to understand why the High Court justices distinguished "merely convergent habitual behaviour in a social group" and "legal rules."

Hart famously discussed "the difference[s] between saying of a group that they have the habit, e.g., of going to the cinema on Saturday nights, and saying that it is the rule with them that the male head is to be bared on entering a church." The convergence of their behaviour suffices to say that the group has a habit, but in itself that doesn't provide evidence of a rule requiring the behaviour, such that deviations "are regarded as lapses or faults open to criticism, and threatened deviations meet with pressure for conformity." He noted that, where there are such normative rules, people not only criticize deviations but also appeal to them as reasons for criticism. Finally, Hart observed that members of the group display internal "acceptance" of the rules: that is, they feel bound by them without experiencing feelings of compulsion. They have "a critical reflective attitude to certain patterns of behaviour as a common standard" that displays "itself in criticism (including self-criticism), demands for conformity, and in acknowledgements that such criticism and demands are justified, all of which find their characteristic expression in the normative terminology of 'ought,' 'must,' and 'should,' 'right' and 'wrong.'" Hart, *Concept of Law*, 55-57.

Gilbert asked,

> What is it for a group to have a rule or prescription about action? According to Hart (1961) the members must take a certain "critical reflective attitude" to some actual pattern of behaviour. They must regard it as a standard to be conformed to by all members. Hart stresses that most members must believe that they are *entitled to criticize* one another for deviance from the standard, and that they are entitled to *demand compliance* if deviance is threatened.

See Gilbert, "Norm," 426. She considered that such beliefs are based on *jointly accepted principles,* as she described in *On Social Facts.*

83 See Barnard and Spencer, *Social and Cultural Anthropology,* 615: "*Norm.* Usually, in any given culture the established mode of behaviour to which conformity is expected. Sometimes the term refers to the average or typical behaviour, referred to as the statistical norm, rather than the expected behaviour, or ideal norm." Gilbert distinguished norms as actual patterns of behaviour from prescribed patterns of behaviour as well as predictive expectations from normative or deontic expectations about what members of a group will do: "Normative expectations involve a belief that the 'expected' behaviour *ought* to occur, in some more than merely predictive sense." Gilbert, "Norm," 425. Gessner wrote that "normative expectations are by definition ... different from actual social behavior and a certain tension between them both exists in all societies." Gessner, "Law as an Instrument," 8492.

Hart's view, which restricts the normative to the ideal and expected, nonetheless is not too unconventional for many social scientists. Giddens, the well-known British sociologist, wrote in his textbook that "norms are definite principles or rules which ... [members of a group] are expected to observe. Norms represent the 'dos' and 'don'ts' of social life." Giddens, *Sociology,* 31. Calhoun took the same view; see Calhoun, ed., *Dictionary of the Social Sciences,* 339. The late Roger Keesing, erstwhile professor of anthropology at the Australian National University and author of a classic textbook, importantly differentiated "public" norms from other rules for behaviour and action; see *Cultural Anthropology,* 317.

84 Although courts want to know about ideal and expected norms or standards, surely they also want to know whether they are acknowledged or observed or, perhaps more often, broken or even ignored.

85 See Haviland, *Cultural Anthropology,* 46-47; and Keesing, *Cultural Anthropology,* 7, two well-known introductory textbooks, for material bearing directly on our ethnographic responsibility to do more than just listen to what people say and to report a fuller picture. Palmer also cautions us that we need to attend to more than just what people tell us because their customary behaviour may differ. Palmer, "Forensic Anthropology," 966.

86 After all, we expect there to be a difference between the ideal and the real in any society and culture.

87   Firth, *Primitive Polynesian Economy,* 258. We also need to be aware that phenomena such as norms and rules, not to mention social life generally, are not tightly scripted. We constantly improvise as we meet new situations and adapt to them. Calhoun, *Dictionary of the Social Sciences,* 339, reminded us, for example, that "Pierre Bourdieu's practice theory focuses especially on the margin of improvisation implicit in any structure of norms, and it emphasizes the degree to which norms are evoked or activated in the context of concrete experience." Many sociologists and anthropologists have rejected the conventional, tightly scripted concept of role in part or in whole; see, for example, Connell "The Concept of Role"; Wrong, "The Oversocialized Conception of Man";and Keesing, *Cultural Anthropology,* 518, who came to use mainly the term *social identity* – "a social position or capacity (e.g., salesperson, customer, physician) that a person assumes in a particular setting." See also Jenkins, *Social Identity,* 134-36; and Luhrmann, "Identity in Anthropology," 7154-59.

88   Supreme Court of Western Australia, No. 1744 of 1993, unreported.

89   Here I concur with Merlan, who talks of the need not to take what is said as "facts," unproblematic except for their truthfulness. We must place what is said in an appropriate interpretive context in which considerations of differential power, gender, ethnicity, and the like are brought into view together with our observations. See Merlan, "Assessment of von Doussa on Anthropology," 1-12.

90   Williams, *Yolngu and Their Land,* 123-24.

91   McCann and Scheingold noted that scholars have identified "three separate [historical] stages, or generations, of rights claims." See McCann and Scheingold, "Rights: Legal Aspects," 13340.

92   MacLean, "Rights," 13334-39.

93   Ibid., quotation at 13334-35.

94   MacLean, 13334-35.

95   It is striking that he did not use the term *norm,* but I think that his *rules* or *standards* are simply norms. Scholars working in the law-and-economics tradition also seem to take norms and rules to be synonymous; see Basu, "Social Norms and the Law," 476-81; and McClennen and Shapiro, "Rule-Guided Behaviour," 363-69.

96   Goodenough, *Culture, Language, and Society,* 76-77. McNeil has expressed skepticism and (perhaps) distaste for a rights-based approach in proving Native title; see McNeil, *Emerging Justice?,* 460-63.

97   See also Hallowell, "Nature and Function of Property"; Hoebel, "Fundamental Legal Concepts"; Maine, *Ancient Law*; and Radcliffe-Brown, "Patrilineal and Matrilineal Succession."

98   Hohfeld, *Fundamental Legal Conceptions.*

99   Hafner, "Legal Reasoning Models," 8675; MacLean, "Rights," 13335.

100 Penner, "Analysis of Rights," 300.

101 Hoebel, "Fundamental Legal Concepts," 95-96. Hoebel was well known for his pioneering work in legal anthropology, including his collaboration with the jurist Karl N. Llewellyn in *The Cheyenne Way.*

102 Hallowell, "Nature and Function of Property," 240.

103 MacLean, "Rights," 13335.

104 Ibid.; Simmonds, "Introduction," xii.

105 Hoebel, "Fundamental Legal Concepts," called them *demand-rights.*

106 The term *jural* has a different sense among anthropologists. Williams noted Fallers' definition of *jural* as "consensual norms backed by sanctions," and she commented that *jural* "refers to an area of behaviour more important than taste, where expectations can be framed in terms of rights and duties, where enforcement relies on appeal to more than the aesthetics of pleasing comportment, and where people expect breaches of norms to be met by sanctions more dire than a raised eyebrow." Williams, *Yolngu and Their Land,* 8. Barnard and Spencer wrote that "the word '*jural*' refers to the legal world of rights and obligations [i.e., duties] and widely used in mid-[twentieth] century British structural-functionalism." Barnard and Spencer, *Encyclopedia,* 610.

107 Simmonds, "Introduction," xiii.

108 Ibid., xiii-xiv. See also MacLean, "Rights," 13335.

109 Simmonds, "Introduction," xiv, xv.
110 McCann and Scheingold, "Rights," 13339.
111 A.M. Honoré, summarized by Becker, *Property Rights,* 18-19. Note also Munzer, *A Theory of Property,* 22; Nygh and Butt, eds., *Butterworths Australian Legal Dictionary,* 49. Honoré proposed that the "full" or "liberal" concept of ownership included eleven kinds of rights:

   1 the right to possess – that is, to exclusive physical control of the thing owned (where the thing cannot be possessed physically due, for example, to its "noncorporeal" nature, "possession" may be understood metaphorically or simply as the right to exclude others from the use and other benefits of the thing);

   2 the right to use – that is, to personal enjoyment and use of the thing as distinct from (3) and (4) below;

   3 the right to manage – that is, to decide how and by whom a thing shall be used;

   4 the right to the income – that is, to the benefits derived from the foregoing personal use of a thing and allowing others to use it;

   5 the right to the capital – that is, the power to alienate the thing and to consume, waste, modify, or destroy it;

   6 the right to security – that is, immunity from expropriation;

   7 the power of transmissibility – that is, the power to devise or bequeath the thing;

   8 the absence of term – that is, the indeterminate length of one's ownership rights;

   9 the prohibition of harmful use – that is, one's duty to forbear from using the thing in certain ways harmful to others;

  10 liability to execution – that is, liability to have the thing taken away for repayment of a debt; and

  11 residuary character – that is, the existence of rules governing the reversion of lapsed ownership rights.

    Note that Honoré used the Hohfeldian terms *power* in (5) and (7), *immunity* in (6), *duty* in (9), and *liability* in (10). I also suggest that (2) and (5) are *privileges* and that (1), (3), and (4) are *claim-rights.* I draw attention to Honoré's formulation of the incidents of ownership because, together with Hohfeld's analysis of rights, it has been important in the development of the "bundle-of-rights" view of property – see, especially, Penner, "'Bundle of Rights.'" In fact, Honoré made use of the Hohfeldian terms, what I have called "rights in particular."

112 McCann and Scheingold, "Rights," 13339-40.
113 Hallowell, "Nature and Function of Property," 248.
114 Penner, "Analysis of Rights," 300.
115 Penner, *The Idea of Property in Law,* 13.
116 Ibid., 13n9.
117 Cited by Hart, *Concept of Law,* 291-92.
118 Smith, "'All Been Washed Away Now,'" 141.
119 Smith, *Between Places,* 141-42.
120 It is conventional among linguists to distinguish cases of homonymy from polysemy in analyzing and describing the meanings of words. In homonymy, "distinct lexical items happen to be pronounced and spelled alike." The English word *bank* provides a clear example, denoting "a financial institution" or the "sloping margin of a river." Huddleston and Pullum, *The Cambridge Grammar of the English Language,* 334. But in polysemy, a lexical item has two or more senses related in some principled way as by metaphor or metonymy. The sentences "the bank is located in Indooroopilly Shoppingtown" versus "the bank foreclosed on their mortgage" provide examples of polysemy. In the first, *bank* denotes a building in which the characteristic activity of banking takes place, and in the second it denotes the corporate social group that engages in that activity. Such semantic analysis can identify instances when anthropologists, judges, and lawyers slip from one sense of a word to another without clearly signalling it, perhaps without realizing it.
121 Nygh and Butt, *Australian Legal Dictionary,* 612-13.
122 Penner, *Idea of Property in Law,* 9-10.

123 For his part, Hallowell, "Nature and Function of Property," 248-49, was in no doubt that "we cannot properly speak of rights, obligations and privileges among animals." He further noted (418n63) the description of social philosopher G.H. Mead: "The dog is not taking the attitude of the other dog. A man who says 'this is my property' is taking an attitude of the other person. The man is appealing to his rights because he is able to take the attitude which everybody else in the group has with reference to property, thus arousing in himself the attitude of others." Mead, *Mind, Self, and Society,* 161-62.
124 Sutton, *Kinds of Rights,* 16-18.
125 McNeil, *Emerging Justice?*
126 Rigsby, "Aboriginal People, Spirituality," 963-73.
127 Brennan, "Ward, Wilson and *Yorta Yorta,*" 1-13.

3
Law's Infidelity to Its Past: The Failure to Recognize Indigenous Jurisdiction in Australia and Canada
David Yarrow

The terms "Aboriginal title" and "Native title" are highly evocative. As title is about property and ownership, Aboriginal title and Native title are immediately presumed to be related. These adjectival forms of property are taken to be somehow different from conventional property forms, although exactly how different is an uncertain matter. Property itself is a powerful concept that brings with it the established doctrine of generations of common law judges and thinkers. And though judges often warn that indigenous "property" should not be conceived in common law terms, the gravitational pull of conventional thinking about property is sometimes irresistible.

An example of such thinking is the long-established divide between public and private law in common law systems. Although the exact location of the boundary is not always clear, and is continuously contested, there is at least an atmosphere of conceptual rigour in the demarcation. Putting it broadly, public law is the law about governments and the things that they do – constitutional law, administrative law, criminal law, and so forth. Private law is the law that applies to the conduct of private citizens as between each other – contracts and trespass, for example. Of course, governments enter the realm of private law all the time to regulate private conduct by legislation, but when they do they are exercising their public law powers. The reverse, however, is not true. Citizens, as property holders, do not have any public law remedies when their rights are violated unless the public law creates such a remedy.[1] So, the thinking goes, indigenous "property" must be the same; it is a private law concept only.

A counterpoint is the position of Indian tribes in the United States or at least those that are federally "recognized" and have status as "domestic dependent nations," by which their sovereignty receives qualified recognition. Although that sovereignty has been subjected to numerous legislative and judicial incursions,[2] it remains true that the law in the United States recognizes at least the potential for a greater degree of indigenous legal autonomy than the law in Australia and Canada, where there has been little or no unambiguous recognition of indigenous sovereignty. This is despite the frequent use of US judicial precedent in Canadian and Australian cases dealing with indigenous "property."

Sovereignty in its domestic form, as opposed to its international law context, encompasses all of the power of government (acting in the name of the sovereign). In constitutional states such as Australia and Canada, that power is distributed among a variety of political institutions in each country's federal system. Talk in terms of sovereignty, however, inevitably brings with it ideas of international law and the status of indigenous people. Without overlooking the many important issues for indigenous people in international law, not the least of which is how they come to be within sovereign nations in the first place, my discussion here is directed only to their situation once they are part of a sovereign Canada or Australia. Therefore, I will describe the domestic distribution of sovereignty through the distribution of jurisdiction. What, then, is jurisdiction? At its broadest (any aspect of domestic sovereignty), it is the power to make decisions about human conduct.[3] The division of jurisdiction between institutions has geographical (territorial jurisdiction), hierarchical (shared power with one institution having overriding authority), and subjective (divisions of jurisdiction over different subject matter) aspects, which I will discuss below.

In functional terms, Aboriginal title and Native title confer at least some form of jurisdiction since they are the foundation of property rights.[4] However, it is unclear whether they confer jurisdiction beyond that – whether they extend to forms of jurisdiction that could take public law. My aim here is to show that Aboriginal title and Native title necessarily involve an element of jurisdiction beyond that of a proprietary form. The basic argument is an egalitarian one: namely, that pre-existing indigenous legal norms and institutions are, for the purposes of jurisdiction, relevantly the same as early modern English local laws and institutions that extensively intermingled property and public law forms of jurisdiction. Moreover, the system of judicial administration permitted local laws that significantly differed from the common law administered in the royal courts at Westminster. Because those laws and institutions were removed only by legislative intervention (albeit with some judicial arrogation of power at the centre), indigenous ones deserve at least the same level of recognition given the absence of clear legislative displacement.

In the colonial era, after initial attempts at accommodation, judicial authorities in Canada and Australia overlooked the possible correlation between indigenous legal systems and English local laws. Rather, they drew on an artificially coherent and idealized version of the common law that denied the possibility of a local, indigenous law. Although contemporary Aboriginal and Native title jurisprudence has departed significantly from colonial period norms and premises in its treatment of indigenous property interests, the same cannot be said for the recognition of indigenous jurisdiction in its public law form.

Earlier Treatment of Jurisdiction

The history of the law of England is rife with competing jurisdictions and different institutional forms for exercising them. In light of the contemporary hierarchy of courts in Australia and Canada, it is often easy to forget that diversity of local law was a central feature of the legal history of England. This diversity was concerned not only with the content of the law (or local custom with the force of law) but also with its administration. Local customary law was administered by local judicial institutions. By the time of British colonial expansion in Australia and Canada, many of these local judicial institutions had been removed or at least displaced by the centralizing force of the royal courts at Westminster.[5] Importantly, the superior courts of the colonies that became Australia and Canada were modelled on the jurisdiction of the courts at Westminster. But local judicial institutions were by no means irrelevant in the late eighteenth century and early nineteenth century. One example was the system of manorial courts.

They were a part of the manor, itself a feudal institution with a history stretching back to the beginning of legal memory in England. The typical manor of the early Middle Ages has been described in a fourfold way: a unit of the administration of public law, a system of agriculture, a unit in the management of property, and an element of jurisdiction.[6] In the feudal era, the manor was a small unit of government, and land within it was held "of the manor" by free and unfree (villein) tenants of its lord. Manors also contained common land in which rights of use were distributed between lord and tenants. In manorial courts, the local customary law of a manor was enforced. Although the courts were notionally administered by the lord, or his steward or bailiff, tenants participated in the operations of a manorial court particularly in its function of regulating the shared commons.[7]

The history of the manorial system is far too extensive for a short summary here. However, for the purpose of contrasting the history of the common law with the recognition of indigenous laws in colonial Australia and Canada, a key point is that the royal courts of Westminster did not exercise any control over relations between the lord of the manor and his unfree tenants for a considerable time. In the eyes of the royal courts, the land of the unfree was possessed by the lord, and it was only the custom of the manor (and its enforcement in manorial courts) that protected the interests of its tenants.[8] Unfree tenants held their land as "tenants by copy of court roll"; hence, their land was termed "copyhold."[9] By the early sixteenth century, the Court of Chancery began to intervene in these disputes,[10] followed by the common law courts.[11] Despite this intervention, the distinction between copyhold land and freehold persisted until 1926,[12] especially for procedures for transferring and dealing with the land.

Manorial courts were in their dying days by the early nineteenth century. The enclosure of manorial land, by which the land became freehold and manorial custom and jurisdiction were abolished, had excluded much of the geographic scope of the operation of manorial courts.[13] But they still had some continuing relevance. As Harry Arthurs describes it,

> By the nineteenth century, certainly by the 1830s, customary law had become less important both because of the decline in the relative (though not absolute) size of the rural population, and because of the elimination through enclosure of common lands and the associated use-rights and, more generally, of other customary rights "prised loose from their sociological context." But the customary law had by no means disappeared entirely. Brougham's famous speech on law reform, in 1828, referred to customary tenures "in a thousand manors, all different from the Common-law that regulates freehold estates, most of them different from each other ... Is it right that such varieties of custom should be allowed to have force in particular districts, contrary to the general law of the land?" As late as the 1850s books were being published, and apparently sold, on local customary law and copyhold tenure, and the relatively slow progress toward freehold tenure, even through the late nineteenth century, inevitably left behind pockets of customary land law.

For the most part, however, the manorial courts had suffered one of two fates by the mid-nineteenth century. On the one hand, the administrative functions of the court leet had largely passed to the new institution of municipal government, although the survival of the Court Leet of the Manor of Manchester offers us a fascinating late glimpse of the institution at work in a new urban and industrial setting. On the other hand, the adjudication of civil disputes by the court baron apparently came to resemble similar functions performed by courts of requests and other local courts; the Court Baron of the Manor of Sheffield, for example, seems to have operated in this fashion throughout the 1830s. The Manchester manorial court was purchased by a new municipal corporation in 1846, and the Sheffield court was replaced by a new county court in 1847, thus bringing to an end two ancient customary tribunals.[14]

The relevance of manorial courts largely ceased with the abolition of copyhold tenure in 1925, although their existence, along with other remnant institutions, was not finally abolished until 1977.[15]

What is the relevance of manorial courts to the jurisdiction of indigenous peoples in colonial Australia and Canada? My point here is certainly not to argue that indigenous peoples should be considered in the same way as the tenants of a medieval manor. Rather, I want to make the more general point that, at the beginning of the British colonial period in both Canada and Australia, tenure, jurisdiction, and plural laws were present in England and not inevitably separated into public and private forms of law. The common law at that time was able to cope with a large measure of legal diversity in England, both the content of local law and its administration by separate institutions. The question then arises why it was not apparently so tolerant of legal diversity in the colonies that became Canada and Australia.

Nineteenth-Century Moments

The typical lens to view the relationship between British colonial and indigenous law is the various rules for the reception of English law developed by the courts in response to the colonial expansion of Britain. Depending on the classification of a particular colony as "settled" or "conquered or ceded," the law of England was received in varying degrees.[16] Although it has been shown persuasively that a principled application of the rules of reception of English law leaves considerable room, in appropriate circumstances, for the continuing operation of indigenous law,[17] rules of reception require assessments of the level of "civilization" of indigenous peoples and evaluations of their religious values (and the extent of compatibility with Christian values) that are inappropriate in modern times. In the Australian and Canadian colonial contexts, English law ceased to be English in the way that it is in England (with its history of pluralism and extensive recognition of local forms of local law); instead, it became a single body of law that limited or displaced the scope and possibility of indigenous law. Rather than examine rules of reception as a basis for indigenous jurisdiction, I will examine here the colonial inability to perceive the existence of indigenous law in a meaningful way and its consequences for indigenous jurisdiction.

Examples from both Australia and Canada demonstrate the uncertainties of the application of English colonial law to indigenous people in certain respects. Although precise details differ, both show that judges initially had some perception of the unsuitability of applying English criminal law to the "internal affairs" of indigenous communities. In both examples, though, this uncertainty was overtaken by an acceptance of the application of English law.

Australia

The assertion of British sovereignty over the east coast of the Australian continent in 1788, together with the creation of a convict colony in New South Wales, made it inevitable that the legal system of the colonists would have to come to terms with the presence of indigenous people. The first legal official of the colony, Judge Advocate David Collins, arrived in Botany

Bay with a copy of Blackstone's *Commentaries* but no legal training.[18] Blackstone's firm endorsement of the "birthright" doctrine,[19] whereby English subjects carried the common law to "settled" colonies, encouraged Collins and later legal officials to apply English law in the new colony. But the penal purpose of the colony, its lack of legal professionals, and its great distance from London, limiting scrutiny by Whitehall and access to appeals in the Privy Council, all conspired to create a wide margin of interpretation for colonial legal officials in their application of English law. Informality, appeals to equity (in the non-legal sense), and individuated justice were the order of the day.[20]

After various judicial misadventures, the imperial Parliament legislated in 1823 to create a Supreme Court in New South Wales and Van Diemen's Land, each with jurisdiction substantially the same as the common law courts of Westminster, in addition to a more general, equitable, ecclesiastical, and criminal jurisdiction.[21] Continuing uncertainty about the application of English law prompted legislation in 1828 specifying its date of enactment (25 July 1828) as the date at which reception of English law was to be decided:

> All laws and statutes in force within the realm of England at the time of the passing of this Act (not being inconsistent herewith, or with any charter or letters patent or order in council which may be issued in pursuance hereof), shall be applied in the administration of justice in the courts of New South Wales and Van Diemen's Land respectively, so far as the same can be applied within the said colonies.[22]

The 1828 act also authorized colonial governors to legislate, declare, or modify the application of English laws. Until such legislation was made, colonial supreme courts were obliged to "adjudge and decide" the application of English laws in New South Wales or Van Diemen's Land.[23] The need for supreme courts to do this, even with a definitive reception date, arose from the continuing need to test the applicability of particular English law to colonial circumstances – whether the law could be applied in the colony.[24] When considering the existence of indigenous jurisdiction, it is also noteworthy that the reception provision directed only that English law be applied "in the administration of justice in the courts" of the colonies.[25] On the face of this provision, complete displacement of indigenous law (and its jurisdiction) by English law could only have been accomplished if the jurisdiction of the courts was exhaustive and exclusive. But, as we will see, there were early doubts that this was the case.

One of the doubts about the operation of English law in New South Wales concerned the application of law to indigenous people for their conduct purely among themselves.[26] The birthright thesis implied that English law was a law of status,[27] and before 1837 colonial authorities there did not regard the indigenous people of the colony as British subjects.[28] Doubts arose about whether the courts of the colony had jurisdiction over crimes between indigenous people.

In June 1829, in the case of *R. v. Ballard*,[29] the New South Wales Supreme Court concluded that it did not have jurisdiction for the killing of one Aboriginal person by another. Chief Justice Forbes wrote that he was "not aware that British laws have been applied to the Aboriginal natives in transactions solely between themselves, whether of contract, tort or crime."[30] Forbes proceeded to justify his conclusion by placing Aboriginal people in the "state of nature" of classical natural law theory: "The most important distinction between the savage [and] civilized state of man" is "that among savages there are no magistrates,"[31] presumably referring to judicial institutions such as the Supreme Court of New South Wales. But this did not prevent him from concluding that Aboriginal people were bound by their own laws, which "are preserved inviolate, [and] are rigidly acted upon."[32] There were also prudential reasons for Forbes's conclusion. Aboriginal people were not acquainted with English law, and its intervention would be resisted.[33] Dowling, the other judge considering the case, pointed to the absence of any indigenous consent to use English law between indigenous people.[34] As Bruce Kercher has observed, *Ballard* shows that Forbes and Dowling were prepared to recognize "a plurality of laws on the Australian continent" and "the obligation of English law both to recognise and protect those other laws."[35] This recognition was qualified in that English law applied to conduct "between" members of the two communities and was coloured by the inability of judges to perceive the complexity of indigenous law by their ascription of "savage" status to Australian indigenous people. But even this qualified form of respect and recognition for indigenous law was quickly discarded by the court.

The court revisited the issue of jurisdiction in 1836 in the case of *R. v. Murrell*.[36] The judgment was delivered by Justice Burton for the unanimous court, concluding that it did have jurisdiction. Burton referred to a number of factors in support of this conclusion, including that the indigenous people of Australia "had not attained at the first settlement of the English people among them to such a position in point of numbers and civilization, and to such a form of Government and laws, as to be entitled to be recognized as so many *sovereign states governed by laws of their own*."[37]

The territory of New South Wales was, in Burton's view, "unappropriated by any one" prior to its occupation by the British crown.[38] The crown had exercised dominion over the territory for many years, and the reception statute described above meant that in the colony "the law of England is the law of the land."[39] Clearly, Burton did not regard the laws of indigenous people as having any bearing on the matter. Those laws had been displaced entirely by English law, and their prior, even continuing, existence was ir-relevant to its application.[40] The question of the applicability of English law to the circumstances of the colony at the time, where the vast majority of indigenous people lived isolated from the colonial legal order, does not ap-pear in Burton's reasons. That legal order was blind to indigenous law because it was "unrecognizable." For considering jurisdiction, *Murrell* is significant for its *volte-face* from *Ballard* in its unwillingness to recognize even some extent of indigenous legal autonomy.

Although claims about the limit to a colonial court's jurisdiction for crimes between indigenous people continued after *Murrell*,[41] the 1830s marked the point of departure for the "decisive shift away from pluralism" in Australian colonies toward a legal monolingualism.[42] By 1889, the Privy Council was able to disregard the early equivocation of the Supreme Court of New South Wales and state in its classic phrase about the legal and human vacuity of the Australian continent before colonization:

> The extent to which English law is introduced into a British colony, and the manner of its introduction, must necessarily vary according to circumstances. There is a great difference between the case of a colony acquired by conquest or cession, in which there is an established system of law, and that of a colony which consisted of a tract of territory practically unoccupied, without settled inhabitants or settled law, at the time when it was peacefully annexed to the British dominions. The colony of New South Wales belongs to the latter class.[43]

Canada
As in New South Wales, the law of England was introduced to the colony of Upper Canada, although the route of its introduction was more circuitous. The introduction of the law of England in Quebec by the Royal Proclamation of 1763[44] was uncertain in its extent[45] and created grievances among the French residents of Quebec.[46] Not unlike that in New South Wales, the recep-tion of English law in Quebec was directed to the administration of justice in courts established by the British.

To avoid uncertainty and ameliorate any grievances, the British Parliament legislated to restore the civil law of Quebec for "property and civil rights" in section 8 of the *Quebec Act* of 1774.[47] For matters of criminal law, the *Quebec Act* preserved the application of the criminal law of England in Que-bec.[48] On the division of Quebec into Upper and Lower Canada by the *Constitutional Act* of 1791,[49] the first act of the legislature of Upper Canada excluded the preserved civil law of Quebec and introduced English law in its place. The reception of English law concerning "property and civil rights" was accomplished by the following provision: "That from and after the passing of this Act, in all matters of controversy relative to property and civil rights, resort shall be had to the laws of England as the rule for decision of the same."[50]

Although it has been generally assumed that Upper Canada "received English law for all purposes,"[51] it is significant that its reception, other than that for "property and civil rights," was, with certain exceptions, based on the Royal Proclamation's emphasis on the administration of justice by courts. One exception was the express reception of English criminal law in 1800 by legislative declaration that "the Criminal law of England, as it stood on the seventeenth day of September, in the year of our Lord, one thousand seven hundred and ninety-two, shall be, and the same is hereby declared to be the Criminal Law" of Upper Canada.[52] This unqualified reception formula did not prevent doubts from arising in the courts of Upper Canada about the extent to which English criminal law applied to indigenous communities. Mark Walters' exhaustive analysis of the *Shawanakiskie* case demonstrates that superior court judges in Upper Canada entertained such doubts.[53]

The *Shawanakiskie* case[54] concerned the killing of an indigenous person by another in the town of Amherstburg, Upper Canada, for which Shawanakiskie was tried and convicted in 1822. After the trial, counsel suggested that other judges had previously concluded that the Indians of Upper Canada enjoyed immunity by reason of treaty.[55] The trial judge, Campbell, placed the matter before Lieutenant Governor Sir Peregrine Maitland. Campbell included his charge to the grand jury in his report. In that charge, he described three categories of territory for considering the application of English law to indigenous people. First was the "uncultivated wilderness," for which indigenous people "have never been considered amenable to our laws or courts of justice for any occurrence purely amongst themselves, and unconnected with European inhabitants or interests." Second was reserve land or lands close to those of colonists, for which any general exemption from British law would be "extremely dangerous." But Campbell suggested a form of limitation to matters that were *mala in se* because indigenous people had no knowledge of merely "municipal laws." Third was land "within the boundaries of any European settlement," which Campbell concluded "there can be no ground for doubt, and I take upon myself to declare that our jurisdiction is full and unquestionable."[56] As Walters notes, a grand jury charge is not a final judgment.[57] But these comments give a clear statement of Campbell's territorial conception of the jurisdiction of colonial courts over the conduct of indigenous people.

Maitland referred the matter of treaty-based immunity to the two other Superior Court judges in Upper Canada, Chief Justice Powell and Justice Boulton. Boulton rejected the possibility out of hand, whereas Powell denied that he had ever judicially determined that a treaty-based immunity existed, but neither did he deny that such an immunity existed.[58] He referred to a grand jury charge in which the imprudence of punishing indigenous people for conduct among themselves by standards of English law is mentioned.[59] Despite these views, the matter was referred to imperial authorities, and after a fruitless search for an exempting treaty a warrant for execution was issued.[60] Walters concludes that the *Shawanakiskie* case shows that some colonial judges were prepared to accept the qualified immunity of indigenous people from colonial British law because their distinct, indigenous laws should determine matters internal to their communities.[61] Although by 1852 Canadian courts had refuted any notion of indigenous legal autonomy,[62] Walters emphasizes the need to ensure that "ideas about the law which developed later in time are not imposed ahistorically upon earlier times: the law of Canada may have eventually denied the rights of Aboriginal nations to exercise Aboriginal customary laws within their own communities, but it would take a generation of judges subsequent to that which dealt with the case of *Shawanakiskie* to articulate that conclusion."[63]

Comparison

It is striking that, in similar ways, the examples considered here show that judicial institutions in both New South Wales and Upper Canada questioned the full application of English criminal law to Aboriginal conduct. In New South Wales, the discriminating factor was Aboriginal status and the continued effect of Aboriginal laws between Aboriginal people. In Upper Canada, the distinction was more political and spatial, with laws applicable between Aboriginal people in Aboriginal spaces being different from those in English ones. Despite this early equivocation about the application of law, both jurisdictions later concluded that the colonial criminal law fully applied to indigenous people even when the reception of statutes applicable to both colonies was directed to the laws as administered by colonial courts rather than at the displacement of indigenous law *per se*. Although neither example here amounts to a robust recognition of an autonomous indigenous law in New South Wales[64] or Upper Canada,[65] it is significant that, even when equivocating about the application of English law, neither recognized the collective indigenous institutions that enforced the law of indigenous people (whether individuals of particular status, families, tribes, etc.). There was no centralized hierarchy for the enforcement of law like the colonial courts system, and indigenous institutions (from the view of colonial authorities) were not sufficiently similar even to be perceived as legal institutions. Without the recognition of separate institutions for the enforcement of law, indigenous laws were in the hands of colonial legal institutions that ultimately dispensed with them. Thus, a limited knowledge of indigenous law encouraged judges to ignore it.

   It is not entirely surprising that courts in Canada and Australia decided, by the middle of the nineteenth century, that English law applied to the exclusion of any continuing indigenous law. Even before the rise of legal positivism in the late nineteenth century, the racial ideology of the British Empire justified deprecating views of indigenous norms. The evolutionist and stadial view of history of the Scottish Enlightenment saw "civilization" proceeding through four stages: hunting, shepherding, agriculture, and commerce.[66] Indigenous people were relegated to the first stage and considered inferior. A chilling example can be found in the 5 December 1855 report of Superintendent General of Indian Affairs Viscount Bury to Governor General of the Province of Canada Sir Edmund Head. Bury "rated" the indigenous people of Canada east and west on a scale of civilization with a score of fifteen being "the average standard of civilization among the general mass of the white population."[67] No indigenous community was rated above ten. A lack of attainment in "point of numbers and civilization" was one of the justifications given by Justice Burton in *Murell* for the non-recognition of indigenous law.

Toward a New History of Title and Jurisdiction

Both Canadian law and Australian law have substantially shifted, in recent decades, in the extent to which indigenous rights in land are recognized. But nowhere is there a recognition of jurisdiction coupled with land ownership. In Australia, the 1992 case of *Mabo v. Queensland (No. 2)*,[68] for the first time ever, declared that indigenous Australians had rights and interests in land arising from their continued observance of traditional law and custom. Shortly after, the prospect that the continuing observance of indigenous law could lead to the recognition of other legal rights was soon repudiated for criminal law matters.[69] Before the Supreme Court of Canada in *R. v. Pamajewon*,[70] the claim of "a broad right to manage the use of their reserve lands" by two First Nations groups was rejected as excessively general.[71] Even the *Delgamuukw* case,[72] in which the Supreme Court recast much of its jurisprudence about Aboriginal title, has no direct acceptance of the authority of Aboriginal law over non-Aboriginal people on Aboriginal title land.

But the communal nature of Aboriginal title, and the capacity for title-holding groups to make decisions about it, necessarily bring rules and procedures within the group that regulate the use of land – a form of self-government.[73] The same rationale applies to the recognition of internal self-government for groups holding Native title in Australia. The strongest indication to date that indigenous jurisdiction exists (in the public law sense) in Canada is the treatment of self-government in the challenge to the *Nisga'a Final Agreement* in *Campbell v. British Columbia (Attorney General)*,[74] in which a single judge of the Supreme Court of British Columbia concluded that Aboriginal self-government survived Confederation, including a limited power to legislate, and that the Nisga'a agreement was a negotiated particularization of the pre-existing right of self-government. In Justice Williamson's view, self-government was intimately connected to the existence of Aboriginal title.

The long history of non-recognition of indigenous jurisdiction finds its origin in the vagaries of the reception of law rules for British colonies and the property-directed nature of Aboriginal title law in Canada (and Native title law in Australia). But the reception of such law rules is, in my view, a fragment of the past. It developed at the height of the British colonial period to facilitate colonial expansion. Where indigenous law continues to be observed and applied by indigenous people, resort to colonial-era rules that purport to nullify, or at least minimize, their laws fails to give equal respect and concern to indigenous people as citizens. Rather than invoke rules of reception, the English history of legal pluralism suggests that the common law can exist side by side with heterodox bodies of local law. That history also underscores the fact that there is no imperative for conceptualizing Aboriginal title separately from jurisdiction. As the *Campbell* case suggests, the one is a necessary corollary of the other.

Full respect for indigenous legal norms, and their parallel administration within the Australian and Canadian legal systems, shifts the focus of legal rules from the superordination of the common law (whether or not some level of recognition of continuing indigenous law arises) to the mutual regard of coexisting legal systems. In that event, the choice of rules of law and boundaries of jurisdiction, combined with the recognition of the authority of indigenous legal institutions, becomes the rules that co-ordinate the separate systems. Although the possible form of co-ordinating rules is unclear at present, the long experience of Quebec civil law in Canada shows the practicality of this treatment of indigenous legal systems. A key difference, however, is the more limited awareness of indigenous legal norms within non-indigenous legal institutions in Australia and Canada. Time and education are required for non-indigenous legal institutions to improve their awareness. In the same way that the philosopher Alasdair MacIntyre describes the meeting of traditions, time is required for mutual recognition, and that recognition does not necessarily arise simultaneously for each culture. Thus, an inability to conceive of indigenous law in the nineteenth century was not a radical incommensurability but a relative position to be overcome (hermeneutically) with the passage of time. Time is an essential resource for mutual comprehension, and cultural components are not static (on either side).[75] As MacIntyre describes it,

> Confrontation by new situations, engendering new questions, may reveal within established practices and beliefs a lack of resources for offering or for justifying answers to these new questions. The coming together of two

previously separate communities, each with its own well-established institutions, practices, and beliefs, either by migration or by conquest, may open up new alternative possibilities and require more than the existing means of evaluation are able to provide.[76]

Acknowledgments
I am grateful for the valuable advice of Kent McNeil and Jeanette Neeson. All mistakes are mine.

Notes
1 See, for example, *Trespass to Property Act,* R.S.O. C.T. 21, which makes entry to premises a criminal offence in certain circumstances.
2 See, for example, Clinton, "Peyote and Judicial Political Activism," 92; and Clinton, "There Is No Federal Supremacy Clause for Indian Tribes," 113-260.
3 In this sense, even proprietary rights are an aspect of domestic sovereignty as they allow the control of some aspects of human conduct. See Cohen, "Property and Sovereignty," 8.
4 Ibid.
5 See Baker, *An Introduction to English Legal History,* 14-27.
6 Pollock and Maitland, *The History of English Law,* 2nd ed., 597.
7 See Neeson, *Commoners,* ch. 3.
8 Gray, *Copyhold, Equity, and the Common Law,* 6.
9 Baker, *Introduction,* 307n5.
10 Gray, *Copyhold,* 13n8.
11 Baker, *Introduction,* 308n5.
12 Ibid., 309.
13 See Mingay, *Parliamentary Enclosure.* Note, however, that even in the enclosure process manorial jurisdiction was preserved unless the lord of the manor gave explicit consent to its extinguishment by an award enclosing manorial land; see, for example, *Inclosure Act 1845* (U.K.), s. 96.
14 Arthurs, "Without the Law," 21-22 (references omitted).
15 Baker, *Introduction,* 27n5.
16 See, generally, Walters, "British Imperial Constitutional Law," 350-413.
17 Ibid., 385-93.
18 Kercher, *Debt, Seduction, and Other Disasters,* 23.
19 Blackstone, *Commentaries on the Laws of England,* 1765; reprint, 701.
20 Kercher, *Debt,* ch. 2.
21 Castles, *Australian Legal History,* 133-38.
22 *Australian Courts Act* (U.K.), 9 Geo. 4 (1828), c. 83, s. 24, 1st para.
23 Ibid., 3rd para.
24 See, for example, Castles, "Reception and Status," 1-32; *Cooper v. Stuart* (1889), 14 *App. Cas.* 273 at 291; Côté, "The Reception of English Law," 29-92; Else-Mitchell, "Foundation of New South Wales," 1-23; and Evatt, "The Legal Foundations of New South Wales," 409-24.
25 For a reception formula not limited in this way, see *Law and Equity Act,* R.S.B.C. 1995, c. 253, s. 2, which provides *Application of English Law in British Columbia*:

> 2. Subject to s. 3, the Civil and Criminal Laws of England, as they existed on 19 November 1858, so far as they are not inapplicable from local circumstances, are in force in B.C., but those laws must be held to be modified and altered by all legislation that has the force of law in B.C. or in any former colony comprised within its geographical limits.

26 See, generally, Bridges, "The Extension of English Law," 264-69; Kercher, "Native Title in the Shadows," 100-19; and Kercher, "Recognition of Indigenous Legal Autonomy," 7-9. The jurisdiction of colonial courts for offences between colonists and Aboriginal people had

been accepted earlier by the Supreme Court of New South Wales in *R. v. Lowe* (unreported, 18 May 1827); see http://www.law.mq.edu.au/scnsw.

27   In a settled colony, Blackstone stated, the "colonists carry with them only so much of the English law as is applicable to the condition of an infant colony." Blackstone, *Commentaries*, 107.

28   Kercher, "Recognition of Aboriginal Status," 83-102. It was only at the direction of the secretary of state for the colonies that colonial officials, including the judges, accepted that indigenous people were British subjects.

29   *R. v. Ballard* (unreported, S.C.N.S.W., 13 June 1829). See the reprinted version in Kercher, "*R v. Ballard*," 410-25 [cited hereafter as "*Ballard, Murrell, and Bonjon Reports*"].

30   Kercher, "*Ballard, Murrell, and Bonjon Reports*," 413.

31   Ibid.

32   Ibid.

33   Ibid.

34   Ibid., 414.

35   Kercher, "Recognition of Aboriginal Status," 92.

36   *R. v. Murrell* (1836), 1 Legge 72. See Kercher, "*Ballard, Murrell, and Bonjon Reports*," 414, for the more extensive report in the New South Wales Archives.

37   Kercher, "*Ballard, Murrell, and Bonjon Reports*," 415-16.

38   Ibid., 416.

39   Ibid.

40   Counsel for Murrell led evidence to show, in a rudimentary way, that there was a system of indigenous law that applied to the alleged killing; see Kercher, "Recognition of Aboriginal Status," 93-94.

41   For example, *R. v. Bonjon*. See Cooke, "Arguments for the Survival of Aboriginal Customary Law," 201-41; Davies, "Aborigines, Murder, and the Criminal Law," 313-45; and Kercher, "*Ballard, Murrell, and Bonjon Reports*," 417.

42   Benton, *Law and Colonial Cultures*, 194-95. In other British colonies in Australia, courts were not as quick as those of New South Wales to assume jurisdiction over criminal matters internal to indigenous communities. In South Australia, the Supreme Court did not conclude that it had jurisdiction until 1851; see Castles, *Australian Legal History*, 529-30.

43   *Cooper v. Stuart* (1889), 14 *App. Cas.* 291.

44   R.S.C. 1985, App. II, No. 1.

45   That part of the Royal Proclamation (GB 1763) that promised to those "inhabiting or resorting to" Quebec the right to "confide in our royal protection for the enjoyment of the benefit of the laws of our realm of England" and, for that purpose, authorized royal governors of Quebec to establish courts to hear and determine "all Causes, as well Criminal as Civil, according to Law and Equity, and as near as may be agreeable to the Laws of England" is generally taken to have imported English law, although the extent is disputed by some; see Côté, "Reception of English Law," 88. Coupland concludes that the introduction of English law in Quebec was done "without adequate knowledge or reflection," which amounted to a "serious blunder"; see Coupland, The Quebec Act, 35.

46   Côté, 72-76.

47   14 Geo. 3 (1773-74), c. 83.

48   Ibid., s. 11.

49   31 Geo. 3 (1790-91), c. 31.

50   *An Act Introducing English Civil Law into Upper Canada*, 32 Geo. 3 (1792), c. 1, s. 3. See *Property and Civil Rights Act*, R.S.O. 1990, c. 29.

51   Côté, "Reception of English Law," 89.

52   *An Act for the Further Introduction of the Criminal Law of England*, 40 Geo. 3 (U.C. 1800), c. 1, s. 1.

53   Walters, "Extension of Colonial Criminal Jurisdiction," 273-310.

54   *R. v. Shawanakiskie* (1822-26), Upper Canada, Ct. of Oyer and Terminer, Western District Assize, cited in ibid. This section is a brief summary of part of his work.

55   Ibid., 293.

56   Ibid., 295-96, citing Public Record Office, CO 42/370, 28-31.

57 Ibid., 296.
58 Ibid., 303. Powell CJ had earlier made extrajudicial statements about the non-application of (British) colonial laws to the Six Nations of the Grand River; ibid., 290-93.
59 Ibid., 300-3.
60 Ibid., 305.
61 Ibid., 309.
62 Ibid., citing *Doe D. Sheldon v. Ramsey* (1852), 9 U.C.Q.B. 105.
63 Ibid.
64 Even though Forbes CJ in *Ballard* expressly considers the existence of indigenous law, his view of it is dismissive and impoverished.
65 In *Connolly v. Woolrich* (1867), 1 C.N.L.C. 70, Justice Monk of the Quebec Superior Court recognized the continuing effect of Cree marriage law for a marriage in Athabaska in 1803. This decision did not, at least historically, prompt greater recognition of an autonomous, indigenous law.
66 Stein, *Roman Civil Law*, ch. 22; Stocking, *Delimiting Anthropology*, ch. 5.
67 "Copies or Extracts of Recent Correspondence Respecting Alterations in the Organization of the Indian Department in Canada," in *Irish University Press Series of British Parliamentary Papers. Colonies: Canada*, 33 vols. (Shannon: Irish University Press, 1968-71), 21: 27-28, at 28.
68 *Mabo v. Queensland (No. 2)* (1992), 66 A.L.J.R. 408.
69 See *Walker v. New South Wales* (1994), 69 A.L.J.R. 111; Odgers, "Criminal Cases in the High Court of Australia," *Criminal Law Journal* 19 (1995): 95-99; and Yeo, "Native Criminal Jurisdiction after Mabo," 9-26.
70 [1996] 2 S.C.R. 821.
71 McNeil, "Aboriginal Rights in Canada," 253-98 at 281-83.
72 [1997] 3 S.C.R. 1010.
73 See *Campbell v. British Columbia (Attorney General)* (2000), 189 D.L.R. (4th) 333 at para. 114 per Williamson J; and McNeil, "Aboriginal Rights in Canada," 286n71.
74 [2000] 189 D.L.R. (4th) 333.
75 See MacIntyre, *Whose Justice?*, ch. 18.
76 Ibid., 355.

4
The Defence of Native Title and Dominion in Sixteenth-Century Mexico Compared with *Delgamuukw*
Haijo Westra

Alonso de la Vera Cruz[1] is far less famous than his eminent and likeminded contemporaries, Vitoria and Las Casas, both of whom he knew well. He was a well-born Spaniard who studied under Vitoria at Salamanca and taught there before leaving for Mexico in 1536, where he became a prominent member of the Augustinian order and the first professor of theology at the University of Mexico. In the first year of existence of that university (1553-54), he gave an important set of lectures, of which we have the *relectio,* typically a repetition of the previous year's lectures made available in written form. Among other issues, they deal with the question of Native dominion, before and after conquest, known as *De dominio infidelium et justo bello.* Despite its obscurity and dependence on Vitoria, the treatise deserves to be far better known than it is because, as its modern editor Ernest Burrus points out, Alonso is far more wide-ranging and extensive in his argumentation and far more knowledgeable about the actual situation in Mexico only decades after the conquest than his famous teacher. He constantly applies his concepts to recent historical developments, actual situations, and colonial practices that he was witnessing himself, whereas Vitoria, the theoretician, had to rely on the reports of others.

Alonso's arguments are based in natural law as developed by the medieval churchmen, particularly Aquinas; on the *jus gentium* that was being transformed into modern international law by Vitoria and others; on divine law as revealed in the Old and New Testaments; on canon law; and on feudal law and custom. With Vitoria, Alonso concludes that the Conquest of Mexico lacked a just cause and was therefore unlawful. He did not have his head in the sand, however, and accepted the conquest as a *fait accompli.*[2] Yet this point of departure profoundly affected his view of Native versus Spanish dominion in Mexico at the moment of contact and afterward.

In *De dominio,* Alonso argues that the preconquest Native community had, and still possessed in his time, full and just dominion in terms of both ownership of and jurisdiction over the land, the two being inseparable. The land belongs to the people, he claims, not the lord. Ownership of and control over common land reside in the community and cannot be rightfully traded without its consent; any such transfer of title is and remains illegal, as does the illegal transfer of title to private land.[3] Mere possession and time do not validate the illegal claim but increase the original injustice, a fundamental difference between natural and common law. Political dominion in the sense of rule/jurisdiction may be conferred on a ruler voluntarily by the community. The transfer of this right is the title by which a ruler is allowed to govern. If he does not govern by common consent or for the common good, he is a tyrant, and his title is illegitimate. Alonso is not prepared to state that Montezuma was a tyrant; therefore, he was unjustly removed.[4]

In terms of land ownership, there are two possibilities. Native ownership may be private or communal. In natural law, rightful ownership is forever. Communal lands cannot be appropriated by the Spaniards, even when uncultivated, without the free consent of the community. The analogy drawn by Alonso is with the unlawful encroachment on communal hunting and fishing rights in medieval and early modern Europe.[5] A Spaniard taking over such communal lands is a thief and is obliged to make restitution for the damage caused.[6] If a Spaniard has bought private land from a local chief at a just price that the chief has not paid the owner, then the Spaniard remains the just owner, but he has to compensate the original owner once he becomes aware of the situation. Just possession yields *bona fide* possession and a clear conscience.[7]

Further addressing the situation on the ground in Mexico in his time, Alonso answers the question of whether Spaniards who purchase land from Natives can do so in good conscience, regardless of the price paid. Whether they buy from an individual or from the community, they are morally obliged to obtain consent and pay a just price; if not, the sale is invalid and the title insecure.[8] The mediation of a trusted and highly regarded individual should be invoked to arrive at a just price in such a case.

One of the arguments put forward by the Spaniards was that the Natives had a superabundance of land, much of which was not used. Alonso allows the validity of such a claim in cases where the land is not claimed in any way by the Natives or where its use is manifestly for the common good. Favouring settled agriculture, he allows for pasturing of Spanish cattle on the lands of the nomadic Chichimecas. As part of their feudal tenure, the Spanish lords exacted a tribute or tax from the Natives. In the context of *De dominio*, Alonso expressly declares the seizing of communal land in lieu of tribute (money) illegal.[9]

Another argument put forward by the Spaniards to justify their rule and appropriation was the principle of prescription. As Burrus suggests in his introduction, *De dominio* may have been intended to ensure that such a claim did not remain uncontested.[10] Prescription, in international law, constitutes acquisition of sovereignty over a territory through its continuous and undisputed exercise. The length of time required varies widely, from two to sixty years. In this case, thirty years had elapsed between the time of conquest and the time of authorship, and the question of Native versus Spanish dominion clearly had not been settled. To begin with, Alonso does not allow claims based on the right of conquest because the conquest was unjust. He also rejects the arguments that the land belonged to those who discovered it as *terra nullius* and that the Natives belonged to the first one to take them over.[11] Instead, Alonso insists throughout that the land and the jurisdiction over it belong to the "people (or peoples) of the New World" (*populus* or *populi Novi Mundi*), implicitly extending the claim on behalf of the Natives beyond Mexico to all of the Americas.

This is a radical stance, and it may have been the cause of subsequent difficulties for Alonso.[12] He was accused of wanting to form his own church, a conventional charge of heresy, and was eventually called to defend himself before the Council of the Indies. But his position was not treasonous in itself. He acknowledges the suzerainty of the king after the fact of conquest (even though denying that the Natives are either *de facto* or *de jure* subjects). Alonso envisages a tutelary overlordship of the king for the protection of the Natives. The king, however, does not own the land of his (non-)subjects and therefore cannot give their land away to enfief the conquistadores as a reward. Therefore, the king's or viceroy's land grants do not hold: they are illegal, and their titles are insecure.[13] As a consequence, the enfiefed Spanish landowners do not have dominion over lands, and they may not seize lands on their own account. A colonial fiefdom does not give just title to seized land. This view of royal jurisdiction, without ownership of the land, was perfectly consistent with feudal law.[14]

What does Alonso propose as a remedy? Restitution (and the issue of restitution is the classical locus for the discussion of dominion in canon law):[15] restitution by unlawful possessors if the community has refused consent, restitution of fields to owners, of communal lands to the community, of stolen goods, of excessive and unjustly (i.e., without dominion) exacted tribute, and of illegally held subjects.[16] Restitution is not only a moral obligation. It is also based on the natural law principle that rightful ownership is forever. Length of time of illegal possession does not validate the *status quo*.

The question of Native title and dominion presented itself early on in North America as well. In Maryland, the Jesuits were granted a parcel of land at Mattapany by one of the Native chiefs, Maquacomen, for use as a mission, but the civil authority, under Lord Baltimore, seized the land.[17] In 1641, the Jesuits through their provincial, Father Knott, argued that the Natives, even though non-believers,[18] were true lords and owners of their lands and other goods (*fundorum aliorumque bonorum suorum ... veri domini ac proprietarii*) and therefore free to dispose of them as they pleased. This view was supported by a learned opinion on the issue by Dr. Francis Silvius of Oxford dated 1641, citing much the same sources as Alonso de la Vera Cruz on natural law and the *jus gentium,* especially Vitoria and Thomas Aquinas. Silvius is categorical in defining Natives as their own and absolute lords (*proprii ac absoluti domini*), citing Vitoria for his opinion that the "barbarians" are owners by public as well as private right and for the conclusion that there is no title in existence that might enable Christians to occupy their lands and possess their goods. Having full ownership and control, Natives were free to keep their lands and possessions or to give, sell, or grant them to whomever they saw fit. The Native land thus donated to the Jesuits was taken over by force by Lord Baltimore, and not returned, with the civil authority arguing that only he could receive or buy (or grant land) as lord and proprietary: that is, as the only one in the colony with full dominion.

Early objections to confiscation did not come solely from the Thomist tradition of natural law and the school of Salamanca. From New England, too, there was a voice of dissent, in this case from a principled non-conformist, Roger Williams, who is said to have held, in 1634, against the royal charter of the Massachusetts Bay Company of 1629, that the king did not have title to Indian lands, that Indian lands were not to be confiscated, that Indians had title to those lands, and that they were to be paid for their lands.[19] He was put on trial for his views. Early American jurisprudence on the subject of Native title remained, in the words of one commentator, "singularly vacillating and ... discordant."[20]

There can be no doubt that Alonso would have regarded the assertion of British sovereignty by the Royal Proclamation of 1763 as illegitimate because it was done without consent, as the contemporary interpretation of John Tabor, the attorney general in 1765, makes clear:

> It is the Policy of our Constitution that wheresoever the King's Dominions extend, he is the Fountain of all Property in Land, and to deny that Right in the Crown in any Place is in Effect denying his right to rule there. Hence it follows that ... the King can grant lands within his Dominions here, with or without a previous Conveyance from the Indians.[21]

This opinion also stresses the inseparability of the right to rule from ownership of the land, necessitating the claim of an underlying title of the crown. The Royal Proclamation actually set aside a territory for the possession and use of Native peoples,[22] but by this very act it stripped them of ownership of and control over the land: that is, of Native dominion. However, as Superintendent of Northern Indians Sir William Johnson pointed out in 1764, the Natives did not consider themselves in any way subjects of the crown:

You may be assured that none of the Six Nations, Western Indians, etc. ever declared themselves to be Subjects, or will ever consider themselves in that light whilst they have any Men, or an open Country to retire to, the very Idea of Subjection would fill them with horror – Indeed I have been Just looking into the Indian Records, where I find in the Minutes of 1751 that those who made ye Entry Say, that Nine different Nations acknowledged themselves to be his Majestys Subjects, although I sat at that Conference, made entrys of all the Transactions, in which there was not a Word mentioned, which could imply a Subjection, however, these matters ... seem not [to] be well known at home [in Britain], and therefore, it may prove of dangerous consequence to persuade them that the Indians have agreed to things which are so repugnant to their Principles that the attempting to enforce it, must lay the foundation of greater Calamities than has yet been experienced in this County, – it is necessary to observe that no Nation of Indians have any word which can express, or convey the Idea of Subjection.[23]

Thus, the Royal Proclamation and subsequent colonial acts and legal decisions allowed for notions of an underlying title of the crown and an overarching jurisdiction over Native lands to take hold and become a colonial reality. For the Supreme Court of Canada in *Delgamuukw,* the same proclamation remains axiomatic and unproblematic: it is referred to as the basis and justification of all subsequent decisions regarding Native lands. Aboriginal title is said to have "survived" the assertion of sovereignty by the crown but only as a "burden" on the crown's title. By contrast, in the political sphere, there has finally been a willingness by the government to give up some jurisdiction in the *Nisga'a Final Agreement* and in the recent treaty with the Dogrib people.

Alonso also would have disapproved of the separation of ownership and title from jurisdiction and self-rule in *Delgamuukw.* By the same token, his insistence on the inherent connection between the two bolsters the original claim in *Delgamuukw* – which was one of Native dominion ("ownership" and "jurisdiction") before it was reduced, on appeal, to one of Native title and self-government. The Supreme Court refused to rule on self-government in *Delgamuukw,* and the signs are not favourable. According to the chief justice in *Pamajewon,* "rights to native self-government, if they exist, cannot be framed in excessively general terms."[24] So the scene is set for a subsequent finding that a limited, *sui generis* Native title, combined with an attenuated form of Native self-government, does not qualify as full dominion, let alone supreme dominion: that is, sovereignty. Yet, as the Royal Commission on Aboriginal Peoples has concluded, the issues of Aboriginal title and Aboriginal self-government are largely inseparable.[25]

Significantly, the court did not pronounce on Native dominion before the Royal Proclamation in *Delgamuukw.* The judgment speaks of pre-existing societies and (Native) systems of law but does not address Native dominion specifically, so it is quietly assumed not to have existed. Aboriginal title is said to derive from prior occupation, not from ownership. The court therefore subscribes, implicitly, to a *dominium nullius* doctrine. There is no question of a right of conquest in Canada, where the Native population at large was not subdued through war and where conquest signifies the victory of one European colonial power (England) over another (France). After the end of the Seven Years War in 1763, the dominion of the British crown was arbitrarily extended beyond the conquered French colony and the lands already under British control to include lands not within British jurisdiction, especially those north and west of the rivers that drain into the Atlantic. Why should historical Native dominion be any less real than the original paper claim of the colonizing power? There was no question of exercising sovereignty over many of these areas for centuries.

As for Alonso's insistence on a fair price for land purchased from the Natives, in British Columbia, for example, individual colonists acquired land and title through a grant of the crown, which cannot be challenged in court proceedings. In other parts of Canada, the courts, in reconsidering historical treaties, *do* examine the motives and willingness of Natives in voluntarily entering into treaties with the crown as well as monetary issues. Canadian courts, however, do not allow Natives to sue for restitution, only for damages.[26] Restitution requires an admission that the confiscation of Native lands was illegal to begin with.

One can only conclude that the Supreme Court failed in its central task, stated in *Van der Peet*: namely, "the reconciliation of the pre-existence of Aboriginal societies with the sovereignty of the Crown,"[27] hampered as it was by the need to justify the Royal Proclamation and the *status quo* that evolved from it. "Let us face it, we are all here to stay," writes the chief justice at the end of the judgment.[28] This phrase betrays the discomfort over the predicament of the colonial past as the basis for today's judgments. In fact, the real problem is no longer the justification of historical colonial rule but the presumption that the assertion of sovereignty by the British crown in 1763 precludes full and just Native dominion and, ultimately, Native sovereignty in Canada today. Of course, Alonso's vision based on justice, equality, and coexistence in postconquest Mexico did not come to pass, but this does not mean that he was wrong. Most striking is that his remarkably progressive vision, 450 years later, still beckons as eminently fair and logical. What a natural law perspective can bring to the present predicament in Canada is a finding whereby Native dominion before the Royal Proclamation is positively affirmed. On that basis, the obvious fact can be admitted that Native dominion was illegitimately reduced during the colonial regime. Restitution could then take the form of recognition of First Nations' dominion and sovereignty.

Notes

1 The works of Alonso de la Vera Cruz have been admirably translated, edited, analyzed, and summarized by E.J. Burrus in *The Writings of Alonso de la Vera Cruz: The Original Texts with English Translation*, 5 vols. (Rome: Sources and Studies for the History of the Americas, Jesuit Historical Institute, 1968-76). I will be citing extensively from volume 2, entitled *Defense of the Indians: Their Rights, Part I: Latin Text and English Translation* (Rome: Sources and Studies for the History of the Americas, Jesuit Historical Institute, 1968), containing the treatise *De dominio infidelium et justo bello* by Alonso, cited hereafter as *De dominio*, the latter followed by paragraph numbers referring to the bilingual edition by Burrus. See also Almandoz Garmendia, *Fray Alonso de Veracruz O.E.S.A. y la encomienda indiana en la historia eclesiástica novohispana, 1522-1556*. A collection of Spanish-language articles entitled *Homenaje a Fray Alonso de la Veracruz en el IV Centenario de su Muerte (1584-1984)*, including "Fray Alonso de la Veracruz, iniciador del derecho agrario en México," by Silvio Zavala, can be accessed at http://www.bibliojuridica.org/.

  For a biography, see Ennis, *Fray Alonso de la Vera Cruz O.S.A. (1507-1584)*. For the legal, philosophical, and ideological background, see, for example, Hanke, *All Mankind Is One*; Hanke, *The Spanish Struggle for Justice in the Conquest of America*; and Pagden, *Lords of All the World*. For North America, see especially MacMillan, *Sovereignty and Possession in the English New World*, and the review with additional bibliography by Christopher Tomlins at http://www.history.ac.uk/.

2 See especially Alonso, *De dominio*, para. 758: "As we are wont to say, many things that are prohibited nevertheless have the status of facts." See also paras. 813, 894, 930. The Spanish king, therefore, is in *de facto* possession of the New World, but this does not entail rightful ownership or the right to dispose of Native lands.

3 See Alonso, *De dominio*, paras. 108, 6, 120-22, cf. 921-27.

4 Ibid., paras. 253, 255-56, cf. 208, 274.

5 Ibid., paras. 459-60, 114-15.

6 Ibid., paras. 149-50, 461, 471, 681, 848, 170.

7 Ibid., para. 294.

8 Ibid., paras. 336-41.

9 Ibid., paras. 148, 112.

10 Ibid., paras. 26-27, Introduction, para. 91*.

11 Ibid., paras. 758, 813.

12 Alonso's questioning of the security of Spanish titles to property in Mexico, as well as his criticism of the feudal tributes exacted from, and the Church tithes imposed on, the Natives, must have raised both secular and ecclesiastical anxieties with regard to property and income in post-conquest Mexico. See also his subsequent treatise, *De decimis* (1554-55), "On the Tithes," which he was expressly forbidden from publishing.

13 Alonso, *De dominio*, paras. 118, 140, 132, 459-61.

14 Ibid., paras. 124, 106-55, 318, 447-48.

15 See Pagden, "Dispossessing the Barbarian," 79-98. Cf. "Restitution," in *Dictionnaire de théologie catholique*, vol. 13 (Paris: Letouzey et Ané, 1937), cols. 2466-2501, and especially col. 2472: "*res clamat domino*" (the rightful owner remains entitled to his property no matter who has obtained possession of it).

16 Alonso, *De dominio*, paras. 178-82, 121-22, 290, 115-17, 171, 189-209, 39.

17 For this case and the original documents, see Hughes, *History of the Society of Jesus, Volume I (1605-1838), Part I*, 448, 454, 477, 483, 489, and especially 490 for the Latin quotation from Father Knott's letter to Lord Baltimore and 491n23 for its source; also see Appendix B for Dr. Silvius (Francis DeBois) on the Maryland question of Mattapany, especially 570 for the Latin quotation, 571, 573, 575. I am indebted for these and the following early American references to Rhonda Barlow.

18 To Alonso, dominion is independent of faith and derives from natural and international law; see *De dominio*, Introduction, paras. 128-30*.

19 See Gaustad, *Liberty of Conscience*, 32-33; see also Glover, "Wunnaumwayean."

20 Hughes, *History of the Society of Jesus*, 574, 573-76.

21 As quoted by Emond, "L'affaire *Delgamuukw*, 849-80 at 869n126.

22 *Delgamuukw v. British Columbia,* [1997] 3 S.C.R. 1010-1141. I have used the English text accessible at http://www.droit.umontreal.ca/ [cited hereafter as *Delgamuukw*].
23 As quoted in Schmaltz, *The Ojibwa of Southern Ontario,* 83.
24 *Delgamuukw,* para. 170.
25 See Canada, *Restructuring the Relationship,* vol. 1, 130. In the challenge to the self-government provision of the Nisga'a Treaty (*Campbell v. British Columbia,* [2000] 4 C.N.L.R. 1 (B.C.S.C.), Justice Williamson actually connected Native title with self-government for the first time.
26 Emond, "L'affaire *Delgamuukw,*" 870-71.
27 *Delgamuukw,* paras. 142, 186.
28 Ibid., para. 186.

5
Beyond Aboriginal Title in Yukon: First Nations Land Registries
Brian Ballantyne

The debate about Aboriginal title appears to consist of two main themes. The first theme is that various judgments define the scope and tests for Aboriginal title. These judgments are critical because, without them, there would be little legal, political, or cultural (at least by the non-Aboriginal community) acceptance of that title: "You have to get the court to make the order, or it just doesn't happen."[1] This theme is widening and deepening. In late 2007, the Supreme Court of British Columbia affirmed the test for Aboriginal title in the course of offering a comprehensive opinion that Tsilhqot'in Aboriginal title did exist inside and outside the claim area in central British Columbia. However, the court was not able to make a declaration of Tsilhqot'in Aboriginal title because the parcels of land being claimed were not well defined.[2]

The second theme in the debate is contributed by lawyers, historians, anthropologists, and others who critique the judgments, legislation, policies, and government pronouncements that affect Aboriginal title. Their contributions were superbly represented at the Conference on Native Title, hosted by the Research Unit for Socio-Legal Studies at the University of Calgary, in September 2003. We heard much about the source, content, and test of Aboriginal title, about legal doctrines and principles in the context of agreements, treaties, legislation, and litigation, and about historical (and, in some cases, contemporary) injustices.[3]

Much rarer in the debate is discussion about what happens after Aboriginal title is affirmed and recognized. As one conference speaker noted, it is imperative that Aboriginal rights be made effective to have any meaning for Aboriginal peoples, for "fine words butter no parsnips."[4] What follows describes efforts to move beyond such fine words (from both the courts and the commentators) on the basis of my observations in Yukon that land claims agreements are a necessary, but not a sufficient, condition to ensure that Aboriginal title has some meaning for Yukon First Nations. After negotiated agreements confirm (among other things) Aboriginal title, there must be capacity building among local communities and the creation of mechanisms, such as rudimentary systems of registering rights in land, that allow First Nations to benefit from such title.

Historical Setting

Aboriginal peoples have lived and prospered in Yukon for thousands of years, and like Aboriginal peoples everywhere they "feel an attachment to their land, a sense of belonging to a part of the earth ... Their land is not a commodity but the heritage of the community, the dwelling place of generations."[5] The land and water were used for travelling over and living on. Even in the absence of surveys, subdivisions, and transfers of land, "they did recognize ownership of plots used for village sites, fishing places, berry and root patches and similar purposes."[6]

The first permanent non-Aboriginal settlement was probably Fort Selkirk, a Hudson's Bay Company trading post at the confluence of the Pelly and Yukon Rivers. Between 1848 and 1852, the fort was the nexus for the hunting and trading economy that involved the Aboriginal peoples of much of Yukon.[7] Since then, Aboriginal peoples' links with the land have been disturbed, but not broken, by various gold and silver rushes, the extraction of other minerals and petroleum, highway and pipeline construction, tourism, the creation of national parks, and the growth of towns. However, this development ethic arose in the absence of any treaties that ceded land or affected the inherent right of self-government enjoyed by the fourteen First Nations, who now represent some 7,000 Aboriginal citizens.

Therefore, negotiations began in the 1970s between the federal government, the territorial government, and the Council of Yukon Indians, resulting in an *Umbrella Final Agreement* (*UFA*) signed on 29 May 1993. The *UFA* set out, among other things, that title to some 16,000 square miles (41,440 square kilometres) of land would vest individually in the fourteen First Nations.

Final Agreements

The *UFA* sets out in section 5.5.1 that "each Yukon First Nation, as owner of Settlement Land, may ... establish a system to record interests in its Settlement Land." Neither the *UFA* nor any of the individual agreements contains anything that explicitly sets out specifications for such an Aboriginal registry. The agreements do give some indirect indications of what a system of recording interests in settlement land needs to take into account.

Settlement land is of three kinds: "Category A," with Aboriginal title to the surface plus fee simple title to minerals; "category B," with Aboriginal title to the surface but without mineral rights; and "fee simple," without mineral rights. Thus, Aboriginal title is retained for category A and category B settlement land but relinquished otherwise, including for fee simple settlement land.

Registration in the Yukon Land Titles Office (LTO) of a less than entire interest in a parcel of settlement land results in that interest taking precedence over Aboriginal rights to that parcel. Registration of an entire interest (i.e., fee simple) in the LTO results in the permanent relinquishment of Aboriginal title and the parcel ceasing to be settlement land. On the one hand, section 5.2.1 sets out that "nothing in settlement agreements shall be construed as affecting any Aboriginal claim, right, title, or interest in and to Settlement Land, except that they are inconsistent with the Settlement Agreements."

On the other hand, section 5.10.1 sets out that

> Each Yukon First Nation and all persons eligible to be Yukon Indian people it represents, shall be deemed to have ceded, released and surrendered to Her Majesty the Queen in Right of Canada all their Aboriginal claims, rights, titles and interests, in and to the Parcels described hereunder and waters therein upon the happening of ... the registration on the Land Titles Office of the fee simple interest in that Parcel of Settlement Land.

Principles of a Land Registry System

The two general types of registry systems – deeds and titles – must effectively identify who owns what rights in a particular parcel; must have the flexibility to support the local land tenure system; must contain a mechanism for resolving disputes; and must support the identification of overriding interests. Any system should be able to screen for ineligible interests to prohibit non-group members from acquiring interests in Aboriginal land. Moreover, any system must be simple to use; be inexpensive to operate provided that integrity of the system is maintained; be easily accessed; and be capable of integration with a land information system.[8]

Land registries operate according to four significant principles. First, a deeds system differs from a titles system in that the former is merely designed to register a pre-existing title, whereas registration in a titles system actually confers title to the land. Second, land titles legislation can amend the principle of *Nemo dat quod non habet*: "No man may give that which he does not have." If the register is conclusive of title, then the first to register (in the absence of fraud by the applicant) gets the best title. Third, registration often constitutes notice to the world. And fourth, registry systems "may limit the classes of interests which are registerable."[9]

Most jurisdictions have established sophisticated registry systems that account for those rights in land that are granted by the crown (usually in

fee simple). Land titles systems enhance security of title, facilitate conveyance, reduce transaction costs, and share the following characteristics: (1) a
wide range of interests can be registered; (2) the effects of registration (and
of non-registration) are set out; (3) the *bona fide* purchaser for value is accorded the most protection (if wrongfully deprived of the interest, then
compensation can be paid); and (4) there are strict limitations on the discretionary power of the registrar.[10]

In many jurisdictions, there is not much of a registry system for interests
in crown land: that is, for those rights in land that are not granted in fee
simple. This is certainly true in Yukon, where systems for territorial and
federal crown land are rather unsophisticated. Systems that register interests
in crown land (not fee simple land) allow only a narrow range of instruments
and interests to be registered. They tend to be resource specific (exemplified
by registries that deal exclusively with mineral rights), and they make the
effects of registration ambiguous and give much discretion to the registrar.

Two fundamental questions must be answered in designing any land
registry for the First Nations of Yukon. First, what is the purpose of a First
Nations registry? Is it to allow for the convenience and protection of land
titles systems that affect security of title and conveyance and transaction
costs? Or is it to allow a First Nation merely to keep an accurate inventory
of its category A and B lands and its fee simple settlement lands? Second,
should such a system be characterized by registration of title (more correctly,
title by registration) or registration of deeds and encumbrances?

These are thorny questions, precisely because the First Nations are both
legislators and proprietors of their settlement lands and thus have an interest
in both assisting their citizens and monitoring their holdings. Thus, the
systems must be flexible enough to deal with unknown tenure structures
that will be utilized by the First Nations, and they must be designed by or
in partnership with First Nations to avoid the pitfall of a top-down impos-
ition of inappropriate systems.[11]

Consultation with First Nations
Between February 2002 and March 2004, I visited nine First Nations in Yukon
– the eight who had entered into final agreements, and one (Kwanlin Dun
First Nation) whose final agreement appeared to be imminent.[12] I spoke twice
with the grand chief of the Council of Yukon First Nations.

Such wide consultation was both a means to an end and an end in itself.
In the first case, site visits and interviews were essential to gather all existing
constitutions, land rights legislation, and instruments used by the First Nations to allocate rights in land and to talk with land administrators about
their needs and concerns. This process allowed an inventory of community
needs, legal tools, and institutional issues to be compiled. Just as important,

the consultation reflected the reality that there is a constitutionally based duty of the crown to consult for any project that affects the rights of First Nations.[13] To the extent that this study was funded by the crown, and to the extent that the focus was on registering First Nations' interests in lands, we had a duty to consult. Finally, the very act of consultation served to educate many of the respondents and thus enhanced the institutional capacity (perhaps only incrementally) of individual First Nations. What follows are the findings from the interviews, classified into five themes.

The first theme is that the need for a land registry was somewhat recognized. Many of the First Nations saw such a need in light of the gradual loss of knowledge of who had what rights for what period of time in which parcel. There is an increasing level of uncertainty (if not ignorance) about why specific sites were chosen by individual First Nations because, in many cases, elders have passed on and there is little oral or written evidence of the selection rationale. Likewise, without a reliable recording system, the potential exists for disputes about which individual or family has rights in parcels, such as the long-term right of exclusive occupation. Loss of such knowledge is exacerbated through changes in parcel size (through erosion or accretion), loss of physical evidence (through forest fires), loss of oral evidence (through the deaths of occupants), problems of intestacy or multiple heirs, and so on.

The second theme is that there was unanimous agreement that the Land Titles Office[14] of Yukon would not be used by the First Nations to register category A or B lands because of the consequent loss of Aboriginal title owing to the *UFA*. Another factor influencing the response was the desire to have an Aboriginal registry, distinct from the LTO located in Whitehorse, because the former need only be akin to a registry of deeds system and need not require surveys to current *Canada Lands Surveys Act* standards.[15]

The third theme is that the merits of a central registry were somewhat acknowledged. Many of the First Nations recognized the merits of a central land registry that served their recording needs. The four advantages of such a registry were either volunteered by some First Nations respondents or acknowledged by others.

First, liability assumed by any such system would be spread across all the participating First Nations rather than borne by only one. Although such risk would likely not extend to offering an assurance fund, as land titles systems do, it would be imprudent to discount operational negligence by the land registry, for "the dividing line between policy and operation is difficult to fix."[16] Of course, if the land registry were to incorporate a dispute resolution mechanism (that dealt, e.g., with encroachments), then it would expose itself to rather more liability.

Second, a central registry would allow for easier access to hard copy records for title searches and for registering instruments by third parties, such as lending institutions and non-Aboriginal users of land. For example, the Bank of Montreal (Whitehorse branch) was keen to see a central registry for ease of access. Centralization would also allow for more efficient co-ordination with other Yukon registries – such as the LTO and those dealing with crown lands.

Third, a central registry would streamline training and retention of staff as only two to four staff would be required to administer a registry for the lands of fourteen First Nations. If one of the staff quit or was unable to work, then the adverse effect on a central registry's capacity would not be critical. However, with fourteen registries – one for each First Nation – the loss of staff would have a significant effect.

Fourth, a single registry could fall within the mandate of the Self Government Secretariat of the Council of Yukon First Nations (CYFN). The CYFN recognized that the integrity of a registry system is critical in terms of enhancing accessibility, deterring frivolous inquiries, and avoiding duplication and inefficiency. If one of the primary goals of the land claims process is to improve the delivery of programs and services, then the CYFN's involvement in a land registry can help to meet that goal; it can also use its political expertise to persuade lending institutions of the registry's utility.

However, this is not to say that the First Nations, without prompting, were overwhelmingly in favour of a central land registry. Indeed, the responses from the eight First Nations and the CYFN fell into four groups. One set of respondents had not considered a registry with vigour. A second set advocated an in-house registry serving only the needs of one First Nation. A third set – the three Northern Tutchone First Nations – suggested that one registry might serve only their needs. However, the fourth and largest contingent of respondents agreed that one registry – with or without the involvement of the CYFN – serving the needs of all First Nations was the most viable option. This group included First Nations as spatially diverse as Champagne and Aishihik, Teslin Tlingit and Vuntut Gwitchin.

The fourth theme is that the First Nations held distinct positions on the occurrence and effect of allocation of parcels. Some respondents indicated that they were unaware that any parcels had been formally allocated to either individuals or families, although there was general agreement that certain sites had been chosen in the land selection process because they were significant to specific families (e.g., as hunting or trapping sites). Neither the First Nations nor other families would disturb a family's peaceful enjoyment of such a site, although no formal authorization existed to occupy the site.

Other respondents indicated that the chief or the chief and council had granted permission to families to use specific or community sites. Sometimes the permission was informal and might have been recorded in a black book or simply in the chief's memory. At other times, the permission took the form of a resolution passed by the chief and council. In both cases, the nature of the rights in land was not defined.

Finally, some First Nations such as Teslin Tlingit, Vuntut Gwitchin, and Champagne and Aishihik had sophisticated legislation dealing with the allocation and recording of rights in land. In these systems, citizens received certificates of allocation for residential and recreational purposes, and long-term leases were granted to non-citizens and for commercial and industrial purposes. Those First Nations that had such sophisticated legislation also had provisions for a land registry in which the rights granted could be recorded.

Only Teslin Tlingit appeared to have formally allocated rights in land through well-defined instruments. Four leases had been issued for residential purposes and were registered in an abstract book. One of the leases was accompanied by a descriptive sketch (a metes and bounds description) prepared by a Canada Lands Surveyor. The abstract book had been perused by two banks, both of which had been approached by the lessees for mortgage financing using the parcels as security. The nascent registry in Teslin was referred to frequently by other First Nations as the one to emulate, although there was little knowledge of how it operated.

The fifth theme is that there was a preference for a parcel-based registry because the land selection process for most respondents had involved parcels of land. The most common reason proposed for having a land registry was to keep track of legal interests in land (i.e., to identify the rights holder, location, and duration) and to allow the land to be used as security in mortgage financing. There was also a consensus that any registry should be multi-purpose to monitor land uses outside settlement lands but within the traditional territories of each First Nation and to accommodate property taxation schemes proposed by the First Nations. This is not to suggest that taxation is inevitable for any First Nation but to note that many First Nations recognized the merits of a land registry if taxation schemes were to be introduced.

Consultation with Government

I also interviewed a series of government administrators in eight departments, all of which dealt with land in Yukon and five of which were responsible for independent land registries (one for fee simple land, two for territorial crown land, one for federal crown land, and one for subsurface interests). The land titles system pursuant to the *Land Titles Act* is the largest system for registering rights in land in Yukon. It contains the originals of some 20,000 certificates of title and approximately 6,000 plans. In 2001 alone, some 1,200 new titles were raised, and 9,000 documents were registered.

The Yukon government also administers at least two other public (although admittedly less formal) land registries for over 200 parcels of territorial crown land administered by the Yukon Lands and Property Assessment Branch. Few of the parcels are defined by survey; most leases are described by a sketch provided by the applicant. All of the dispositions create legal interests in crown land that are less than fee simple interests. Some of the leases and licences for occupation have mortgages recorded against them. Similarly, the Yukon Aviation and Marine Branch administers about sixty leases of land around airports, some of which through subleases have served as security for mortgage purposes. In both cases, the registry consists of a series of file folders.

The Northern Affairs Program of Indian and Northern Affairs Canada (INAC) administers some 2,500 active files, each of which pertains to a parcel of federal crown land. Most of the parcels are leased for terms of between five and sixty years, and some of the leases have mortgages deposited against them as subleases. Finally, the Mining Recorder has about 70,000 active claims and leases recorded in one of the four Yukon Mining District Offices. They serve as interests in land against which lending institutions often advance financing.

All of this suggests that non-Aboriginal interests in land are now found in many land registries across Yukon. Some systems serve to create a title to land through registration; others simply record various instruments that convey rights in land and thus provide systems of priority and notice. This diversity of systems does not deter the use or economic development of land, nor does it seem to deter the lending institutions. Indeed, these systems serve as excellent examples to First Nations of the merits of a registry system for their own lands.

Review of First Nations Legislation

Because some of the First Nations legislation was in draft form, and due to the confidential nature of some land registration policies and accords, the following principles have been assembled without reference to specific First Nations.[17]

First Nations constitutions affirm the centrality of land, stressing the importance of both traditional land use and economic development. Thus, the first objective of one constitution was "to ensure the land, environment and traditional territory of the ... people are maintained, protected and respected." This objective was to be met by ensuring that "there shall be no sale of settlement lands" and that any grant of any proprietary right in settlement land shall require both fourteen days notice and the approval of all council officers. A second constitution incorporated twelve objectives, four of which dealt specifically with land, including controlling "the disposition of rights and interests in and to the traditional lands and resources" of the First Nation. It also prohibited the sale of settlement lands, gave first preference for leasing land to its members, and required that leases, permits, and licences be approved by the Tribal or Elders Council.

These themes continued in the land policies reviewed. One asserted that "settlement lands will be allocated according to the best or most suitable use that will generate the greatest benefits" for all citizens. A second asked the assembly for guidance on "how we are going to share the use of this land amongst ourselves," recognizing that there was a need "to establish and maintain a registry of interests in, and rights to, Settlement Land."

The review included six statutes that dealt with settlement lands. One First Nation had a Register of Land and Resources whose purpose was to hold duplicate originals of certificates of allocation, leases, licences of occupation, copies of other permits or licences, and associated instruments. The statute that created the register provided for the issuance by the General Council of a certificate of allocation that gave the holder the "right to exclusive occupation and use of the allocated settlement land." However, the regulations under the statute provide that "no instrument shall be considered to create an interest, either at law or in equity, in a parcel of Settlement Land unless and until the instrument is filed in the register as set out in the regulation." Thus, the certificate of allocation created the interest but only after being filed in the register.

The other lands acts echoed this theme. One allowed that "the Council shall establish a registry of grants and authorizations ... of any encumbrance, covenant, caveat, notice, interest or right established under law which may affect Settlement land directly." Protection of the registry was provided from claims of loss: "No action may be brought by any person ... for loss or damage caused by or arising from the reliance by any persons on the records of the registry." The limited responsibility of the register was implicit in all statutes. Another First Nation warned explicitly that "the Register of Settlement Land is a record of information only and does not create, deprive, increase or diminish any right it records." Neither the First Nation nor the registrar "shall be liable for information contained in the Register of settlement land which is not accurate." The final First Nation was less restrictive, providing that "a person shall be entitled to rely upon the Register as a conclusive record."

Synthesis of Findings

Examining registry principles, interviewing First Nations and others, reviewing legislation, and assessing Aboriginal registries suggest that a flexible land registry system that allows for a phased approach to interests and parcels should be adopted in Yukon. First, although a land registry system is allowed for in the *Umbrella Final Agreement* and despite six First Nations making specific provision for a registry in their legislation, there was not widespread acceptance of the need for – nor understanding of the characteristics of – a registry.

Second, the merits of a centralized registry were not accepted; indeed, there was wide divergence on which form a registry should take and where it should be located. Thus, a viable prototype would examine the relative advantages of either one central registry (as exemplified by the existing Land Titles Office) or a limited series of four or five regional registries, each serving a group of First Nations. The group could be defined by cultural affiliations (as suggested by the Northern Tutchone peoples), by geographic proximity, or by level of sophistication in land use (as exemplified by the Teslin Tlingit and the Champagne and Aishihik First Nations).

Third, building capacity in registering interest in Aboriginal land should follow the lead of those First Nations that have developed good relationships with the lending institutions by negotiating lease and non-disturbance agreements. Again, the Teslin Tlingit and the Champagne and Aishihik First Nations serve as models in this respect. Much effort can be saved by heeding lessons already learned in system development and implementation.

Fourth, the prototype should be a deeds system because the systems that are extant, proposed, or merely referred to all anticipate that title to the land will not be a function of registration. Like the registries used to administer the disposition of resource rights on crown lands, each First Nation will grant rights in land through its council or assembly (or a delegate) and will then merely record the grants (e.g., a lease or a certificate of allocation) in a registry. That is, although the registries may require that instruments be registered, the registries themselves do not confer title to land, guarantee the rights, or offer compensation through an insurance mechanism. The rights in land are determined through a good root of title.

Fifth, there was much diversity among First Nations in terms of how land rights are allocated. Only one had a functioning registry (and it had recorded rights in only four parcels), and the Whitehorse banks were still developing their own lending and security policies. Thus, the prototype registry must recognize the need for a phased approach to rights, where provisional allotments might mature to full allotments. This phased approach applies to a spectrum of land descriptions (from initially relying on the surveys that are part of the land claims process to subsequently expecting that all new parcels be surveyed) and for rights evolving from merely being recorded to actually being registered. Finally, such a phased approach means that linkages with existing Yukon registries can be made over time.

Principles of a Land Registry for Yukon First Nations

Principle 1: Interests and Preferences

The main function of a register is to disclose information about the ownership of and interests in First Nations land. Interest has two meanings: it refers both to legal interests and to the preferences (or informal interests) that citizens have shown in specific parcels of land. There is sufficient disclosure of a legal interest if the document that creates the interest is recorded. For instance, a certificate of allocation will not be granted to a First Nations citizen by the registry or the registrar. It will, however, be recorded in the registry so as to disclose to the world that citizen X has a legal interest in parcel Y. It is for any third-party investigating title to parcel Y to decide what interest, if any, the recorded document (certificate of allocation) has conferred.

However, if a legal interest is recorded simply by recording a summary of the transaction on which it is based, the summary may be insufficient to disclose the nature of the interest. Such summaries should thus be limited to recording a First Nations citizen's preferences in specific sites and not to recording legal interests.

For example, over the nine-year period from March 1994 to March 2003, the parcel known as Specific Land Selection C-3 B had recorded against it eighteen preferences by First Nations citizens. The citizens received no certificates of allocation, leases, or permits, and thus no documents could be registered that conveyed title. Nevertheless, the following two summaries set out which families have which preferences (informal, non-legal interests) in which land and for which purpose:

1 First Nation citizen A would like to make a land selection within C-3 for residential purposes, looking at 5 ha;
2 First Nation citizen B: 150m x 200m, just town side of dump.

The recording of such summaries is an invaluable function of the registry. Many sites have particular emotional, spiritual, and economic importance to a citizen or a family; an important purpose of the registry is to enable the protection of such ties to the land. If the ties are not recorded, then as the older generation passes on it becomes increasingly difficult to determine which family used which parcels, to justify those family/land links to the First Nations government, and to resolve disputes between families competing for the same parcel of land.

Principle 2: Parcel Based

The registry should be parcel based, meaning that legal interests (documents) and emotional preferences (summaries) should relate to individual parcels of land as defined in the *Final Agreement* for each First Nation or to subsequent plans of subdivision. Furthermore, plans of subdivision must be recorded in the registry so that the original copies are filed. Training of registry staff in examining documents and plans is critical, as is educating users of the registry (e.g., citizens and third parties) about its structure, function, and processes.

Principle 3: Well-Crafted Regulations

Regulations that address all aspects of subdivision and building permits would serve two purposes. First, they would occupy the field, meaning that Yukon government standards and requirements need not be followed. Second, the public consultation process that accompanies the adoption of such regulations would raise awareness and expertise among citizens, so as to encourage greater responsibility for parcels and houses.

Most significantly, each First Nation must identify the types of rights that it wishes to grant in its land. This analysis does not directly address that issue or those rights because a land registry is used only to record those interests and not to create them. The legal interests are created by the First Nation, either by the chief and council or through delegation to a lands committee or lands manager.

Principle 4: Mortgages

A land registry for use by Yukon First Nations will be driven by two forces: the desire by citizens to use their rights in land as collateral against borrowing money in the form of a mortgage, and the requirement by lending institutions that leases to parcels of land be assumed in the event of foreclosure. The registry is not a party to the agreements. However, the reason for the registry is driven by the agreements; the former records the latter and assures the banks that every other legal interest is also recorded against that parcel.

This does not mean that the land is lost to the First Nation. Lending institutions merely acquire the lease to the parcel of land (usually having a term of thirty years) in the event that the First Nation lessee is unable to continue to repay a mortgage. This ability to foreclose on a lease is aided by a non-disturbance agreement between the First Nation (the grantor), the mortgagor (the lessee), and the lending institution (usually a bank). Certainly, such foreclosures are rare because banks ensure that the mortgagor is a good credit risk. The bank is also not keen to assume the lease; it prefers that the mortgage is repaid.

Moreover, the absence of a First Nation's own land registry does not necessarily preclude land from being used as collateral. The Champagne Aishihik and Nacho Nyak Dun First Nations had parcels of land against which mortgages have been granted – but only for those parcels of fee simple land now registered in the LTO.[18]

Conclusion

In the context of Yukon First Nations that wish to move beyond simply the recognition of Aboriginal title, a land registry is as much about process as it is about product. It is a culmination of a series of things – agreements, legislation, policies, forms, books, filing cabinets, and computers – and processes, such as those that build capacity and inform citizens. Both the things and the processes allow the registry to meet local requirements. However, the land registry is based on a First Nation adopting coherent land management and housing policies that constitute a framework for creating and allocating rights in land. That is, Aboriginal title takes the First Nation only part of the way. The step beyond Aboriginal title is the allocation of rights by the First Nation to its individuals and families. Without the allocation of rights in land, there is no need for a registry to record such rights; registration is unnecessary.

Acknowledgment

This chapter is based on research and analysis undertaken before mid-2004. I acknowledge that the Yukon First Nations land registries, the implementation of final agreements in Yukon, and the duty to consult have all evolved since then. This chapter does not necessarily reflect the views of my current employer – SGB, NRCan.

Notes

1 Peter Hutchins, "A Practitioner's Guide to Aboriginal Litigation since *Calder*," keynote address to the conference on Native Title in Canada, Australia, and the United States, University of Calgary, 18 September 2003.
2 *Tsilhqot'in Nation v. British Columbia*, [2007] B.C.S.C. 1700.
3 There is also much ideology in the literature on Aboriginal title. See, for example, Strack, "Customary Title," 44-51.
4 Scott, *The Legend of Montrose*, 307.
5 Berger, *A Long and Terrible Shadow*, xi.
6 Duff, *Indian History of British Columbia*, cited in ibid., 149.
7 Johnson and Legros, *Journal of Occurrences at the Forks of the Lewes and Pelly Rivers*.
8 Ballantyne and Dobbin, *Options for Land Registration*.
9 Bankes, "The Registration and Transfer of Interests in Crown Lands," 89-107 at 93.
10 Ibid., 99.
11 Ballantyne and Dobbin, *Capstone Study*, 18.
12 Final agreements have now been reached with eleven First Nations.
13 Ross, "The Dene Tha' Consultation Pilot Project," 1-4.
14 *Yukon Land Titles Act*, S.Y. 1991, c. 11.
15 *Canada Lands Surveys Act*, R.S.A. 1985, c. L-6.
16 *Just v. British Columbia*, [1989] 2 S.C.R. 1228.
17 Legislation reviewed:

   • Champagne and Aishihik First Nations Constitution, 2000;
   • Vuntut Gwitchin First Nation Constitution;
   • Champagne and Aishihik First Nations Lands Policy, Draft 5;
   • Selkirk First Nation Land and Resource Policy, 2.11.98;
   • Champagne and Aishihik First Nations Lands Act, 14 June 2001;
   • Little Salmon/Carmacks First Nation Settlement Land Act, Draft 6, 10 August 1999;
   • First Nation of Nacho Nyak Dun Land and Resources Act;

- Teslin Tlingit Settlement Land Act, 20 November 1998;
- Teslin Tlingit Settlement Land Use Regulations, 2000;
- Tr'ondek Hwech'in Land and Resources Act;
- Vuntut Gwitchin Land and Resources Act, Draft 6, 17 March 2000.

18 Greg Fekete, Association of Canada Lands Surveyors' CPD Seminar, Whitehorse, June 2004.

Part 2:
Native Land, Litigation, and Indigenous Rights

6
The "Race" for Recognition: Toward a Policy of Recognition of Aboriginal Peoples in Canada

Paul L.A.H. Chartrand

At the time when the British came into contact with the Aboriginal peoples in its former colonies, from several of which Canada was formed, the Aboriginal peoples were cognizable, as were the newcomers to the locals. It was easy for the British to discern that the Aboriginal peoples were socially, politically, and culturally distinct peoples. There was a clear cognizance on each side of the distinct existence of the other. Today circumstances have changed, requiring a re-cognition.

The power balance between the two sides had shifted so much that in 1969 a Canadian prime minister could declare that the historical treaties that recognized the Indians' legal capacity to enter into treaty relations as distinct social and political peoples could be ignored. The colonial policy of dismantling the historical nations resulted in the disintegration of traditional social and political institutions. Communities were realigned to conform to the unilateral legislative dictates of the *Indian Act,* which placed those whom the government chose to define as Indians on reserved lands and organized them as "bands" for purposes of federal administration of Indian affairs. Over the years of such administration, many individuals were removed from the ranks of reserve Indians, and today their descendants comprise a significant portion of the Aboriginal ancestry population of Canada. In addition, there are large numbers of persons descended from Aboriginal people who were never recognized in treaties or by federal administrations. Others are descendants of the small historical Métis people, who were recognized in the *Manitoba Act* of 1870, which they negotiated, and in federal lands legislation applicable across western Canada. In the northern regions, the Inuit people, although expressly excluded from the *Indian Act,* are recognized in executive policies and recent legislated agreements.

In 1982, an amendment to the Constitution expressly recognized the existing Aboriginal and treaty rights of the Aboriginal peoples of Canada, including the Inuit, Métis, and Indian peoples. Treaty and Aboriginal rights are group rights and give rise to obligations of governments to respect them and make them effective. To abide by the law of the Constitution, which binds governments to these responsibilities, it is essential that the groups that have these rights, and the persons who belong to them and are consequently entitled to enjoy the benefits of such rights, be politically and legally recognizable among all Canadian citizens. There is a need for a rational policy of recognition that works. That policy must extend to all Aboriginal peoples recognized in the Constitution.

Recognition by the government is necessary because it is the government that controls the state apparatus that controls Aboriginal peoples. If power were balanced between the two sides, then they would be able to work out the nature of their government-to-government relationships. Where all the power is on one side and the government is obliged to respect the law, a constitutionally valid policy of recognition is a constitutional imperative.

This chapter aims to illustrate and assess the need for a rational legislated policy by identifying some of the major difficulties that have arisen in its absence. Among them are the tensions that occur when executive, legislative, and judicial branches of government have views that do not conform to one another.

The rhetoric of "race" as denoting the descendants of the historical nations encountered by the ancestors of contemporary Canadians has worked, and continues to work, a pernicious effect on the public dialogue. It is important to debunk some of this rhetoric and to make clear the distinction between citizenship rights and Aboriginal rights.

The courts have the task of identifying and defining Aboriginal people for a range of purposes reflected in various statutes and in various constitutional provisions. These enactments vary widely in their objectives and are intended to apply to different groups of people. There is an immense gulf between the philosophical foundations of some provisions, such as the equality provision of section 15 in the *Charter of Rights and Freedoms,* on the one hand, and section 35, the Aboriginal rights provision, on the other hand. It is apparent from the decisions of the Supreme Court of Canada (SCC) that the judges have not yet been required to give much attention to these differences. They have not only adopted the "race" language for some purposes, but they have also coined a variety of new terms to add to the list of words with unclear meanings that are directed at the identity of Aboriginal peoples. Since many, if not most, Aboriginal rights cases are put together only after an Aboriginal person has been charged with an offence,[1] the resulting jurisprudence fails to confront directly some basic questions about the identity of Aboriginal peoples themselves.[2]

This commentary suggests that a legislated policy of recognition for Aboriginal peoples that is built on the constitutional principles applicable to

Aboriginal rights is required in Canada. The following is a discussion of the need for such a legislated federal policy for the Aboriginal peoples whose rights have been recognized and affirmed in the *Constitution Act* of 1982.

Negotiated Legislated Recognition

Recognition is a legal concept imported during the colonial period from international law into domestic American and Canadian law to deal with the fact that North America was already populated by peoples organized into distinct political units referred to by the settlers as "tribes" and "nations."[3]

Recognition legislation is required to make effective, to respect, or to implement the Aboriginal and treaty rights that are vested in the Aboriginal peoples identified in the Canadian Constitution. Right now the only legislation behind current Aboriginal federal policy is the *Indian Act*,[4] which derives its authority from section 91(24) of the *Constitution Act* of 1867.[5] The *Indian Act* does not recognize the Inuit or the Métis, who are expressly included in section 35 of the *Constitution Act* of 1982. In addition to its other shortcomings, the *Indian Act* does not recognize all Indian people either, including only those entitled to be registered by the federal government.[6]

The 1982 constitutional recognition can only be made effective by a proactive legislated scheme of recognition that includes all Aboriginal peoples. Without such a policy, the courts will continue to identify Aboriginal peoples by defining their Aboriginal rights – essentially a default process. In effect, judges and government officials will continue to make decisions about the inclusion or exclusion of individuals and groups or communities. The justiciability of questions of group definition and the political legitimacy of judicial answers are both at issue here.

A legislated scheme of recognition that follows legitimate discussions and negotiations with the political representatives of the Aboriginal peoples is a better policy option than waiting for the results of judicial decisions on Aboriginal rights. Negotiated solutions between legitimate political representatives will yield a more democratic and effective scheme of recognition.[7]

Issues of Recognition

Aboriginal rights have their origins in history and in the relations between colonial governments and local Aboriginal people. Without a sense of history, it can be difficult for contemporary Canadians to perceive the basis for the recognition of a special category of Aboriginal rights that are not held by all Canadian citizens. Some opponents of Aboriginal rights as well as some judges have taken advantage of this lack of knowledge to use the rhetoric of "race-based privileges" as a red herring to divert constructive public dialogue.[8]

Identifying and recognizing the Aboriginal peoples of Canada is a very contentious political and legal issue. The same holds for any former British colony where the rights of the indigenous population are at issue. The situation is further complicated where the historical indigenous societies have been largely dismantled, over time, by the effects of policy and practice. This disintegration makes it difficult in some cases to recognize the descendants of the distinct societies encountered by earlier colonists.[9]

The general public has particular difficulty in understanding the rights of the Aboriginal peoples as group rights vested in communities. Western societies are more familiar with conceptions and institutions of individual rights that enable individual citizens to relate directly to a central state. Where Aboriginal individuals have intermarried and do not live in discrete communities, it can be difficult to appreciate the various relationships (e.g., social, political, economic, and legal) between individuals and their communities or nations and between individual rights and group rights. Also, where Aboriginal individuals are intermarried with people from other cultures, and scattered among the general population, the notion of community may have disappeared from the view of outsiders, even if the urban Aboriginal person still identifies with a home community and nation and is understood by that community and nation to be a member.

Treaties signed with the Indian nations were based on the concept of recognition and are an acknowledgment of their capacity to enter into legally binding relations as groups that were territorially, socially, and politically distinct from the new arrivals. However, once states acquired sufficient power, it was convenient for them to ignore the legal implications of political recognition. In recent times, policies of disintegration and assimilation have wrought changes in Aboriginal societies that make it even easier to ignore the distinct social and political character of these historical nations. Although it is almost ignored in Canada, the term and concept of "recognition" have been adopted and have currency in the United States, where jurisprudence has characterized Indian tribes as "domestic, dependent nations." The American policy of recognition applies to those tribes recognized as having a measure of sovereign authority to govern themselves and their members.

If recognition applies primarily to the idea of recognizing the capacity of a politically distinct entity to enter into legal relations with the state, then the concept is particularly useful in the context of Aboriginal self-government. Although supported by some judicial statements and the application of their internal logic, the constitutional status of the Aboriginal right of self-government remains an open question. Recognition will be particularly important in the context of new treaties that recognize the capacity of the Aboriginal treaty party to enter into legal relations with Canadian governments. The modern treaty policy includes the recognition of some powers of self-government in negotiated treaties, and it is in the context of a treaty policy that the concept is most useful.[10]

There is another advantage created by a policy of recognition that identifies the groups entitled to enter into treaty negotiations on the basis that they have Aboriginal rights. Basically, such recognition of groups with Aboriginal and treaty rights would make it possible to distinguish other persons of Aboriginal ancestry who may be entitled to the benefits of discretionary government programs or services but who do not necessarily belong to a rights-bearing community and are consequently not entitled to the enjoyment of Aboriginal or treaty rights. In Canada, the distinction requires that the groups designated by section 15 of the *Charter of Rights and Freedoms* not be conflated with groups designated by section 35 of the *Constitution Act* of 1982.

Since recognition as a member of a group with Aboriginal rights carries some benefits, official recognition has become a desirable goal for many individuals, as evidenced by the numerous claims in Canadian courts. This race for recognition is beating a path to the courthouse following the failure of political negotiations directed at constitutional reform in regard to Aboriginal peoples in the 1980s and early 1990s. Given that the decisions of the courts are bound to influence future governments' recognition policy and practice, it is important to identify the issues at stake.

Three Categories of Aboriginal People
It is appropriate to introduce the three categories of Aboriginal people mentioned in section 35 of the *Constitution Act* of 1982 and to explain their situation within the current recognition legislation in Canada. The introduction follows the historical policies and practices of the federal government with respect to the people in each category and considers some of the basic issues that might be better addressed in a new, legislated policy of recognition.

The Indian People
The group most widely known to the international audience is the Indian people. After the period of entering into treaties with eastern Indian nations, Canada continued the treaty process where it was convenient and necessary to establish Canadian territorial control. Treaties were entered into across most of Canadian territory but excluded almost all of British Columbia, the Yukon, and the northern portions of Quebec and the Northwest Territories. This historical treaty process continued well into the second half of the twentieth century as new groups signed adhesions to treaties that were negotiated into the 1920s. Recently, the treaty negotiation process was renewed following constitutional recognition and affirmation of Aboriginal and treaty rights in 1982.

Historically, treaties were entered into with groups that were politically recognized as comprising local indigenous inhabitants. In both treaty and non-treaty areas, the groups that were politically recognized as Indians were placed on lands set aside for their use as a matter of federal policy and practice.

Many Indian people came to be outside this federal system of Indian recognition. Sometimes this exclusion occurred as a result of simply missing some Indian groups. Other times it occurred because of the exclusive oper-ation of the membership code in the *Indian Act*. As with any membership code, the act included certain persons and excluded others. The code centred on the male head of the nuclear family. Those related to him, including a non-Indian spouse, were defined as Indian. In this way, many ethnic non-Indian women became recognized as statutory or "status" Indians. By the same token, a daughter of a male Indian head of family lost "status" or code membership by marrying a person who was not a status Indian. The act also contained various other "enfranchisement" provisions that had the effect, over the years, of removing many individuals from the membership of recognized Indian "bands."[11]

Assuming that identity as an Aboriginal person for legal purposes requires consent of the individual, those unregistered persons and their descendants, if they wish to identify as Indians, fall within the category of non-recognized Indians. Outsiders have known them generally as "non-status Indians."

In summary, with regard to the category "Indians" among all Aboriginal peoples of Canada, the Canadian policy of recognition in the *Indian Act* membership code extends recognition to those who are associated with the male heads of families descended from those members of Indian bands that were politically recognized in the era of signing treaties or setting aside re-serve lands. Other Indians are generally not recognized by executive or legislative acts.

A major exception was a 1985 amendment to the *Indian Act* that recognized over 100,000 individuals to be added to the federal registration system.[12] This amendment purported to comply with the sex equality provision in section 15 of the Charter.[13] The amended act now excludes all non-registered spouses, splitting up nuclear families and eventually excluding descendants of families of such mixed marriages. Such a code, which fails to grant status to spouses from outside the group, encourages endogamous marriages and therefore, in theory, works best with arranged marriages. Given the social unpopularity and probable unconstitutionality of arranged marriages in Canada, the amended act illustrates the point that any code intended to define an Aboriginal people must be carefully crafted to reflect the basic social, moral, and political values of the group and to conform to Canadian constitutional standards. The reflection of the group's preferred values can only be done legitimately by the group itself, not by a unilaterally imposed defining statute, as done by the *Indian Act*.[14]

The Inuit People

Inuit people form the second group of Aboriginal peoples expressly mentioned in section 35. They are distinct from the Indian people and inhabit their traditional territories in the northern regions of Canada. Although excluded from the *Indian Act*, the Inuit have been recognized by executive and legislative policies and actions. Government policies and programs have been established in respect to them as northern residents in the federal Northwest Territories and Nunavut and as provincial residents in the northern portions of Quebec by means of legislation. There is no general federal legislation concerning Inuit people, as there is for Indian people, but the federal department Indian and Northern Affairs Canada includes Inuit matters within its mandate.

The Métis People

The third category of Aboriginal peoples recognized in 1982 is the Métis people. They have a well-documented history in the prairie and northern rivers and lakes region of western Canada. They emerged as a new indigenous nation prior to the establishment of Canadian colonial rule in the late eighteenth century and particularly the nineteenth century. As related earlier, the Métis emerged from a unique set of social, economic, political, and geographic factors at a specific time.[15] It is widely emphasized in the historical literature that members of the new nation resulted from marriages between Europeans involved in the fur trade and members, usually women, of several western Indian nations. Because of this intermarriage, Métis have sometimes been incorrectly identified by outsiders as a "mixed-blood" or racial group. *Métis* is a French-derived word that in its generic sense refers to "mixed-bloods"; the pejorative term "half-breed" is the English equivalent. This connotation is inapt to describe a group within a constitutional category that recognizes the rights of distinct historical nations. The Métis people in section 35 must refer to an Aboriginal people, and their identification and definition must follow from the same constitutional analysis as the other peoples in section 35. Neither the text nor the purpose of section 35 allows for differentiation between peoples. Accordingly, the constitutional meaning of "the Métis people" must be found by using the same approach as applicable to other Aboriginal peoples and in light of general constitutional principles.

The purpose of section 35 is to recognize Aboriginal rights, whose source lies in the history of Aboriginal-crown relations. History reveals that the group consciousness of the Métis as a distinct nation was not only compelled by the development of entire communities based on a particular economic lifestyle but also crystallized over the years by political action that clearly demarcated the existence of a new people distinct from both Europeans and Indians. The unique set of circumstances in the fur trade history, economy, and regions provided the opportunity for entire families and communities to develop away from local Indian communities, living along rivers and lakes and developing a unique political and social community far removed from the European communities then existing in eastern Canada. The identity of the new people was forged in the same fires of collective consciousness that characterized the evolution of other new peoples: that is, warfare. The Métis were involved in a number of well-known historical military skirmishes against new European settlers in Red River early in the nineteenth century, against the incoming Canadian government in Manitoba in 1869-70, and again against Canadian intrusion farther west along the Saskatchewan River as late as 1885. Throughout the era of the great buffalo hunts in the first half of the nineteenth century, the Métis made peace with Indian nations, with whom they shared the open spaces of the Prairies, but peace was punctuated until the 1850s by occasional military skirmishes in the Dakotas.

The Métis were specifically recognized in the Canadian Constitution by the *Manitoba Act* of 1870,[16] which provided them with three categories of local rights, including rights to land. This recognition flowed from the political action of the new nation in asserting its right to defend its interests against Canadian intrusion and from the negotiations that followed initial armed resistance. The *Manitoba Act* is part of the contemporary *Constitution Act* of 1982.[17] The interpretive canon that the Constitution speaks with one voice suggests that the Métis in section 35 are members of the same group. These people were part of a much larger group that had developed a regional identity as far west as the Rocky Mountains.[18]

This brief historical introduction has been essential to note and emphasize the distinction between "mixed-blood populations" or mestizos, which are an unexceptional feature of European colonial expansion into indigenous peoples' territories, and the emergence of a new indigenous people not belonging to the European colonial order.[19] The Métis were not part of the new order but functioned as part of the distinct indigenous order prior to the effective establishment of European political or legal authority. The Métis of Canada represent an exceptional development, a new people distinct from local Indian groups and distinct from the communities of "non-status Indians" that federal law and policy have failed to recognize. Because of the failure to recognize the unique history of the Métis people, and because of the etymology of the term, the false notion of "race" or "mixed-blood" status came about and continues to be used.

In its recent decision on Métis Aboriginal rights recognized in section 35, the SCC views Métis communities as descendant communities of historical groups that are, as such, social and political communities and not "racial" groups united merely by birth.[20] The judicial test for proof of Aboriginal rights in Canada is based on the idea that those rights are vested in historical communities that are social and political in nature.[21] The judicial conception of Aboriginal rights is predicated on the social and constitutional value of culture: not biological cultures evoked by the term "racial groups" but human communities formed by social and political relationships.

The test adopted by the SCC for identifying a Métis rights-bearing community in the recent *Powley* decision seems at first blush to make it difficult at best to distinguish Métis from Indian communities.[22] This ambiguity may not be important for many Aboriginal individuals who appear to seek official recognition under any label. Social scientists have explained that a good indicator of the political weakness of a marginalized group is a situation in which people allow the state to shift their identity easily, and that seems to be the situation with many individuals who switch identities or plead "alternative" identities in Aboriginal rights cases.[23] At the same time, there is a strong sense of history and nationalism among the descendants of the western Métis, whose ancestors had vigorously defended their identity and territory. The legitimacy of judicial decisions on Métis definitions with members of this group may be quite different from the legitimacy with others who seek recognition under any label. Initial reactions to the *Powley* and *Blais*[24] decisions do not lead to easy conclusions, in part because of the difficulty in anticipating the precise social and political significance of these legal decisions on a subject never before addressed by the SCC.

Types of Rights

I have considered the distinctions between the categories of Aboriginal peoples mentioned in the *Constitution Act* of 1982, but it is also important to distinguish between Aboriginal persons who are members of communities with Aboriginal or treaty rights and other Canadian citizens who have Aboriginal ancestors but who do not belong to Aboriginal communities. A rational policy of recognition would accomplish this purpose. It would make clear the distinction between Aboriginal and citizenship rights.

On the one hand, Aboriginal rights have their source in the history of the group to which the individual belongs. The Aboriginal person is entitled to enjoy activities recognized as Aboriginal rights because the person belongs to the Aboriginal group or community or people. Aboriginal rights derive not from the history of an individual's personal antecedents but from the history of a distinct people of a specific place within Canada. The history is that of the people's existence as a people on specific lands, giving rise to specific Aboriginal rights in specific places.

In theory, Aboriginal and treaty rights also have their source in the history of political relations between the government, symbolically called "the crown" in Canada, and the Aboriginal peoples. In this sense, the law recognizes the interests of Aboriginal people that have been at stake in their relationship with the crown as legal rights. The crown legally acquired a fiduciary or trust-like relationship with Aboriginal peoples because of its duty to recognize and protect their interests while making decisions in the general public interest. Aboriginal rights are vested in Aboriginal communities or nations and protect the integrity of the community or nation from government policies and actions adverse to communal interests. Since Aboriginal rights are made effective by the actions of individuals who enjoy them, it is not difficult to confuse Aboriginal rights with individual or personal rights.

On the other hand, citizenship rights belong to all citizens within the legitimate state. Citizenship rights engage the legal and political relationship between citizens and the state, a subject that has been at the forefront of political theory in European thought. Aboriginal persons are also citizens of the state in which they reside, and as such they are entitled to the discretionary benefits of government actions aimed at the redress of past wrongs or suffering. This is remedial justice intended to be satisfied on the attainment of the desired equality results. The notion that all Canadian citizens are equal in dignity, rights, and duties is often confused with the specificity of Aboriginal rights. This confusion underlies some misconceived arguments such as "race-based" privileges and "one law for all."

The one-law-for-all argument is central to the notion of equality of citizens, and applies to Aboriginal persons as citizens, subject to recognition of the validity of affirmative action that discriminates in favour of disadvantaged individuals recognized in section 15 of the Charter. It is not applicable, however, to a comparison between the rights of the non-Aboriginal citizen and the rights of an Aboriginal member of a rights-bearing Aboriginal community.

The *Indian Act*
These difficulties in the race for recognition are compounded by results of the administration of membership provisions of the *Indian Act* over time by the federal government. Research and analysis have shown that the maladministration of the membership code in the act has resulted in an irrational scheme of status Indian definition.[25] On this basis, it has been suggested that any attempt, judicial or otherwise, to build a concept of Métis identity at the definitional boundary of Indian identity is bound to fail since a rational scheme cannot be built on an irrational foundation.[26]

The statutory definitions of "Indian" in the act will likely need to change in the future as the act itself undergoes transformation. The 1985 amendments introduced the category of "band member," a band being comprised of individuals who are included by way of band decisions instead of by application of the act. The process of change may gain impetus because the courts are likely to dismantle the act since it conflicts with Charter values.[27] Thus, the archaic *Indian Act* seems like a house of cards that is sure to tumble by the combined effects of judicial decisions and legislated amendments.

Identifying Aboriginal Peoples

Section 35 of the *Constitution Act* of 1982 recognizes and affirms the existing Aboriginal and treaty rights of the Aboriginal peoples of Canada. The Supreme Court has not yet commented directly on the nature of the Aboriginal peoples, but it seems reasonably clear that they are conceived of, for the purposes of section 35, as being essentially social and political communities. For example, in *Delgamuukw* the court explained that Aboriginal rights are communal in nature; it adopted a term of art, "the Aboriginal perspective," which includes the legal systems of the Aboriginal peoples and which makes clear the social and political nature of the Aboriginal societies.[28] This is the view also espoused in the final report by the Royal Commission on Aboriginal Peoples: "Aboriginal peoples are not racial groups; rather they are organic political and cultural entities. Although contemporary Aboriginal groups stem historically from the original peoples of North America, they often have mixed genetic heritages and include individuals of varied ancestry. As organic political entities, they have the capacity to evolve over time and change their internal composition."[29]

Whenever the SCC concludes that a group has Aboriginal rights, it necessarily contributes to the identification and definition of that group. Accordingly, the process of defining Aboriginal rights also defines the Aboriginal people who have them. But the courts have to define Aboriginal people for a range of purposes as they construe the meanings of various constitutional and legislative terms that refer to Aboriginal people. The court has adopted a purposeful approach to the construction of such language, an approach that conforms to the notion that definitions are only useful in relation to specific purposes. Often one hears the question who is an Aboriginal person? The question can be answered usefully only in relation to the purpose of the definition. The *Indian Act* exemplifies a statute that recognizes both groups (i.e., bands) and individuals (i.e., Indians) for the purposes of administering federal policy with respect to Indians residing on reserves.

In Canada, then, there are as many definitions of Aboriginal people as there are constitutional or legislative provisions that reflect particular purposes, and the relationship between the various terms has not been developed. In the absence of precisely defined terms, the courts have adopted a variety of interchangeable terms to refer to the Aboriginal groups that have Aboriginal rights, with the most commonly used terms appearing to be, in no particular order, "nation," "people," "community," "society," and "group." It is beyond the scope of this chapter to analyze fully the terms and their meanings that the SCC has adopted, but the following list of some of the terms that have been coined or interpreted by the court offers an insight into the complexity and open-ended nature of questions being asked about the identity and definition of Aboriginal peoples.

1 Characterization of Aboriginal peoples recognized as having Aboriginal and treaty rights protected by section 35, *Constitution Act, 1982*.[30]
2 Interpretation of the subject matter "Indians" in the constitutional provision allocating exclusive legislative power with respect to this matter to Parliament, section 91(24), *Constitution Act, 1867*.[31]
3 Characterization of "Indians" who live on reserves and are subject to the terms of the *Indian Act*.[32]
4 Identification of "Aboriginal persons" for sentencing purposes under the *Criminal Code*[33] – the *Gladue* decision.[34]
5 Characterization of Aboriginal people for purposes of applying the equality provision in the Charter to certain provisions in the *Indian Act*.[35]
6 Definition of "Indians" within the meaning of the game laws paragraph in the *Constitution Act, 1930*,[36] who are entitled to hunt and fish for food in the Prairies.

As a matter of constitutional law, it is established that Métis, Indians, and Inuit are all "Aboriginal peoples" for the purposes of section 35. It is established that Indians and Inuit are "Indians" for the purposes of section 91(24) and that Inuit are not "Indians" for the purposes of the *Indian Act*, but some "Métis" might be.[37] The complexities abound, making it difficult for individuals and groups seeking official recognition.

One complexity revealed in this list is that the courts have adopted the concept of "race" to characterize the "Indians" in the *Indian Act* and the meaning of "Indians" in the constitutional provision granting exclusive legislative jurisdiction to Parliament. This characterization is adequate only in referring to a group of people who have been, or may be, politically singled out for special policy treatment in federal legislation subject to constitutional limits. The racial characterization would be inadequate, however, for the historical Aboriginal groups, including Indian groups, with Aboriginal or treaty rights, as discussed earlier. The racial characterization is inapt to distinguish between local cultures and societies that have vested Aboriginal rights.[38] The sphere of Aboriginal definition is further complicated by the inclusion of "racial ancestry" in the Charter, a provision whose meaning and purposes are quite distinct from those of section 35, which recognizes and affirms the rights of Aboriginal peoples.

The SCC has not always observed the approach that carefully links definitions with specific legislative and constitutional purposes. The sentencing provisions of the *Criminal Code* have come under particular attack from some quarters as being unfair discrimination on the basis of "race."[39] In *Gladue*, the court appeared to take the view that "Aboriginal persons" within the meaning of the code are all members of section 35 Aboriginal communities that are part of the "Aboriginal peoples" with Aboriginal or treaty rights. This interpretation is problematic because the sentencing provision addresses conditions of social and economic marginalization as a factor to be considered in sentencing. Nothing in the code indicates Parliament's intention to limit the application of the sentencing provision to members of section 35 rights-bearing communities.

In Aboriginal rights cases, the courts have emphasized that such rights are vested in communities and not in individuals. In sentencing cases, the courts have not examined whether the individual belongs to a section 35 rights-bearing community. Instead, they have examined the personal circumstances of the individual to decide on an appropriate sentence. It would be a strange result if isolated individuals who appear before the court to be sentenced for crimes are required to prove membership in a rights-bearing community when the issue of Aboriginal rights is immaterial to the legislated mandate of the court to sentence the individual. The better view is that the *Criminal Code* addresses the case of individual Aboriginal persons qua Canadian citizens, not qua members of Aboriginal groups with Aboriginal rights. In *Gladue*, the court did not consider the difference between section 15 and section 35 purposes.

In its final report, the Royal Commission on Aboriginal Peoples proposed that Canada's governing authority over the Aboriginal peoples of Canada ought to be legitimized by the inclusion of Aboriginal "nations" within the Canadian federal system that allocates governing power and authority. This approach would recognize a measure of self-governing authority within the Canadian Constitution for Aboriginal peoples who were kept out of the original process of establishing Canada's constitutional framework. The task could be accomplished by construing section 35 of the *Constitution Act, 1982*, which provides recognition and affirmation of the Aboriginal and treaty rights of the Aboriginal peoples of Canada, as protecting an Aboriginal right of self-government. The commission recommended that, for the purposes of negotiating "nation-to-nation" treaties, the federal government negotiate with Aboriginal political leaders a framework of guiding principles for the recognition of Aboriginal "nations."[40]

Canada's official policy statements recognize this possibility, but at the time of writing, treaty negotiations have proceeded only within the traditional scope of the federal policy of recognition and have not included the Aboriginal peoples recognized in section 35, who now lack official executive or legislative recognition. This official stance is exemplified by the appointment of a federal "interlocutor" for Métis and non-status Indians rather than dealing with Métis and non-status Indian affairs under the auspices of the federal Indian and Northern Affairs department.[41] This political approach rejects the view that Aboriginal people other than status Indians recognized in federal legislation are included in its jurisdictional mandate and, by the absence of federal legislation with respect to Métis, Inuit, or Indians, outside the scope of the *Indian Act*. A change to the approach is a necessary first step in developing a defensible policy of recognition that applies to all the Aboriginal peoples recognized by the Constitution.[42]

Conclusion

In 1982, a Canadian constitutional amendment recognized and affirmed the collective rights of Aboriginal peoples. Those Aboriginal and treaty rights are being defined mainly in judicial decisions. I have proposed in this chapter that a constitutionally valid policy of recognition is a constitutional imperative. I have illustrated the need for a rational legislated policy by identifying some of the major difficulties that have arisen in its absence, where the government has continued to rely on the archaic *Indian Act* as the foundation of Aboriginal policy. A new legislated policy foundation is required to conform to the demands of the Constitution.

Recognition legislation is required to make effective and to implement the Aboriginal and treaty rights vested in the Aboriginal peoples identified in the Canadian Constitution. A legislated scheme of recognition that follows legitimate discussions and negotiations with the political representatives of the Aboriginal peoples is a better policy option than waiting for the results of judicial decisions on Aboriginal rights. Negotiated solutions between legitimate political representatives will yield a more democratic and effective scheme of recognition.

A major goal of this chapter has been to show that the concept of "race" must not inform the process of identifying or defining the historical groups, whether called "nations" or "peoples" or otherwise, in which are vested collective Aboriginal and treaty rights. The concept has no scientific basis and is being jettisoned by social scientists.[43] It has no place within the sphere of collective rights.

It does not follow that the concept of "race" can or will be eliminated from the intellectual and rhetorical contributions to policy or legal developments, whether in relation to indigenous peoples or generally. It may be better if elimination were possible, but the concept is here to stay. It is embedded in international law and in the law of the constitutions of modern states, such as Canada, the United States, and Australia.[44]

The concept finds its philosophical home as a companion to debates on the concept of "equality," usually among citizens of states, and debates on corrective justice, or "affirmative action" projects, whose aim is to correct the practical disadvantages faced by some groups of citizens. As such, it is a rhetorical device that denotes groups comprised of individual persons whose individual rights are at stake. I explained this above in the context of differentiating between the concept of "race" in Canada's *Charter of Rights and Freedoms* and the collective rights of the Aboriginal peoples that are guaranteed in a distinct part of the Constitution. States often designate their affirmative action policies in relation to indigenous peoples by expressions such as "closing the gap," which illustrates the corrective justice feature of such policies. Recognition of the collective rights of indigenous peoples is not a corrective measure or an affirmative action measure. Aboriginal rights, which are historically based and vested in distinct contemporary social and political communities, do not come within the ambit of such rhetorical labelling or philosophical justification. One result of a rational policy of recognition respecting Aboriginal "peoples" with collective rights is that it would distinguish in a practical way those persons who are entitled to the benefits and burdens of belonging to rights-bearing groups from other citizens who may be entitled to the benefits of affirmative action or corrective justice policies.

The experiences in Australia, Aotearoa/New Zealand, and the United States indicate that the distinction between indigenous "peoples" or "nations" with collective rights, on the one hand, and individuals who are singled out for other particular legislative purposes, on the other hand, is likely to remain elusive for some time, and the concept of "race" is not likely to be jettisoned as a foundational concept on which state policies will be structured. As in Canada, the distinction between the collective "Aboriginal" rights of indigenous peoples and the individual rights of all citizens, which include indigenous persons, is overlooked by legislators and judicial decision makers. Where the distinction is not noticed, the concept of "race," with its attendant vexed questions about "equality," the merits (constitutional or otherwise) of "affirmative action," and "special race-based" privileges, is granted easy entry into the dialogue.

The recent adoption by the United Nations General Assembly of the *Declaration on the Rights of Indigenous Peoples*[45] brings the attention of states to precepts that emerge from the recognition of the right of self-determination and other collective rights of indigenous peoples.[46] This development highlights the need to properly conceptualize and distinguish between collective rights of "peoples" and individual rights of citizens of states. The precepts relating to "racial equality" in international law and treaties must be balanced and reconciled with the precepts relating to the "third generation" of collective human rights. It is within states that just and rational balancing and reconciliation of rights are to take place.

In Australia, the concept of "race" is embedded in the law of the Constitution and in the *Racial Discrimination Act,* which guides Aboriginal policy and legislation.[47] "Native title" groups, those recognized by legislation and the common law as having Aboriginal title, have appropriately not been defined by the concept.[48]

In Aotearoa/New Zealand, the concept of "race" informs legislated defin-itions enacted for specific state purposes,[49] but policy and practice tend to defer to the more sophisticated and richer concept of "belonging" of the indigenous Māori people.[50]

In the United States,[51] courts have held that American Indian tribes con-stitute separate peoples with their own political institutions,[52] but they have also firmly tied the concept of "race" to particular legal purposes.[53] Here, too, as in Australia, the concept is embedded within the Constitution and has been used by the courts to scrutinize and strike down both state and federal statutes enacted in favour of indigenous people.[54]

In Canada, the number of persons reporting an Aboriginal identity in official census reports has soared since the Constitution affirmed the col-lective rights of Aboriginal peoples. It is not necessary to assume that persons identify themselves thus to gain access to what may be perceived as new legal entitlements in order to observe that these numbers are one indicator of the practical significance of designing rational policies of recognition. There may be a race for recognition, but defensible and practical policies of recognition must treat the concept of "race" with the utmost caution and never apply it to recognition of the right of self-determination or other col-lective rights of indigenous peoples.

Notes

1 Aboriginal rights cases are often related to fishing, hunting, and trapping but might also include activities such as organized gambling. The courts tend to recharacterize the broader Aboriginal rights claimed by Aboriginal peoples into narrower, activity-based practices. See, generally, *R. v. Van der Peet*, [1996] 4 C.N.L.R. 177 (S.C.C.) [*Van der Peet*]; and *R. v. Pamajewon*, [1996] 4 C.N.L.R. 164 (S.C.C.).

2 In the recent *Powley* case, the SCC did not find it necessary to consider the meaning of a "people," deciding only that the defendant belonged to an Aboriginal rights-bearing com-munity. *R. v. Powley*, [2003] S.C.J. No. 43 [*Powley*]. The courts have used a variety of terms, apparently interchangeably, to describe the groups or communities that have been found to have Aboriginal rights, with the result that there is no single term with precise legal meaning to identify Aboriginal peoples and their constituent communities. In this com-mentary, the term *group* or *community* will be used to denote a rights-bearing community. These terms are intended to refer solely to a group of Aboriginal people in which is vested an Aboriginal right.

3 Giokas, "Domestic Recognition in the United States and Canada," 126 at 127.

4 *Indian Act*, R.S.C. 1985, c. 1-5 [*Indian Act*].

5 *Constitution Act, 1867* (U.K.), 30 and 31 Vict., c. 3, reprinted in R.S.C. 1985, App. II, No. 5 [*Constitution Act, 1867*].

6 Under international law, states are not concerned with the citizenship of other states. Given this, Canada's *Indian Act* scheme of recognition is "not a true group recognition instrument because in its definition of 'Indian' it also concerns itself with the question of who is a 'citizen' of the recognized group." Giokas and Groves, "Collective and Individual Recogni-tion in Canada," 41 at 50.

7 It must be disclosed that the author was a commissioner on the Royal Commission on Aboriginal Peoples, which, in its 1996 final report, included recommendations along these lines. See Canada, *Restructuring the Relationship*.
8 See, for example, *R. v. Kapp* (2003), B.C.P.C. 0279, File No. 108246, Vancouver Registry. Social science has concluded that "race" belongs to the history of ideas and not science. There are no biological "races," and the term is meaningful only to denote a group of people singled out for political purposes. For fuller discussions, see Canada, *Restructuring the Relationship*, 176; and Chartrand and Giokas, "Defining the Métis People," 281-85.
      It is impossible to overemphasize the significant extent to which the "race" rhetoric is raised in contemporary Canada to oppose government actions that single out Aboriginal people. It is effective in part because of its faulty association with the American civil rights movement and South African apartheid. Civil rights apply to citizenship rights questions such as equality of all citizens, not to special, constitutionally affirmed, historical group rights issues. Apartheid was forced on a majority; Aboriginal rights inhere in contemporary groups as a result of historical facts and reasons, do not follow "racial descent" of individuals, and are available only with the consent of the group that has them. Aboriginal peoples are in their nature social and political communities with rights whose sources lie in history and the Constitution. Persons of Aboriginal ancestry may belong to such groups, or they may not. If they do not, they do not enjoy Aboriginal rights but may benefit from affirmative action directed at persons disadvantaged on account of "racial origins" by virtue of s. 15 of the *Charter of Rights and Freedoms*.
9 Indian bands constructed by the *Indian Act* consisting of descendants of the various Aboriginal peoples who have been commonly called "Indians" are the most visible Aboriginal communities as they reside on exclusive reserves set aside for them. The term *First Nations* is replacing *Indian* in both academic and popular usage.
10 *Nisga'a Final Agreement*, S.B.C. 1999, c. 2, and *Nisga'a Final Agreement*, S.C. 2000, c. 7.
11 According to the Native Women's Association of Canada (NWAC), the various enfranchisement measures caused approximately 25,000 people to lose their registered status between 1878 and 1985. See NWAC, "The Background to Bill C-31," in "Equality for All in the 21st Century," Second National Conference on Bill C-31, Edmonton, 1999, 103.
12 However, given that the average marrying-out is at about 25 percent, operation of the amended *Indian Act* provisions will actually ensure a significant reduction in the status Indian population within two generations. According to Harry Daniels, "we merely have to ask what would happen if all status Indians alive today married a non-Indian or someone without status, and their children did the same: after two generations, there would be no status Indians left in Canada." Harry Daniels, "Bill C-31: The Abocide Bill," paper presented at the NWAC Conference on Bill C-31, 23 March 1998, 12-13. See also Stewart Clatworthy and Anthony H. Smith, "Population Implications of the 1985 Amendments to the *Indian Act*," paper prepared for the Assembly of First Nations, December 1992, 19.
13 *Canadian Charter of Rights and Freedoms*, Part I of the *Constitution Act, 1982*, being Schedule B to the *Canada Act 1982* (U.K.), 1982, c. 11 [Charter].
14 See Napoleon, "Extinction by Number," 114. According to Napoleon, the 1985 *Indian Act Amendment*, known as Bill C-31, maintained the same divisive "classes" of Indians. In effect, the amendment changed the category of status and non-status Indians to categories of 6(1) (real Indians) and 6(2) (half Indians). The way in which this formula applies is that a child of

- two 6(2) parents becomes a 6(1);
- two 6(1) parents becomes a 6(1);
- a 6(1) parent and a 6(2) parent becomes a 6(1);
- a 6(1) parent and a non-Indian (or non-registered Indian) becomes a 6(2); and
- a 6(2) parent and a non-Indian (or non-registered Indian) becomes a non-Indian.

As a result of this amendment, bands can adopt membership codes that are distinct from that of the federal Indian Register (now Indian Register, Indian and Northern Affairs Canada). Basically, this scheme separates band membership from the central federal registration system. As of 1985, Indians listed with the federal registry can still be refused membership by their band, effectively creating a new group of bandless Indians.

If a band does not adopt its own membership code, the *Indian Act* criteria apply by default, thereby granting status to Indian people who can substantiate having at least one parent qualified to be registered. At the end of 1995, only 240 of the 600 bands in Canada adopted membership codes. Most of these newly adopted band membership codes incorporate the restrictive criteria of blood quantum or genetic descent.

Regarding future generations, the amended *Indian Act* simply shifts the burden of discrimination away from the Indian woman who regained status in 1985 to her grandchildren – this is because, when she was reclassified as an Indian, she only became a 6(2), while her brothers, who never lost their status, remained 6(1)s. In other words, the woman's "watered down" 6(2) Indian status has direct implications for her children and grandchildren. See also Giokas and Groves, "Collective and Individual Recognition."

15 Some important sources that describe this history and explain the circumstances of the emergence of a new Aboriginal people are Devine, "Les Desjarlais"; Foster, "Wintering, and Ethnogenesis of the Western Plains Métis"; and Peterson and Brown, *The New Peoples*.

16 *Manitoba Act (an Act to Amend and Continue the Act 32 and 33 Victoria, Chapter 3; and to Establish and Provide for the Government of the Province of Manitoba)*, S.C. 1870 (33 Vict.), c. 3, reprinted as *Manitoba Act, 1870*, in R.S.C. 1985, App. II, No. 8 [*Manitoba Act, 1870*].

17 52. (1) The Constitution of Canada is the supreme law of Canada, and any law that is inconsistent with the provisions of the Constitution is, to the extent of the inconsistency, of no force and effect.

52. (2) The Constitution of Canada includes (a) the *Canada Act 1982*, including this Act; (b) the Acts and orders referred to in the schedule; and (c) any amendment to any Act or order referred to in paragraph (a) or (b).

The *Manitoba Act, 1870*, is listed in the schedule mentioned in s. 52(2)(b).

18 The Métis had a number of cultural symbols of their distinct identity, including a flag and a "national anthem" composed by Pierriche Falcon to celebrate an early victory over British intruders in the Red River region in 1816. The publications mentioned in note 15 will introduce the reader to the history.

19 Brown and Schenck, "Metis, Mestizo, and Mixed-Blood," 231.

20 *Powley*. The case, particularly if viewed in light of the decisions at the various court levels, is nevertheless illustrative of the judicial inexperience with Métis issues and history. Although the following is by no means a complete analysis, three basic criticisms of the case may be mentioned.

1 The judges appear to attempt to draw guidance from the equality principles of s. 15 of the Charter that are primarily aimed at affirmative action and remedial justice. S. 35 rights have absolutely nothing to do with remedial justice, past wrongdoing, or disadvantage.

2 Another significant aspect of this decision is the establishment of the "effective control date" as the legal date at which Métis rights must be proved to have existed. In contrast, the date for proving Aboriginal rights derived from Indian cases is "European contact." There is no sound legal reasoning behind either of these dates because they completely miss the basic constitutional theory behind Aboriginal rights. The crown encountered Aboriginal peoples with intact legal orders, and, in exchange for their allegiance, the crown agreed to protect them. How can the "effective control date" be proven? It raises questions similar to those raised by the "date of contact" criteria (e.g., Does the contact of one colonial person count? How many contacts should there be? What does contact mean?).

3 Finally, the defendant, Powley, was a mixed-blood descendant of enfranchised Indians. Although the case was not argued on this basis, the facts reveal grounds for a challenge to the *Indian Act* policy of enfranchisement that resulted in removing Powley's grandmother from membership in an Indian band. The facts and the case illustrate the problems in attempting to define Métis people at the boundary of *Indian Act* definitions where no rational solution is possible.

21 *Van der Peet.*

22 The meaning of "Métis" is also ambiguous when applied to individuals for various purposes, as exemplified by the roughly 25,000 persons who identified themselves as "Métis" in the 1996 Canadian census. See Giokas and Chartrand, "Who Are the Métis in Section 35?" This statistic also illustrates the need for a policy that can distinguish between Métis and Indian persons for various policy purposes.

23 *R. v. Chiasson*, [2002] 2 C.N.L.R. 220 (N.B. Prov. Ct.), affirming *R. c. Chiasson*, [2004] N.B.B.R. 80 (QB).

24 *R. v. Blais*, [2003] 4 C.N.L.R. 219 (S.C.C.).

25 According to Giokas and Chartrand, "Who Are the Métis in Section 35?," 104,

> There is no consistent basis for Canada's approach to recognition of Indians. Rather than recognizing the institutions that maintained the identity of the original Indian "nations" or groups with which treaties were entered into, or in some other way establishing a functional relationship with Indian communities, Canada instead unilaterally legislated one general definition of "Indian" for all its purposes, without regard for membership in distinct "nations" or other communities.

The authors describe the attempts to define Métis at the edges of the current Indian definition as a "fool's errand" and instead suggest approaching Métis identity in a principled manner. Administration of the membership code of the act has had an irrational result because it has put beyond reach all the usual factors used to denote a human group: namely, blood, kinship, and lifestyle factors. "There is little logic or utility to trying to define 'Métis' in the absence of a serious, sustained, and rational approach to the status system under the *Indian Act,* including a review of its validity and legitimacy in respect to the identification of 'treaty nations' and other First Nations communities" (106).

26 Ibid.

27 *Corbiere v. Canada,* [1994] 1 C.N.L.R. 71 (S.C.C.) [*Corbiere*]. At issue was the *Indian Act* residency requirement that limited voting in band elections to those members residing on reserves. The SCC unanimously ruled that the words "and is ordinarily resident on the reserve" in s. 77(1) of the *Indian Act* infringed s. 15 of the *Charter of Rights and Freedoms* by denying equality to off-reserve band members. The court struck the offending words, and the section is to be read as if the words are not present. According to Giokas and Groves, *Corbiere* has serious implications for the entire *Indian Act* because electors vote on a range of issues, such as land surrenders, land designations, distribution of capital and revenue monies, bylaws, et cetera. Additional s. 15 Charter challenges may be expected that could lead to the dismantling of the fragile *Indian Act*: "The sheer volume of equality issues tied up in the *Indian Act* may be such as to prevent limited amendments of the type called for by the Court in *Corbiere*. If so, the administrative regime established by the *Indian Act* and financed through INAC may well begin to crumble in the ensuing decades in the face of this anticipated litigation." Giokas and Groves, "Collective and Individual Recognition," 72-73.

28 1997 CanLII 302 (S.C.C.) at 115, 141, and 155. In respect to discussion of the Aboriginal perspective, at 155-57 inc., [1997] 3 S.C.R. 1010, 153 D.L.R. (4th) 193, [1999] 10 W.W.R. 34, [1998] 1 C.N.L.R. 14, and 66 B.C.L.R. (3d) 285.

29 Canada, *Report of the Royal Commission on Aboriginal Peoples,* vol. 2, *Restructuring the Relationship,* Part One (Ottawa: Supply and Services Canada, 1996), ch. 3, at 177.

30 *R. v. Sparrow,* [1990] 1 S.C.R. 1075 [*Sparrow*] (re Aboriginal rights test); *Delgamuukw v. British Columbia,* [1997] 3 S.C.R. 1010 [*Delgamuukw*] (re historical, culturally distinct, social and political communities).

31 The *British North America Act* ... by using the word "Indians" in s. 91(24) creates a racial classification and refers to a special group for whom it contemplates the possibility of special treatment. It does not define the expression "Indian." This Parliament can do within constitutional limits by using criteria suited to this purpose but among which it would not appear unreasonable to count marriage and filiation and, unavoidably, intermarriages, in the light of either Indian customs and values ... or of legislative history.

A.G. Canada v. Canard, [1976] 1 S.C.R. 170, at 207, per Beetz J. The scope of this legislative power has been subsequently limited by the fiduciary relationship of the crown with Aboriginal peoples, as the court has elaborated in R. v. Guerin, [1984] 2 S.C.R. 335, 1984 CanLII 25 (S.C.C.), 13 D.L.R. (4th) 321, [1984] 6 W.W.R. 481, and Sparrow, [1990] 1 S.C.R. 1075, 1990 CanLII 104 (S.C.C.), 70 D.L.R. (4th) 385, [1990] 4 W.W.R. 410, 56 C.C.C. (3d) 263, [1990] 3 C.N.L.R. 160, and 46 B.C.L.R. (2d) 1. See also R. v. Dick, [1985] 2 S.C.R. 309 (provincial laws cannot covertly or colourably single out Indians for special treatment and impair their status as Indians); and Delgamuukw (re s. 35 protecting a core of "Indianness," that essential characteristic of Indian people).

32 See, for example, R. v. Sikyea (1964), S.C.R. 642 (re application of the Migratory Birds Act, R.S.C. 1952, c. 179, to restrict the right to hunt under the terms of Treaty 11); R. v. Drybones, [1970] S.C.R. 282 (re liquor on reserves and the Canadian Bill of Rights); and R. v. Hayden, [1983] M.J. No. 27 (Man. C.A.) (re "place" becomes "race," treatment post s. 15).

33 Criminal Code, R.S. 1985, c. C-46.

34 R. v. Gladue, [1999] 2 C.N.L.R. 252 (S.C.C.) [Gladue].

35 Corbiere (re Aboriginality and residence). For an analysis of the "signal failure" of the genealogical or race test developed by judges to interpret legislative definitions of Aboriginal people in Australia, see De Plevitz and Croft, "Aboriginality under the Microscope," 104-20. The authors show that science cannot prove Aboriginal descent as a "quantum of genes," as judicial tests attempt to do. Cultural identification is sufficient.

36 Constitution Act, 1930, formerly the British North America Act, 1930 (U.K.), 20 and 21 Geo. 5, c. 26, reprinted in R.S.C. 1985, App. II, No. 26.

37 The ambiguity about this point arises from some puzzling statements made by the SCC in Powley about persons who have been members of Indian bands not losing their Métis identity. It is also illustrated in a practical sense by the case of many "Métis" who have acquired status as "Indians." Some Métis might be Indians, depending on what is a Métis and again depending on the purpose.

38 Kruger and Manuel v. The Queen, [1977] 75 D.L.R. (3d) (S.C.C.); R. v. Adams, [1996] 4 C.N.L.R. 1 (S.C.C.); and R. v. Côté, [1996] 4 C.N.L.R. 26 (S.C.C.).

39 Gladue. This view of the meaning of the provision is clearly wrong. S. 718 of the Criminal Code mandates the court to seek alternatives to imprisonment for all offenders, not only for Aboriginal people. The task to which the attention of the court is drawn by the legislature in relation to Aboriginal people is to consider the background of the individual in assessing the sentence because of the particular conditions in which the Aboriginal people in Canada live.

40 Canada, Restructuring the Relationship, vol. 2 of Report of the Royal Commission on Aboriginal Peoples, Part 2, 177, 180, 182, 184. Recognition legislation would guide the process, but the agreement of the federal executive government would be required to recognize any particular nation.

41 Recently, the office of the interlocutor has been administered from within the department, but the policy approach remains the same.

42 This point is argued fully in Giokas and Groves, "Collective and Individual Recognition."

43 See, for instance, Rigsby, "'Race,'" 57-61: "When race appears today in anthropological discourse, it is not as an analytic or explanatory concept, but rather it presents as a concept in need of historical exegesis and analytical deconstruction and interpretation."

44 Montagu, Man's Most Dangerous Myth; cf. Harris, "Whiteness as Property," 1707-91 at 1715; For example, the Charter of the United Nations, art. 1, cl. 3, requires that all members promote human rights "without distinction as to race, sex, ... ," and the International Convention on the Elimination of Racial Discrimination is obviously based on the idea of "race." UN Doc. A/RES/2106 (1967) [CERD]; Charter; See notes 54-59 and 50-51.

45 Adopted by General Assembly Resolution 61/295 on 13 September 2007 (A/RES/61/295).

46 The collective right of self-determination is affirmed in art. 3 and that of self-government in art. 4. Among the other articles that affirm collective rights, the following do so most unambiguously: 5, 7, 8, 11, 14, 18, 20, 26, 28, 29, 32, 35, 37, 39, 40.

47 The act purports to adopt the CERD precept, which provides that, "when circumstances so warrant," parties shall take "special and concrete measures to ensure the adequate

development and protection of certain racial groups or individuals belonging to them, for the purpose of guaranteeing them the full and equal enjoyment of human rights." This means that such special measures do not violate the mandate of equality and are required to attain substantive equality. See McRae, Nettheim, Beacroft, and McNamara, *Indigenous Legal Issues*, 441-50.

48 See *Corporations (Aboriginal and Torres Strait Islander) Act 2006* (Cth.); Mantzaris and Martin, *Native Title Corporations*; McRae et al., *Indigenous Legal Issues*, especially chap. 9; *Patmore v. Independent Indigenous Advisory Committee*, [2002] F.C.A.F.C. 316; *Shaw v. Wolf* (1998), 83 F.C.R. 113; and Strelein, *Compromised Jurisprudence*.

49 *Te Ture Whenua Māori Act 1993/Māori Land Act 1993*, Public Act 1993 No. 4, s. 2: "Maori means a person of the Maori race of New Zealand; and includes a descendant of any such person." The same definition is found in the legislation that establishes special Māori electoral provisions; see *Electoral Act 1993*, Public Act 1993 No. 87, ss. 3, 45; Kukutai, "The Problem of Defining an Ethnic Group for Public Policy," 86-108; Maaka and Fleras, *The Politics of Indigeneity*; Moeke-Pickering, *Maori Identity within Whanau*; and *Te Waka Hi Ika o Te Arawa v. Treaty of Waitangi Fisheries Commission*, [2002] 2 N.Z.L.R. 17.

50 See Kingsbury, "Competing Conceptual Approaches," 101-34 at 122; and Tomas, "Key Concepts of Tikanga Maori (Maori Custom Law)."

51 Brownell, "Who Is an Indian?" 275-320 at 275, 308; Goldberg, "Descent into Race," 1373-94.

52 *United States v. Antelope*, 430 U.S. 642, 646. See also *Cherokee Nation v. Georgia*, 30 U.S. (5 Pet.) 1 (1831); *Morton v. Mancari*, 417 U.S. 535 (1974); and *Santa Clara Pueblo v. Martinez*, 436 U.S. 49 (1978).

53 *United States v. Rogers*, 45 U.S. (4 Howe) 567 (1846) (importing "race" into the definition for purposes of federal criminal jurisdiction).

54 See Western Attorneys General, "Indian Status and the Fifth Amendment," 43-47; *Rice v. Cayetano*, 528 U.S. 495 (2000); See comment on *Williams v. Babbitt*, 115 F. 3d 657 (9th Cir. 1997), by Tsosie, "Tribalism, Constitutionalism, and Cultural Pluralism," 357.

7

The Sources and Content of Indigenous Land Rights in Australia and Canada: A Critical Comparison

Kent McNeil

The content of indigenous land rights is heavily influenced, if not determined, by the source of these rights. This has been confirmed by important decisions of the High Court of Australia and the Supreme Court of Canada in the past twenty years. This chapter will examine the divergent approaches that these courts have taken to the sources of indigenous land rights and critically assess the consequences of each approach for the content of the rights.

Indigenous land rights can, of course, be derived from positive enactments. In Canada, the Royal Proclamation of 1763 was regarded as the source of Indian title in *St. Catherine's Milling and Lumber Co. v. The Queen*.[1] Similarly, in Australia, various statutes enacted since 1975 have provided legislative bases for Aboriginal land rights. The focus in this chapter is on sources that arise from or are recognized by the common law. Generally, three potential sources have been identified by the courts in Australia and Canada. The first source is indigenous legal systems. Under this approach, any land rights that indigenous peoples enjoyed under their own legal systems continued as rights and interests enforceable in common law courts after colonization by the British crown. This approach involves an application of what is generally known as the "doctrine of continuity." The second source is the common law itself, which acknowledges that persons in exclusive occupation of land have a title that is good against anyone who cannot show a better title. Applying this common law rule in the colonial context, indigenous peoples who were in exclusive occupation of land at the time of British colonization would have title to the lands that they occupied at that time, regardless of the nature of their land rights under their own legal systems. This title can be designated as "common law title." The third source, added by the Supreme Court of Canada in 1996, is composed of traditions and land use practices that were integral to distinctive indigenous cultures at the time of contact with Europeans. These rights can be described as "integral to the distinctive culture rights."

With some modifications, each of these approaches has its place. I think that indigenous peoples should be able to rely on the source of land rights that best suits their particular circumstances. In situations where they can prove exclusive occupation at the time of crown acquisition of sovereignty, they should be able to rely on the doctrine of common law title. In other situations (e.g., where exclusive occupation cannot be shown), they should be able to rely on their own laws and customs and the doctrine of continuity. Finally, in circumstances where their ways of life depended on practices or traditions that were not necessarily supported by legal rules or norms, respect for those ways of life should result in legal protection being accorded to those practices and traditions after European colonization. I will now turn to an examination of the case law in Australia and Canada to determine the extent to which this range of choices has actually been accorded to indigenous peoples.

The High Court of Australia's Pronouncements on the Sources and Content of Indigenous Land Rights

Mabo v. Queensland (No. 2)[2] is the leading case on indigenous land rights in Australia. Prior to that landmark decision, Australian courts denied the existence of indigenous land rights apart from statutory rights.[3] *Mabo* overruled this judicial denial and held that indigenous Australians did in fact retain rights to lands occupied and used by them in accordance with their traditional laws and customs at the time of crown acquisition of sovereignty. But to what extent do those rights *depend on* those laws and customs? Unfortunately, Justice Brennan's principal judgment in *Mabo* contains certain ambiguities in this regard that have resulted in a narrowing of the range of sources of land rights available to indigenous Australians.

The ambiguities appear from a comparison of the following passages in Brennan's judgment. At one point, he said this: "Native title has its origin in and is given its content by the traditional laws acknowledged by and the traditional customs observed by the Indigenous inhabitants of a territory. The nature and incidents of native title must be ascertained as a matter of fact by reference to those laws and customs."[4] Elsewhere in his judgment, however, he seems to have envisaged another source of Native title where land was exclusively occupied by indigenous peoples at the time the crown acquired sovereignty:

> If it be necessary to categorize an interest in land as proprietary in order that it survive a change in sovereignty, the interest possessed by a community that is in exclusive possession of land falls into that category. Whether or not land is owned by individual members of a community, a community which asserts and asserts effectively that none but its members has any right to occupy or use the land has an interest in the land that must be proprietary

in nature: there is no other proprietor ... The ownership of land within a territory in the exclusive occupation of a people must be vested in that people: land is susceptible of ownership, and there are no other owners.[5]

Brennan then clarified how this proprietary interest arising from exclusive occupation might relate to the traditional laws and customs of the community:

> Where a proprietary title capable of recognition by the common law is found to have been possessed by a community in occupation of a territory, there is no reason why that title should not be recognized as a burden on the Crown's radical title when the Crown acquires sovereignty over that territory. The fact that individual members of the community ... enjoy only usufructuary rights that are not proprietary in nature is no impediment to the recognition of a proprietary communal title ... That being so, there is no impediment to the recognition of individual non-proprietary rights that are derived from the community's laws and customs and are dependent on the community title. A fortiori, there can be no impediment to the recognition of individual proprietary rights.[6]

It appears from these passages that Brennan offered two bases for indigenous land rights. First, Native title can arise directly from the traditional laws and customs of indigenous Australians. This appears to be a straightforward application of the doctrine of continuity. This option seems to be particularly applicable where indigenous peoples *were not* in exclusive occupation of land at the time of crown sovereignty. But if they *were* in exclusive occupation of land, then they would have a communal proprietary title that does not seem to arise from their own laws and customs. In that situation, their communal title appears to be due to the juridical effect that the common law accords to exclusive occupation of land.[7] Nonetheless, indigenous laws and customs could be used as evidence to support this occupation. Moreover, they would continue to apply internally to govern the land rights of the members of the indigenous community *inter se*.[8]

The communal title of the Meriam people in the *Mabo* case was based on exclusive occupation. Justice Moynihan, the finder of fact in the case, concluded that Meriam law and custom did not make provision for a communal title in the Meriam people as a whole.[9] As Brennan observed, Moynihan "found that there was apparently no concept of public or general community ownership among the people of Murray Island, all the land of Murray Island being regarded as belonging to individuals or groups."[10] Nonetheless, the order of the High Court, which Brennan said was a declaration of "the native communal title of the Meriam people,"[11] provided "that the Meriam people are entitled as against the whole world to possession, occupation, use and enjoyment of the lands of the Murray Islands."[12] Because Meriam laws and customs did not make provision for the communal title declared by the High Court, they could not be the source of that title. Thus, the explanation for the court's order must be found in Brennan's observation that "the ownership of land within a territory in the exclusive occupation of a people must be vested in that people: land is susceptible of ownership, and there are no other owners."[13] The source of the Meriam people's communal title was their exclusive occupation of the Murray Islands as a whole, albeit in accordance with laws and customs that provided for landholding by individuals and groups. But occupation is a matter of fact, not law.[14] For the factual occupation of the Meriam people as a community to be transformed into a legally enforceable communal title, a law or custom leading to that result would have to be applied. As Meriam laws and customs were found not to contain a concept of communal title based on occupation of the Murray Islands by the Meriam people, the order must have been based on the common law.[15] No other system of law appears to have been considered by the court in this context.[16]

By *sourcing* the Meriam people's land rights in their exclusive occupation, and apparently using the common law to give juridical effect to that occupation, the High Court was able to declare the *content* of their title to be an entitlement "as against the whole world to possession, occupation, use and enjoyment of the lands of the Murray Islands."[17] This description of the beneficial content of their interest is equivalent to the beneficial content of a common law fee simple estate arising from exclusive occupation of land.[18] Thus, it appears that the content as well as the source of their communal land rights vis-à-vis the rest of the world were derived from the common law, not from Meriam laws and customs, though the latter continued to operate internally to define the content of the land rights of individuals and groups within the Meriam community. However, the circumstances of the colonial context caused the court to create a common law property interest that is different from a common law fee simple estate in some respects. Although the title declared to exist in *Mabo* appears to be as extensive as a fee simple in duration and incidents, it differs from it in substantial ways: it is vested in a community rather than in individual persons or corporations, it is inalienable other than by surrender to the crown, and it is vulnerable to extinguishment by crown grant or appropriation.[19]

Regardless of the fact that the court's order in *Mabo* reveals that indigenous land rights based on exclusive occupation of land at the time of crown acquisition of sovereignty are neither sourced in nor defined by the indigenous people's traditional laws and customs, the High Court has virtually ignored this aspect of *Mabo* in subsequent decisions. Although the common law title approach on which the court's order in *Mabo* was apparently based does not appear to have been foreclosed by the court's subsequent decisions in *Wik Peoples v. Queensland*[20] and *Yanner v. Eaton*,[21] more recent decisions have relied exclusively on the traditional laws and customs of indigenous peoples for the source and content of their Native title. This narrowing of the options available to indigenous peoples for proving and defining their title has occurred in the context of the *Native Title Act 1993* (Cth), enacted after *Mabo* (and amended extensively in 1998) for the express purpose, among others, of providing for "the recognition and protection of native title."[22] In particular, the High Court has focused on section 223(1), which provides the following definition of Native title:

> The expression "native title" or "native title rights and interests" means the communal, group or individual rights and interests of Aboriginal peoples or Torres Strait Islanders in relation to land or waters, where: (a) the rights and interests are possessed under the traditional laws acknowledged, and the traditional customs observed, by the Aboriginal peoples or Torres Strait Islanders; and (b) the Aboriginal peoples or Torres Strait Islanders, by those laws and customs, have a connection with the land or waters; and (c) the rights and interests are recognized by the common law of Australia.

The exclusion from this statutory definition of the common law basis for indigenous land rights that appears to have been applied in *Mabo* has permitted the court to take the same exclusionary approach in the following judgments, to the detriment of the indigenous peoples of Australia.[23]

Fejo v. Northern Territory[24] arose from an application under the *Native Title Act 1993* for determination of Native title to lands and waters around Darwin and the Cox Peninsula. Six High Court judges delivered a joint judgment that upheld the extinguishment of Native title by crown grant of a fee simple estate.[25] In the course of their judgment, the justices stated that

> Native title has its origin in the traditional laws acknowledged and the customs observed by the Indigenous people who possess the native title. Native title is neither an institution of the common law nor a form of common law tenure but it is recognised by the common law. There is, therefore, an intersection of traditional laws and customs with the common law. The underlying existence of the traditional laws and customs is a necessary prerequisite for native title but their existence is not a sufficient basis for recognizing native title.[26]

In *Commonwealth v. Yarmirr*,[27] involving an application under the *Native Title Act 1993* for determination of Native title to the sea and seabed in the Croker Island region north of Arnhem Land in the Northern Territory, the majority quoted the above passage from *Fejo* and stated that "the relevant starting point is the question of fact posed by the Act: what are the rights and interests in relation to lands or waters which are possessed under the traditional laws acknowledged and the traditional customs observed by the relevant peoples?"[28]

This approach to Native title claims brought under the *Native Title Act 1993* was affirmed in *Western Australia v. Ward*,[29] in which Chief Justice Gleeson and Justices Gaudron, Gummow, and Hayne said that

> Paragraphs (a) and (b) of s 223(1) indicate that it is from the traditional laws and customs that native title rights and interests derive, not the common law. The common law is not the source of the relevant rights and interests; the role accorded to the common law by the statutory definition is that stated in para (c) of s 223(1). This is the "recognition" of rights and interests.[30]

The effect of this approach is that indigenous Australians – other than the Meriam people of the Murray Islands, it seems – are entitled only to the land rights and interests provided by their specific laws and customs at the time of crown acquisition of sovereignty in Australia.[31] This is a rigid application of the doctrine of continuity.[32] Chief Justice Gleeson and Justices Gummow and Hayne put it this way in *Members of the Yorta Yorta Community v. Victoria*: "What survived [the crown's acquisition of sovereignty] were rights and interests in relation to land or waters. Those rights and interests owed their origin to a normative system other than the legal system of the new sovereign power; they owed their origin to the traditional laws acknowledged and the traditional customs observed by the Indigenous peoples concerned."[33]

These justices also declared that "the normative or law-making system" that existed prior to crown sovereignty "could not thereafter validly create new rights, duties, or interests. Rights or interests in land created after sovereignty and which owed their origin and continued existence *only* to a normative system other than that of the new sovereign power, would not and will not be given effect by the legal order of the new sovereign."[34]

Moreover, the majority in *Yorta Yorta* held that an indigenous people who ceased to acknowledge and observe their traditional laws and customs in relation to land or waters, at any time after British acquisition of sovereignty, lost their Native title rights and interests because the continuing existence of those rights and interests depends on continuation of the laws and customs. Sourcing Native title in traditional laws and customs can thus have a two-pronged negative impact for indigenous Australians: it can narrow the content of their rights and interests from the exclusive possession, occupation, use, and enjoyment found to exist in *Mabo* to more limited rights and interests defined by their traditional laws and customs, and it can facilitate the loss of their rights and interests through the disappearance of their traditional laws and customs as a result, for example, of cultural assimilation.[35]

The restrictive approach that the High Court has taken to the source and content of Native title on applications brought under the *Native Title Act 1993* raises an intriguing question: Given that this approach depends on the definition of Native title in section 223(1), can indigenous claimants avoid that definition by bringing a legal action outside the Act, such as an action for declaration of a common law title, that would acknowledge the existence of a title of the sort declared to exist in *Mabo*? Although nothing in the Act expressly prohibits this, it might be argued that, other statutory land rights aside, the definition in section 223(1) was intended to include all forms of indigenous land rights in Australia and so precluded the continued existence of rights not encompassed by the definition.

There are at least three reasons why this argument should fail. First, in the *Wik* case, Justice Drummond of the Federal Court decided that a claim to "Aboriginal and possessory title" filed before enactment of the *Native Title Act 1993* did not have to be converted into an application for determination of Native title under the Act, especially if there were aspects to the claim that did not fall within the Act's scope.[36] It was on this basis that the action proceeded, eventually leading to the High Court decision referred to above.[37] Second, if my point is correct that the Act's definition of Native title, as interpreted by the High Court, excludes the kind of title declared to exist in *Mabo*, then an important category of indigenous land rights would have been extinguished by statutory definition if no indigenous land claims could be brought outside the Act. Such a conclusion is inconsistent with general principles of statutory interpretation[38] and with the court's pronouncement that any statutory extinguishment of Native title has to be clear and plain.[39] It also runs counter to clear intentions of the Act itself: namely, to give effect to *Mabo* and protect Native title.[40] Finally, section 9 of the *Native Title Act 1993* states that "Part 15 contains definitions of certain expressions that are used in this Act." As section 223 is contained in Part 15, it appears that the definition was intended to apply to determinations of Native title under the Act, not outside it.[41] Thus, the disjuncture between the title declared to exist in *Mabo* and the judicially interpreted definition of Native title in the Act could be avoided by bringing actions for the declaration or protection of indigenous land rights outside the Act.[42]

The Supreme Court of Canada's Pronouncements on the Sources and Content of Indigenous Land Rights

In Canada, the leading case on indigenous land rights is *Delgamuukw v. British Columbia*,[43] decided by the Supreme Court in 1997. That decision contains both similarities to and differences from Justice Brennan's judgment in *Mabo* with respect to the sources and content of those rights. In the principal judgment, Chief Justice Lamer said that Aboriginal title is based on exclusive occupation of land at the time of crown assertion of sovereignty.[44] If exclusive occupation at that time is proven, then the Aboriginal people in question have a right of exclusive occupation and use that is not limited to their traditional uses of the land. Aboriginal laws can be used as evidence of exclusive occupation,[45] but the existence of Aboriginal title does not depend on those laws. It is derived instead from the juridical effect that the common law accords to exclusive occupation of land and thus is a form of common law title. Because Aboriginal title does not depend on Aboriginal law, it does not vary from one Aboriginal group to another except in one respect: Aboriginal title holders cannot use their land in ways that would be incompatible with the connection to the land relied on to establish their Aboriginal title.[46]

Apart from the limitation on use just mentioned, the Aboriginal title described by Lamer in *Delgamuukw* closely resembles the title declared to exist in *Mabo*. In both instances, exclusive indigenous land rights appear to arise from the juridical effect that the common law attributes to exclusive occupation. Both decisions acknowledged (at least implicitly) that traditional laws would govern landholding within an indigenous community, but in neither case was the communal title of the people as a whole derived from or defined by those laws.[47]

Although the *Delgamuukw* decision involved Aboriginal title, the Supreme Court has made clear that indigenous land rights are not limited to the rights of exclusive occupation and use that arise from that title. In situations where Aboriginal peoples do not prove exclusive occupation at the time of crown assertion of sovereignty, they may have site-specific rights to use certain lands for limited purposes, such as hunting or fishing. Lamer first articulated this concept of site-specific land rights in 1996 in *R. v. Adams*.[48] In *Delgamuukw*, he reaffirmed the distinction between Aboriginal title and site-specific rights.[49] However, the tests for the existence of each are not the same. Although Aboriginal title depends on exclusive occupation of land at the time of crown assertion of sovereignty, site-specific rights depend on practices, customs, or traditions integral to the distinctive cultures of Indian and Inuit peoples at the time of contact with Europeans.[50] In *R. v. Sappier* and *R. v. Gray*, the Supreme Court applied this test and decided that the Mi'kmaq and Maliseet peoples of New Brunswick have an Aboriginal right to harvest wood for domestic purposes, such as building houses and making furniture, on crown lands traditionally used by those peoples for these purposes.[51]

Although site-specific rights bear some resemblance to non-exclusive Native title rights in Australia, there are important differences. As we have seen, the Australian courts have decided that non-exclusive Native title rights are based on traditional laws and customs. Those rights are enforceable in common law courts through application of the doctrine of continuity. As a result, the relevant date for proof of those rights is the time of crown sovereignty, when the common law was received. By contrast, site-specific rights in Canada are not based on the enforceability of traditional laws and customs by common law courts by means of the doctrine of continuity. Rather, they are based more broadly on practices, customs, and traditions that could, but need not, have been followed as a result of rights and interests supported by legal norms arising within Aboriginal societies.[52] However, only those practices, customs, and traditions that were *integral* to the distinctive cultures of those societies qualify for common law enforcement as Aboriginal rights. The contact time frame for proof of these practices, customs, and traditions also reveals that what is being protected are distinctive aspects of Aboriginal societies, not legal rights and interests within them. This time frame does not work in the context of the doctrine of continuity, as only those rights and interests existing at the time of crown sovereignty could be continued through that doctrine's application.[53]

Given that neither exclusive Aboriginal title nor site-specific land rights are based on the continuation of rights and interests as they existed in Aboriginal legal systems prior to crown sovereignty, does the doctrine of continuity have any relevance to indigenous land rights in Canada? Although the Supreme Court has not relied directly on this doctrine in its development of the law of Aboriginal rights, it may do so in the future.[54] There are at least two reasons to think that this question may still be open to judicial consideration in appropriate circumstances.[55]

First, in *R. v. Powley*[56] the Supreme Court decided that the Métis can establish site-specific rights to hunt by proving practices, customs, and traditions integral to their distinctive culture (or cultures) post-contact, at the time that Europeans gained control over the region in question. Problematic as the court's creation of a third time frame for establishing Aboriginal rights in Canada may be,[57] the fact that the court did so reveals that it is willing to craft new approaches to Aboriginal rights to take account of circumstances not previously considered by it.

Second, in numerous cases, Canadian courts have upheld the validity of adoptions and marriages that have taken place in accordance with Aboriginal customary laws.[58] None of these cases has gone to the Supreme Court. Nonetheless, given the consistency and duration of these lower court decisions, and the importance of maintaining family relationships, it is very unlikely that the Supreme Court would overrule them. So far, however, it is unclear how these decisions fit into the court's jurisprudence on Aboriginal rights. The only case I am aware of that specifically addressed the issue is *Casimel v. Insurance Corporation of British Columbia*,[59] a unanimous 1993 decision of the BC Court of Appeal. In that case, the court held that an adoption in accordance with the customary law of the Stellaquo Band of the Carrier Nation was valid and conferred the status of parents on the adoptive mother and father so that they could recover parental survivor benefits under the *Insurance (Motor Vehicle) Act*.[60] In the course of his judgment, Justice Lambert referred to the Court of Appeal's earlier decision in *Delgamuukw v. British Columbia*,[61] where, he said, "all five judges who heard that appeal concluded that Aboriginal rights arose from such of the customs, traditions and practices of the Aboriginal people in question as formed an integral part of their distinctive culture at the time of assertion of sovereignty by the incoming power."[62] Applying that test to the customary adoption in question, Lambert concluded that "such a customary adoption was an integral part of the distinctive culture of the Stellaquo Band of the Carrier People ... and as such, gave rise to Aboriginal status rights that became recognized, affirmed and protected by the common law and under section 35 of the *Constitution Act, 1982*."[63]

Although we have seen that the Supreme Court took a somewhat different approach to Aboriginal title to land in the *Delgamuukw* appeal,[64] in *R. v. Van der Peet* the court nonetheless accepted the BC Court of Appeal's "integral to the distinctive culture" test (with the substitution of European contact for crown assertion of sovereignty) in relation to other Aboriginal rights.[65] Recognition of Aboriginal customs in relation to adoption and marriage through application of that test may, however, go beyond a strict application of the doctrine of continuity, as what is being recognized is not just the continuity of *rights* in existence at the time of crown sovereignty, but also the continuation of Aboriginal *customs* that can give rise to new "status rights" (as Lambert called them in *Casimel*).[66] Moreover, as the courts in the adoption and marriage cases have generally not required proof of the existence of these customs at the time of either contact or crown sovereignty, the decisions can be regarded as either endorsing yet another time frame or acknowledging limited authority to modify or create customs, which would seem to entail a right of self-government.[67] Nonetheless, given that courts have been willing to recognize customary adoptions and marriages that took place *after* crown assertion of sovereignty, it seems clear that they would recognize customary adoptions and marriages that took place *before* that time if the matter ever came up. As recognition of those pre-sovereignty adoptions and marriages would undoubtedly involve application of the doctrine of continuity, one would expect the doctrine to apply as well to other rights in existence at the time of crown sovereignty.[68]

As the *Casimel* decision predated the Supreme Court's decisions in both *Van der Peet* and *Delgamuukw*, and did not take account of the distinction between customs and rights, it is apparent that the courts still need to explain how the marriage and adoption cases relate to the Supreme Court's developing jurisprudence on Aboriginal rights. However, it is sufficient to make the point that there may be yet another category of indigenous land rights in Canada that is based not on exclusive occupation of land or site-specific practices, customs, or traditions integral to distinctive Aboriginal cultures, but on rights and interests in relation to land that existed in Aboriginal law at the time of crown sovereignty and continued thereafter.[69]

Comparative Analysis and Conclusions

The foregoing examination of leading decisions of the High Court of Australia and the Supreme Court of Canada on indigenous land rights has revealed three potential sources of these rights: (1) indigenous laws and customs; (2) exclusive occupation and the legal effect given to it by the common law; and (3) indigenous practices, customs, and traditions not dependent on rights and interests in indigenous legal systems. I will now assess the implications of each of these approaches for indigenous land rights.

Several reasons can be given why reliance on indigenous laws and customs as the source of land rights is appropriate in the right circumstances. This approach provides validation for indigenous legal systems by acknowledging their existence both before and after crown acquisition of sovereignty. It also provides the means for enforcement in common law courts of rights and interests arising from those systems. Moreover, this approach is consistent with long-standing principles of British imperial law and the international law of state succession.[70]

Nonetheless, reliance on indigenous laws and customs can also be problematic.[71] It obliges indigenous peoples to demonstrate in non-indigenous courts that their own legal systems provided them with rights and interests in relation to land prior to crown sovereignty. Apparently, it is not sufficient for them to prove that they engaged in land use practices, even if those practices were important or indeed essential to their ways of life. Instead, they have to show that their laws or customs gave them a "right" to engage in those practices or created an "interest" that provided them with some kind of entitlement to do so.[72]

The High Court seems to be aware of the injustice that can result if this standard of "legality" is placed too high. In *Yarmirr*, the joint judgment referred to Viscount Haldane's familiar, cautionary words in *Amodu Tijani v. Secretary, Southern Nigeria*,[73] in which his lordship said that "there is a tendency, operating at times unconsciously, to render [Native] title conceptually in terms which are appropriate only to systems which have grown up under English law. That tendency has to be held in check closely."[74] After pointing out that neither use of the word *title* nor reference to "rights and interests in relation to land or waters" in section 223(1) of the *Native Title Act 1993* should "be seen as necessarily requiring identification of the rights and interests as what the common law traditionally recognized as items of 'real property,'" or even what "the common law would traditionally identify as necessary or sufficient to constitute 'property,'" the joint judgment in *Yarmirr* continued:

> Nor is it necessary to identify a claimed right or interest as one which carries with it, or is supported by, some enforceable means of excluding from its enjoyment those who are not its holders. The reference to rights and interests enjoyed under traditional laws and customs invites attention to how (presumably as a matter of traditional law) breach of the right and interest might be dealt with, but it also invites attention to how (as a matter of custom) the right or interest is observed. The latter element of the inquiry seems directed more to identifying practices that are regarded as socially acceptable, rather than looking to whether the practices were supported or enforced through a system for the organized imposition of sanctions by the relevant community. Again, therefore, no a priori assumption can or should be made that the only kinds of rights and interests referred to in par (a) of s 223(1) are rights and interests that were supported by some communally organized and enforced system of sanctions.[75]

Although this passage reveals that the court is conscious of the cross-cultural difficulties inherent in identifying rights and interests in indigenous societies, it nonetheless appears that the traditional laws and customs must give rise to rights or interests that are in some sense normative. In *Yorta Yorta*, Chief Justice Gleeson and Justices Gummow and Hayne said this:

> When it is recognized that the subject matter of the inquiry is rights and interests (in fact rights and interests in relation to lands or waters) it is clear that the laws and customs in which those rights or interests find their origins must be laws and customs having a normative content and deriving, therefore, from a body of norms or a normative system – the body of norms or normative system that existed before sovereignty.[76]

The justices then raised the jurisprudential issue inherent in this inquiry:

> To speak of such rights and interests being possessed under, or rooted in, traditional law and traditional custom might provoke much jurisprudential debate about the difference between what HLA Hart referred to as "merely convergent habitual behaviour in a social group" and legal rules. The reference to traditional customs might invite debate about the difference between "moral obligation" and legal rules. A search for parallels between traditional law and traditional customs on the one hand and Austin's conception of a system of laws, as a body of commands or general orders backed by threats which are issued by a sovereign or subordinate in obedience to the sovereign,

may or may not be fruitful. Likewise, to search in traditional law and traditional customs for an identified, even an identifiable, rule of recognition which would distinguish between law on the one hand, and moral obligation or mere habitual behaviour on the other, may or may not be productive.

This last question may, however, be put aside when it is recalled that the Native Title Act refers to traditional laws acknowledged and traditional customs observed. Taken as a whole, that expression, with its use of "and" rather than "or," obviates any need to distinguish between what is a matter of traditional law and what is a matter of traditional custom. Nonetheless, because the subject of consideration is rights or interests, the rules that together constitute the traditional laws acknowledged and the traditional customs observed, and under which the rights or interests are said to be possessed, must be rules having normative content. Without that quality, there may be observable patterns of behaviour but not rights or interests in relation to land or waters.[77]

The distinction that the justices drew between laws and customs amounting to "rules having normative content" on the one hand, and "observable patterns of behaviour" on the other, reveals an apparent willingness to draw a line between behaviour engaged in as a right, or at least out of moral obligation, and behaviour that is merely routine.[78] This distinction puts indigenous claimants in the difficult position of having to prove to the satisfaction of non-indigenous judges that their pre-crown sovereignty connections with and uses of the land had normative bases, and hands judges the awkward task of determining whether those underpinnings were sufficiently normative to give rise to enforceable rights and interests. Linguistic differences obviously exacerbate these difficulties, as the concepts of one culture often cannot be adequately expressed or described in the language of a different culture.[79]

These cultural, jurisprudential, and linguistic difficulties obviously give rise to serious problems of proof. Such problems are exacerbated because indigenous Australians, in addition to being required to prove that they had laws and customs at the time of crown acquisition of sovereignty that gave rise to specific rights and interests in relation to land, have to show that their rights and interests have been maintained through retention of their laws and customs up to the present.[80] Given that they did not keep written records, these requirements place an intolerable burden of proof on them, making it difficult for them to establish land rights in this way.[81] Although this burden could be reduced somewhat by relying on presumptions similar to those available to non-indigenous claimants in analogous circumstances,[82] and perhaps by developing specific presumptions for the unique circumstances of indigenous peoples, the application of presumptions in the context of proof of indigenous rights has just begun to receive judicial attention.[83]

Reliance on indigenous laws and customs and the doctrine of continuity entails another risk: namely, freezing indigenous rights in the pre-colonial past. As we have seen, a strict application of the doctrine of continuity means that only those rights and interests in existence at the time of crown acquisition of sovereignty would qualify for post-sovereignty recognition by the common law.[84] Even though the indigenous laws and customs supporting those rights and interests would have to continue to the extent necessary for their maintenance, the doctrine of continuity would have to be modified to permit *new* rights and interests to be created under those laws and customs after sovereignty. Moreover, for the laws and customs themselves to change so that indigenous societies could adapt to changing circumstances, including the dramatic changes caused by the impact of British colonization, some degree of internal self-government would have to be accorded to indigenous peoples.[85] Unfortunately, courts in Australia in particular have been reluctant to acknowledge any post-colonization rights of self-government.[86]

Despite these problems, I think that indigenous peoples should have the option of basing their land rights on their own laws and customs and the doctrine of continuity. This option would provide them with a legal basis for their rights equivalent to that enjoyed by other peoples who were brought under the sovereignty of the crown, such as the French Canadians.[87] In Canada, it would also provide an alternative to the *Van der Peet* approach of proving practices, customs, and traditions that were integral to their distinctive cultures at the time of European contact. If the rights and interests existed as such under their legal systems, then there should be no reason to impose an additional requirement that those rights and interests be integral to their distinctive cultures. Moreover, the time frame for proof of the rights would be the time of crown sovereignty rather than European contact.[88]

Turning to the second option, where indigenous peoples were in exclusive occupation of land at the time of crown acquisition of sovereignty, they should have a common law title of the kind that was declared to exist in *Mabo* and described in *Delgamuukw*. Since this title is based on the legal effect given to exclusive occupation by the common law, it should not vary from one group to another, regardless of the content of their own laws and customs. It should always amount to a right "against the whole world to possession, occupation, use and enjoyment" (as the court declared in *Mabo*)[89] or "to exclusive use and occupation ... for a variety of purposes, which need not be aspects of those aboriginal practices, customs and traditions which are integral to distinctive aboriginal cultures" (as Chief Justice Lamer said in *Delgamuukw*).[90]

These expressions of the meaning of indigenous title to land by the High Court and the Supreme Court amount to essentially the same thing. This title is equivalent to a fee simple estate in the sense that it encompasses the entire beneficial interest in the land, including the surface, subsurface, and airspace, for a potentially unlimited period of time.[91] But it has certain *sui generis* aspects arising from the unique circumstances of the indigenous peoples, as detailed by Lamer in *Delgamuukw*: it originates from exclusive occupation at the time of crown acquisition of sovereignty; it is inalienable other than by surrender to the crown (or, I would argue, transfer to other indigenous groups);[92] and it is communal.[93] In Canada, unlike in Australia, the Supreme Court has also said that there is an inherent limit on this title that prevents the lands from being used in ways that are incompatible with the indigenous attachment to the land on which the title is based.[94] However, this limit is supported neither by the common law relating to possessory titles nor by the *Mabo* decision. Moreover, it can be regarded both as paternalistic and as an unnecessary impediment to economic development that would be in the interests of the indigenous peoples who hold the title.[95]

The third option is to base indigenous land rights on the practices, customs, and traditions of the indigenous peoples, as the Supreme Court did in *Van der Peet*.[96] This approach has a place where neither exclusive occupation of land nor indigenous laws or normative customs in relation to the claimed land uses can be shown. The main advantage is therefore evidential: it allows for proof of indigenous land rights in situations where the first two approaches might not. However, by limiting these rights to matters integral to the distinctive cultures of the indigenous peoples, the Supreme Court has restricted their scope in a way that seems to relate more to their constitutional status than to the source of these rights in indigenous ways of life.[97] If the intention is to preserve the cultures and livelihoods of indigenous peoples,[98] then it is hard to understand why there should be a distinction, as Lamer has held, between "integral" and "incidental" aspects of indigenous cultures.[99] Moreover, one can question the capacity of judges to distinguish between aspects of indigenous cultures that were important enough to be integral and aspects that were not.[100] The European contact time frame for proof is also problematic, as it appears to be based on the view that the only truly "Aboriginal" aspects of indigenous cultures are those features that existed prior to European influence.[101] But shorn of these objectionable features, there is a place for an approach that bases land rights on indigenous practices and non-legal customs and traditions. The goal here would be the preservation of aspects of indigenous cultures and livelihoods that are not adequately protected by either indigenous laws and normative customs or common law title based on exclusive occupation.[102]

Depending on the circumstances, indigenous peoples in Australia and Canada should therefore be able to rely on any or all of the three options described above. For example, in asserting a right to fish in a particular location, they should be able to rely on one or more of the following: (1) rights or interests derived from their own laws and normative customs that continued after crown acquisition of sovereignty; (2) pre-crown sovereignty practices, non-legal customs, or traditions that gave them a site-specific right to fish at the place in question; (3) common law title derived from exclusive occupation of the land where the fishing took place at the time of crown sovereignty.[103] This is in keeping with common law practice, whereby a person who claims a right in relation to land can generally rely on any potential source of the right, either exclusively or in the alternative.[104] The range of options would also serve to alleviate some of the evidential burden faced by indigenous peoples, so that fewer legitimate claims are rejected for lack of adequate proof.

The content of the right to fish would then depend on the right's source. If the right was based on indigenous laws or normative customs, the dimensions of the right would be defined by those laws and customs. If it was based on practices, non-legal customs, or traditions, then the content of the right would be determined by the nature of the practice, custom, or tradition. Finally, if the right was based on common law title, then it would be a right encompassed by (but not separate from) the broader right of exclusive occupation, possession, enjoyment, and use of the land that flowed from that title.

Outlining the range of options in this way still does not resolve the "frozen rights" problem that arises from specifying a moment in time when the rights become enforceable in common law courts. Whatever the source of indigenous land rights, in my opinion the appropriate time for determining their existence is the date of crown acquisition of sovereignty. In the case of rights based on indigenous laws and normative customs, the reason for accepting this date is that the doctrine of continuity applies at that time to continue under crown sovereignty the rights and interests that were already in existence in indigenous societies. Where rights based on indigenous practices, non-legal customs, or traditions are concerned, these rights did not exist as such under indigenous legal systems. They arise at common law, which applies in this context at the time of crown acquisition of sovereignty.[105] Finally, common law title arises at the time of crown sovereignty because this is when the title vests as a burden on the underlying title acquired at the same moment by the crown.[106] However, acceptance of crown acquisition of sovereignty as the appropriate date for initially determining indigenous land rights does not necessarily entail acceptance of standard views of when this might have occurred in any particular part of Australia or Canada. Although I cannot pursue the matter here, my view is that the crown could not have acquired sovereignty over territories occupied by indigenous peoples, either in imperial British law or in international law,

until it either received a cession of sovereignty from them or effectively occupied the territory in question.[107]

But does acceptance of acquisition of crown sovereignty as the date for
determining the existence of indigenous land rights mean that those rights
are frozen as of that date? I think that the answer depends in part on which
of the three potential sources is relied on and in part on whether one is
considering the external or internal dimensions of the rights. By "external
dimensions," I mean the scope of the communal rights held by the indigenous community vis-à-vis the rest of the world, including the crown. By
"internal dimensions," I mean the manner in which the rights are distributed among and enjoyed by the members of the indigenous community
themselves.

If indigenous laws and normative customs are the source of the rights in
question, the content of the rights vis-à-vis the rest of the world would be
determined by those laws and customs. To continue the example used above,
let us assume that an indigenous community in Canada proved that, at the
time of crown sovereignty, they had an exclusive right under their laws and
customs to take fish from a certain lake for whatever purpose they, as a community, deemed appropriate. That would be the scope of their right exter-
nally. They would not be able to take beaver from the lake, or harvest wild
rice there, unless they proved a separate right to do so at the time of crown
sovereignty. Moreover, they would not be able to change their laws and
customs after that time to give themselves rights to other resources in the
lake.[108] Accordingly, it appears that the external dimensions of their rights
would be frozen at the time of crown sovereignty. However, their own laws
and customs would also apply internally to determine which members of
the community could take fish, what those fish could be used for, how they
would be distributed within the community, and so on. There does not appear to be any reason why the internal dimensions of their exclusive right
to take fish should be fixed at the time of crown sovereignty. Indeed, freezing the internal dimensions of their right in this way could have serious
consequences for the community because it would prevent them from
changing their laws and customs to meet changing conditions, such as the
availability of fish in the lake and the current needs of the community.
Acknowledging the authority of the indigenous community to alter their
laws and customs after crown sovereignty so as to change the internal dimensions of their right to take fish from the lake necessarily involves recognition of a right of self-government in relation to this right.[109]

Moving on to the second potential source, if the same indigenous community proved in the alternative that they had an exclusive right to take
fish from the lake for any purpose they deemed appropriate because that
was their practice, non-legal custom, or tradition at the time of crown sovereignty, then the content of the right would similarly be determined by the

extent of that practice, custom, or tradition.[110] As in the case of a fishing right based on indigenous laws and normative customs, the external dimensions of this right would also seem to be frozen as of the time of Crown sovereignty, and so could not be changed to include other resources that might be found in the lake. But given the right's communal nature, the community would still have to make decisions about how the right is exercised by members. For this reason, the internal dimensions of the right, or at least of its exercise, would not be fixed at the time of crown sovereignty. From one perspective, it may be more difficult in theory to conceive of this decision-making authority as governmental because it would not involve changing pre-existing indigenous laws and normative customs. Nonetheless, as the existence of a communal right seems to necessitate a community structure and a decision-making process to regulate exercise of the right by community members, self-government appears to be a logical and practical consequence in this context as well.[111]

Finally, let us consider the result if the indigenous community proved that they had common law title because they were in exclusive occupation, at the time of crown sovereignty, of land that encompassed the lake. Their right vis-à-vis the rest of the world would be an exclusive right of occupation, possession, use, and enjoyment of that land, including the lake. They would have an exclusive right not only to take fish but also to harvest any other resources, such as beaver and wild rice, that the lake might contain.[112] The external dimensions of the right would be frozen, but given its exclusive and all-encompassing scope this would not be a serious limitation. The internal dimensions of their right would be a matter for the community to determine from time to time through an ongoing decision-making process, in accordance with their own culture and their current priorities and needs. In this situation, their governmental authority would include, but not be limited to, regulating fishing in the lake by community members. Given their exclusive right to occupation, possession, use, and enjoyment of all the land exclusively occupied by them at the time of crown sovereignty, and the communal nature of this entitlement, they would have general governance authority in relation to the land and its use.[113]

It therefore appears that, whichever of the three approaches is used, the external dimensions of the land rights in question would be limited to the content of those rights at the time of crown acquisition of sovereignty. Within the community, however, the rights would be dynamic in that they could be changed through exercise of the decision-making authority vested in the community. This authority is governmental in nature because it is either a continuation of the community's authority to make laws and normative customs for members or a necessary consequence of the communal nature of their land rights. So, although the source of the rights determines their content as against the rest of the world, it does not determine their internal dimensions. Within the community, the dimensions of the rights depend on the decisions made from time to time by the community through exercise of their powers of self-government.

Acknowledgments

I would like to thank David Yarrow for his very helpful comments on a draft of this chapter and the Social Sciences and Humanities Council of Canada and the Killam Trusts for supporting this research. I would also like to point out that the analysis here is presented within the confines of the case law on indigenous rights in Australia and Canada. This does not mean that I endorse these confines, as I have argued elsewhere that a more expansive approach should be taken, starting from the premise that indigenous land rights are rights to territory that include both property and jurisdiction. See, e.g., "Aboriginal Rights in Canada: From Title to Land to Territorial Sovereignty," *Tulsa Journal of Comparative and International Law* 5 (1998): 253-98 at 291-98, reprinted in McNeil, *Emerging Justice?*, 58-101 at 95-101, and "The Post-*Delgamuukw* Nature and Content of Aboriginal Title," also in McNeil, *Emerging Justice?*, 102-35.

Notes

1 (1888) 14 App. Cas. 46 (P.C.) [*St. Catherine's Milling*]. The proclamation is reproduced in R.S.C. 1985, App. II, No. 1.
2 (1992) 175 C.L.R. 1 [*Mabo*].
3 See *Milirrpum v. Nabalco Pty. Ltd.* (1971), 17 F.L.R. 141 (N.T.S.C.).
4 *Mabo*, 58; see also per Deane and Gaudron JJ at 87-88, 110; cf. per Toohey J, especially at 187-92.
5 Ibid., 51; see also per Deane and Gaudron JJ at 86, Toohey J at 184-92, 194-95, 207-14. Although Brennan J's use of the word *right* in the part of this passage stating that "a community which asserts and asserts effectively that none but its members has any right to occupy or use the land" might be taken to mean that the possession must have been pursuant to a system of traditional laws and customs that acknowledged such a right, this interpretation is inconsistent with the order of the court because there was no evidence of such a communal right in Meriam law and custom. See notes 9-16 below and accompanying text.
6 Ibid., 51-52; see also 61-62.
7 See also ibid., per Toohey J at 206-14.
8 See Pearson, "Concept of Native Title at Common Law," 150-62 at 154; and Pearson, "Principles of Communal Native Title."
9 See *Eddie Mabo et al. v. The State of Queensland,* Determination Pursuant to Reference of 27 February 1986 by the High Court of Australia to the Supreme Court of Queensland to hear and determine all issues of fact raised by the pleadings, particulars, and further particulars in High Court Action B12 of 1982 ["Factual Findings in *Mabo*"]. I am grateful to Margaret Stephenson for providing me with a copy of these findings of fact.
10 *Mabo*, 22; see "Factual Findings in *Mabo*," ch. 9, especially 9. See also per Toohey J in *Mabo* at 191, where he observed that "the findings of Moynihan J. do not allow the articulation of a precise set of rules."
11 *Mabo*, 75.
12 Ibid., 217. See also Grattan and McNamara, "The Common Law Construct of Native Title," 50-85 at 70. Note that the order excluded certain lands for reasons not relevant to the issues discussed in this chapter.
13 *Mabo*, 51.
14 See McNeil, *Common Law Aboriginal Title,* 7, 197; and Pollock and Wright, *Possession in the Common Law,* 10-16.
15 In fact, the common law of England does not provide for *communal* title either, as unincorporated communities lack the legal capacity to hold property. But in Canada, at least, this has not prevented the Supreme Court from deciding that Aboriginal title can be vested in Aboriginal groups as communities. See *Delgamuukw v. British Columbia,* [1997] 3 S.C.R. 1010

at para. 115 (Lamer CJ) [*Delgamuukw*]; and discussion in McNeil, "The Post-*Delgamuukw* Nature and Content of Aboriginal Title," in McNeil, *Emerging Justice?*, 102-35 at 122-27. The High Court in *Mabo* was similarly able to modify *the common law* to provide the Meriam people with a communal title. The court would not, however, have had the authority to create a communal title *in Meriam law* where no such title existed.

16 Potentially, international law might be applicable, but nothing in the *Mabo* judgments suggests that the court was relying on international law in this context. Nor does the court appear to have applied norms derived from natural law.

17 *Mabo*, 217.

18 See McNeil, *Common Law Aboriginal Title*, 6-78.

19 For a critique of the court's views on extinguishment, see McNeil, "Racial Discrimination," 357-408.

20 (1996) 141 A.L.R. 129 [*Wik*].

21 (1999) 166 A.L.R. 258 [*Yanner*]. For discussion of this aspect of these decisions, see McNeil, "Relevance of Traditional Laws and Customs" in McNeil, *Emerging Justice?*, 416-63 at 423-32. Significantly, neither of these decisions involved an application for determination of Native title under the *Native Title Act 1993*: *Wik* was initiated before the Act came into force (though a parallel claim was subsequently brought under the Act), and *Yanner* involved a prosecution for taking crocodiles in violation of the *Fauna Conservation Act 1974* (Qld). However, the *Yanner* decision did involve the application of s. 211 of the *Native Title Act*, which shields certain Native title rights, such as non-commercial hunting and fishing, from some Commonwealth, state, and territorial laws.

22 S. 3(a).

23 Noel Pearson has argued that the High Court, by equating Native title with specific rights and interests arising under traditional laws and customs, has misinterpreted s. 223(1). See Pearson, "The High Court's Abandonment," 1-31; Pearson, "Land Is Susceptible of Ownership,"; and Pearson, "Where We've Come from," 1-17 at 12-14. See also the judgment of McHugh J in *Members of the Yorta Yorta Community v. Victoria* (2002), 194 A.L.R. 538 (H.C.A.) at paras. 129-34 [*Yorta Yorta*].

   I am more inclined to think that the drafters of the Act misinterpreted *Mabo* because they ignored the fact that there was no basis in Meriam laws and customs for the communal Native title that the court declared to exist on the Murray Islands (see text accompanying notes 9-16), with the result that they mistakenly limited the definition in s. 223(1) to rights and interests possessed under traditional laws and customs. I find support for this view in the fact that Richard H. Bartlett, a leading commentator on Native title, provided just such an assessment of the relationship between *Mabo* and s. 223(1) in *Native Title in Australia*, 215: "The language of the Justices [in *Mabo*] indicated that the determination of the content of native Indigenous title required an inquiry as to traditional laws and customs. Brennan J.'s formulation was codified in the Native Title Act 1993 s. 223(1)(a)." But whether the fault lies with the High Court or the Commonwealth Parliament, I agree with Pearson that s. 223(1), as interpreted by the court, has had a very negative impact on the land rights of indigenous Australians.

24 (1998) 195 C.L.R. 96 [*Fejo*].

25 Kirby J wrote a concurring judgment. For critical commentary, see McNeil, "The Vulnerability of Indigenous Land Rights," 271-301 at 278-81.

26 *Fejo*, 128 [footnotes omitted].

27 (2001) 208 C.L.R. 1.

28 Ibid., para. 15.

29 (2002) 191 A.L.R. 1 [*Ward*].

30 Ibid., para. 20. See also *Yorta Yorta*, paras. 74-76.

31 Australian courts have so far refused to accept the continuation of rights not related to land. For example, in *Walker v. New South Wales* (1994), 182 C.L.R. 45 (H.C.A.), Mason CJ denied that traditional laws and customs relating to criminal matters had any application after crown acquisition of sovereignty.

32 Compare the more flexible approach taken by the New Zealand Court of Appeal in *Attorney-General v. Ngati Apa*, [2003] 3 N.Z.L.R. 643, where the court said that the tikanga Māori on

which Māori land rights are based includes practice and usage as well as custom. See McNeil, "Legal Rights and Legislative Wrongs," 83-118 at 87-89.

33 *Yorta Yorta*, para. 37. Although acknowledging that some alteration of traditional laws and customs could occur after crown sovereignty, Gleeson CJ, Gummow J, and Hayne J denied that the possibility of alteration entailed any lawmaking authority. Ibid., para. 44. See Highland, "The Mote in the Common Law's Eye."

34 *Yorta Yorta*, para. 43.

35 According to the High Court, once lost in this way these rights and interests cannot be revived. Ibid., paras. 87-89. For critical commentary, see Young, *Trouble with Tradition*.

36 *Wik Peoples v. Queensland* (1994), 120 A.L.R. 465 (F.C.). I am grateful to David Yarrow for bringing this trial court decision to my attention.

37 *Wik*.

38 Two principles are applicable here. First, statutes are to be interpreted, if at all possible, so as not to interfere with vested rights, especially property rights. See Gifford, *Statutory Interpretation*, 180-81; Pearce and Geddes, *Statutory Interpretation in Australia*, 106-7; and Sullivan, *Driedger on the Construction of Statutes*, 370-76. Second, definitions in statutes should not be given substantive effect. See Edgar, *Craies on Statute Law*, 213; and Evans, *Statutory Interpretation*, 52.

39 *Mabo*, 64 (Brennan J); *Western Australia v. Commonwealth* (1995), 183 C.L.R. 373 at 423 [*Western Australia*]; *Ward*, paras. 74-78.

40 See *Native Title Act 1993* (Cth), Preamble and s. 3(a). See also Pearson, "High Court's Abandonment"; and *Western Australia*.

41 This interpretation is consistent as well with the principle that statutes are to be interpreted, if at all possible, so as not to oust the jurisdiction of the courts (in this context, the courts' jurisdiction to entertain actions based on the common law). See Bennion, *Statutory Interpretation*, 74-76; and Edgar, *Craies on Statute Law*, 122-24. As pointed out by these authors, some judges have gone even further and said that a statutory intention to limit the jurisdiction of the courts must be express.

42 For such actions to succeed, judges would probably have to be convinced that the definition of Native title in s. 223(1) does not encompass the kind of title declared to exist in *Mabo*. This might be difficult, especially given the following passage from the judgment of Gleeson CJ, Gummow J, and Hayne J in *Yorta Yorta*, para. 75:

> Native title is not a creature of the common law, whether the Imperial common law as that existed at the time of sovereignty and first settlement, or the Australian common law as it exists today. Native title, for present purposes, is what is defined and described in s. 223(1) of the *Native Title Act*. *Mabo (No 2)* decided that certain rights and interests relating to land, and rooted in traditional law and custom, survived the Crown's acquisition of sovereignty and radical title in Australia. It was this native title that was then "recognized and protected" in accordance with the *Native Title Act* and which, thereafter, was not able to be extinguished contrary to that Act. [footnotes omitted]

It is apparent from this passage that the justices regarded the definition of Native title in the Act to be the same as the concept of Native title described in *Mabo*. However, the inconsistency between the definition in the Act and the title actually declared to exist in *Mabo* remains unexplained by the High Court.

43 Unlike in Australia, however, earlier decisions in Canada acknowledged the existence of indigenous land rights. See *Calder v. Attorney-General of British Columbia*, [1973] S.C.R. 313; *Guerin v. The Queen*, [1984] 2 S.C.R. 335; and *St. Catherine's Milling*.

44 In *Delgamuukw*, para. 145, Lamer CJ accepted that assertion of sovereignty had occurred in British Columbia in 1846 at the time of the *Oregon Boundary Treaty* between Britain and the United States. See also *Tsilhqot'in Nation v. British Columbia*, [2008] 1 C.N.L.R. 112 (B.C.S.C.) at paras. 585-602.

45 Cf. *R. v. Marshall; R. v. Bernard*, [2005] 2 S.C.R. 220 [*Marshall/Bernard*], where the majority appears to have downplayed the role of indigenous law in this context. For critical commentary, see McNeil, "Aboriginal Title and the Supreme Court."

46 *Delgamuukw,* paras. 125-32. See Slattery, "Making Sense of Aboriginal and Treaty Rights," 196-224 at 212; and Slattery, "A Taxonomy of Aboriginal Rights," 111-28 at 118.

47 *Delgamuukw* is clearer on this than *Mabo.* One interpretation of the latter case is that, though the content of indigenous land rights does not depend on indigenous laws and customs, it is exclusive occupation under those laws and customs that gives rise to those rights. See Pearson, "Land Is Susceptible of Ownership."

48 [1996] 3 S.C.R. 101 [*Adams*].

49 *Delgamuukw,* para. 138. See also *Marshall/Bernard.*

50 *R. v. Van der Peet,* [1996] 2 S.C.R. 507 [*Van der Peet*]. For Métis, the time frame is different: see the text accompanying notes 56-57.

51 *R. v. Sappier; R. v. Gray,* [2006] 2 S.C.R. 686 [*Sappier/Gray*].

52 See *Delgamuukw,* para. 148 (Lamer CJ).

53 See McNeil and Yarrow, "Constitutional Recognition," 177-212 at 204-6.

54 Significantly, McLachlin J (now CJ) relied on the doctrine of continuity as a means of identifying Aboriginal rights in her dissenting opinion in *Van der Peet,* paras. 261-69. See also McNeil and Yarrow, "Constitutional Recognition," 204-11, for evidence of further reliance on the doctrine of continuity in Canada.

55 The doctrine of continuity is an established feature of both British imperial and international law. See Barsh, "Indigenous Rights and the *Lex Loci,*" 91-126; McNeil, *Common Law Aboriginal Title,* 161-92; O'Connell, *State Succession,* vol. 1, 237-68; and Walters, "'Golden Thread' of Continuity," 711-52.

56 [2003] 2 S.C.R. 207.

57 See McNeil and Yarrow, "Constitutional Recognition," 202; and Slattery, "Making Sense of Aboriginal and Treaty Rights," 217-18.

58 E.g., see *Connolly v. Woolrich* (1867), 17 R.J.R.Q. 75 (Que. S.C.), affirmed sub nom. *Johnstone v. Connolly* (1869), 17 R.J.R.Q. 266 (Que. Q.B.); *R. v. Nan-E-Quis-A-Ka* (1889), 1 T.L.R. 211 (N.W.T.S.C.); *R. v. Bear's Shin Bone* (1899), 4 T.L.R. 173 (N.W.T.S.C.); *R. v. Williams* (1921), 30 B.C.R. 303 (B.C.S.C.); *Re Noah Estate* (1961), 32 D.L.R. (2d) 185 (N.W.T.T.C.); *Re Adoption of Katie* (1961), 32 D.L.R. (2d) 686 (N.W.T.T.C.); *Re Beaulieu's Adoption Petition* (1969), 3 D.L.R. (3d) 479 (N.W.T.T.C.); *Re Deborah* (1972), 5 W.W.R. 203 (N.W.T.C.A.); *Re Wah-Shee* (1975), 57 D.L.R. (3d) 743 (N.W.T.S.C.); *Deer v. Okpik,* [1980] 4 C.N.L.R. 93 (Que. S.C.); *B.C. Birth Registration No. 1994-09-040399 (Re),* [1998] 4 C.N.L.R. 7 (B.C.S.C.). For discussion of the older cases, see Norman K. Zlotkin, "Judicial Recognition of Aboriginal Customary Law in Canada: Selected Marriage and Adoption Cases," *Canadian Native Law Reporter* 4 (1984): 1-17.

59 [1994] 2 C.N.L.R. 22 [*Casimel*]. In *Re Tagornak Adoption Petition,* [1984] 1 C.N.L.R. 185 (N.W.T.S.C.), Marshall J relied on s. 35(1) of the *Constitution Act, 1982,* to support his declaration of a customary adoption, but did not explain how the adoption related to Aboriginal rights.

60 R.S.B.C. 1979, c. 204.

61 [1993] 5 C.N.L.R. 1.

62 *Casimel,* 25.

63 Ibid., 32.

64 See the text accompanying notes 43-46.

65 See note 50 and accompanying text.

66 Cf. the quotations from *Yorta Yorta* accompanying notes 33-34.

67 See *Hineiti Rirerire Arani v. Public Trustee of New Zealand,* [1920] A.C. 198 (P.C.) at 204-5, where Lord Phillimore observed in relation to Māori customary adoptions that

> It may well be that ... the Maori as a race may have some internal power of self-government enabling the tribe or tribes by common consent to modify their customs, and that the custom of such a race is not to be put on a level with the custom of an English borough or other local area which must stand as it always has stood, seeing that there is no quasi-legislative internal authority which can modify it.

See also *Campbell v. British Columbia,* [2000] 4 C.N.L.R. 1 (B.C.S.C.) at paras. 97-104 (*Campbell*). For discussion, see Walters, "'Golden Thread' of Continuity."

68 The doctrine of continuity has been applied to the rights of French Canadians that predated crown acquisition of sovereignty over French Canada. See *Drulard v. Welsh* (1906), 11 O.L.R. 647 (Ont. Div. Ct.), reversed on other grounds (1907), 14 O.L.R. 54 (C.A.).

69 See McNeil and Yarrow, "Constitutional Recognition," 207-11.

70 See note 55.

71 For detailed discussion, see Young, *Trouble with Tradition*.

72 E.g., see *Mason v. Tritton* (1994), 34 N.S.W.L.R. 572 (N.S.W.C.A.); *Derschaw, Clifton, and Murphy* (1996), 90 A. Crim. R. 9 (W.A.S.C.); *Dillon v. Davies* (1998), 156 A.L.R. 142 (Tas. S.C.), all of which denied the existence of a Native title right to fish because the practice of fishing had not been shown to be supported by traditional laws and customs. For critical discussion, see McNeil, "Relevance of Traditional Laws and Customs," 454-58.

73 [1921] 2 A.C. 399 (P.C.).

74 *Yarmirr*, para. 11, quoting ibid. at 403.

75 *Yarmirr*, paras. 12-13, 16. See also *Yorta Yorta*, paras. 39-40 (Gleeson CJ, Gummow and Hayne JJ).

76 *Yorta Yorta*, para. 38.

77 Ibid., paras. 41-42 [footnotes omitted]. The H.L.A. Hart quotations are from *The Concept of Law*, 10, 13. The other reference is to Austin, *Province of Jurisprudence*, 11.

78 This distinction appears as well in the cases cited in note 72.

79 See Wurm, "Aboriginal Languages and the Law," 1-10 at 10 (describing the reverse situation):

> Aborigine languages cannot as a rule be used to express the juristic ideas and principles involved in the operation of a white man's court of law, seeing that many of these ideas and principles are completely outside the aborigine's conceptual world, and no symbols can be available in any language for notions not forming part of the conceptual system, i.e., the culture, of its speakers.

For some linguists, the problem is even more fundamental because the very structure of a language is entwined with the worldview of a people. See Lucy, *Language Diversity and Thought*; Sapir, *Culture, Language, and Personality*, especially 160-66; and Whorf, *Language, Thought, and Reality*.

80 See *Yorta Yorta* and critical commentary in Young, *Trouble with Tradition*, especially 281-380. See also *Bodney v. Bennell*, [2008] F.C.A.F.C. 63.

81 In Canada, the Supreme Court has acknowledged these difficulties in relation to both Aboriginal rights in general and Aboriginal title to land in particular, and adapted the rules of evidence to make it easier to prove these rights through the use of oral histories. See *Van der Peet*, para. 68; and *Delgamuukw*, paras. 80-108.

82 Such as the presumption that a custom that has been shown to exist as far back as living memory extends has existed since time immemorial, which in England means since AD 1189. See McNeil, "Continuity of Aboriginal Rights," 127-50 at 139.

83 See *Gumana v. Northern Territory*, [2005] F.C.A. 50 at paras. 195-202; *Griffiths v. Northern Territory*, [2006] F.C.A. 903 at paras. 570-85. For further discussion, see McNeil, "The Onus of Proof," reprinted in McNeil, *Emerging Justice?*, 136-60.

84 See the text accompanying notes 34 and 66.

85 See the quotation from *Hineiti Rirerire Arani* in note 67.

86 Although the High Court in *Mabo* envisaged that change in traditional laws and customs could take place after sovereignty (see per Brennan J at 61, Deane and Gaudron JJ at 110), the implications of this for self-government seem to have been lost on the court. See *Walker*; *Coe v. Commonwealth* (1993), 68 A.L.J.R. 110; and *Thorpe v. Commonwealth (No. 3)* (1997), 71 A.L.J.R. 767. The High Court attempted to justify this in *Yorta Yorta*; see note 33.

87 See note 68.

88 See McNeil and Yarrow, "Constitutional Recognition," 203-11, where the constitutional status of these rights is also discussed.

89 217; see the text accompanying note 12.

90 Para. 117.

91 As in the case of other common law interests, this title would nonetheless be subject to common law restrictions, such as those imposed by the riparian rights of other landholders and the law of nuisance.

92 See *Delgamuukw,* para. 198 (La Forest J); and Kent McNeil, "Self-Government and the Inalienability of Aboriginal Title," *McGill Law Journal* 47 (2002): 473-510 at 501-2.

93 *Delgamuukw,* paras. 112-15. For discussion, see McNeil, "Post-*Delgamuukw.*"

94 *Delgamuukw,* paras. 125-32 (Lamer CJ).

95 See McNeil, "Post-*Delgamuukw,*" 116-22.

96 See text accompanying note 50.

97 See *Van der Peet,* paras. 15-32. For critical analysis, see McNeil and Yarrow, "Constitutional Recognition."

98 See, especially, *Sappier/Gray.*

99 *Van der Peet,* para. 70. Cf. McLachlin J's dissenting judgment at paras. 255-59.

100 See Barsh and Henderson, "The Supreme Court's *Van der Peet* Trilogy," 993-1009.

101 See *Van der Peet,* paras. 17-20, 60-62; cf. McLachlin and L'Heureux-Dubé JJ's dissenting judgments. See also Borrows, "Frozen Rights in Canada," 37-64; and McNeil and Yarrow, "Constitutional Recognition," 199-203.

102 For support for the argument that indigenous peoples have a right to a livelihood in accordance with their own ways of life, see Slattery, "Aboriginal Sovereignty and Imperial Claims," 681-703. International law also supports this position. For example, the *International Covenant on Civil and Political Rights* (1966), 999 U.N.T.S. 171 (in force 1976), provides in art. 1, s. 2, that "in no case may a people be deprived of its own means of subsistence."

103 In *Adams* and *R. v. Côté,* [1996] 3 S.C.R. 139 [*Côté*], the Supreme Court held that a site-specific right can be established without proving the occupation necessary for Aboriginal title. See also *Sappier/Gray.* However, as discussed above, the court has not yet considered whether indigenous land rights can also be based on indigenous laws and customs and the doctrine of continuity. See text accompanying notes 48-69.

104 E.g., a person defending his or her possession against someone claiming a better right to possession can rely on (1) the possessory title that everyone in possession of land has; (2) the presumption of title arising from possession; and/or (3) a title by inheritance, purchase, or gift. See McNeil, *Common Law Aboriginal Title,* 6-78.

105 In the parts of Canada acquired by conquest and cession from France, the common law did not apply to private, civil matters involving the French inhabitants until it was introduced, as those matters continued to be governed by French law. However, it appears that from the moment of crown acquisition of sovereignty the rights of indigenous peoples in Canada were determined by English, not French, law. See *Adams*; and *Côté.*

106 See *Delgamuukw,* para. 145 (Lamer CJ); and McNeil, *Common Law Aboriginal Title,* 196-221. Acquisition of crown sovereignty appears to be the time for determining the existence of common law title in the parts of Canada acquired from France as well. See *R. v. Bernard,* [2003] 4 C.N.L.R. 48 (N.B.C.A.); *R. v. Marshall,* [2004] 1 C.N.L.R. 211 (N.S.C.A.); and *Marshall/ Bernard,* para. 71.

107 Regarding Canada, see McNeil, "Aboriginal Nations and Quebec's Boundaries: Canada Couldn't Give What It Didn't Have," in McNeil, *Emerging Justice?,* 1-24; McNeil, "Negotiated Sovereignty," 35-55; and McNeil, "Sovereignty and the Aboriginal Nations of Rupert's Land," 2-8. Note too that using effective occupation (which in this context really means effective exercise of jurisdiction) as the date of crown sovereignty might also help to resolve the dilemma of the land rights of the Métis, as their emergence as a distinct people (or peoples) probably predated effective crown exercise of jurisdiction in most, if not all, regions of what is now Canada. For example, see *Powley.*

108 If they had no rights to these other resources under their own laws and customs, then entitlement would be determined from the time of Crown sovereignty by the common law and legislation applicable in the jurisdiction where the lake is located. The common law, for example, provides generally that the first person (as long as he or she is not a trespasser) to kill or capture a wild animal acquires the property in it. If an indigenous community could create a new law after crown acquisition of sovereignty, giving themselves an exclusive

right to take beaver, for example, from the lake, then doing so would infringe the common law rights of others to take beaver. No doubt the authority of the indigenous community to take away rights of others in this way would be questionable.

109 To date, the strongest support for such a right in Canadian jurisprudence can be found in *Campbell*, where Williamson J upheld the self-government provisions in the Nisga'a Treaty (1998), in part because he decided that the decision-making authority that the Nisga'a have over their communal land rights is governmental in nature. Williamson J relied on Lamer CJ's observation in *Delgamuukw*, para. 115, that the indigenous peoples of Canada have this decision-making authority. See also *R. v. Marshall*, [1999] 3 S.C.R. 533 at para. 17, where the court held that indigenous communities also have authority over their treaty rights to fish, apparently including authority to control fishing by their members. For detailed discussion, see McNeil, "Judicial Approaches to Self-Government since *Calder*," 129-52.

110 For examples (though using the date of European contact rather than sovereignty), see *Adams; Côté; Sappier/Gray;* and *R. v. Gladstone*, [1996] 2 S.C.R. 723.

111 For further discussion, see McNeil, "Aboriginal Rights in Canada," reprinted in McNeil, *Emerging Justice?*, 58-101 at 89-95; and McNeil, "Judicial Approaches to Self-Government," especially 139-43.

112 At common law, a person who has title to land encompassing a non-tidal body of water has title to its bed and to plants growing in it, as well as an exclusive right to take game and fish from it.

113 See the cases cited in note 109. However, in Canada the inherent limit placed on use of Aboriginal title lands by Lamer CJ in *Delgamuukw* would prevent this governance authority from being exercised in ways that would be irreconcilable with the attachment to the land on which the title was based: see text accompanying notes 94-95.

8

Common Law, Statutory Law, and the Political Economy of the Recognition of Indigenous Australian Rights in Land

Nicolas Peterson

The development of Native title in Australia has been widely criticized as a disappointment by Aboriginal people and as legally impoverished by various legal commentators. Rosemary Hunter has argued that recognition of Native title is more about self-legitimation of the courts, the law, and the legal process than it is about returning land to Aboriginal people. More recently, Elizabeth Povinelli has advanced the view that, although the Australian liberal democratic state has at last come to recognize Aboriginal rights, it has done so in a way that undermines the *bona fides* of that recognition by imposing a narrow criterion of authenticity. Thus, though the state appears to be accepting of difference, ultimately the kinds of difference embodied by Aboriginal people are unacceptable to liberal moral sensibilities, making the preconditions for recognition high. Most outspoken of all has been Noel Pearson, an indigenous lawyer who has attacked the conceptualization of indigenous ownership by the High Court. Why should indigenous ownership be, he asks, any less comprehensive than that of land holders in the English legal tradition? "What people," he goes on to say, "do not conceive of their occupation and possession of land as being anything less than what the holder of a fee simple would conceive of?"[1]

In pragmatic terms, at issue here is that, for many areas of Australia, Native title is not returning a great deal of land and sea to Aboriginal people, and when it does recognize people's rights in land and sea the rights are usually quite limited.[2] In effect, it is only those rights and interests that can be demonstrated to have been continuously activated since sovereignty and not to have been extinguished by valid acts of government. This is inevitably a process of attrition since new rights or interests, or revivals, cannot have their source in the pre-sovereignty system of laws and customs. Although this is not such a high hurdle in many parts of remote Australia, over 72.6 percent of the Aboriginal population lives in urban areas largely in settled Australia.[3] Generally, these people are better educated, have had much longer histories of contact, and are of mixed descent, whereas those in the remote parts of the continent are, for the most part, poorly educated, often did not settle down until the 1940s, and are of full descent. The general public tends to accept the existence of continuities between past and present practice in respect of land in the case of the latter but is quite skeptical about their existence among the former.

The High Court *Mabo* decision of 3 June 1992, which recognized the existence of Native title in Australia for the first time, has been described as a magnificent declaration of national recognition and a "redemptive confession and atonement on behalf of the nation,"[4] but the decision is undermined in the minds of many commentators because the High Court chose to define Native title in terms of indigenous people's laws and customs rather than as more or less equivalent to fee simple. This definition makes it much more difficult for Aboriginal people in the settled parts of Australia, where their lives have been radically transformed, to have their Native title rights recognized. The consequence is that the period of large numbers of groups seeking court determinations of the existence of Native title is likely to come to an end soon.[5]

Land rights are, of course, more about sociopolitical issues and relations than about purely legal ones, especially in Australia, where recognition of Native title has been so long in coming. Indeed, it would be surprising if the delay between the first settlement of Europeans in 1788 or 178 years before the granting of even statutory land rights, and 204 years before the recognition of community Native title, did not have some consequences for what was done, how it was done, and for whom it was done. A country that has conducted itself without regard to indigenous rights for so long is clearly in a different position from one that, however neglectful, dishonest, or venal it has been, has often recognized Aboriginal title from the beginning.

Although for indigenous Australians recognition of their rights in land is above all an act of natural restorative justice, this is clearly only one of the reasons for recognizing such rights by the community at large. Recognition of rights in land is also expected to make a difference to the lives of Aboriginal people and to go a considerable way toward resolving the social and political problems that come between them and the wider community. Among other things, land rights are expected to promote social harmony by removing, as far as possible, legitimate causes of complaint, to provide an economic base for people who are economically depressed, to sustain indigenous cultural life and links with the land, and to enhance Australia's standing in the world community.[6] In terms of making a difference, perhaps the most important sociopolitical consequence of this recognition has been the effective incorporation of Aboriginal people into local, regional, economic, and political structures. No longer are they simply people to be consulted; they are people who have to be negotiated with. The other side of this coin, however, is that the legal system, in turning reserves and other lands into Aboriginal property, has to define the areas, rights holders, and their rights and interests with the clarity required by a capitalist economy, and in so doing it simplifies and transforms them.

That the wider community has always expected land rights to make a practical difference in Aboriginal people's lives, and to go some way toward solving "the Aboriginal problem," was made explicit in the review of the Northern Territory statutory land rights regime in 1998. The whole thrust of the report was that the Northern Territory's *Aboriginal Land Rights (Northern Territory) Act* of 1976 needed amending to ensure that land ownership contributed more to the economic well-being of Aboriginal people there.[7] Although there is no one Aboriginal problem, of course, most of the public debate and the calls for public funds are in relation to Aboriginal people's generally poor standing in the areas of health, housing, income, education, and employment.[8]

To understand the way in which Native title in Australia is being recognized, it is instructive to look at the background to the recognition and to place that recognition in its widest sociopolitical context by asking the obvious question: Why did the Australian state start granting statutory land rights after 178 years of failing to do so?

Statutory Land Rights

Although no land rights would ever have been granted to Aboriginal people had they not continuously made an issue of land rights from the moment of colonization, in one way or another, and made the significance of land to them unequivocally clear to those who would listen, the proximate causes of the recognition relate to factors indirectly connected to Aboriginal activism. The history of Aboriginals' struggle for recognition of their land rights and of the reservation of land for the use and benefit of Aboriginal people is long and complex. Although many factors contributed to the beginning of a change of heart, two factors, one local and one global, were crucial.[9]

By the early 1960s, Aboriginal people had achieved equal rights, in a formal sense, marked by the right to vote in federal elections in 1962 and in all states by 1965.[10] Except for Queensland, all discriminatory legislation was also removed by the latter date. This formal achievement of equal rights raised, among other questions, the issue of what was to be done with the lands reserved for the use and benefit of Aboriginal people. In South Australia, the position of attorney general and minister of community welfare and Aboriginal affairs in a Labor government was held by a reformist, Donald Dunstan, a long-time campaigner for Aboriginal rights and abolition of the white Australia policy. He was committed to transferring reserved lands to Aboriginal ownership and achieved this, in a formal sense, with the establishment of an Aboriginal land trust in 1966, thus making South Australia the first state to enact statutory legislation and putting pressure on the other states to do likewise.[11] Transferring land long reserved for the use and benefit of Aboriginal people was, politically, relatively unproblematic.

The Northern Territory Legislative Assembly, dominated by pastoral and conservative interests, went the other way in 1967-68. It prepared legislation to open up Aboriginal land to commercial development. However, all Northern Territory legislation until 1978 had to be approved by the federal government, and such was the outcry that the legislation was vetoed in Canberra.[12]

Equal rights not only put land issues directly into active consideration by Australian politicians but also, once achieved, led to Aboriginal people looking beyond Australia's borders for recognition of their distinctive status and to becoming involved in the politics of indigenism. Ronald Niezen has suggested four factors that encouraged the promotion of indigenous rights in the post-World War II era from a Canadian perspective. First, the struggle against fascism contributed to a greater receptiveness at the international level to measures for the protection of minorities, leading to the development of the United Nations conventions between 1948 and 1966 that make up the *International Bill of Human Rights*.[13] Second, the principle of self-determination became a right recognized by the UN. Third, by the mid-twentieth century, it was clear that assimilation policies had failed. And fourth, the rise of an indigenous middle class led to the establishment of specifically indigenous national government organizations that had a powerful advocacy role.

These factors are undoubtedly important in the rise of indigenism, but they do not account for the focus on indigenous land issues, particularly in the First World, during the 1970s. This focus arose out of the unresolved issues relating to what was, in effect, a new phase in the appropriation of indigenous land. The global prosperity of the 1950s underwrote a wave of prospecting and development in remote areas worldwide. This activity not only brought miners into contact with indigenous populations but also caused conflict, which in Australia focused on damage to sacred sites by geologists such as chipping significant stones or destroying ancestrally significant trees. The discovery of resources to develop led to the need for proprietal certainty, which was what set off the new round of land rights settlements.

Thus, the fact that Alaska had been purchased by the United States from Russia in 1867 left unclear the issue of Native title along the path of the pipeline taking oil from the Beaufort Sea to Anchorage. The oil industry, to secure its own property rights, led the drive to create a set of property rights for the indigenous population, which resulted in the *Alaskan Native Claims Settlement Act* of 1971. Hydro development, and the threat of prolonged court cases working out the content of Aboriginal title in Quebec, drove the

Quebec provincial government and the Canadian federal government to negotiate the *James Bay and Northern Quebec Agreement* of 1975.

In Australia, it was the development of a bauxite mine in northeastern Arnhem Land in the Northern Territory that led to the test case on Native title, *Milirrpum and Others v. NABALCO and the Commonwealth of Australia,* decided in 1971. The decision went against the Aboriginal people, with Justice Blackburn ruling that communal Native title did not exist.[14] Although a negative decision, it paradoxically strengthened the moral claims of Aboriginal people since it was widely seen as unjust. Edward Woodward, counsel for the plaintiffs, advised against appealing the decision. In his view, there was a danger that, even if the Aboriginal people won the appeal, they could end up with weaker rights than they could achieve through the political process.[15] The High Court at the time was unsympathetic to Aboriginal rights and unlikely to have gone beyond Blackburn, who had said some positive things about Aboriginal relations to land – as in finding that there was an identifiable land law. This was both a legal and a political judgment. After twenty-two years, the Conservative federal government that also controlled the Northern Territory was clearly on its last legs, and the Labor Party had made its commitment to land rights legislation part of its platform.

Events proved Woodward right. In the following year, the Labor Party was elected, and Woodward, who in the meantime had become Justice Woodward, was appointed to conduct a royal commission into the appropriate ways to recognize traditional rights and interests in relation to land "and to satisfy in other ways the reasonable aspirations of the Aborigines to rights in or in relation to land."[16] Priority was given to the Northern Territory because Aboriginal people constituted about 27 percent of the population versus no more than 2.2 percent elsewhere, and the Territory was virtually an internal colony. It was always intended to extend what was done there to the rest of the continent.[17]

The primary active role for the legal process in the *Aboriginal Land Rights (Northern Territory) Act* of 1976 that resulted from the royal commission was in regard to land claims. Aboriginal people were able to make claim to unalienated crown land outside the existing system of reserves. It was thought necessary to have what were actually inquiries, but conducted as adversarial court hearings, before land was transferred to Aboriginal ownership. There was considerable opposition to land rights, and the public needed to be reassured that there were people with genuine connections to the land. This opposition has to be understood in terms of the common public view that in many areas any Aboriginal people with connections to the land had died out and that so-called carpet-baggers – Aboriginal people from southern Australia – were coming north to make claims.

There were both positive and negative aspects of this claims process, of which four were principal positives. First, substantial resources became available to Aboriginal people to visit often remote and normally inaccessible areas to map them, and in the course of this process a great deal of cultural knowledge about the country that was in danger of dying out was reproduced. Second, much family and local history was documented that otherwise might not have been. Third, people, who for the most part had a slim grasp of the wider legal system within which they were encapsulated, came to be much better informed about it in regard to legal processes, the operation of courts, and the functions of lawyers. And fourth, the legal process brought a moral authority to Aboriginal claims that were tested in a court-like situation.

The negative aspects of the process were several. First, because people had to articulate their rights and interests explicitly, simmering disputes were forced out into the open, in some cases aggravating conflict between individuals and groups. Second, the claims process required testing of the existence of traditional relations to land and led to the incipient codification of the indigenous system through a demonstration that the claimants met a legal definition of traditional ownership. Furthermore, because this legal definition did not match exactly the diversity and complexity of the range of indigenous systems in the Northern Territory, it created some difficulties, although the way in which the legislation was drawn up largely prevented any people with interests in areas successfully claimed from being disenfranchised. Third, some Aboriginal people were unable to make claims because their land was alienated, and a small number of people's claims were not recognized. Fourth, and in some ways most important, legal discourse and processes subtly and, perhaps inevitably, led to some undermining of the intentions of the legislation.

The commission had been concerned not to codify indigenous land law but to place a protective legal carapace around Aboriginal land and leave Aboriginal people to deal with internal relations. The purpose of this approach was to maintain maximum flexibility in the hope that there would be organic development of new arrangements as required by contemporary land use and developments. However, to assist people with administration and development of their land, two land councils were set up, the Northern Land Council for the northern half of the Northern Territory and the Central Land Council for the southern half, each located in the major town of its region. Each was provided with its own senior and junior counsel. Significantly, the senior counsel for the Northern Land Council was Gerard Brennan, later to become chief justice of the High Court and author of the lead judgment in the *Mabo* case.

The inspiration for these councils came substantially from Canadian indigenous political organizations and the emergence of the National Indian

Brotherhood in the years 1968-70. The Australian land councils were not building on any indigenous structures because Australian Aboriginal societies are highly egalitarian, for the most part, without any overarching political structures that would assist in their articulation with the wider society. Indeed, the land councils "went beyond anything natural to Aboriginal social organization."[18] These structures, the commission believed, were needed to help Aboriginal traditional owners represent and protect their interests, as well as manage their land, and were central to the whole conceptualization of the report.

The need for the land councils further entrenched the idea of "traditional owner" in the act as a way of keeping these centralized professional bureaucracies accountable to the actual landowners. Thus, before any action in relation to an area of land could be taken, the Land Council officers had to go out and speak to the traditional owners. The claims process, the permission seeking, and then the distribution of royalty payments all led to the concept of traditional owners having rather more significance than originally intended. This significance was reinforced by the legal process, understandably pushing the rights of rights holders as far as they could and resulting in a kind of creeping codification, although with one exception there has never been any attempt to map clan territories to devolve their titles.[19]

Thus, the Northern Territory legislation, the high-water mark of land rights in Australia, was beneficial legislation for the most tradition-oriented and poorest Aboriginal people, the great majority of whom were actually living on or near the land with which they had traditional connections. It was legislation concerned with the future rather than the past, and it was based substantially on the drafting instructions written by Brennan on the basis of the thinking of the commission.

Native Title

The second test case for the existence of communal Native title, the *Mabo* case, was well chosen. It was among the Torres Strait Islanders who inhabit the islands between Cape York and the south coast of Papua New Guinea, many of whom practised small-scale horticulture as well as making extensive use of the sea. Subsequently, however, there has been absolutely no national planning or co-ordination among Aboriginal people in the sequencing of Native title applications with an eye to taking the best case to court to establish precedents. This was one of the many failures of the Aboriginal and Torres Strait Islander Commission, which, from early on in the process, had control of the funding for the preparation of Native title applications and hearings.[20]

It is sobering to realize that the success of the *Mabo* litigation was completely contingent on the passing of the *Racial Discrimination Act* of 1975, which enacted, in domestic legislation, the 1966 ratification of the *United Nations Convention on the Elimination of Racial Discrimination. Mabo* was contingent on this legislation because the Queensland government in 1979 had passed its own act that sought to abolish the possibility of any Native title in Torres Strait. However, this piece of legislation, having been passed after 1975, was found by the High Court to be in conflict with the *Racial Discrimination Act,* thus keeping the *Mabo* case alive.

To regulate the relationship between the recognition of Native title and the existing Australian land tenure system, the *Native Title Act* of 1993 was passed. A main purpose of the act was to try to steer people toward mediation and away from costly and lengthy legal proceedings. However, because many issues were left unclear in the *Mabo* decision, the reality has been that legal advisers preferred to go to court until litigation provided a clearer picture of how the courts understood the scope and nature of Native title.[21] The first important decision was the High Court *Wik* decision in 1996, which ruled that there could be coexistence of Native title on pastoral leases. Subsequent key cases have been *Ward v. Western Australia* and the *Yorta Yorta* case finalized in 2002.[22]

Two crucial aspects of the agreement between Aboriginal leaders involved in negotiations over the nature and content of the *Native Title Act* and the Labor government of the time were the social justice package and the right to negotiate. The social justice package was to fund Aboriginal people who were unable to get their Native title rights recognized because of either their extinguishment by legitimate acts of government or historical factors that had completely disrupted their relations to land. At the time of the *Mabo* judgment, it was widely predicted that few people in settled Australia would be recognized as Native title holders. From one point of view, this was seen as a fundamental anomaly: those people who had suffered most intensely and for the longest time from the impacts of colonization had the least chance of having their Native title rights survive.[23] From another point of view, many of the people who self-identified as Aboriginal in settled Australia were too like other Australians to justify rights to land on traditional grounds. For example, in Queensland, New South Wales, Victoria, and Tasmania, between 74 percent and 90 percent of all indigenous couple families have one partner who is not indigenous.[24]

The right to negotiate allowed anyone wanting to carry out an activity on land that was the subject of an application for the recognition of Native title to negotiate with the applicants, provided that their application had passed the registration test and been accepted by the National Native Title Tribunal registrar, even though the existence of Native title had not yet been determined by the court.[25]

With the conclusion of the *Yorta Yorta* case, it became clear that the original assessment that few groups would have their Native title recognized in settled

Australia was accurate. This outcome has precipitated considerable criticism of the original *Yorta Yorta* trial judgment from Aboriginal people and their supporters but caused little comment in the wider community. The decision will undoubtedly generate a literature by anthropologists and historians, in particular, on issues such as custom, tradition, continuity, and adaptation.

The positive aspects of the Native title process are similar to the statutory regime. Resources become available for professional researchers to pull together a great deal of historical material that the indigenous applicants are usually unaware of or that they have been unable to access. Family trees are drawn up and photographic archives uncovered. If the application is litigated, then the court provides a forum in which people can, to some extent, tell their stories and achieve recognition; the whole process, more or less regardless of outcome, brings a moral authority to the people's claim. Because, as a result of the process, the Aboriginal applicants are much better informed about the full scope of their group's history, have often gained access to nineteenth-century ethnographic material about their ancestors previously unknown to them, and heard other applicants speaking, they come away better able to formulate their case in public.

The negative aspects of the legal process evident in the statutory regime of the Northern Territory have been intensified among applicants seeking recognition of their Native title in settled Australia. Making an application, and going through the original hearings, raise people's expectations, increase their historical consciousness, and strengthen their sense of injustice, all of which makes dealing with the loss of a case more difficult. The fully adversarial nature of the Native title court process, in which there may be several hundred objectors to an application at the outset, is gruelling but is partially offset by the possibility of avoiding it by opting for the mediation process, which, while still involving the same parties, is increasingly leading to agreements of various kinds before cases reach the courts.[26]

Many Aboriginal people are naive about the extent of documentation and scholarship that exists in relation to them in various archives, so that cherished beliefs and local understandings may be shown to be wrong, often to the embarrassment of particular indigenous people in a community. They are also rarely aware of the demanding nature of the cross-examination process. Past movement of people away from the area of their land interests, often forced on them several generations ago by governments, differentiates "traditional people" (potential Native title rights holders) from "historical people" (those from elsewhere), creating enormous tensions. Preparation of a Native title application often radically transforms situations in which such people have been getting along with each other, setting family network against family network.

However, the right to negotiate, even though it was modified in the 1998 amendments to the *Native Title Act* of 1993, combined with the threat of extended court proceedings, has given many groups recognition and limited benefits that they did not have before. Increasingly, there is an emphasis on negotiation, both with private interests and local and regional tiers of government and with the state, especially in Western Australia.[27] The increasing significance of negotiation is thus a *de facto* recognition that dealing with legitimate grievance should be in the political, rather than the legal, domain.

But what constitutes a legitimate Aboriginal grievance in the eyes of the public or government today is complex and changing. On all social indicators, Aboriginal people, collectively, come out poorly, even in settled Australia, and there is widespread support for efforts to improve the situation. Increasingly, the boundary between who is, and who is not, Aboriginal in settled Australia is becoming blurred in the public's eyes. As in North America, in Australia substantial numbers of people are now choosing to identify themselves on the census form as indigenous who have not done so previously, so that between 1991 and 1996, and between 1996 and 2001, the census population grew by 33 percent and 16 percent respectively, far beyond the rate of natural increase. Whatever the rhetoric, the lives of many of these Aboriginal people in settled Australia are materially not greatly different from those of what are locally known as "Aussie battlers" – or poor ordinary Australians. Because of the absence of radical cultural difference, and because of the decline in physical difference as a result of intermarriage, public support for the claims of Aboriginal people in settled Australia for land rights and other group rights is not strong, and in all probability it is likely to decline.

In the remote regions of northern and central Australia, the grievances are not so much over land, since many communities have rights to considerable tracts of land, but arise from frustration over the lack of a clear vision for the future. Rapidly increasing populations in remote places give rise to enormous social problems in many of the communities, problems that came to a head in June 2007 with the Northern Territory Emergency Response, widely known as the Intervention, by the Howard government. The ostensible reason for this radical policy change and practical administrative change was the response to a report on the high level of abuse of Aboriginal children, but the underlying issue was the government's belief that Aboriginal policy needed a huge shake-up.[28] In these regions, issues around self-government, often confused with and spoken of in terms of self-determination, are seen as the major issues by both Aboriginal people and advocates for them.

Conclusion
The long delay in the legal recognition of Aboriginal prior ownership of the continent of Australia has, unsurprisingly, resulted in this recognition being highly constrained by the extent and complexity of non-indigenous land

interests and the political reality of indigenous people's minority status at about 2.2 percent of the population. Given the form that Native title has taken, the rights and interests that successful applicants are going to end up with in settled Australia will be in shreds and patches. What benefit will inalienable, collectively owned, leftover land likely have in the twenty-first century for such people? What many Aboriginal people in such situations want, and what would improve their life circumstances, is real estate – land for housing and business enterprises. Yet communal Native title, at best, can only provide for such needs unsatisfactorily. The future requires the development of creative new policies that work toward negotiated rather than litigated solutions and recognize these contemporary realities.

In the longer run, the major benefit of the recognition of Native title may well be the boost that it is giving to the push for self-government. Unlike in Canada, in Australia there is no recognition of an inherent right to self-government. But the growth in the proportion of Aboriginal people in parts of regional Australia, such as in Cape York, the Northern Territory, central Australia, and the Kimberley, and the fact that Aboriginal people are now the largest land holders in these regions, give a practical sense to the idea of an indigenous order of government alongside state and federal levels. Regional agreements are already firmly on the agenda. In their strongest form, they can lead to all government resources for a region being channelled through a single regional body, as among the James Bay Cree in Canada. This has not happened anywhere in Australia yet but is closest to happening in the Torres Strait, which is something of a special case.[29]

Much academic and indigenous writing not only makes strong forms of self-government/self-determination the ultimate goal in the politics of indigenism but also usually implies or assumes that it will make a radical difference in people's life circumstances. However, the academic writing on this topic is either thinly disguised advocacy or highly abstract legal or political theorizing that is unrealistic about the practical implementation of, and the kinds of beneficial impacts that will flow from, such self-government. Any sophisticated social analysis is completely lacking, with the focus solely on power and legal relations, to the neglect of the economic and the cultural.[30]

There is little reason or evidence to suppose that the social, cultural, economic, and other problems that Aboriginal people are facing today, created and reproduced by the influences of modernity, commoditization and related factors, are going to be much more easily or better addressed by indigenous governments than they have been by existing ones. This is not an argument against self-government, which is probably important. It is, however, a criticism of the utopian benefits implied to flow from such arrangements. Although Native title and statutory land rights are fundamental foundations for the future that have brought, and will bring, increasing degrees of autonomy and self-government over time, their contribution to the social and economic problems facing Aboriginal people, especially in the remote regions, may be limited. A better future in those regions lies not in the realm of Native title but in a much more complex existential domain.

Notes

1 Hunter, "Aboriginal Histories, Australian Histories," 1-16; McNeil, "The Relevance of Traditional Laws and Customs to the Existence and Content of Native Title at Common Law,"; Pearson, "Where We've Come from and Where We're at with the Opportunity that Is Koiki Mabo's Legacy to Australia," the 2003 Mabo Lecture, Native Title Representative Bodies Conference, Alice Springs, 3 June 2003, http://www.capeyorkpartnerships.com; Povinelli, *The Cunning of Recognition*.
2 About a quarter of the Aboriginal population lives on Aboriginal land; see Altman, *Sustainable Development Options on Aboriginal Land*, 2.
3 At the 1996 census, 72.6 percent of the population was living in urban areas with a population of more than 1,000 people. For the delineation of settled Australia, see Rowley, *The Remote Aborigines*, endpapers.
4 H. Wootten, "Native Title in a Long Term Perspective: A View from the Eighties," paper delivered at the Native Title Representative Bodies Conference, Geraldton, Western Australia, 3 September 2002.
5 As at the time of writing, there is likely to be an increase in the number of cases coming before the federal court because it has tightened up on procedures forcing many groups that have lodged applications for hearing, but regularly asked for postponements because they have not completed the research, to appear in court. Many of these cases are not strong, from a legal point of view, also a reason for the continuous delays.
6 Following Justice Woodward, *Aboriginal Land Rights Commission: Second Report, April 1974* (Canberra: Government Printer, 1974), 2.
7 Reeves, *Building on Land Rights*.
8 See Altman, Hunter, and Johns, "Monitoring 'Practical' Reconciliation: Evidence from the Reconciliation Decade 1991-2001," 2003, http://www.anu.edu.au/caepr; and recent discussion papers of the Centre for Aboriginal Economic Policy Research, Australian National University, http://www.anu.edu.au/caepr.
9 For New South Wales, see Goodall, *Invasion to Embassy*; for Queensland, see Anderson, "Queensland," 53-114; and for Victoria, see Felton, "Victoria," 168-220.
10 The details are complex. See Peterson and Sanders, eds., *Citizenship and Indigenous Australians*. One thing that is clear, however, is that the 1967 referendum that removed any references to Aboriginal people from the Constitution had nothing to do with citizenship, although it is often spoken of as when people acquired citizenship rights. It was/is, however, extremely important symbolically, and it opened the way for the Commonwealth to take responsibility for Aboriginal affairs in the states, something for which supporters of Aboriginal people had long been campaigning.
11 In his political memoirs, Dunstan records that he also wanted to include ownership of minerals but was prevented from doing so by the upper house. He did, however, sign an indenture on behalf of the state, providing in perpetuity that the Aboriginal Land Trust would be paid all royalties derived by the state from minerals on trust lands. Dunstan, *Felicia*, 109-11.
12 Rowse, *Obliged to Be Difficult*, 55.
13 That is, the *Universal Declaration of Human Rights* (1948), the *International Covenant on Economic, Social, and Cultural Rights* (1966), and the *International Covenant on Civil and Political Rights* (1966). See Niezen, *Origins of Indigenism*, 4-46.
14 I am unclear whether the same sort of factors accounted for the establishment of the Waitangi Tribunal in 1975. The proximate conflict was over land in the centre of Auckland at Bastion Point.

15 McNeil, *Common Law Aboriginal Title*, 295-96, comments that, since the "plaintiffs in *Milirrpum* lost on almost every issue (of fact as well as law), it is perhaps not surprising that they did not appeal."

16 Woodward, "Aboriginal Land Rights Commission," 1.

17 The first attempt to do so was in Victoria when the Victorian Aboriginal Land Council was formed in April 1975. In opening the meeting, Senator Cavanagh, minister for Aboriginal affairs, said this:

> The situation in Victoria is far removed from that applying in the Northern Territory and many of Mr Justice Woodward's recommendations may therefore not be applicable ... The associations which Victorian Aborigines hold for land are of a different nature to the traditional religious ties held by many Aboriginal people in other areas of Australia ... I believe that your Council's best approach will be to seek to identify the land needs of the Victorian Aboriginal Community as it now exists. Broadly, I imagine that these needs will be: land for housing, principally in urban areas; land for community purposes; and land for economic development.

Cited in Moore, "The Victorian Aboriginal Land Council," 241-49 at 243. Dissensions within the Aboriginal community prevented them from taking up this offer. It is significant that such dissensions are still a problem. The state representative body charged with helping Aboriginal people in Victoria with Native title has not managed to get one case into the courts despite the expenditure of more than $15 million Australian, largely because of these kinds of problems. Although the representative body has chosen to try to reach negotiated agreements, they have, so far, not eventuated.

18 Woodward, "Aboriginal Land Rights Commission," 65. This was the source of a major political campaign against the bill. See Peterson, "Reeves in the Context of the History of Land Rights Legislation," 25-31 at 27-29.

19 This was on the old Finke River Mission lease at Hermannsburg west of Alice Springs.

20 The continuing difficulties with the Aboriginal and Torres Strait Islander Commission's leadership and with its oversight of funds finally led the government to abolish it in 2005.

21 As of 31 March 2009, 121 court determinations of Native title have been made: 86 that native title exists, and 35 that it does not. There are 367 registered Indigenous Land Use Agreements. For up-to-date official information about the Native title process, summaries of judgments, etc., see http://www.nntt.gov.au/.

22 For the full transcripts of the judgments in these cases, see http://www.austlii.edu.au/. Until the results of the appeal in what has popularly come to be known as the "Single Noongar Application," but formally as *Bennell v. State of Western Australia*, [2006] F.C.A. 1243, were handed down on 23 April 2008, it looked as though this case would be groundbreaking. The original case recognized that Native title still survived in some small parts of the Perth metropolitan area, to the surprise of many observers. The appeal, *Bodney v. Bennell*, [2008] F.C.A.F.C. 63, against this original decision was, however, upheld.

23 Wootten "Native Title in a Long Term Perspective," 3.

24 Birrell and Hirst, "Aboriginal Couples at the 2001 Census," 23-28.

25 Although there is no uniform opinion on the basis for inclusion of this provision in the Native title agreement, it was in recognition of the fact that much of Australia would not be subject to Native title, *including*, it was widely assumed, pastoral leases, and that the area open to application should not be further reduced by alienation before people could have the applications dealt with. At the same time, it was also to help reduce delays to development.

26 These agreements include Indigenous Land Use Agreements, which can range from being geographically extensive and comprehensive to highly localized and specific, and specific contractual arrangements between Aboriginal people and particular parties.

27 Following a change of government in Western Australia in February 2001, a review was commissioned of the government's position in relation to Native title applications and processes. See Wand and Athanasiou, *Review of the Native Title Claims Process in Western Australia*. This review strongly endorsed the new government's proposed move from litigation to negotiation. For an account of the situation in Western Australia, particularly as it

relates to the position of historians in the application process, see Choo and Hollbach, eds., *History and Native Title*.

28   Because the Intervention happened with an election looming, some saw it as an election ploy. However, anybody who had been following the articles published in the conservative *Quadrant* magazine over the previous five years could see that this was not the case. Many articles by authors who had the government's ear clearly set out the conservatives' critique of previous governments' policies and recommended specific action. It was not the election but the moral authority provided by the report, "Little Children Are Sacred," coming on top of information about other horrific events, that was seized on by the government to enact changes that went way beyond anything recommended in the report.

29   On an indigenous order of government, see Sanders, *Indigenous Order of Australian Government*. On regional agreements, see Edmunds, ed., *Regional Agreements*. On the Torres Strait situation, see Arthur, "Towards Regionalism," 59-82.

30   For some recent examples, see Ivison, *Postcolonial Liberalism*; Keal, *European Conquest and the Rights of Indigenous Peoples*; and Niezen, *Origins of Indigenism*.

9
Claiming Native Title in the Foreshore and Seabed
Jacinta Ruru

Komuruhia te poioneone kia toe ko te kirikiri kotahi.
Ahakoa tana kotahi, e honoa ana ia ki te whenua, mai i te
Whenua ki te rangi, te rangi ki te whenua, ki te maunga, ki
te moana, ki te tangata e tu ake nei;
Ko au tenei te kirikiri nei.

Rub away the earthen clump to leave but one lone grain of dirt;
Whilst it is but one, yet it is inextricably joined to the land,
From the land to the sky, the sky to the land, to the
Mountain, to the sea, to the people;
Tis I who is that one lone grain.

> – Waitangi Tribunal, *Report on the Crown's
> Foreshore and Seabed Policy*

Once upon a time, a man and a woman embraced so tightly that their children were doomed to live in perpetual darkness. Desperate to escape the tight embrace, the children revolted. That man now stands above us as our sky father (Ranginui), that woman lies with us as our earth mother (Papatuanuku), and those children, who succeeded in decorating their parents with, for example, trees, waters, rainbows, animals, and eventually human beings, became the gods of this natural world order. Or, at least, this is how Māori, and the indigenous peoples of Aotearoa me Te Waipounamu (New Zealand), view the creation of the world in which we live today.[1]

To Māori, as to many other indigenous peoples, the environment is personified with a life force that views all things, including human beings, as interrelated. The environment gives Māori their spiritual, cultural, political, and economic identity. Extensive traditional use laws exist that centre on ensuring natural balance. The importance for environmental balance is viewed in literal terms. For instance, the survival of Māori is dependent on the survival of the sea: it is a source of food; it links past generations with future generations through the passing on of knowledge and traditions; it provides the means by which to gain *mana* (prestige) through the sharing of its bounty; and it provides a geographical and spiritual link to the world order.[2] It is a landscape that embodies our earth mother. The indivisible entity of land and water makes Māori who they are.

Since colonization, the ability of indigenous peoples to maintain and respect the relationship with their environment has been under threat. In the context of New Zealand, the British settlers brought with them a different way of viewing the world. Essentially, human beings are separate from nature and have superiority and dominion over it. Nature is capable of being exclusively owned; nature is relied on for political and economic ends. Human beings can exert rights over nature free of onerous responsibilities to the spiritual world.[3] The beach, foreshore, and seabed are special and distinct from dry land. Land under, or bordering, water should be freely accessible; it should not be subject to exclusive private ownership. Divisible, land and water are separate entities.

Not surprisingly, the ownership lines since drawn on the landscape separating the high-water mark from tidal land and the seabed are but one example of where the clash of worldviews has come to a head. This is particularly so for New Zealand. On 19 June 2003, New Zealand's then top domestic appeal court, the Court of Appeal, indicated, in a unanimous decision – *Ngati Apa v. Attorney-General*[4] – to the horror of the government and the public majority but to the relief of Māori, that Māori should be allowed the opportunity to prove, in the courts, customary ownership of the foreshore and seabed. Determined not to allow them to have such an opportunity, the government introduced legislation that clearly and plainly extinguished Native title in the foreshore and seabed.[5] This chapter provides a background and an assessment of the foreshore and seabed mayhem in New Zealand and seeks to put the current controversy into a historical and comparative context.

Historical and Contemporary Background

All land in New Zealand was once Māori customary land (land held by Māori in accordance with *tikanga* Māori – Māori laws and customs).[6] As accepted by Chief Justice Elias in the *Ngati Apa* foreshore and seabed case, Māori customary land was property in existence when a colonial government was established by the crown in 1840.[7] The *Treaty of Waitangi,* signed in 1840 between Māori and British representatives, did not create, alter, or extinguish this property. The treaty simply gave the British crown the right to govern. Māori retained chieftainship over their own affairs, they were guaranteed the same rights and privileges as British citizens living in New Zealand, and the crown was given the right of pre-emption to purchase Māori land.[8] It was the English common law, imported into New Zealand after the signing of the treaty, that ensured the continuation of Māori property rights in their customary lands despite the change in sovereignty. New Zealand's now-named High Court clarified this fact back in 1847. The judges in the case of *R. v. Symonds* held that Māori customary interests were to be solemnly respected and not to be extinguished at least in times of peace without their free consent.[9]

Twenty years after the signing of that treaty, in the early 1860s, the government sought the means to encourage the conversion of the property in land owned by Māori to enable sales to new settlers. It established the now-named Māori Land Court.[10] The court's mandate was to enable the speedy British settlement of New Zealand. The crown's right of pre-emption was thus waived in favour of a process whereby Māori were to apply to the court for a fee simple title that would, in effect, change the status of Māori customary land to Māori freehold land. Once a freehold title was issued, Māori were encouraged to alienate (sell, gift, lease, mortgage, etc.) their land to the new settlers. The founding legislation clearly envisioned the "assimilation as nearly as possible to the ownership of land according to British law" to result in "the peaceful settlement of the Colony and the advancement and civilization of the Natives."[11]

A decade after establishment of the Māori Land Court, the judiciary did an about-face on Native title. In 1877, Chief Justice Pendergast, in *Wi Parata v. The Bishop of Wellington*,[12] declared that the doctrine of Native title had no application in New Zealand because there were no laws or rights in property existing before 1840: "In the case of primitive barbarians [Māori], the supreme executive of Government must acquit itself, as best it may, of its obligation to respect Native proprietary rights, and of necessity must be the sole arbiter of its own justice."[13]

Although the Privy Council in 1901, on an appeal from a New Zealand court, disapproved of *Wi Parata*,[14] the case has continued to resonate in New Zealand's courts. In particular, in 1963, the precedent set in *Wi Parata* led the Court of Appeal, in *In re the Ninety Mile Beach*,[15] to hold that all foreshore in New Zealand that lies between the high- and low-water marks, and in respect of which contiguous landward title has been investigated by the Māori Land Court, is land in which Māori customary property has been extinguished. The reasoning of the judgment was as follows: "In my opinion it necessarily follows that on the assumption of British sovereignty ... the rights of the Māoris to their tribal lands depended wholly on the grace and favour of Her Majesty Queen Victoria, who had an absolute right to disregard the Native title to any lands in New Zealand, whether above high-water mark or below high-water mark."[16]

In stark contrast, the more recent Native title decisions reiterate not the *Wi Parata* or *Ninety Mile Beach* line of reasoning but the *R. v. Symonds* precedent. For instance, in 1986, Justice Williamson of the High Court, in *Te Weehi v. Regional Fisheries Officer*,[17] endorsed the view that "the treatment of its indigenous peoples under English common law had confirmed that the local laws and property rights of such peoples in ceded or settled colonies were not set aside by the establishment of British sovereignty."[18] Likewise, in 1993, President Cooke of the Court of Appeal stressed that, though the colonizing power acquires a radical title, that title "is subject to the existing Native rights."[19] Similarly, in 1995, the High Court stressed that Native title "does not disappear by a side wind." Thus, "where action taken by the Crown which arguably might extinguish Aboriginal title is not plainly so intended the Court will find that the Aboriginal title has survived."[20] Against this historical and contemporary Native title background, the foreshore and seabed issue has been relitigated in recent years.

Native Title Litigation

In New Zealand, the *Resource Management Act* of 1991 regulates the use of land, air, and water. The institutions of regional and local government are primarily responsible for regulating this use via issuing district, regional, and coastal plans, policy statements, and resource consents.[21] The general rule is that, for a person to use land in a manner that would contravene a rule in a plan, that person must first obtain resource consent.[22] In terms of the foreshore and seabed, the act explicitly states that this land referred to as the coastal marine area[23] can only be occupied if expressly allowed by a rule in a regional coastal plan or by a resource consent.[24]

In the 1990s, several *hapu* (subtribes) at the top of the South Island sought to establish a marine farm. In accordance with the *Resource Management Act,* they applied to the Marlborough District Council for a resource consent. It was denied. In an attempt to challenge the council's mandate, the *hapu* sought to have the land declared Māori customary land – land held according to *tikanga* Māori and protected as their property by the doctrine of Native title. The *hapu,* in December 1997, asked the Māori Land Court to make an order under the *Te Ture Whenua Māori Act* of 1993 (the *Māori Land Act*) to declare that certain land either temporarily or permanently under water in the Marlborough Sounds was Māori customary land.

The Māori Land Court has jurisdiction to determine and declare, by status order, land in New Zealand.[25] The *Māori Land Act* states that no land can acquire or lose the status of Māori customary land other than in accordance with the act or as expressly provided in any other act.[26] That direction is a reflection of the common law doctrine of Native title: clear and plain legislation is required to extinguish Native title. Although all land was once Māori customary land, it is said that the percentage of this land type on dry soil today is so little that it cannot be quantified.[27] Today it is more common for land to bear the status of Māori freehold land, general land owned by Māori, general land, crown land, or crown land reserved for Māori.[28]

The *Māori Land Act,* in stark contrast to its predecessors, endorses a new philosophy that recognizes that Māori customary land and Māori freehold land comprise *taonga tuku iho* (land of special importance that is handed down through the generations) to its owners, and thus the Māori Land Court should now promote and assist owners to retain that land and to effectively use, manage, and develop it.[29] Therefore, the law makes it incredibly difficult to alienate Māori land. Māori customary land is simply inalienable,[30] and Māori freehold land can be alienated but only in accordance with stringent laws that usually include confirmation by the Māori Land Court.[31]

The Māori Land Court's interim decision,[32] which was favourable to the *hapu*, distinguished the *Ninety Mile Beach* case on the basis that it applied only where the Māori Land Court had investigated adjoining lands above the high-water mark. Judge Hingston held that he was not prepared to extend the *Ninety Mile Beach* ratio to situations where "Māori were separated from their customary lands adjacent to the foreshore by purchase, the customary rights to the foreshore not included in the sales or not having been expressly extinguished since sale by an Act or other statutory instrument."[33] Hingston commented that the effect of the *Ninety Mile Beach* case was an example of "extinguishment of customary rights by a 'side wind'"[34] and that he was not going to fall into that trap.

The Marlborough District Council appealed Hingston's interim decision to the Māori Appellate Court. Concerned with several legal implications, the court opted to state a case for the High Court to answer.[35] The High Court released its decision in 2001.[36] It found in favour of the council: the foreshore and seabed are not Māori customary land but crown land. The *hapu* then appealed. The full bench of the Court of Appeal heard the case in July 2002 and a year later released its unanimous decision in *Ngati Apa.* All five judges disagreed with the High Court conclusion and held instead that the Māori Land Court does have jurisdiction to investigate and determine, if the evidence warrants, that foreshore and seabed are Māori customary land.

The Court of Appeal decision effectively reiterated the 1901 Privy Council declaration that *Wi Parata* was wrong in law and overruled the *Ninety Mile Beach* case. It had little problem defining foreshore and seabed as "land." It held that legislation simply stating that the foreshore and seabed are to "be and always to have been vested in the Crown" is not sufficient to constitute clear and plain intent to extinguish Native title in the foreshore and seabed.[37] It concluded that the Māori Land Court should be allowed to hear evidence of the Māori claimants' association with the foreshore and seabed and determine, if warranted, that the foreshore and seabed are Māori customary land – land held according to *tikanga* Māori and thus protected by the doctrine of Native title.

With regard to Native title, the Court of Appeal held as common law doctrine that any property interest of the crown in land over which it acquired sovereignty depends on pre-existing customary interests.[38] As Chief Justice Elias summarized, "the transfer of sovereignty did not affect customary property. They are interests preserved by the common law until extinguished in accordance with the law."[39] The content of such customary interest is a question of fact discoverable, if necessary, by evidence. As a matter of custom, the burden on the crown's radical title might be limited to use or occupation rights held as a matter of custom.[40] Nonetheless, the court stated that customary rights might be so complete as to reduce any radical right in the sovereign to one that extends only to comparatively limited rights of administrative interference.[41]

In reaching these conclusions, the court relied on overseas jurisprudence, including *Delgamuukw v. British Columbia*[42] and *Mabo v. Queensland (No. 2).*[43] The court endorsed the reasoning in *Delgamuukw* by stating that "the Supreme Court of Canada has had occasion recently to consider the content of customary property interests in that country. It has recognised that, according to the custom on which such rights are based, they may extend from usufructuary rights to exclusive ownership with incidents equivalent to those recognised by fee simple title."[44]

The New Zealand Court of Appeal thus extended this reasoning to land under water. Native title can exist in regard to land under water, and it can exist to the extent of exclusive ownership akin to a fee simple title. Avoiding any declaration that such land exists in reality in New Zealand, the Court of Appeal simply held that Māori should not be prevented from bringing an application of this nature to a hearing before the Māori Land Court.

Reaction to the *Ngata Apa* Decision

New Zealand is an island country bordered by the Tasman Sea and the Pacific Ocean. Since 1840, there has been little history of individual private ownership of the beach, foreshore, or seabed. Instead, the crown has presumed itself to be the owner.[45] Believing that dry land and land under water are separate entities, the crown has not subjected itself to the general rule that its title must be a matter of record before possession can be legal. Land under water was thought exempted from this rule. After all, it was land that historically had little physical property apart from the odd pier or retaining wall. Public access and use were thought more fundamental to this type of land. The presumption of crown ownership protected that ideology. But the Court of Appeal has effectively displaced that presumption in favour of the common law doctrine of Native title. Not surprisingly, public reaction has been unprecedented.

Within days of the *Ngati Apa* decision, government and media sensational-
ized the issue into one of Māori seeking ownership of the beach *per se* to
either halt public access to it or sell it to the highest bidder. Lost was the
reason for the litigation – *hapu* simply seeking to assert a potential legal
property right to have better opportunities to legally associate with the
foreshore and seabed (not the beach) and to participate in their commercial
use. Less than a week after the decision, Prime Minister Helen Clark announced that the "government is proposing to enshrine in law Crown
ownership of the foreshore and seabed."[46] This announcement signalled the
passing of clear and plain legislation that would abruptly extinguish potential
Māori property rights in land under salt water. The Labour-led government
devised a proposal premised on four principles: access, regulation, protection, and certainty. The principles, enshrined in the *Protecting Public Access
and Customary Rights* consultative paper published in August 2003, were as
follows:

> The foreshore and seabed should be public domain, with open access and
> use for all New Zealanders;
>> The Crown is responsible for regulating the use of the foreshore and the
> seabed, on behalf of all present and future generations of New Zealanders;
>> Processes should exist to enable the customary interests of whanau, hapu
> and iwi in the foreshore and seabed to be acknowledged, and specific rights
> to be identified and protected; and
>> There should be certainty for those who use and administer the foreshore
> and seabed about the range of rights that are relevant to their actions.[47]

This consultative paper – littered with numerous emotive shots of children
playing on the foreshore – attracted more than 2,100 written submissions.[48]
From Māori, it attracted a clear and unanimous rejection, as evidenced at
hui meetings held throughout the country.[49] Māori immediately responded,
on one front, by applying to the Māori Land Court for status orders to declare
parts of the foreshore and seabed in their *takiwa* (territory) as Māori customary land and, on another front, by lodging applications for urgency with
the Waitangi Tribunal. The tribunal is a permanent commission of inquiry
that has jurisdiction to inquire into claims that Māori are, or are likely to
be, prejudicially affected by acts or omissions of the crown that are inconsistent with the principles of the *Treaty of Waitangi*.[50]

In the meantime, on 19 December 2003, the government announced its
policy on the foreshore and seabed. Its *Summary of the Foreshore and Seabed
Framework* begins as follows: "The policy proposes a new framework to
provide a clear and unified system for recognizing rights in the foreshore
and seabed, as well as practical initiatives to develop effective working relationships between whanau, hapu and iwi, who hold mana and ancestral

connection over an area of foreshore and seabed, and central and local government decision makers."[51] The summary outlined the policy in the following manner. It retained the four principles of access, regulation, protection, and certainty. It proposed two new land titles: public domain and customary land. The public domain land title would vest full legal and beneficial ownership of the foreshore and seabed in the people of New Zealand.[52] The customary land title would recognize *whanau, hapu,* or *iwi* connection over particular areas of the foreshore or seabed and identify specific customary rights.[53] Customary title would not alter reasonable and appropriate public access.[54] The Māori Land Court would award customary title based on recommendations made by a newly formed independent, nationally roving commission. The job of the commission would be to identify those who held *mana* and ancestral connection over particular foreshore and seabed areas.[55] The policy also proposed the creation of sixteen regional working groups to be comprised of central government, *whanau, hapu,* and *iwi,* and local government.[56] The purpose of these groups would be to reach an agreement in each region on the ways in which *whanau, hapu,* and *iwi* would participate in the management of the coastal marine area. Once regional agreements were concluded, they would be formally recognized by the crown, making them legally enforceable.[57]

In the week following the government's release of its policy, 23 December 2003, the Waitangi Tribunal confirmed that it would hear, in urgency, the *hapu* claim concerning the foreshore and seabed.[58] The tribunal heard the claim in January 2004 and published its recommendations in March.[59] Its overriding recommendation was that the government should go back to the drawing board and engage with Māori in proper negotiations about the way forward. This is how the tribunal viewed the government's policy:

> It removes the ability of Māori to go to the High Court and the Māori Land Court for definition and declaration of their legal rights in the foreshore and seabed.
>
> In removing the means by which the rights would be declared, it effectively removes the rights themselves, whatever their number and quality.
>
> It removes property rights. Whether the rights are few or many, big or small, taking them away amounts to expropriation.
>
> It does not guarantee compensation. This contradicts the presumption at law that there shall be no expropriation without compensation.
>
> It understates the number and quality of the rights that we think are likely to be declared by, in particular, the Māori Land Court under its Act. We think that the Māori Land Court would declare that customary property rights exist, and at least sometimes these would be vested as a fee simple title.
>
> In place of the property rights that would be declared by the courts, the policy will enact a regime that recognises lesser and fewer Māori rights.

It creates a situation of extreme uncertainty about what the legal effect of the recognition of Māori rights under the policy will be. They will certainly not be ownership rights. They will not even be property rights, in the sense that they will not give rise to an ability to sue. They may confer priority in competing applications to use a resource in respect of which a use right is held, but it is not clear whether this would amount to a power of veto.

It is therefore not clear (particularly as to outcomes), not comprehensive (many important areas remain incomplete), and gives rise to at least as many uncertainties as the process for recognition of customary rights in the courts.

It describes a process that is supposed to deliver enhanced participation of Māori in decision-making affecting the coastal marine area, but which we think will fail. This is because it proceeds on a naïve view of the (we think extreme) difficulties of obtaining agreement as between Māori and other stakeholders on the changes necessary to achieve the required level of Māori participation.

It exchanges property rights for the opportunity to participate in an administrative process: if, as we fear, the process does not deliver for Māori, they will get very little (and possibly nothing) in return for the lost property rights.[60]

The tribunal concluded that the policy was in serious breach of the principles of the *Treaty of Waitangi* and of wider norms of domestic and international law. It stated that the serious breaches gave rise to serious prejudices:

The rule of law is a fundamental tenet of the citizenship guaranteed by article 3 [of the *Treaty of Waitangi*]. Removing its protection from Māori only, cutting off their access to the courts and effectively expropriating their property rights, puts them in a class different from and inferior to all other citizens.

Shifting the burden of uncertainty about Māori property rights in the foreshore and seabed from the Crown to Māori, so that Māori are delivered for an unknown period to a position of complete uncertainty about where they stand, undermines their bargaining power and leaves them without recourse.

In cutting off the path for Māori to obtain property rights in the foreshore and seabed, the policy takes away opportunity and mana, and in their place offers fewer and lesser rights. There is no guarantee to pay compensation for the rights lost.[61]

Despite the tribunal's analysis and strong recommendations, the government labelled the report "disappointing."[62] It rejected the central conclusions, stating that "those conclusions – particularly surrounding supposed breaches of the Treaty of Waitangi and the rule of law – depend upon dubious or incorrect assumptions by the Tribunal."[63] The government simply stressed the notion of parliamentary sovereignty – the idea that Parliament is supreme and unhindered in its lawmaking abilities.

As the government began drafting the *Foreshore and Seabed Bill,* serious disquiet began to mount. A Māori Land Court judge, in defiance of the proposed legislation but in accordance with the law post *Ngati Apa,* announced that the court would proceed with hearing Māori applications for ownership of the foreshore and seabed. Prime Minister Clark responded on national television, openly criticizing the judge and adding rather cynically that she thought the court had "rather better things to do with its time."[64] There were, however, more pressing concerns for the prime minister – the dissension of several of her Māori members of Parliament. Associate Māori Affairs Minister Tariana Turia, after months of speculation, announced in early May her resignation from Parliament in opposition to the government's foreshore and seabed policy.[65] Similarly, Māori Member of Parliament (MP) Nanaia Mahuta announced that, though she would not resign as a Labour MP, she would cross the floor and vote against the proposed legislation.[66] The dissension left Labour with a precarious balance of power, forcing it to renegotiate with smaller political parties to ensure the votes to pass the bill.[67] But before the vote was put to the house, on 5 May 2004 over 20,000 Māori converged on the capital city of Wellington to express outrage and to encourage other Māori MPs to vote against the bill. It was the biggest political march (*hikoi*) in New Zealand's history. *Hapu* and *Iwi* throughout the country participated in the *hikoi.* Nonetheless, the prime minister refused to acknowledge the *hikoi* participants and steadfastly refused to retract her earlier statement the same week that many of the marchers were "haters and wreckers."[68]

The *Foreshore and Seabed Act* of 2004

The *Foreshore and Seabed Act* was passed by the Labour government on 18 November 2004, with initial sections coming into force on 17 January 2005. The sensitivities were such that an axe was thrown at the prime minister's constituency office in Auckland on the day of the act's passage. Opposed by the National Party as too favourable to the Māori, a preliminary report of the United Nations Committee on the Elimination of Racial Discrimination dated 12 March 2005 condemned the act.[69] It conducted an on-site investigation, and its final report in March 2006 was equally highly critical.[70]

The law vested ownership of the foreshore and seabed that are not currently subject to a specified freehold interest in the crown. They are labelled crown land and not "public domain" or "customary land" as previously contemplated.[71] Integral to the public foreshore and seabed are public access and recognition of ancestral connection and customary rights.[72] No roving commission or regional working groups will be established. Instead, the process for establishing connection and rights sits with the Māori Land Court and the High Court via applications to be heard and with certain ministers of the crown via direct negotiation.

In essence, the Māori Land Court now has jurisdiction to issue customary rights orders to a group of Māori if they are able to prove that they have had, since 1840, and continue to have, an ancestral connection to the area.[73] The statutory test requires the claimants to prove that (1) they are an established and identifiable group of Māori whose members are *whanaunga*; (2) the activity, use, or practice has been integral to *tikanga* Māori since 1840 and has been carried on, exercised, or followed in a substantially uninterrupted manner since 1840 in accordance with *tikanga* Māori; and (3) it is not prohibited by law.[74] The High Court can also issue customary rights orders under similar conditions. The substantial difference is that the High Court is able to make an order in favour of any established and identifiable group, Māori or non-Māori, whose members share a distinctive community. But the group must still show connection since 1840.[75]

The effect of a customary rights order is to confer a right on the holder to carry out the recognized customary activity and to enable protection of the activity under the *Resource Management Act*.[76] The group holding the order can carry out certain defined customary activities without first obtaining a resource consent. Importantly, a customary rights order may entitle the holder to derive a commercial benefit but only to the scale, extent, and frequency of the recognized customary activity as at 1840.[77]

Moreover, a Māori group can apply to the High Court to find that, but for the legislation, they would have held territorial customary rights to a particular area of the public foreshore and seabed. The act defines territorial customary rights to mean a collection of rights that would have been recognized at common law and would have amounted to a right to exclusive occupation and possession of a particular area.[78] If the court holds that a group has a territorial customary right, then it is no longer able to give effect to those rights but must refer its order to the attorney general and minister of Māori affairs.[79] The ministers must enter into discussions with the group, the purpose of which is to consider the nature and extent of any crown redress. Redress is at the discretion of the ministers.[80]

Conclusion

Although the crown's presumption that it owns the foreshore and seabed was born in an era when this type of land could only be occupied by piers or retaining walls, the new era provides significant opportunities to generate immense revenue from occupying the foreshore and seabed through marine farm construction.[81] In this new era, tension between the crown's presumption and the common law doctrine of Native title exists. The *Foreshore and*

Seabed Act provided a legal response that will clearly extinguish Native title in favour of crown ownership. But what it means in reality for Māori, and how the law will work in a comparative context, requires comment.

First, the act claims that it creates new rights for Māori and gives new powers to the courts. Although this claim is true, it obscures the reality that in giving new rights the act has potentially removed significant other rights: namely, property rights. The act is even more mischievous in that what an ancestral connection order and a customary rights order will give Māori will be very little. For example, all persons exercising functions and powers under the *Resource Management Act* in relation to managing the use, development, and protection of natural and physical resources must already have particular regard to *kaitiakitanga*[82] and recognize and provide for the relationship of Māori and their culture and traditions with their ancestral lands, water, sites, *waahi tapu* (sacred places), and other *taonga* (treasures) as a matter of national importance.[83]

In effect, the law will create a series of legal hoops for Māori to jump through but with no real prize at the end. All three orders – ancestral connection, customary rights, and territorial customary rights – establish onerous threshold tests for Māori. Adoption of the "connection since 1840" rule will be especially difficult to surpass. A like rule has emerged in Australia with recent court decisions contemplating that interruption of enjoyment or exercise of Native title rights or interests can be fatal.[84] Moreover, though the act provides political redress, the restricted ambit limits its relevancy – only where the High Court accepts that a right would have amounted in common law to exclusive occupation and possession. Bearing in mind that political redress is discretionary, compensation to Māori is unlikely to occur on any grand scale. More fundamentally, the cost, time, and energy required to seek any one of the three orders will be significant initial barriers for Māori.

Second, to discuss the New Zealand experience in a comparative context, reference needs to be made to Australia. The tension created by Native title existing in the foreshore and seabed has recently arisen in Australia. In 2001, the Australian High Court, in *Commonwealth of Australia v. Yarmirr*,[85] held that Native title rights do exist over the sea and seabed in the Croker Island region of the Northern Territory but only to the non-exclusive extent. In effect, Native title comprises free access to the sea and seabed within a claim area in accordance with traditional laws and customs for limited purposes of travelling through or within the area, fishing and hunting, visiting and protecting places that are of cultural and spiritual importance, and safeguarding cultural and spiritual knowledge. This significant decision, dubbed "The *Mabo* of the Seas," limited Native title in the sea and seabed to usufructuary-type rights. Unlike the New Zealand Court of Appeal in its *Ngati*

Apa decision, the Australian High Court did not foresee the possibility of the nature and extent of Native title extending to exclusive ownership.

In 2004, the Queensland Federal Court, in *The Lardil Peoples v. State of Queensland,*[86] endorsed the *Yarmirr* approach by refusing to hold that the claimants have exclusive ownership of the land and water below the high-water mark in a Queensland coastal and sea area.[87] Likewise, it emphasized rights of access and rights to fish, hunt, and gather in accordance with and for the purposes allowed by traditional laws and customs.[88] Interestingly, it rejected any notion that the claimants could have a general right to construct structures in the intertidal zone or the adjacent seas or even a specific right to construct, maintain, and repair rock fishtraps – a traditional use of the foreshore.[89] Justice Cooper found that the location of the rock fishtraps in the intertidal zone did not survive the assertion of sovereignty, and even if it did survive sovereignty it was not a right recognized by common law.[90] As Cooper stated,

> The common law recognised, in respect of the foreshores and the beds of tidal rivers, a full beneficial title in the Crown in such lands by virtue of the Crown prerogative. The title of the Crown was presumed and any person claiming title to the foreshores or to the beds of tidal rivers had to prove a prior grant from the Crown ... or adverse possession of the land against the Crown ... The Crown title to the foreshore ... was not a radical title but an absolute one.[91]

Cooper then substantiated that position in reference to legislation. Section 77 of the *Harbours Act* of 1955 (Queensland) states that this land, "unless and until the contrary is proved, [is] deemed to be the property of the Crown."[92] He concluded that the effect of this section was to "extinguish any right or interest of the applicants, if it had not been earlier extinguished at sovereignty, which was inconsistent with the Crown right, title, interest or estate in the land in the foreshore (inter-tidal zone) or land lying under the sea within Queensland waters."[93]

That judgment is remarkably different from the New Zealand Court of Appeal approach in its 2003 *Ngati Apa* decision. The Queensland judgment better aligns with New Zealand's Court of Appeal approach in *Ninety Mile Beach* taken back in 1963. The *Lardil* decision falls into the "extinguishment by a side-wind" trap, fails to be alive to the distinction between sovereignty and property, and equates the crown interest with absolute title, not radical title. Surprisingly, though the New Zealand Court of Appeal in its *Ngati Apa* decision discussed the leading Canadian and Australian Native title case law, it did not refer to the *Yarmirr* case.[94] Even though the more recent *Lardil* decision failed to reference *Ngati Apa*, this is less surprising in that no overseas case law was cited in that decision. The New Zealand Court of Appeal oversight may or may not be poignant.

Despite the different approaches between the New Zealand and Australian judiciaries, the actual outcomes for the indigenous peoples of each country will be similar: rights limited to traditional precolonial use and spiritual association.⁹⁵ The *Foreshore and Seabed Act* ensures this outcome in New Zealand. In the end, legal fictions and presumptions and geographical lines drawn in the sand have won. In New Zealand, the law was amended to give reality to the crown's presumption of legal title in the foreshore and seabed. The law endorses the need to divide land under water from land above water. It will create special rules that give effect to the British-derived cultural association with land under water: the crown must own the land to ensure the right of public access. With landscape divisions being such, claiming Native title in the foreshore and seabed will not be easy. That "one lone grain" has just found out how hard that task will be.⁹⁶

Notes

Epigraph: Waitangi Tribunal, *Report on the Crown's Foreshore and Seabed Policy*, http://www.waitangi-tribunal.govt.nz, 1-181 at 12-13.

1 For a good introduction to Māori custom, see any of the Waitangi Tribunal reports, including the recent *Te Whanganui a Tara me ona Takiwa: Report on the Wellington District* (Wellington: Wai 145, 2003), chap. 2. See also Hayes, "Defining Kaitiakitanga," 893-99; New Zealand Law Commission, *Maori Custom and Values*; Roberts et al., "Kaitiakitanga," 7-20; and Tomas, "Implementing Kaitiakitanga."

2 See Waitangi Tribunal, *Report on the Crown's Foreshore and Seabed Policy*, chap. 2.

3 Klein, "Belief-Views on Nature," 81-119.

4 [2003] 3 N.Z.L.R. 643 [*Ngati Apa*]. Note that the *Supreme Court Act* of 2003 established a new court of final appeal in New Zealand. The Supreme Court replaced the Judicial Committee of the Privy Council located in London on 1 January 2004 and commenced hearings on 1 July. New Zealand's proposed and enacted legislation can be viewed at http://www.legislation.govt.nz.

5 *The Foreshore and Seabed Act* (2004, No. 93) s. 5, provides an extensive definition of the foreshore and seabed, including stating that it (a) means the marine that is bounded (i) on the landward side by the high-water line at mean high-water spring tide; and (ii) on the seaward side by the outer limit of the territorial sea; and includes (b) the beds of rivers that are part of the coastal marine area within the meaning of the *Resource Management Act* of 1991; (c) the bed of Te Whaanga Lagoon in the Chatham Islands; (d) the air and water space above the areas described in paragraphs (a) to (c); and (e) the subsoil, bedrock, and other matters below the areas described in paragraphs (a) to (c). Note that in New Zealand Māori interests in fisheries and fishing have been negotiated. See the Deed of Settlement, 25 September 1992, signed by the crown and Māori; the *Treaty of Waitangi (Fisheries Claim) Settlement Act* (1992, No. 121); and the *Māori Fisheries Act* (2004, No. 78).

6 Defined in s. 129(2)(a) of *Te Ture Whenua Māori Act/Māori Land Act* (1993, No. 4).

7 *Ngati Apa*, 651.

8 For a copy of the treaty, see the first schedule to the *Treaty of Waitangi Act* (1975, No. 114).

9 [1847] N.Z.P.C.C. 387.

10 See the *Native Lands Acts* of 1862 and 1865. Its original name was the Native Land Court.

11 Preamble of the *Native Lands Act* (1862).

12 [1877] 3 N.Z. Jur. (N.S.) 72.

13 At 78. To better understand the political reality of New Zealand in the 1870s and the reason for Chief Justice Pendergast's decision, see McHugh, "A History of Crown Sovereignty in New Zealand," 189-211.

14 *Nireaha Tamaki v. Baker,* [1901] A.C. 561. The Privy Council in this case rejected the thinking in *Wi Parata* on the basis that it was "rather late in the day" for an argument to be made that Native title had no application.

15 [1963] N.Z.L.R. 461.

16 At 468.

17 [1986] 1 N.Z.L.R. 680.

18 At 687.

19 *Te Runanganui o Te Te Ika Whenua Inc Society v. Attorney-General,* [1994] 2 N.Z.L.R. 20 at 23-24.

20 *Faulkner v. Tauranga District Council,* [1996] 1 N.Z.L.R. 357 at 363.

21 See ss. 30-31, 63, 72.

22 S. 9.

23 See s. 2 of the *Resource Management Act.*

24 S. 12 of the *Resource Management Act.*

25 S. 131(1) of the *Māori Land Act.*

26 Ibid., s. 130.

27 See Boast et al., *Māori Land Law;* and the Maori Land Court website, http://www.courts. govt.nz/maorilandcourt/.

28 See s. 129(1) of the *Māori Land Act.*

29 See ibid., Preamble, and ss. 2, 17. For examples of previous statutes, see the founding legislation, *Native Lands Acts* (1862 and 1865); and two subsequent significant statutes, *Native Land Act* (1909) and *Māori Affairs Act* (1953).

30 S. 145 of the *Māori Land Act.*

31 See ss. 146, 147-48, 150A-C, 151-52 of the *Māori Land Act.*

32 *In Re Marlborough Sounds Foreshore and Seabed* (unreported), Māori Land Court, 22A Nelson MB 1, 22 December 1997 (Hingston J).

33 At 4.

34 At 9.

35 *Crown Law Office v. Māori Land Court (Marlborough Sounds),* 1998/3-9 Te Waipounamu A.C.M.B., 19 October 1998 (Durie CJ, Smith, Carter, Isaac JJ).

36 *Re Marlborough Sounds Foreshore and Seabed Decision,* [2002] 2 N.Z.L.R. 661.

37 See s. 7 of the *Territorial Sea and Exclusive Economic Zone Act* (1977, No. 28); and s. 9A of the *Foreshore and Seabed Endowment Revesting Act* (1991, No. 103).

38 At 655-66.

39 At 651.

40 At 656.

41 Ibid.

42 [1997] 3 S.C.R. 1010.

43 [1992] 175 C.L.R. 1.

44 *Ngati Apa,* 656, per Elias CJ.

45 See McNeil, *Common Law Aboriginal Title,* 105.

46 Cited in NZPA Political Reporter, "Law to Confirm Status of Seabed and Foreshore," *Otago Daily Times,* 24 June 2003, 1.

47 Government of New Zealand, *Protecting Public Access and Customary Rights: Government Proposals for Consultation* (Wellington: Government Publications, 2003), 4. To view the official foreshore and seabed website, see http://www.beehive.govt.nz/foreshore/home.cfm.

48 Department of Prime Minister and Cabinet, *Report on the Analysis of Submissions,* (Wellington: Government Publications, December 2003), 3.

49 For information on these *hui,* see http://www.tokm.co.nz/ and http://www.teope.co.nz/.

50 See s. 6(1) of the *Treaty of Waitangi Act* (1975).

51 Department of Prime Minister and Cabinet, *Summary of the Foreshore and Seabed Framework,* para. 1. See the document at http://www.beehive.govt.nz/foreshore/summary.cfm.

52 At para. 3.
53 See paras. 7 and 14-20.
54 At para. 8.
55 At para. 9.
56 At para. 12.
57 At para. 13.
58 Waitangi Tribunal, *Report on the Crown's Foreshore and Seabed Policy.*
59 Note that the tribunal can recommend to the crown action to compensate for or remove the prejudice or to prevent other persons from being similarly affected in the future. The recommendation may be in general terms or may indicate in specific terms the action that, in the tribunal's opinion, the crown should take. See s. 6(3-4) of the *Treaty of Waitangi Act* (1975); and Byrnes, *The Waitangi Tribunal and New Zealand History.*
60 Waitangi Tribunal, *Report on the Crown's Foreshore and Seabed Policy,* xiii-xiv.
61 Ibid., xiv-xv.
62 See Deputy Prime Minister Michael Cullen's official speech, "Waitangi Tribunal Report Disappointing," 8 March 2004, http://www.beehive.govt.nz/.
63 Ibid.
64 TV ONE Network News, 12 March 2004; and "Helen Clark Hits Out at Judge over East Coast Claim," *New Zealand Herald,* 13 March 2004, http://www.nzherald.co.nz/. See the response of the judge and the New Zealand Bar Association at http://www.nzherald.co.nz/ and http://www.nzherald.co.nz/.
65 For example, "Turia Quits Labour, Stripped of Portfolios," *New Zealand Herald,* 1 May 2004, http://www.nzherald.co.nz/.
66 For example, "Mahuta Stays On as Bill Goes Through," *New Zealand Herald,* 6 May 2004, http://www.nzherald.co.nz/.
67 For example, "Colin James: Foreshore and Seabed Bill Puts MMP on Shaky Ground," *New Zealand Herald,* 11 May 2004, http://www.nzherald.co.nz/.
68 For example, "Clark Defends Refusal to Meet Hikoi," *New Zealand Herald,* 5 May 2004, http://www.nzherald.co.nz/.
69 Decision 1 (66): New Zealand CERD/C/DEC/NZL/1 (17 Feburary-11 March 2005). See: http://www.converge.org.nz/pma/fs110305.htm.
70 United Nations Economic and Social Council, Distr. GENERAL E/CN.4/2006/78/Add.3 (13 March 2006). See: *www.converge.org.nz/pma/srnzmarch06.pdf.*
71 Ss. 4(a) and 13(1). Note that the government believes that very little of the foreshore and seabed is in private ownership; apparently, only about fifty-nine freehold titles exist.
72 S. 4.
73 See ss. 46-51.
74 S. 50(1).
75 See ss. 66-77.
76 Ss. 52, 76.
77 Ibid.
78 S. 32.
79 S. 36.
80 Ss. 37, 38.
81 See the *Māori Commercial Aquaculture Claims Settlement Act* (2004).
82 S. 7(a) of the *Resource Management Act.*
83 S. 6(e) of the *Resource Management Act.*
84 In *Mabo v. Queensland (No. 2)* (1992), 175 C.L.R. 1 at 70, it was established that, for a court to make a declaration of Native title, it must be satisfied that the connection has been "substantially maintained." Recent High Court judgments have narrowly interpreted this rule: for example, *Members of the Yorta Yorta Aboriginal Community v. Victoria and Others* (2002), 194 A.L.R. 538.
85 [2001] H.C.A. 56.
86 [2004] F.C.A. 298.
87 See para. 245.
88 Ibid.

89 See para. 186.
90 At paras. 220-21.
91 At para. 221.
92 At para. 223.
93 At para. 224.
94 See also the commentary by Brookfield, "Maori Customary Title," 34-38.
95 This argument is explored in more detail by Ruru, "What Could Have Been," 116-44. For more commentary on the *Foreshore and Seabed Act,* see Boast, *Foreshore and Seabed*; Brookfield, "Maori Claims and the 'Special' Juridical Nature of Foreshore and Seabed," 179-216; Charters and Erueti, eds., *Māori Property Rights*; McHugh, "Aboriginal Title in New Zealand," 139-202; Ruru, "A Politically Fuelled Tsunami," 57-72; and Tomas and Johnston, "Ask That Taniwha," 10-52.
96 See proverb, note 1.

10
Waterpower Developments and Native Water Rights Struggles in the North American West in the Early Twentieth Century: A View from Three Stoney Nakoda Cases
Kenichi Matsui

The Native struggle for water and waterpower rights in the face of hydroelectric developments, or what Ward Churchill calls "hydrological rape,"[1] entailed both legal wrangling and cross-cultural negotiation for legitimacy. In such contested places, indigenous peoples, government officials, and entrepreneurs interacted, fought, collaborated, or negotiated in an attempt to determine the extent to which Native peoples were entitled to water, riverbed, and waterpower. The major focus of this chapter is to examine some social aspects of Native water rights history germane to the three hydroelectric developments on the Stoney Reserve in the Treaty 7 region, or present-day southwest Alberta. These three dams were constructed at the Horseshoe Falls, Kananaskis Falls, and Ghost River sites on the Bow River east of Calgary from 1907 to 1930. The dams are highly significant in the history of Native water rights issues not only because they were the earliest hydroelectric developments on Native reserves in western Canada but also because, through the negotiation process with the Stoney Nakoda (or Stoney),[2] government experts and authorities intensely debated the Native water rights question and, to some extent, incorporated Native demands. I approach this history from a historical rather than case law perspective by placing it within a context of cross-border studies. I also endeavour to explain how Treaty 7 Native water rights were similar to or distinct from those of neighbouring states of the American west or the province of British Columbia. By making this cross-border comparison, I intend to shed some light on the complex history of Native water rights issues in the North American west during its formative period.

The Early Development of Native Water Rights
In the early twentieth century, both American and Canadian officials were uncertain about how to define and deal with Native water rights, especially in relation to waterpower developments. The first successful operation of hydroelectric enterprise that combined alternating power generators, turbines,

and long-distance transmission lines for urban and industrial expansion came only in the 1890s in the Niagara Falls area.[3] Within a decade, private industry had quickly seized this opportunity and spread the technology across many parts of the North American west. However, such a large indus- trial endeavour often required an industrial monopoly of the entire river system, and federal and provincial officials were not ready to respond to these new demands.[4]

Many states in the American west,[5] New Zealand,[6] Australia,[7] and the North-West Territories (under dominion jurisdiction at the time and encom- passing present-day Alberta and Saskatchewan)[8] established statutes to regulate water rights before 1900, but these statutes mainly regulated irriga- tion and storage dam developments as they related to agricultural activities.[9] As early as 1892, the British Columbia government addressed waterpower developments in the *Water Privileges Act,*[10] but the major drafter of the federal *North-West Irrigation Act* (1893), William Pearce of Calgary, and other irriga- tion experts, such as J.S. Dennis in Ottawa, paid scant attention to this BC legislation. The *Irrigation Act,* therefore, did not make provisions related to waterpower rights.[11] At the time that he prepared the legislation, Pearce was the superintendent of mines in the Department of the Interior (1885-1901) and arguably the most informed of government personnel about irrigation laws. He had thoroughly studied irrigation practices in India, Italy, and Egypt as well as Australian irrigation law, which Minister of Public Works Alfred Deakin of Victoria (later prime minister) had proposed successfully in 1886. Pearce, however, paid little attention to waterpower developments. It is ironic that, while Deakin took ideas from Canadian engineers George Chaf- fey and William Benjamin of Ontario, who successfully combined irrigation and waterpower generation for the settlements of California and Australia in the 1880s, Pearce neglected to learn from what these Canadians had achieved.[12]

In the actual implementation of water laws, one important difference existed between British Columbia and the North-West Territories before 1930. After British Columbia became a Canadian province in 1871, the provincial government consolidated former colonial legislation and established statutes related to water rights. It aggressively attempted to adjudicate Native water rights and fought against federal jurisdiction over reserve lands and the railway belt, although these areas were proclaimed to be under the exclusive jurisdiction of the federal government in accordance with subsection 91(24) of the *British North America Act* and Article 13 of the *Terms of Union.* As early as 1888, the *British Columbia Land Act* authorized the chief commissioner of lands and works to appropriate water for Native peoples for agricultural purposes. The *Water Clauses Consolidation Act* of 1897 and the *Water Act* of 1912 amendment maintained this provision, although the latter stipulated that an Indian agent could acquire water licences for Native peoples for domestic, irrigation, or industrial purposes. The 1914 *Water Act* eliminated the industrial purpose of water rights for Native peoples and provided licences to Indian agents only for domestic and irrigation purposes.[13]

However, these provisions did not mean that Native peoples gained rightful legal protection under these laws. On the contrary, after 1909, provincial authorities such as the commissioner of lands and works and the Board of Investigation pushed aside Native applications in favour of non-Native ones. Department of Indian Affairs (DIA) officials constantly requested provincial authorities to protect Native water rights, though their attempts often met with aggressive rejections by provincial authorities.[14] In 1921, the province passed the *Indian Water Claims Act*, which declared provincial jurisdiction over Native water rights and authorized the provincial Board of Investigation to hear and determine all Native claims for the purposes of diverting, storing, and using water. The board would decide terms and conditions of Native water rights as it considered "just and reasonable."[15]

Native peoples in the Prairies, on the other hand, did not face this interjurisdictional strife until 1930.[16] Assuming that the *North-West Irrigation Act* and the *Dominion Lands Act* applied to Native peoples, the federal authorities did not make an effort to include provisions regarding Native rights to water in these acts or other related dominion legislation. It was only after passage of the *Natural Resources Transfer Agreements* in 1930 that the provinces of Alberta, British Columbia, and Saskatchewan similarly attempted to gain control over Native water rights under provincial waterpower laws.[17]

In the United States, the judiciary began defining Native water rights as well. The Supreme Court rendered a landmark decision in 1908 concerning Native water rights for the Gros Ventre and Assiniboine peoples on the Fort Belknap Reservation in northern Montana. In rendering this so-called *Winters* decision, Chief Justice Joseph McKenna confirmed that it was the federal government, not the state government, that had the jurisdiction over Native water rights. When the federal government and Native peoples reserved land by treaty or agreement, they reserved water as well. The nature of Native water rights defined by the court combined riparian water rights and the doctrine of prior appropriation. If the reservation land was attached to river or other water sources, then Native peoples had the right to claim riparian rights to water. The priority date (the date to claim prior and superior rights to water in accordance with the doctrine of prior appropriation) of Native water rights was recognized as the date that the reservation was set aside.[18]

The *Winters* decision did not clearly address to what extent Native peoples could claim their rights to waterpower because the case arose mostly out of concerns about Native rights to irrigation. However, McKenna implicitly touched on the waterpower question by declaring that "Indians had command of the lands and the waters – command of all their beneficial use, whether kept for hunting, 'and grazing herds of stock,' or turned to agriculture and the arts of civilization."[19] In the 1920s, the *Winters* doctrine appealed to some prominent dominion legal experts, such as H.W. Grunsky, legal adviser for the dominion Water Power Branch, and A.S. Williams, legal officer and future deputy superintendent of the DIA, who promoted adoption of this doctrine in Canada as a means to transform Native people into family farmers.[20] Despite their efforts, the *Winters* doctrine had limited political impact on Native irrigation practices and laws, especially in British Columbia.[21]

The Stoney Nakoda and Three Hydroelectric Dam Projects
Under these circumstances, the debate over Native rights to waterpower on the Stoney Reserve became a major legal and political quagmire. In November 1905, the Canadian Pacific Railway (CPR) competed with four other companies for the right to build dams and power plants near the Kananaskis and Horseshoe Falls sites solely for power generation purposes.[22] The DIA and Department of the Interior officials were not sure how to deal with these applications. This was especially the case after the minister of the interior, Clifford Sifton, ruled in 1905 that the *North-West Irrigation Act,* then the sole legislation dealing with water rights in the North-West Territories, was not applicable and that the applications had to be dealt with in "some other manner."[23] Without clear instructions from Sifton about the proper approach to deal with waterpower development issues, many federal and local officials turned to the *Irrigation Act* for guidance.[24]

Federal authorities often lamented the fact that the dominion government lacked a proper statute to deal with such schemes. They also regretted that they had not thoroughly investigated the legal questions regarding waterpower rights on dominion lands, especially as they related to Native rights. With the provinces of Alberta and Saskatchewan officially joining Confederation in 1905, some DIA authorities became even more confused about the jurisdiction questions concerning waterbed and water rights.[25] For example, William A. Orr, whose legal opinion on land issues had considerable weight in the DIA, thought that local governments had jurisdiction over water. A close examination of his correspondence indicates that he made this wrong assumption largely because he did not know that section 21 of the *Alberta Act* of 1905 stipulated that the revised *North-West Irrigation Act* of 1898 still applied to water resources on all crown lands in Alberta.[26]

Those officials who relied on the *Irrigation Act* for answers to the waterpower rights question knew that the act contained two subsections regarding the construction of dams, reservoirs, and other reclamation works but no provision for waterpower projects. After Sifton's ruling, the federal government amended the *Dominion Lands Act* in 1908, but the amendment provided only modest extensions to the clauses dealing with the subject in the *North-West Irrigation Act*.[27] It was under this cloudy statutory regime that waterpower companies made their applications to the Department of the Interior for rights to waterpower on dominion lands and the Stoney Reserve in the Treaty 7 region.

In the meantime, under the *Indian Act*, as early as 1903 the DIA initiated negotiations with the Stoney Nakoda for the surrender of portions of their reserve lands that were needed for anticipated hydroelectric developments. The department instructed its agent in Morley, H.E. Sibbald, a former missionary teacher, to discuss the proposition with the Stoney Nakoda. Chief John Chiniquay, the only one of the three Stoney Nakoda chiefs whom Sibbald consulted, flatly rejected the proposition. Although the chief had been known for his support for the Methodist mission in Morley and the establishment of an agricultural way of life for his people, he and his son Thomas opposed the plan partly because the reserve was too small to sell any portion of it.[28]

After this rebuff, the DIA sent the elderly and much more experienced missionary John McDougall to negotiate the surrender in April 1906. Initially, McDougall met intense hostility from the Stoney Nakoda. The disrespectful action taken by the DIA in allowing the CPR survey party to enter Stoney Nakoda land without permission in the preceding winter was fresh in their memory. The scale of the surveys was also impressive enough for some Stoney Nakoda observers to think that the waterpower site must be of tremendous value.[29] After one month of consideration, the chiefs and councillors relented and agreed to the proposition if some of their conditions were met. The Stoney Nakoda leaders proposed that, in exchange for surrendering Kananaskis Falls and Rapids, covering a distance of one mile and spanning the river, they would receive $110,000. When making this demand, the leaders claimed their rights both to waterpower and the riverbed. They also asked for compensation of $12 per acre for the land to be surrendered adjacent to the river.[30]

On 6 June 1906, the superintendent general of the DIA, Frank Pedley, sent a message to the Stoney Nakoda on the reserve through McDougall, saying that "as far as they have a proprietary interest in the water powers their interest will be fully protected by the Department when these are disposed of." The message also said that the "government is anxious that the Indians should receive for the use of the water power everything that the interests developing the power can afford to pay." Pedley recommended that the Stoney Nakoda offer a selling price of $25 in annual payment for the waterpower up to 1,000 developed horsepower and an additional dollar for power generated in excess of that amount.[31] This was the same rate that the city of Buffalo paid at the time.[32]

In January 1907, the Montreal-based Alexander and Budd syndicate approached the DIA to develop the Horseshoe Falls site. Consulting engineer Charles H. Mitchell, who represented the syndicate, accepted the lower, negotiated price of $10 per acre but also agreed to pay the Stoney Nakoda through the DIA an annual waterpower rental fee of $1,500.[33] Three chiefs, five councillors, and eleven other male members endorsed the agreement in February.[34] The DIA accepted the proposal and sent a cheque for the sum of $3,350. Agent Fleetham distributed the amount on a per capita basis on 13 March. On 14 May, an order-in-council formally approved the surrender.[35]

In the following years, the syndicate faced some financial difficulties, and their payment to the DIA was delayed for two years. The Montreal syndicate completed the Horseshoe dam in 1910 but later in the same year merged with other corporations to become the Calgary Power Company.[36] Lawyer and future prime minister Richard B. Bennett from Calgary and Montreal financier William Maxwell Aitken[37] led the new company and immediately sought to gain control of all the power sites on the Bow River.[38] Subsequently, the new company proposed developing two other hydro projects, one at the Kananaskis Falls site in 1912 and the other at the Ghost River site in 1927. The basic components of the agreements for these two later projects were largely modelled after the Horseshoe Falls agreement. These agreements also adopted a payment system identical to that arranged under the terms of Treaty 7.

Although the Stoney Nakoda, the DIA, and the company had sharply disagreed about the prices to be paid for reserve land surrenders and power rental payments, it is significant that the Stoney Nakoda's rights to waterpower had not been challenged. In fact, the Stoney Nakoda had effectively advanced their water rights in the second agreement for the Kananaskis Falls development by using the legal concept of "riparian" rights, and the dominion government had accepted it. The records do not clearly demonstrate whether the Stoney Nakoda and Samuel Bray, chief surveyor for the DIA, had knowledge of the *Winters* doctrine at the time.[39]

The Stoney Nakoda were initially reluctant to lose additional tracts of reserve land and were deeply offended when the Calgary Power Company entered their land to conduct surveys without their consent. However, they took the initiative to draft the second agreement in April 1913 with the help of Bray. As with the first approach, they demanded a per capita payment, annual rental, and monetary compensation for the surrendered land but increased the per capita payment to $25 per head in cash on completion of the surrender of 212 acres. Stoney Nakoda leaders insisted on this higher price even though their Indian agent, J.W. Waddy, thought that this amount was too high for DIA approval. The water rental clause for $1,500 per annum appeared again, but this time the Stoney Nakoda leaders based it on a claim of riparian rights. They also increased the amount of money for the 212 acres to $16,500 or about $77.83 per acre. This higher demand infuriated Bennett, who wrote to J.D. McLean, secretary of the DIA, "I think you will agree with me that, with the restriction in question, $16.50 is an absurd price for the land."[40]

The Stoney Nakoda leaders rejected Bennett's argument and remained adamant in their demands. They knew that rich Canadians such as Bennett, Aitken, and Isaak Walton Killam were involved in this project. Chief Inspector of Indian Agencies Glen Campbell also recommended to his superiors in Ottawa that "if this property were owned by one of your own shareholders he would not even consider $100 per acre." Departmental secretary J.D. McLean took this advice and demanded that the Calgary Power Company pay $100 per acre as well as the rental payment.[41] In 1914, Chief Walking Buffalo, Councillor Jonas Benjamin, and Dan Wildman Jr. travelled to Ottawa to negotiate with the DIA and Bennett. They met Bennett and the company representatives and, after a lengthy negotiation, had the company finally agree with most of what the Stoney Nakoda proposed.[42]

In 1919, the *Dominion Water Power Act* came into force. It applied to all dominion lands except the BC railway belt, where administrative control was delegated to the provincial authorities under the *Dominion Railway Belt Water Acts* of 1913 and 1914. The 1919 act replaced the water power provisions of the *Dominion Lands Act* of 1908. It authorized the director of waterpower, who was under the minister of the interior, to investigate, survey, and undertake all water power works in dominion lands. The *Dominion Water Power Regulation Act* of 1921 dealt in considerable detail with waterpower development. As in the BC *Water Act,* first enacted in 1909 and amended several times in the following years, the *Dominion Water Power Regulation Act* adopted a water licensing system instead of employing the patent system that had been included in section 35 of the *Dominion Lands Act* of 1908. Although the *Water Act* made water and waterpower provincial properties, the *Dominion Water Power Act* and *Regulations* regarded them as national properties, partly following the precedent set in the dominion *North-West Irrigation Act* and the American *Reclamation Act* of 1902.[43]

The new dominion waterpower law affected the third agreement negotiation for the Ghost River plants between 1927 and 1938. In accordance with this legislation, the Calgary Power Company applied for these power plant sites in November 1927. In January of the following year, the director of the Dominion Water Power and Reclamation Service, J.T. Johnson, notified the DIA that the Department of the Interior had given preliminary approval to the Ghost River development plan because it basically followed Service's comprehensive scheme for the "complete development" of the Bow River. DIA officials held a day-long meeting with the Stoney Nakoda regarding the Ghost River development on 8 May. At this meeting, the Stoney Nakoda agreed to sell 1,229 acres of reserve land for the payment of $20,000 (about $16 per acre). In addition, they requested the right to purchase 1,500 acres of additional land, known as the Potts Estate, situated on the southeast boundary of the reserve. In June, the Calgary Power Company reduced the size of land for surrender to 1,144 acres but promised to pay the amount proposed in May.[44] In late January 1929, voting for final approval took place in the United Church on the reserve. The *Calgary Herald* took an interest and reported the proceedings as follows:

> Prior to the actual voting a long discussion took place. Through an interpreter, Inspector Christianson explained in detail what the purpose of the voting was and why it was necessary. The two Stoney chiefs, Hector Crawler and John Dixon, with their councillors, joined vigorously in the debate and harangued their braves at length. At the conclusion of the discussion each voter stepped forward and affixed his signature or his mark to the official document which set forth that they agreed to surrender their ancient rights to the property.[45]

In total, eighty-eight Stoney Nakoda signed the document. The legal representative of the Potts Estate, Chambers, was also present and notified DIA officials that the legal papers to transfer the land to the DIA were completed. The Department of the Interior issued the final licence to the company for the Ghost River development under the revised *Water Power Act* of 1927. The terms of the licence specified that it would be valid for fifty years commencing on 31 December 1929.[46]

In September 1930, after passage of the transfer agreements, representatives from the DIA, Department of the Interior, Dominion Water Power and Reclamation Service, and Calgary Power Company met in Calgary to discuss whether the Department of the Interior was still entitled to the rental payment from the Ghost River development and whether the DIA should receive payments on behalf of the Stoney Nakoda directly, through the Department of the Interior, or via the province.[47] These questions arose because the Calgary Power Company had arranged to make a rental payment at once to the Department of the Interior, which was supposed to transfer half of the amount to the DIA. Uncertain whether the company should deal with the Department of the Interior or the Province of Alberta, it had held back a substantial portion of the Stoney Nakoda's rental payment.[48]

Although this delay in the middle of the Great Depression outraged many Stoney Nakoda, who strongly urged federal officials to obtain a prompt resolution of the jurisdictional question, the federal Department of Justice delayed its response for almost three years. In July 1933, Deputy Minister of Justice W. Stuart Edwards offered the opinion that "a portion of the water power rental is payable to and administrable by the Dominion for the benefit of the Indians, and that the Province (although the Director of Water Resources of the Province has indicated that the Province claims the whole amount of such rental) has no well-founded right or claim to receive such portion of the rental." In November 1933, the Stoney Nakoda finally received their share of arrears water rental payment for the period 1930-33.[49]

Conclusion

As we have seen, although no dominion statute defined the extent to which the indigenous peoples could claim their water rights on their traditional territories, and no parliamentary committee investigated them, the Stoney Nakoda clearly had obtained federal recognition of their rights to water, waterpower, and waterbed. This recognition was in stark contrast to the opposition in British Columbia, where the province strenuously opposed Native water rights and the attempts of federal officials to assert jurisdiction to deal with Native water rights on reserve lands. In the Treaty 7 region, Native rights to waterpower became *de facto* rights partly because the province of Alberta could not challenge them before 1930. These *de facto* rights were based on several sources, including Treaty 7, the *Indian Act*, the *Dominion Lands Act* (1908), the *Dominion Water Power Acts* (1919 and 1927), the *Dominion Water Regulations*, and most importantly the three Stoney Nakoda surrender agreements. The negotiating skills of the Stoney Nakoda leaders, which had improved considerably since Treaty 7 negotiations, became part of the driving force to incorporate these different sets of statutes to their advantage at that time.

Today experts in Aboriginal rights tend to emphasize court decisions and statutes. But, as we have seen, the history of Stoney Nakoda water rights highlights the need to consider the social, political, and economic contexts of hydroelectric developments. The examination of these contexts in turn will help us more fully to understand the complex history of Native water rights issues.

Acknowledgments
This chapter is a revised and abridged version of Chapter 6, "Hydroelectric Dams and Stoney Water Rights, 1907-1939," in *Native Peoples and Water Rights: Irrigation, Dams, and the Law in Western Canada* (Montreal/Kingston: McGill-Queen's University Press, 2009).

Notes
1   Churchill, *Struggle for the Land*, 292.
2   In Department of Indian Affairs documents, the Stoney Nakoda appear as "the Stoney" or "Stoneys." As of 2008, those members on the Stoney Reserve call themselves "Nakoda First Nations," consisting of three peoples or bands (Bearspaw, Chiniki, and Wesley). Their traditional territory encompassed not only the Morley area but also north and south along the Rocky Mountains and beyond. They are related to the Lakota and Dakota peoples in the Great Plains region.
3   Hunter, *A History of Industrial Power*, 205-30, 318-72; Jackson, Burtniak, and Stein, *The Mighty Niagara*, 201-39.

4 Armstrong and Nelles, *Monopoly's Moment*, 3-7; Dales, *Hydroelectricity and Industrial Development*, 13-23.

5 For example, see Hundley Jr., *Water and the West*; Mead, *Irrigation Institutions*; Pisani, *To Reclaim a Divided West*; Reisner, *Cadillac Desert*; Wilkinson, *Crossing the Next Meridian*; and Worster, *Rivers of Empire*.

6 Schroder, "On the Crest of a Wave," 1-54 at 38-39; Wheen, "A Natural Flow," 71-110.

7 Fisher, *Water Law*; Hill, *Water into Gold*.

8 Burchill, "The Origins of Canadian Irrigation Law," 353-62; den Otter, *Irrigation in Southern Alberta*; Mitchner, "William Pearce"; and the William Pearce Collection, series 7, University of Alberta Archives.

9 Perhaps one notable exception is the *Onehunga Water Reserves Act* of 1879 by New Zealand Parliament (Local Act No. 6), which protected "Bycroft's Springs" from pollution by setting aside two acres of land as a municipal reserve.

10 *Statutes of British Columbia*, 55 Vict. (1892), c. 47.

11 Pearce and his friend, surveyor J.S. Dennis, extensively researched irrigation practices in Australia, Egypt, and Italy, attended the Irrigation Congress held in Los Angeles in 1893, and met with prominent irrigation promoters such as George G. Anderson of Colorado, Elwood Mead of Wyoming, J.W. Mackie of California, Francis Newlands of Nevada (who drafted the federal *Reclamation Act*), and William Smythe, chairman of the International Irrigation Congress. See William Pearce to T. Myne Daly, Minister of the Interior, 24 October 1893, William Pearce Collection, series 7, 2-8; Elwood Mead, "Water Rights in Wyoming, 1898," William Pearce Collection, series 7, 1-11; and Mead, *Irrigation Institutions*.

12 In 1884, Alfred Deakin, a cabinet minister, solicitor-general, and commissioner for public works and water supply (and soon to be the minister of public works), toured California, Colorado, New Mexico, Kansas, and Utah to investigate irrigation laws and practices. He met Canadian-American irrigation promoter George Chaffey, who, on Deakin's invitation, went to Australia in the following year and established large settlements in Victoria based on irrigation agriculture. The partnership was instrumental in establishing irrigation law in Australia. See Alexander, *The Life of George Chaffey*, 47-56, 70-74; and Hill, *Water into Gold*, 54-72.

13 *Statutes of British Columbia*, 51 Vict. (1888), c. 10; 61 Vict. (1897), c. 45; 2 Geo. 5 (1912), c. 49; 4 Geo. 5 (1914), c. 81.

14 Matsui, "Reclaiming Indian Waters," 56-93.

15 *Statutes of British Columbia*, 12 Geo. 5 (1921), c. 19.

16 Matsui, "Reclaiming Indian Waters," 56-92.

17 Ibid., 128-65.

18 Several historians and legal scholars have already provided detailed accounts of the *Winters* doctrine. See Bartlett, *Aboriginal Water Rights in Canada*; Hundley Jr., "The Dark and Bloody Ground of Indian Water Rights," 454-82; Hundley Jr., "The 'Winters' Decision and Indian Water Rights," 17-42; and Shurts, *Indian Reserved Water Rights*.

19 *Winters v. United States*, 207 U.S. 576-77 (1908). See also *United States v. Rio Grande Dam and Irrigation Company*, 174 U.S. 690, 702, 703 (1899); and *United States v. Winans*, 198 U.S. 371 (1904).

20 Matsui, "Reclaiming Indian Waters," 87-88.

21 Matsui, "'White Man Has No Right to Take Any of It,'" 75-101.

22 Other applicants included Frank Oliver (1903 for Horseshoe Falls), O.G. Devenish of Montreal-based Guardian Assurance Company (for the Kananaskis site), Alexander Smith of Smith and Johnson on behalf of E.R. of Ontario (for the Kananaskis site), and W.M. Alexander and W.J. Budd of the Montreal-based Builders' Supply and Construction Company (1906 for Horseshoe Falls).

23 J.D. McLean to Commissioner of Irrigation, 7 November 1905; Commissioner of Irrigation to J.D. McLean, 13 November 1905; J.A. Markle, Inspector, to J.D. McLean, 13 November 1905, in LAC RG 10, vol. 7604, file 12119.

24 Canada, "Annual Report of the Department of the Interior," *Sessional Papers* (1914), 210.

25 In New Zealand, Te Awara in the Rotorua region of Northern Island sought clarification from courts in 1909 regarding Māori customary rights to lakes and lakebeds. In *Tamihana*

Korokai v. Solicitor General (1912) 15 G.L.R. 96, the Supreme Court confirmed Te Arawa's ownership of lakebeds. The subsequent negotiation between the crown and Te Arawa resulted in a 1922 agreement that recognized the crown's fee simple title to the lakebeds of fourteen lakes in the region, to which the Māori tribes had claimed ownership, in exchange for the protection of Māori customary fishing rights (along with forty fishing licences) and burial reserves. See Schroder, "On the Crest of a Wave," 39-40; and *Te Arawa Lakes Settlement Act,* Public Act 43 (2006).

26 *Statutes of Canada,* 4-5 Ed. 7 (1905), c. 3, ss. 21, 82; 57-58 Vict. (1894), c. 30, ss. 12(7-8); 61 Vict. (1898), c. 35.

27 S. 35 of the *Dominion Lands Act* 7-8 Ed. 7 (1908) authorized the governor in council to sell or lease land required for the development of waterpower. However, at this time, there was no licensing system and no specific agency designated to administer waterpower applications. Only signatures were required to certify the maps, plans, and books of reference for power development. *Statutes of Canada,* 7-8 Ed. 7 (1908), c. 20, "Dominion Lands Act Amendment," s. 35.

28 Sibbald to David Laird, 17 August 1903; David Laird to J.D. McLean, Secretary, DIA, 25 August 1903, in LAC RG 10, vol. 3686, file 13, 119 (2-4).

29 John McDougall to DIA, 25 May 1906, in ibid.

30 Stoney Chiefs and Councillors to DIA, 22 May 1906, in ibid.

31 DIA to John McDougall, 6 June 1906; Frank Pedley to John McDougall, 13 June 1906, in ibid.

32 Jackson, Burtniak, and Stein, *The Mighty Niagara,* 219.

33 Frank Oliver to John McDougall, 24 July 1906; Builders' Supply and Construction Ltd. to Minister of the Interior, 21 Dec. 1906; Secretary of the Department of the Interior to J.D. McLean, DIA, 11 January 1907; J.D. McLean to Alexander and Budd, 18 January 1907; Charles H. Mitchell to Frank Pedley, 27 January 1907; Charles H. Mitchell to Frank Pedley, 29 January 1907, in LAC RG 10, vol. 3686, file 13, 119 (2-4).

34 The major signatories were Chiefs Jonas Two Youngman, Peter Wesley, Moses Bearspaw, Councillors John Mark, James Swampy, Hector Crawler, Amos Bigstoney, and George McLean or Walking Buffalo. See the agreement of 20 February 1907; and T.J. Fleetham to Frank Pedley, 21 February 1907, in ibid.

35 Frank Pedley to T.J. Fleetham, 4 March 1907; "Cash Statement" by T.J. Fleetham on 13 March 1907; and Clerk of the Privy Council to Frank Pedley, 14 May 1907, in ibid.

36 Frank Pedley to Frank Oliver, 21 January 1908; Jones, Nicholas, and Pescod, Barristers, Solicitors, Notaries, etc. to DIA, 27 January 1908; W.J. Budd to Frank Pedley, 13 February 1908, in ibid.

37 "Max" Aitken established himself as an investment banker in Montreal at the end of 1906. In 1910, he moved to London, England, and won a parliamentary seat for the Conservatives. One year later he was knighted and known as Lord Beaverbrook. The Calgary Power Company began with $3,000,000. Aitken later sold his holding to Isaak Walton Killam. See Taylor, *Beaverbrook,* 15-16.

38 Hawkins, *Electrifying Calgary,* 121-47.

39 Here I do not mean to suggest that the Stoney Nakoda had not held any concept of law regarding the use and ownership of the Bow River. Likely, they had traditionally regarded the river, riverbank, and riverbed as one undivided entity. I believe that the Stoney Nakoda found the "riparian" claim somewhat similar to their traditional notion of water rights and used this Western legal idea to their advantage.

40 *Stoney Agreement,* 15 April 1913; Samuel Stewart, Assistant Deputy and Secretary, DIA, to George Cousins, Solicitor for the Calgary Power Company, 3 May 1913; R.B. Bennett to J.D. McLean, 28 May 1913, in LAC RG 10, vol. 8057, file 772/32-3-3, pt. 1.

41 Dominion Water Power Branch to Frank Pedley, 10 July 1913; G.S. Worsley, Inspector, NWMP, "Memorandum re: Trouble between Indians and Calgary Power Company," 6 July 1913; G.S. Worsley, Inspector, NWMP, to Agent Waddy, 8 July 1913; J.D. McLean to V.W. Drury, Calgary Power Company, 21 July 1913, in ibid.

42 MacEwan, *Tatanga Mani*, 170-72; General Manager, Calgary Power Company, to J.D. McLean, 6 September 1913; Indian Agent at Morley to J.D. McLean, 13 December 1913; the 1914 agreement of surrender, LAC RG 10, vol. 8057, file 772/32-3-3, pt. 1.

43 *Statutes of Canada*, 9-10 Geo. 5 (1919), c. 19; 11-12 Geo. 5 (1921); J.B. Challies, "Report of the Superintendent of the Water Power Branch," 15 July 1915, in Canada, *Sessional Papers* (1916), 5-6.

44 M. Christianson to W.M. Graham, Indian Commissioner, 9 May 1928; *Stoney Agreement*, 8 May 1928; "Calgary Power Co. Buys Indian Land along Bow River," *Calgary Herald*, 28 May 1928, in LAC RG 10, vol. 8057, file 772/32-3-3, pt. 2. The *Calgary Herald* reported that over fifty men signed, but this number was slightly exaggerated.

45 "In Formal Manner Stoneys Vote Sale of Morley Land," *Calgary Herald*, 21 January 1929, in ibid.

46 Another important change to the licence, authorized by the 1927 amendment, was the provision that declared it to be illegal for a member of the House of Commons of Canada, in this case R.B. Bennett, to benefit from the licence. See terms of the final licence, Department of the Interior (1930), in LAC RG 10, vol. 8057, file 772/32-3-3, pt. 3. S. 48 of the *Water Power Regulations* determined the annual waterpower rental rate for the Stoney Nakoda. Until 17 January 1932, the company would pay fifty cents per installed horsepower. After this date to 17 January 1952, the rate for the annual payment depended on the annual load factor. If the company operated with a higher percentage load factor, then it would pay less money per horsepower.

47 "Memorandum First Drafted at a Conference at the Office of Mr. O.M. Biggar, K.C., on 26 Sept. 1930, at Which Were Present Mr. A.S. William, Solicitor of the Department of the Indian Affairs; Mr. J.C. Caldwell, Director of Indian Lands; Mr. W.W. Cory, Solicitor to the Department of the Interior, and Mr. M.F. Cochrane, Water Power and Reclamation Engineer of the Water Power and Reclamation Service," 30 September 1930, in LAC RG 10, vol. 8057, file 772/32-3-3, pt. 3.

48 Indian Agent Hinton to Secretary of the DIA, 17 January 1933; Memorandum of Harold W. McGill to Duncan Campbell Scott, 27 January 1933; M. Christianson to Secretary of the DIA, 8 March 1933; Duncan Campbell Scott to A.E. Miller, Office of the Prime Minister, 7 April 1933, in ibid.

49 W. Stewart Edwards to H.H. Rowatt, 19 July 1933, in ibid; Indian Agent to Secretary of the DIA, 21 March 1938, in LAC RG 10, vol. 8057, file 772/32-3-3, pt. 2.

Power and Principle: State-Indigenous Relations across Time and Space
Peter W. Hutchins

Constitutional protection of indigenous difference ought to extend beyond protection of certain customs, practices, and traditions integral to Aboriginal cultures to include protection of interests associated with territory, sovereignty, and the treaty process.

> – Patrick Macklem, *Indigenous Difference and the Constitution of Canada*

Without a guardian of the pledged word, only force counts.

> – Alain Supiot, *Homo Juridicus: On the Anthropological Function of the Law*

Power and principle frame the portrait of state-indigenous relations – irrespective of era, irrespective of place. With this portrait, Western courts have struggled for a century and a half. Aboriginal litigation of course has one predominant characteristic – almost inevitably it involves the state as plaintiff or defendant. Politics is introduced into the brew; principle is often siphoned off.

I was honoured to be asked to give the keynote address at the conference *Delgamuukw, Mabo,* and *Ysleta*: Native Title in Canada, Australia, and the United States at the University of Calgary on 18 September 2003. I used the Thirty Years War as a metaphor for the experience that I had lived (and at least to that date had survived) as a practitioner seeking justice in state-indigenous relations. Although not combative by nature (!), I was drawn to the parallel by the fortuitous chronology (*Calder* in 1973 and the conference in 2003) and other analogies. The title of my address, "The Thirty Years War: A Practitioners' Guide to Aboriginal Litigation since *Calder,*" might have seemed somewhat dark and exaggerated. There could well have been protests that there had been no war and certainly not one for thirty years. It did occur to me that the title could have been "The Hundred Years War: A Practitioners' Guide ... since *St. Catherine's Milling*" or "The Hundred and Seventy Years War: A Practitioners' Guide ... since *Cherokee Nation v. Georgia.*"

From the chapters in this volume, it appears that litigation arising in Australia and New Zealand has also been a field of battle for the struggle of indigenous peoples toward *state* acceptance of Native title, self-governance, human rights, and human dignity. In these few pages, I wish to examine the strengths and failings of our judicial systems as they have confronted and continue to confront the challenges presented by the conflicts. For indigenous peoples, majority populations, and the states in which they cohabit, much is at stake, particularly for those who harbour what Michael Ignatieff terms a "longing to live in a fair world."[1]

Courts may be the guardians of principled and just outcomes. Writing in 1761 as a young lawyer, John Adams, the second president of the United States, saw an indelible link between the practice of law and a fairer world:

> Now to what higher object, to what greater character, can any mortal aspire than to be possessed of all this knowledge, well digested and ready at command, to assist the feeble and friendless, to discountenance the haughty and lawless, to procure redress to wrongs, the advancement of right, to assert and maintain liberty and virtue, to discourage and abolish tyranny and vice?[2]

Charles Dickens had a bleaker view of the denizens of the courts:

> This is the Court of Chancery ... which gives to monied might the means abundantly of wearying out the right; which so exhaust[s] finances, patience, courage, hope; so overthrows the brain and breaks the heart; that there is not an honourable man among its practitioners who would not give – who does not often give – the warning, "Suffer any wrong that can be done you rather than come here!"[3]

What are they, then, these judicial systems? Are they instruments "to discountenance the haughty and lawless, to procure redress to wrongs"? Or are they instruments that give "to monied might the means abundantly of wearying out the right"? The young Adams spoke of what the law should be; the jaded Dickens regretted that power and the instruments of power often distort the law and break the heart.

Sovereignty Now Is a Cinch

Let's be honest. Since the initial European-indigenous meetings in North America, Australia, and New Zealand, the prize has been lands and their

resources. Indigenous peoples lived on and among them; European colonizers coveted them. Had Europeans applied their own common law to these
meetings, the hostilities would have been over before they began. Kent
McNeil in his chapter implies just this:

> The second source is the common law itself, which acknowledges that per-
> sons in exclusive occupation of land have a title that is good against anyone
> who cannot show a better title. Applying this common law rule in the col-
> onial context, indigenous peoples who were in exclusive occupation of land
> at the time of British colonization would have title to the lands that they
> occupied at that time, regardless of the nature of their land rights under
> their own legal systems. This title can be designated as "common law title."

By definition, the first peoples used and occupied – possessed – lands and
resources exclusively at the moment that the courts have referred to as
"contact." Haijo Westra in his chapter asks the right question: "Why should
historical Native dominion be any less real than the original paper claim of
the colonizing power?" The courts have obfuscated the illegality and im-
morality of these historical moments, asserting, as the Supreme Court of
Canada did in *Sparrow*, that

> It is worth recalling that while British policy towards the native population
> was based on respect for their right to occupy their traditional lands, a
> proposition to which the Royal Proclamation of 1763 bears witness, there
> was from the outset never any doubt that sovereignty and legislative power,
> and indeed, the underlying title, to such lands vested in the Crown.[4]

The same court more recently in *Haida*,[5] though propounding what has
become the buzzword in contemporary jurisprudence (*reconciliation*), used
an interesting language of counterpoint in describing the law's sleight of
hand, indeed black magic, in depriving indigenous peoples of their dominion
and property: "This process of reconciliation flows from the Crown's duty
of honourable dealing toward Aboriginal peoples, which arises in turn from
the Crown's assertion of sovereignty over an Aboriginal people and *de facto*
control of land and resources that were formerly in the control of that
people."[6]

Use of the expressions *assertion of sovereignty* and *de facto control of land and
resources* to describe the crown's involvement in this colonial conjuring may
well hold significance as a moment of truth in Canadian jurisprudence.

Meanwhile in this volume, we read Westra's description of the judgment
of the process of the seventeenth-century professor of theology at the University of Mexico, Alonso de la Vera Cruz: "Mere possession and time do not
validate the illegal claim but increase the original injustice, a fundamental

difference between natural and common law." The great tradition of Jacques Cartier planting the flag and Captain James Cook sighting the northwest coast of what is now Canada is alive and well in the scramble for sovereign legitimacy in the Arctic, with the important difference that Canada now asserts sovereignty through the Inuit rather than in spite of them. Two texts illustrate this progressive change. The first is of a 1951 Canadian government telegram:

> Press release the flag was raised today in fine *comma* clear weather that marked the opening of the Craig Harbour detachment of the RCMP *stop* this outpost which is situated on Ellesmere Island Northwest Territories of Canada *comma* is seventy six degrees twelve north latitude *comma* is now the most northerly active establishment of the RCMP stop the ceremony opened with an address by Alex Stevenson OIC Eastern Arctic Patrol *stop* Captain Chouinard ... arrived from ship by helicopter to present flag on behalf of Department of Transport ... two constables will maintain establishment assisted by two eskimo families *stop* prayers by Rev. G. A. Ruskell ... visiting Anglican Missionary stop service included appropriate anthems *stop* ship passengers *comma* eskimo families in attendance *stop* snow clad mountains *comma* icebergs *comma* glaciers tundra and white caribou formed backdrop for impressive occasion *stop* film board unit coverage *stop* <u>sovereignty now is a cinch.</u> (emphasis added)[7]

The second is a statement from 1985 by Prime Minister Joe Clark (then Minister of External Affairs), in which he asserted:

> Canada is an Arctic nation. The international community has long recognized that the Arctic mainland and islands are part of Canada like any other, but the Arctic is not only a part of Canada, it is a part of Canadian greatness. Canada's sovereignty in the Arctic is indivisible. It embraces land, sea and ice ... From time immemorial Canada's Inuit people have used and occupied the ice as they have used and occupied the land.[8]

Let me conclude on this point by recalling that the Inuit have an understanding of Arctic sovereignty that contrasts profoundly with that held by the still flag-planting State. The version put forward by the indigenous peoples of the Arctic is one in which their rights and roles in their land are fully recognized. In a 2002 speech outlining an Inuit perspective on Arctic sovereignty, Sheila Watt-Cloutier, then President of the Inuit Circumpolar Council (Canada), used Prime Minister Clark's above words for support of her point that Inuit have been instrumental in exerting Canadian sovereignty in the Arctic and went on to urge the involvement of Inuit as part of the Canadian delegation asserting Canada's Arctic sovereignty at the international level.[9] Affirmation of the Inuit's role in Arctic governance grew stronger in April 2009 when Inuit across the circumpolar Arctic came together to adopt the *Declaration on Sovereignty in the Arctic*.[10] This landmark *Declaration* notes that the five coastal Arctic states "have neglected to include Inuit in Arctic sovereignty discussions"[11] and asserts that, "[t]he inextricable linkages between issues of sovereignty and sovereign rights in the Arctic and Inuit self-determination and other rights require states to accept the presence and role of Inuit as partners in the conduct of international relations in the Arctic."[12]

Establishing Checks and Balances

Once comfortably installed on indigenous lands, the sovereign, with the assistance of some early jurisprudence, proceeded to ensure that the crown sat atop the hierarchy of rights and power in the newfound lands. With crown sovereignty established, the courts set about placing the chess pieces, establishing checks and balances.

Initially, the courts reinforced the crown's position. As late as 1929, the court in *R. v. Syliboy* asserted that

> A civilized nation first discovering a country of uncivilized people or savages held such country as its own until such time as by treaty it was transferred to some other civilized nation. The savages' rights of sovereignty even of ownership were never recognized. Nova Scotia had passed to Great Britain not by gift or purchase from or even by conquest of the Indians but by treaty with France, which had acquired it by priority of discovery and ancient possession; *and the Indians passed with it.* (emphasis added)[13]

By 1985, Chief Justice Brian Dickson, forcefully rejecting this language, stated for the Supreme Court of Canada that "it should be noted that the language used by Patterson J., illustrated in this passage, reflects the biases and prejudices of another era in our history. Such language is no longer acceptable in Canadian law and indeed is inconsistent with a growing sensitivity to native rights in Canada."[14] We have come a long way since *Syliboy* with *Calder, Haida,* and the reasonably recent *Tsilhqot'in* case in British Columbia, although a very long stretch of road lies ahead. The classic Canadian approach to all things is perhaps most aptly expressed by Chief Justice Antonio Lamer in *Van der Peet*:

> *The challenge of defining aboriginal rights stems from the fact that they are rights peculiar to the meeting of two vastly dissimilar legal cultures; consequently there* will always be a question about which legal culture is to provide the vantage point from which rights are to be defined ... A morally and politically

defensible conception of aboriginal rights will incorporate both legal perspectives.[15]

As Bruce Rigsby observes in his chapter, legal recognition by the colonizing nation of the rights and interests that Aboriginals might have in lands and waters came late in Australia. The Thirty Years War in that jurisdiction started badly with the 1971 decision in *Milirrpum*,[16] and, as I understand from the chapters here, peace has not yet been declared. Matters started peacefully enough in New Zealand with the 1847 decision in *R. v. Symonds*,[17] but as Jacinta Ruru points out in her chapter the battle front has shifted over the years, starting with the 1877 judgment in *Wi Parata v. The Bishop of Welling-ton*[18] declaring that Native title had no application in New Zealand. The front again moved with the disapproval of *Wi Parata* by the Privy Council in 1901 on appeal, and then again with the continued resonance of *Wi Parata* in New Zealand courts, particularly the 1963 Court of Appeal decision in *In re the Ninety Mile Beach*.[19] Today the courts appear to have come full circle, for, as Ruru writes, "the more recent Native title decisions reiterate not the *Wi Parata* or *Ninety Mile Beach* line of reasoning but the *R. v. Symonds* precedent."

Time and Education

One remarkable thing about the protracted period of conflict is that much of the Canadian populace, and I must assume those of Australia and New Zealand as well, have remained oblivious to the struggle and uncomprehend-ing of its causes or outcomes.

During the turbulent Oka Crisis of 1990, I was asked by Assembly of First Nations National Chief Georges Erasmus to go into the Mohawk community of Kanesatake, situated about sixty kilometres from Montreal, and assist the besieged population to organize and seek help. Together with two other advisers, Peter DiGangi and Roger Jones, I was spirited behind the lines across the Lake of Two Mountains in the dead of night, and for several days we worked to help the traumatized community. When I say the community was besieged, this is no exaggeration. It was surrounded by army and police and occupied by warriors and various elements from elsewhere determined to make a last stand. At night, helicopters patrolled the skies and cast their searchlights over the village. Roads in and out were blocked, and supplies had to be negotiated past the roadblocks. It was a frightening place.

After several days, once again we had to slip away across the Lake of Two Mountains. As I sat in the small boat reflecting on the community-turned-war zone, I suddenly looked up to see a singular and, in the circumstances, bizarre scene. We were surrounded by a small armada of swank sailboats filled with swank crews. We had wandered into the midst of the Hudson Sunday Regatta. The flapping of sails replaced the beating of rotors, and suddenly the war zone was in another country and another time – the perfect metaphor for the thirty years of struggle of Aboriginal peoples in the face of public stasis. Perhaps more judicial reprimand would help concentrate society's mind as well as prick its conscience. When faced with the fact that just application of the law might not accord either with precedent or with society's views, the judiciary often must attempt to craft a compromise.[20] In this they require, indeed deserve, a population manifesting its "longing to live in a fair world" – in a principled world. Although this transformation is taking place, we cannot depend on politics or legislatures to insist on principle; our last best hope is the judicial system.

Perhaps, as David Yarrow observes in his chapter, "time and education are required for non-indigenous legal institutions to improve their awareness." Yarrow quotes Allistair McIntyre, contending that time is required for mutual recognition between cultures and apparently questioning whether we have, at present, the suitable means for mutual cultural evaluation: "The coming together of two previously separate communities, each with its own well-established institutions, practices, and beliefs, either by migration or by conquest, may open up new alternative possibilities and require more than the existing means of evaluation are able to provide."

Lost in the Thickets and Brambles

In his signature prose, Lord Denning had this to say about clinging rigidly to bad precedent:

> Let it not be thought from this discourse that I am against the doctrine of precedent. I am not. It is the foundation of our system of case law. This has evolved by broadening down from precedent to precedent. By standing by previous decisions, we have kept the common law on a good course. All that I am against is its too rigid application – a rigidity which insists that a bad precedent must necessarily be followed. I would treat it as you would a path through the woods. You must follow it certainly so as to reach your end. But you must not let the path become too overgrown. You must cut out the dead wood and trim off the side branches, else you will find yourself lost in thickets and brambles. My plea is simply to keep the path to justice clear of obstructions which would impede it.[21]

As courts feel their way toward more principled positions in state-indigenous relations, they have, I fear, far too often found themselves lost in Lord Denning's thickets and brambles. In Canada, high hurdles must be cleared to establish the legal legitimacy of claims to Aboriginal rights and title.[22] The high and low priesthoods of the law refer to these obstacles as "legal tests" to be passed or failed. The challenge is made more interesting as the tests are occasionally adjusted in the midst of the race.[23] One obvious example is the "*Van der Peet* test," derived from Chief Justice Lamer's determination that "in order to be an Aboriginal right an activity must be an element of a practice, custom or tradition integral to the distinctive culture of the Aboriginal group claiming the right" at the time of European-indigenous contact.[24] The test carries the burden of proof to a new level: no evidence (in an unwritten record) of integrality and distinctiveness at the moment of "contact" (established in eastern Canada as 1640), no rights to assert against the state.

I have written elsewhere that the *Van der Peet* test, as it was applied subsequently in *Mitchell v. M.N.R.*, reflected the increasingly misguided attempts by courts to impose judicial positivism on history and culture.[25] Mark Walters, in his excellent paper entitled "The Right to Cross a River? Aboriginal Rights in the *Mitchell* Case," wrote that "within the space of three paragraphs in *Mitchell* the law of Aboriginal rights in Canada was reduced to doctrinal shambles."[26]

Perhaps we should ponder for our subject US Supreme Court Justice Ruth Bader Ginsburg's observation of the court's approach to the abortion issue: "I am not a big fan of these tests. I think the court uses them as a label that accommodates the result it wants to reach."[27] Sadly, that describes many of the judicial pronouncements over the past thirty years in our three jurisdictions.

Things do not appear to be much better in Australia. Nicolas Peterson opens his chapter commenting that, "while the state appears to be accepting of difference, ultimately the kinds of difference embodied by Aboriginal people are unacceptable to liberal moral sensibilities, making the preconditions for recognition set high."

Liberal sensibilities, not to mention conservative convictions, are indeed challenged. In the tug-of-war between power and principle, look at what has been and continues to be at issue: universal human rights versus special rights and privileges; individual versus collective rights; acquired rights versus expropriated rights; Western liberal democracy versus clans, kinship, and heredity; natural resource extraction versus the seasonal round of harvesting; the crown as protector of indigenous cultures and economies versus the crown as facilitator of settlement and development; Aboriginal peoples with treaties versus those without them; universal principles of human rights versus the exercise of self-determination; domestic laws and politics versus international laws on human rights and constraints on state power; and, perhaps most importantly, as raised in this volume, claims to "tradition" versus claims to "modernity."[28] These are all principles and positions devoutly held and bitterly contested. The jurisprudence is replete with these struggles.

Clearly, serious social science intervention might assist in keeping "the path to justice clear of obstructions." It is at this point that the crying need for a multidisciplinary approach to these matters becomes most apparent. Arthur Ray, in his contribution to this volume, provides fascinating insights into the role of social science "experts" in this tug-of-war. Justices involved in Aboriginal litigation are being placed in a near-impossible situation. When Ray was awarded the 2005 Bora Laskin Fellowship to examine what he calls "Canada's biggest unresolved human rights issue, Aboriginal land claims," he pointed out how the complexities of Aboriginal litigation are making unrealistic demands on trial judges who must develop a PhD level of knowledge on the subject almost overnight and sort through many different points of view to make decisions about new historical facts.

Justice Ian Binnie of the Supreme Court of Canada has acknowledged the dilemma for the courts if required by litigants to make a final determination on the facts:

> The courts have attracted a certain amount of criticism from professional historians for what these historians see as an occasional tendency on the part of judges to assemble a "cut and paste" version of history ...
>
> While the tone of some of this criticism strikes the non-professional historian as intemperate, the basic objection, as I understand it, is that the judicial selection of facts and quotations is not always up to the standard demanded of the professional historian, which is said to be more nuanced. Experts, it is argued, are trained to read the various historical records together with the benefit of a protracted study of the period, and an appreciation of the frailties of the various sources. The law sees a finality of interpretation of historical events where finality, according to the professional historian, is not possible. The reality, of course, is that the courts are handed disputes that require for their resolution the finding of certain historical facts. The litigating parties cannot await the possibility of a stable academic consensus. The judicial process must do as best it can.[29]

With respect, I am not sure that "the law sees a finality of interpretation of historical events." Chief Justice Dickson in *Simon* did not seem to think so. Nor does it appear that Lord Denning did. Perhaps the litigating parties as well as the law and history would benefit from judicial restraint. In responding to Ray's observations on the challenges facing courts involved in Aboriginal litigation, Marc Renaud, president of the Social Sciences and Humanities Research Council of Canada, cautioned that "these decisions have real consequences: for the rights of Aboriginal people, for governments who sometimes pay millions of dollars in compensation, and for our understanding of Canadian history. The work of Prof. Ray will help us learn how we can reduce the potential costs of land claim disputes, both in terms of money and human dignity."[30] We must provide the judicial process with the tools to seek, at least within the parameters of a given case, a relatively stable academic consensus.

Many answers are harboured in the rich, sensitive, at times plaintive chapters in this book. Lou Knafla has skilfully distilled their essence in his introductory chapter. I look to them as an invaluable critique or perhaps a call to arms against the disciplinary silos that have been in construction for over fifty years – what Peterson alludes to when he asserts that "sophisticated social analysis is completely lacking, with the focus solely on power and legal relations, to the neglect of the economic and the cultural."

Without a Guardian of the Pledged Word, Only Force Counts

I return with mixed feelings to the words that I spoke six years ago to open the conference at the University of Calgary. I knew then that there had been defeats in the unequal battles waged in the Canadian courts since *Calder*. I had come to understand as well that any advance in favour of indigenous peoples had been prompted, if not ordered, by court decisions, particularly those of the Supreme Court of Canada. What I had yet to appreciate was the mediating role of the courts, which has the potential to replace final judgments. Brian Ballantyne has the right idea in opening his chapter:

> The debate about Aboriginal title appears to consist of two main themes. The first theme is that various judgments define the scope and tests for Aboriginal title. These judgments are critical because, without them, there would be little legal, political, or cultural (at least by the non-Aboriginal community) acceptance of that title: "You have to get the court to make the order, or it just doesn't happen." This theme is widening and deepening.

But I now ask, are there only two possible outcomes: war through litigation or an unequal peace resulting from negotiations in which the settler state makes its paper claims over the lands of indigenous peoples? Peterson contends that "the future requires the development of creative new policies that work toward negotiated rather than litigated solutions." In my opinion, that depends entirely on what is referred to as "litigated solutions." The siren call of negotiations, friendly settlements, and their ilk issues from the courts and the state – from the courts as a naive consummation devoutly to be wished; from the state as a Faustian bargain to entice indigenous peoples away from their "indigenous difference";[31] and, if I may speak as a member of the world's second oldest profession, from the law's protection. The deal with the devil is that one will enter into discussions with the state not on the basis of rights but on the basis of "interests," not mediated by the courts, but mano-a-mano. I doubt that Rigsby had *La damnation de Faust* playing in his ears when he wrote the following, but his caution is well worth pondering:

We and our lawyer brethren, I believe, have been too willing to overempha-
size the spiritual aspect of Aboriginal traditional ownership of land, to the
disregard and perhaps devaluation of its social and material features. I cannot say whether a rights-based approach in our ethnography and Native
title research and writing will produce the determinations that our clients
desire, but I can say that, without a rights-based approach, *we are not even
in the game anymore.* (emphasis added)

I suggest that, five years on, the path to our own *Peace of Westphalia* will
lie in the supervisory capacity of the courts. This may surprise those who
view the courts as often "getting it wrong" or litigation as being one more
battle to survive and negotiation the preferred route. Negotiation can be a
frustrating, ruinous, and seemingly unending road if the power and discretion of the crown are left unchecked. There will be no progress without the
assistance of the courts, assistance that can take many forms – with due
respect to Arthur Ray, Bruce Rigsby, Paul Chartrand, Nicolas Peterson, Jacinta
Ruru, and Kenichi Matsui – indeed to some extent every contributor to this
volume.

Other reforms being discussed have been inspired by initiatives by courts
in Australia and New Zealand, in particular those that create greater space
for Aboriginal peoples' laws and ways of sharing their knowledge. These
initiatives include the recent amendments to Australia's *Evidence Act 2005*
that make it easier for members of an Aboriginal or Torres Strait Islander
group to give evidence of their traditional laws and customs.[32] Another
amendment makes it possible for a witness to give evidence in narrative
form[33] without facing the barrage of questions on cross-examination that
many elders and other respected members of Aboriginal communities have
found nothing short of harrowing and demeaning. Inspiration also comes
from the practice in Australia of judges travelling to the territories at the
centre of title claims to hear "on country evidence," which places the court
on the very lands that hold so much meaning to the Aboriginal claimants.
This displacement allows at least portions of cases to be heard on Aboriginal
peoples' own lands and on their own terms. Canadian courts are following
suit. During the recent trial of the ground-breaking *Tsilhqot'in* case, the court
took the unconventional, yet highly respectful, step of holding evening
sessions in order to hear stories that could only be told by the Tsilhqot'in
people after the sun had set.[34] In my own legal practice, I have seen how
efforts to hold court in Aboriginal communities have been met with considerable gratitude and resulted in much-needed empowerment.

Westphalia was an important step in Western historical evolution, but the
price was high. The evolution of Aboriginal law and the recognition of
Aboriginal rights, title, and self-government have been great achievements,

but Aboriginal peoples are still healing from the wounds inflicted by centuries of policies and laws aimed at the eradication not only of their rights but also of their very existence. Hopefully, the process of healing will be helped by the recent acceptance of responsibility for the devastation caused by the removal of Aboriginal children from their families and the regimes of residential schools.[35] We will see. In the meantime should we not ask why it happened in the first place?

Courts, at least those in Canada, must become considerably more assertive in requiring best efforts to settle matters *under court supervision,* something almost invariably resisted by the state. What I am proposing, in effect, is that the bench, the bar, and other disciplines swept up in Aboriginal litigation work together to ensure that the judicial process as it applies in state-indigenous litigation becomes less adversarial and more professorial. Perhaps the disputes handed to the judiciary can be resolved, at least in part, through the techniques of mediation, involving a partnership of law, social science, and Aboriginal perspective. One important structural feature of this partnership must be the willingness of the courts to retain jurisdiction to see matters through to the end. I fear, however, that a significant population of litigation counsel will not only have to be led to this stream but also induced to drink from it.

The trust confided in the courts, whether exercising inherent or statutory jurisdiction, resides in the hope that they will wield power in the vindication of justice and principle – the principle exposed so skilfully and passionately in the pages of this volume. Just and secure arrangements must reflect a genuine clasping of hands,[36] not a winner and a loser. But that result will not be achieved by leaving power unsupervised to negotiate with principle. The respective perspectives on what is right and lawful may first have to be laid before the courts supported by law – customary law, common law, indigenous law, the rule of law, constitutionalism, and international law – for without that "we are not even in the game anymore." Once this is done, the parties should submit to mediation by the courts, preferably voluntary, if necessary imposed, involving not just counsel but also clients, principals, and the considerable assistance of other relevant disciplines introducing the knowledge and wisdom resulting from social science research. We would no longer be dealing with "might is right" but with informed, directed, and motivated attempts to give expression to our "longing to live in a fair world." All parties would know that failure in this quest may result in resolution by judicial dictate while at the same time being cognizant of the reality that those judicial pronouncements will, in the future, emanate from a process no longer held hostage to political or financial power. Hopefully, this will be a legacy of the current promising judicial reform and members of the bench and bar who continue to strive for that reform.

The *Columbia Encyclopedia* characterized the aftermath of the Thirty Years War in these words: "The war ended the era of conflicts inspired by religious passion, and the Peace of Westphalia was an important step toward religious toleration. The incredible sufferings of the German peasantry were remembered for centuries."[37] Let us not forget that virtually every case comprising the jurisprudence discussed in this volume involved indigenous individuals, communities, and nations with a great deal at stake, each required to make considerable sacrifices. Behind every court case is a client. The battles are fought on that client's behalf. The law is forged through their struggles. And let us understand that the battle is not over when the war is won, for we are left to deal with the scars long after the last shots have been fired. It is a testament to the strength of indigenous peoples around the world that they have survived brutal assaults on their culture and their lives and have continued to fight back. It is true that the courts in the three jurisdictions discussed in this volume have dithered, but for me they still hold out the best hope for nudging power toward principle. It was in the Supreme Court of Canada's landmark *Sparrow* decision that the court acknowledged "it is clear, then, that s. 35(1) of the *Constitution Act, 1982,* represents the culmination of a long and difficult struggle in both the political forum and the courts for the constitutional recognition of aboriginal rights."[38]

The judges' calling was well expressed by the young John Adams. To allow the law to work its magic, the courts need appropriate forums and the wise counsel of visitors from indigenous cultures and those professions that strive to establish connections and comprehension between cultures. The appropriate forums, I am suggesting, must include court-supervised dispute resolution through mediation, facilitation, and persuasion (gentle or not so gentle). Judges and litigation counsel seeking the principled path and the helping hand of the social science professions (including legal academics), as indeed they should, would do well to contemplate and act on the contents of this important volume.

Acknowledgments
With sincerest appreciation for the editorial and research assistance of Robin Campbell, BCL/LLB, Faculty of Law, McGill University and articling student with Hutchins Caron and Associés.

Notes
1 Ignatieff, *The Rights Revolution,* 2.
2 Cited in McCullough, *John Adams,* 53.
3 Dickens, *Bleak House,* 18-19.
4 *R. v. Sparrow,* [1990] 1 S.C.R. 1075 at 1103 [*Sparrow*].
5 *Haida Nation v. British Columbia (Minister of Forests),* [2004] 3 S.C.R. 511, [2004] S.C.C. 73 [*Haida*].
6 Ibid., para. 32.
7 Telegram, 1951, from Alex Stevenson to J.G. Wright Dalb, Ottawa, Indian and Northern Affairs Canada.

8 Minister of External Affairs Joe Clark, Canada's "Statement on Sovereignty," Canada, House of Common Debates, Vol. V, 1985 (10 September 1985).

9 Watt-Cloutier, "Inuit, Climate Change, Sovereignty, and Security in the Canadian Arctic," Inuit Circumpolar Council, 25 January 2002, http://www.inuitcircumpolar.com/index. php?ID=91&Lang=En.

10 Inuit Circumpolar Council, "A Circumpolar Inuit Declaration on Sovereignty in the Arctic," adopted 28 April 2009, http://inuitcircumpolar.com/files/uploads/icc-files/PR-2009-04-28-Signed-Inuit-Sovereignty-Declaration-11x17.pdf *(Declaration on Sovereignty in the Arctic)*.

11 Ibid., at provision 2.6.

12 Ibid., at provision 3.3.

13 *R. v. Syliboy*, [1929] 1 D.L.R. 307 at 313 (N.S. Co. Crt) [*Syliboy*]. Interestingly, the question about Indians passing with it is still with us, as demonstrated in the positions argued in *Reference re: Secession of Quebec*, [1987] 2 S.C.R. 217.

14 *Simon v. The Queen*, [1985] 2 S.C.R. 387 at 399.

15 *R. v. Van der Peet*, [1996] 2 S.C.R. 507 at para. 42 [*Van der Peet*].

16 *Milirrpum v. Nabalco Pty. Ltd.* (1971), 17 F.L.R. 141 (N.T.S.C.).

17 *R. v. Symonds* (1847), N.Z.P.C.C. 387. The court held that Māori customary interests were to be solemnly respected and not to be extinguished, at least in times of peace, without their free consent.

18 *Wi Parata v. The Bishop of Wellington* (1877), 3 N.Z., Jur. (N.S.) 72.

19 *In re the Ninety Mile Beach*, [1963] N.Z.L.R. 461.

20 Denning (Lord Denning), *The Discipline of Law*, 314; see also *Makivik Corp. v. Canada (Minister of Canadian Heritage) (T.D)* [1999] F.C. 38 at 106 where Richard A.C.J. states that "[t]he courts should design their remedies to facilitate negotiations."

21 Ibid.

22 Hurdles abound in Aboriginal law. As I discussed in a paper given after the Supreme Court's decision in *Mitchell*, another example is the legal test for the admissibility of oral history evidence. The test has been used by some adjudicators to bar or devalue the Aboriginal claimants' evidence, thereby taking away the factual foundation of their case and preventing their perspective from being taken into account. See Peter W. Hutchins and Tanya Whiteside, "Mixed Messages, Double Standards, Eurocentrism, and High Hurdles: Evidentiary Challenges in Aboriginal Litigation," paper presented at the conference Aboriginal Law: Litigation Issues, organized by the Continuing Legal Education Society of British Columbia, Vancouver, 29 October 2004.

23 For more on this point, see Hutchins and Choksi, "From Calder to Mitchell," 241-83.

24 *Van der Peet*, para. 46.

25 See Hutchins and Choksi, "From Calder to Mitchell."

26 Mark Walters, "The Right to Cross a River? Aboriginal Rights in the *Mitchell Case*," paper presented at the Pacific Business and Law Institute National Conference on Canadian Aboriginal Law, Toronto, 25-26 October 2001, 242.

27 Cited in Bazelon, "The Place of Women on the Court."

28 On this aspect, see Young, *The Trouble with Tradition*.

29 *R. v. Marshall*, [1999] 3 S.C.R. 456 at paras. 36-37.

30 Cited in Social Sciences and Humanities Research Council of Canada, "Land Claims Too Costly for Some Aboriginal Groups."

31 Macklem, *Indigenous Difference*.

32 *Evidence Act of 1995 (as Amended)*, (Cth.) (Australia), s. 72.

33 Ibid., s. 29(2).

34 *Tsilhqot'in Nation v. British Columbia*, 2007 B.C.S.C. 1700 at para. 167.

35 In his February 2008 speech, Australian Prime Minister Kevin Rudd apologized for "the laws and policies of successive Parliaments and governments that have inflicted profound grief, suffering, and loss" on Aboriginal peoples, for the removal of children and the breakup of families, and for the "degradation inflicted on a proud people and a proud culture"; Motion by Australian Prime Minister Kevin Rudd, 13 February 2008, House of Representatives, 42nd Parliament, Parliamentary Debates, First Session, First Period, Official Hansard, No. 1, http://www.aph.gov.au/hansard/reps/dailys/dr130208.pdf. In Canada, Prime Minister

Stephen Harper's apology to the Aboriginal peoples of Canada rightly noted that the "burden of this experience has been on your shoulders for far too long. The burden is properly ours as a government and as a country." Speech by Canadian Prime Minister Stephen Harper, 11 June 2008, House of Commons, 39th Parliament, 2nd Session, Edited *Hansard*, No. 110, http://www2.parl.gc.ca/HousePublications/Publication.aspx?Language=E&Mode=1& Parl=39&Ses=2&DocId=3568890. With these apologies, majorities within states are also finding their way toward healing from this painful legacy as we all move along this more principled path.

36 Morris, *The Treaties of Canada*, 208:

And now, Indians of the plains, I thank you for the open ear you have given me; I hold out my hand to you full of the Queen's bounty and I hope you will not put it back. We have no object but to discharge our duty to the Queen and towards you. Now that my hand is stretched out to you, it is for you to say whether you will take it and do as I think you ought -- act for the good of your people.

37 *Columbia Encyclopedia*, 4th ed.
38 *Sparrow*, 1105.

Acknowledgments

The editors gratefully acknowledge the support of several institutions. Grants from the Social Sciences and Humanities Research Council of Canada and the University of Calgary's Research Grants Committee and Centre for Public Policy – together with the Faculties of Social Sciences, Humanities, and Law – supported the original conference from which this book stems. Additional funding from Vice President of Research and Social Sciences Dean Steve Randall to the Socio-Legal Studies Research Unit that developed the project was critical for its completion.

The chapters in this book, apart from the introduction, originated as papers in a conference entitled *Delgamu'ukw, Mabo, and Ysleta*: Native Title in Canada, Australia, and the United States, hosted by the University of Calgary in September 2003. Fourteen papers were given by graduate students and younger and older scholars before a large audience of academics, students, and First Nations people. They were critiqued in the long discussions that followed each session and in a wrap-up session led by Robin Fisher (chair), Tolly Bradford, Brian Calliou, and Rod Martin.

During the publication process, which stretched over several years, these essays were revised several times. We wish to thank the anonymous readers for UBC Press and the Aid to Scholarly Publishing Programme. As editors of this volume in the prominent UBC Press Law and Society Series, we wish to thank the general editor, Wes Pue, and acquisition editor Randy Schmidt for their continual encouragement as well as Megan Brand for shepherding the work through to publication.

The editors wish to thank Adam Westra and Alison Mercer for assistance with compilation of the bibliography and accept responsibility for any remaining errors or omissions. The comprehensive index and tables were compiled by Maggie and Louis Knafla, and the editors wish to thank the artist Luc Nadeau and La Guilde Graphique for the book cover.

Selected Bibliography

Abel, Kerry, and Jean Friesen, eds. *Aboriginal Resource Use in Canada: Historical and Legal Aspects*. Winnipeg: University of Manitoba Press, 1991.

Alexander, Joseph Aloysius. *The Life of George Chaffey: A Story of Irrigation Beginnings in California and Australia*. Melbourne: Macmillan, 1928.

Almandoz Garmendia, José Antonio. *Fray Alonso de Veracruz O.E.S.A. y la encomienda indiana en la historia eclesiástica novohispana, 1522-1556. Edición crítica del texto 'De dominio infidelium et justo bello' y apéndice documental por José Antonio Almandoz Garmendia; con un prólogo por Ernest J. Burrus*. Madrid: J. Porrua Turanzas, 1971.

Altman, Jon C. *Sustainable Development Options on Aboriginal Land: The Hybrid Economy in the Twenty-First Century*. Discussion Paper No. 226. Canberra: Centre for Aboriginal Economic Policy Research, 2001.

Altman, Jon C., Boyd Hunter, and Melissa Johns. "Monitoring 'Practical' Reconciliation: Evidence from the Reconciliation Decade 1991-2001," 2003. http://www.anu.edu.au/caepr.

Alvord, Clarence Walworth. *The Mississippi Valley in British Politics: A Study of the Trade, Land Speculation, and Experiments in Imperialism Culminating in the American Revolution*. 2 vols. Cleveland: Arthur H. Clark Company, 1917.

Anaya, James, and Claudio Grossman. "The Case of *Awas Tingni v. Nicaragua:* A New Step in the International Law of Indigenous Peoples." *Arizona Journal of International and Comparative Law* 19, 1 (2002): 1-14.

Anderson, Chris. "Queensland." In *Aboriginal Land Rights: A Handbook*, ed. Nicolas Peterson, 53-114. Canberra: Australian Institute for Aboriginal Studies, 1981.

Armstrong, Christopher, and H. Viv Nelles. *Monopoly's Moment: The Organization and Regulation of Canadian Utilities, 1830-1930*. Philadelphia: Temple University Press, 1986.

Arneil, Barbara. *John Locke and America: The Defence of English Colonialism*. Oxford: Clarendon Press, 1996.

Aronowitz, Stanley. "Global Capital and Its Opponents." In *Implicating Empire: Globalization and Resistance in the 21st Century World Order*, ed. Stanley Aronowitz and Heather Gautney, 179-95. New York: Basic Books, 2003.

Aronowitz, Stanley, and Heather Gautney, eds. *Implicating Empire: Globalization and Resistance in the 21st Century World Order*. New York: Basic Books, 2003.

Arthur, William. "Torres Strait." In *Regional Agreements: Key Issues in Australia*, ed. Mary Edmunds, 59-82. Canberra: Australian Institute of Aboriginal and Torres Strait Islander Studies, Native Title Research Unit, 1998.

Arthurs, Harry William. *"Without the Law": Administrative Justice and Legal Pluralism in Nineteenth-Century England*. Toronto: University of Toronto Press, 1984.

Asch, Michael. *Aboriginal and Treaty Rights in Canada: Essays on Law, Equality, and Respect for Difference*. Vancouver: UBC Press, 1997.

–. "From *Calder* to *Van der Peet:* Aboriginal Rights and Canadian Law." In *Indigenous Peoples' Rights in Australia, Canada, and New Zealand,* ed. Paul Havemann, 428-46. Oxford: Oxford University Press, 1999.

Attwood, Bain, and S.G. Foster, eds. *Frontier Conflict: The Australian Experience.* Canberra: National Museum of Australia, 2003.

Austin, John. *The Province of Jurisprudence Determined.* 2nd ed. New York: Burt Franklin, 1970.

Baerreis, David. "The Ethnohistoric Approach and Archaeology." *Ethnohistory* 8 (1961): 49-77.

Baker, John Hamilton. *An Introduction to English Legal History.* 4th ed. London: Butterworths, 2002.

Ballantyne, Brian, and James Dobbin. *Capstone Study: Flexibility and Rigour in the CLS System.* Ottawa: Legal Surveys Division, Geomatics Canada, 2002.

–. *Options for Land Registration and Survey Systems on Aboriginal Lands in Canada.* Ottawa: Legal Surveys Division, Geomatics Canada, 2000.

Bankes, Nigel D. "The Board of Investigation and the Water Rights of Indian Reserves in British Columbia, 1909-1926." In *Aboriginal Resource Use in Canada: Historical and Legal Aspects,* ed. Kerry Abel and Jean Friesen, 89-107. Winnipeg: University of Manitoba Press, 1991.

–. "The Registration and Transfer of Interests in Crown Lands." In *Public Disposition of Natural Resources: Essays from the First Banff Conference on Natural Resources Law,* ed. Nigel D. Bankes and J. Owen Saunders, 89-107. Calgary: Canadian Institute of Resources Law, 1983.

Banner, Stuart. *How the Indians Lost Their Land: Law and Power on the Frontier.* Cambridge, MA: Belknap Press, 2005.

Barfield, Thomas, ed. *The Dictionary of Anthropology.* Oxford: Blackwell Publishers, 1997.

Barnard, Alan. *History and Theory in Anthropology.* Cambridge, UK: Cambridge University Press, 2000.

Barnard, Alan, and Jonathan Spencer, eds. *Encyclopedia of Social and Cultural Anthropology.* London: Routledge, 1996.

Barnsley, Paul. "Free Peltier Campaign Fails." *Windspeaker* 18, 10 (2001).

Barsh, Russel Lawrence. "Indigenous Rights and the *Lex Loci* in British Imperial Law." In *Advancing Aboriginal Claims: Visions/Strategies/Directions,* ed. Kerry Wilkins, 91-126. Saskatoon: Purich Publishing, 2004.

Barsh, Russel Lawrence, and James Youngblood Henderson. "The Supreme Court's *Van der Peet* Trilogy: Naïve Imperialism and Ropes of Sand." *McGill Law Journal* 42 (1997): 993-1009.

Bartlett, Richard H. *Aboriginal Water Rights in Canada: A Study of Aboriginal Title to Water and Indian Water Rights.* Calgary: Canadian Institute of Resources Law, 1986.

–. *The Indian Act of Canada.* Saskatoon: Native Law Centre, University of Saskatchewan, 1980.

–. *The* Mabo *Decision and the Full Text of the Decision in* Mabo and Others v. State of Queensland: *With Commentary by Richard Bartlett.* Sydney: Butterworths, 1993.

–. *Native Title in Australia.* Sydney: Butterworths, 2000.

–. "Native Title in Australia: Denial, Recognition, and Dispossession." In *Indigenous Peoples' Rights in Australia, Canada, and New Zealand,* ed. Paul Havemann, 408-27. Oxford: Oxford University Press, 1999.

Basu, Kaushik. "Social Norms and the Law." In *The New Palgrave Dictionary of Economics and the Law,* ed. Peter Newman, 476-81. London: Macmillan Reference, 1998.

Battiste, Marie, and James (Sa'ke'j) Youngblood Henderson. *Protecting Indigenous Knowledge and Heritage: A Global Challenge.* Saskatoon: Purich Publishing, 2000.

Bazelon, Emily. "The Place of Women on the Court." *New York Times Magazine,* 12 July 2009, MM22.

Becker, Lawrence C. *Property Rights: Philosophical Foundations.* London : Routledge and Kegan Paul, 1977.

Bennion, Francis. *Statutory Interpretation: A Code.* 3rd ed. London: Butterworths, 1997.

Benton, Lauren A. *Law and Colonial Cultures: Legal Regimes in World History, 1400-1900.* Cambridge, UK: Cambridge University Press, 2002.

Berger, Thomas R. *A Long and Terrible Shadow: White Values, Native Rights in America, 1492-1992.* Vancouver: Douglas and McIntyre, 1991.

Binnema, Theodore, Gerhard Ens, and Roderick C. Macleod, eds. *From Rupert's Land to Canada.* Edmonton: University of Alberta Press, 2001.

Birrell, Bob, and John Hirst. "Aboriginal Couples at the 2001 Census." *People and Place* 10, 3 (2002): 23-28.

Bishop, Charles A. "Limiting Access to Limited Goods: The Origin of Stratification in Interior British Columbia." In *The Development of Political Organization in Native North America,* proceedings of the American Ethnological Society, ed. E. Tooker, 148-61. Washington, DC: the American Ethnological Society, 1979.

–. The *Northern Ojibwa and the Fur Trade: An Historical and Ecological Study.* Toronto: Holt, Rinehart, and Winston, 1974.

Blackstone, William. *Commentaries on the Laws of England.* 4 vols. Oxford: Clarendon Press, 1765; reprint, Buffalo: William S. Hein, 1992.

Blue, Gregory, Martin Bunton, and Ralph Croizier, eds. *Colonialism and the Modern World: Selected Studies.* Armonk, NY: M.E. Sharpe, 2002.

Boast, Richard. *Foreshore and Seabed.* Wellington: Lexis Nexis, 2005.

Boast, Richard, Andrew Erueti, Doug McPhail, and Norman F. Smith. *Maori Land Law.* 2nd ed. Wellington: Lexis Nexis, 2004.

Borrows, John. "'Because It Does Not Make Sense': Sovereignty's Power in the Case of *Delgamuukw v. The Queen* 1997." In *Law, History, Colonialism: The Reach of Empire,* ed. Diane Kirkby and Catherine Coleborne, 190-206. Manchester: Manchester University Press, 2001.

–. "Frozen Rights in Canada: Constitutional Interpretation and the Trickster." *American Indian Law Review* 22 (1997): 37-64.

–. *Recovering Canada: The Resurgence of Indigenous Law.* Toronto: University of Toronto Press, 2002.

–. "Wampum at Niagara: The Royal Proclamation, Canadian Legal History, and Self-Government." In *Aboriginal and Treaty Rights in Canada: Essays on Law, Equality, and Respect for Difference,* ed. Michael Asch, 155-72. Vancouver: UBC Press, 1997.

Bowe, Heather. "Linguistics and the Yorta Yorta Native Title Claim." In *Language in Native Title,* ed. J. Henderson and D. Nash, 101-59. Canberra: Native Title Research Unit, Aboriginal Studies Press, 2002.

Bowe, Heather, and Stephen Morey. *The Yorta Yorta (Bangerang) Language of the Murray Goulbourn Including Yabula Yabula.* Canberra: Pacific Linguistics, 1999.

Boyer, Paul. "Cultural Assimilation." In *International Encyclopaedia of the Social and Behavioral Sciences,* ed. Neil J. Smelser and Paul B. Baltes, vol. 5, 1032-35. Amsterdam: Elsevier, 2001.

Brennan, Frank. *The Wik Debate: Its Impact on Aborigines, Pastoralists, and Miners.* Sydney: New South Wales University Press, 1998.

Bridges, Barry. "The Extension of English Law to Aborigines for Offences Committed Inter Se, 1829-1842." *Journal of the Royal Australian Historical Society* 59 (1973): 264-69.

Bright, Susan, and John Dewar, eds. *Land Law: Themes and Perspectives.* New York: Oxford University Press, 1998.

Brookfield, F.M. (Jock). "Maori Claims and the 'Special' Juridical Nature of Foreshore and Seabed." *New Zealand Law Review* 2 (2005): 179-216.

–. "Maori Customary Title in Foreshore and Seabed." *New Zealand Law Journal* 34 (2004): 34-35.

Brown, Jennifer S., and Theresa Schenck. "Metis, Mestizo, and Mixed-Blood." In *A Companion to American History,* ed. Philip Deloria and Neal Salisbury. Oxford: Blackwell Publishers, 2002.

Brownell, Margo S. "Who Is an Indian? Searching for an Answer to the Question at the Core of Federal Indian Law." *Michigan Journal of Law Reform* 34, 1-2 (2001): 275-320.

Buck, Andreas Richard, John McLaren, and Nancy E. Wright, eds. *Land and Freedom: Law, Property Rights, and the British Diaspora*. Aldershot: Ashgate, 2001.

Burchill, C.S. "The Origins of Canadian Irrigation Law." *Canadian Historical Review* 29, 4 (1948): 353-62.

Burrus, Ernest J. *Defense of the Indians: Their Rights, Part I: Latin Text and English Translation. The Writings of Alonso de la Vera Cruz, Vol. 2: The Original Texts and English Translation*. Rome: Sources and Studies for the History of the Americas, Jesuit Historical Institute, 1968.

Butt, Peter, Robert Eagleson, and Patricia Lane. *Mabo, Wik, and Native Title*. 4th ed. Sydney: Federation Press, 2001.

Byrnes, Giselle. *The Waitangi Tribunal and New Zealand History*. Melbourne: Oxford University Press, 2004.

Calhoun, Craig, ed. *Dictionary of the Social Sciences*. Oxford: Oxford University Press, 2002.

Canada. *Report of the Royal Commission on Aboriginal Peoples: Restructuring the Relationship*. Vol. 2, Part One. Ottawa: Supply and Services Canada, 1996.

Castellino, Joshua, and Niamh Walsh, eds. *Indigenous Peoples and Human Rights*. Leiden: Martinus Nijhoff, 2005.

Castles, Alex C. *An Australian Legal History*. Sydney: Law Book Company, 1982.

–. "The Reception and Status of English Law in Australia." *Adelaide Law Review* 2 (1963): 1-32.

Chartrand, Paul L.A.H., ed. *Who Are Canada's Aboriginal Peoples? Recognition, Definition, and Jurisdiction*. Saskatoon: Purich Publishing, 2002.

Chartrand, Paul L.A.H., and John Giokas. "Defining the Métis People: The Hard Case of Canadian Aboriginal Law." In *Who Are Canada's Aboriginal Peoples? Recognition, Definition, and Jurisdiction*, ed. Paul L.A.H. Chartrand. Saskatoon: Purich Publishing, 2002.

Choo, Christine. "Historians and Native Title: The Question of Evidence." In *Law, History, Colonialism: The Reach of Empire*, ed. Diane Kirkby and Catherine Coleborne, 261-76. Manchester: Manchester University Press, 2001.

Choo, Christine, and Shawn Hollbach, eds. *History and Native Title*. Perth: University of Western Australia Press, 2003.

Churchill, Ward. *Struggle for the Land: Native North American Resistance to Genocide, Ecocide, and Colonization*. Winnipeg: Arbeiter Ring, 1999.

–. "The Tragedy and the Travesty: The Subversion of Indigenous Sovereignty in North America." In *Struggle for the Land: Native North American Resistance to Genocide, Ecocide, and Colonization*, ed. Ward Churchill, 37-90. Winnipeg: Arbeiter Ring, 1999.

Clemmer, Richard O., L. Daniel Meyers, and Mary Elizabeth Rudden, eds. *Julian Steward and the Great Basin: The Making of an Anthropologist*. Salt Lake City: University of Utah Press, 1999.

Clinton, Robert N. "Peyote and Judicial Political Activism: Neo-Colonialism and the Supreme Court's New Indian Law Agenda." *Federal Bar News and Journal* 38 (1991): 92-101.

–. "There Is No Federal Supremacy Clause for Indian Tribes." *Arizona State Law Journal* 34 (2002): 113-260.

Cohen, Morris R. "Property and Sovereignty." *Cornell Law Quarterly* 13 (1927): 8-30.

Columbia Encyclopedia. 4th ed. New York: Columbia University Press, 1975.

Connell, Robert William (formerly; now Connell, Raewyn). "The Concept of Role and What to Do with It." *Australian and New Zealand Journal of Sociology* 15, 7 (1979): 7-17.

Connor, Michael. *The Invention of Terra Nullius: Historical and Legal Fictions on the Foundation of Australia*. Paddington, NSW: Macleay Press, 2005.

Cooke, Simon. "Arguments for the Survival of Aboriginal Customary Law in Victoria: A Casenote on *R. v. Peter* (1860) and *R. v. Jemmy* (1860)." *Australian Journal of Legal History* 5 (1999): 201-41.

Côté, J.E. "The Reception of English Law." *Alberta Law Review* 15 (1977): 29-92.

Coupland, Reginald. *The Quebec Act: A Study in Statesmanship*. Oxford: Clarendon Press, 1925.

Culhane, Dara. *The Pleasure of the Crown: Anthropology, Law, and First Nations*. Burnaby: Talon Books, 1998.

Cullen, Michael. "Waitangi Tribunal Report Disappointing." Official speech delivered 8 March 2004. http://www.beehive.govt.nz/.

Curr, Edward M. *The Australian Race: Its Origin, Languages, Customs, Place of Landing in Australia, and the Routes by Which It Spread Itself over That Continent.* 4 vols. Melbourne: Government Printer; London: John Ferres, Trübner, 1886.

–. *Recollections of Squatting in Victoria Then Called the Port Phillip District (from 1841 to 1851).* Melbourne: G.R. Robertson, 1883.

Dales, John H. *Hydroelectricity and Industrial Development: Quebec, 1898-1940.* Cambridge, MA: Harvard University Press, 1957.

Daunton, Martin, and Rick Halpern, eds. *Empire and Others: British Encounters with Indigenous Peoples, 1600-1850.* Philadelphia: University of Pennsylvania Press, 1999.

Davies, Susanne. "Aborigines, Murder, and the Criminal Law in Early Port Phillip, 1841-1851." *Historical Studies* 22 (1987): 313-45.

Demsetz, Harold. "Property Rights." In *The New Palgrave Dictionary of Economics and the Law,* ed. Peter Newman, 144-55. London: Macmillan Reference, 1998.

Denning, Alfred Thompson (Lord Denning). *The Discipline of Law.* London: Butterworths, 1979.

De Plevitz, Loretta, and Larry Croft. "Aboriginality under the Microscope: The Biological Descent Test in Australian Law." *Queensland University of Technology Law and Justice Journal* 3, 1 (2003): 104-20.

Devine, Heather. "Les Desjarlais: The Development and Dispersion of a Proto-Métis Hunting Band, 1785-1870." In *From Rupert's Land to Canada,* ed. Theodore Binnema, Gerhard Ens, and Roderick C. Macleod. Edmonton: University of Alberta Press, 2001.

Dick, Darren. "Comprehending 'the Genius of the Common Law': Native Title in Australia and Canada Compared Post-*Delgamuukw.*" *Australian Journal of Human Rights* 5, 1 (1998): 79-105.

Dickens, Charles. *Bleak House.* New York: Signet Classics, 1853 [2003 rpt.].

Dixon, Robert M.W. *The Rise and Fall of Languages.* Cambridge and New York: Cambridge University Press, 1997.

Dorsett, Shaunnagh, and Lee Godden. *A Guide to Overseas Precedents of Relevance to Native Title.* Canberra: Australian Institute of Aboriginal and Torres Strait Islander Studies, 1998.

Duff, Wilson. *Indian History of British Columbia.* 2nd ed. Victoria: Royal British Columbia Museum, 1972.

Dunstan, Don. *Felicia: The Political Memoirs of Don Dunstan.* Melbourne: Macmillan, 1981.

Edgar, Samuel Gairdner Gibson. *Craies on Statute Law.* 7th ed. London: Sweet and Maxwell, 1971.

Edmunds, Mary, ed. *Regional Agreements: Key Issues in Australia.* Canberra: Australian Institute of Aboriginal and Torres Strait Islander Studies, Native Title Research Unit, 1998.

Elliott, David, ed. *Law and Aboriginal Peoples in Canada.* 2nd ed. Concord, ON: Captus Press, 2005.

Else-Mitchell, Rae. "The Foundation of New South Wales and the Inheritance of the Common Law." *Journal of the Royal Australian Historical Society* 49 (1963): 1-23.

Emond, André. "L'affaire *Delgamuukw* ou la réactualisation du droit américain au regard des conditions d'existence et d'extinction du titre aborigène au Canada." *Les cahiers du droit* 39 (1998): 849-80.

Ennis, Arthur. *Fray Alonso de la Vera Cruz O.S.A. (1507-1584): A Study of His Life and Contribution to the Religious and Intellectual Affairs of Early Mexico.* Louvain: E. Warny, 1957.

Erueti, Andrew, and Claire Charters, eds. *Māori Property in the Foreshore and Seabed: The Last Frontier.* Wellington: Victoria University Press, 2007.

Evans, Jim. *Statutory Interpretation: Problems of Communication.* Auckland: Oxford University Press, 1988.

Evans-Pritchard, Edward Evan. *The Nuer: A Description of the Modes of Livelihood and Political Institutions of a Nilotic People.* Oxford: Clarendon Press, 1940.

Evarts, Reverend Jeremiah. *Cherokee Removal: The "William Penn" Essays and Other Writings.* Ed. Francis Paul Prucha. Knoxville: University of Tennessee Press, 1981.

Evatt, Herbert V. "The Legal Foundations of New South Wales." *Australian Law Journal* 11 (1938): 409-24.

Fairweather, Joan G. *A Common Hunger: Land Rights in Canada and South Africa.* Calgary: University of Calgary Press, 2006.

Fels, Marie H. *Good Men and True: The Aboriginal Police of the Port Phillip District.* Victoria: Melbourne University Press, 1988.

Felton, P. "Victoria." In *Aboriginal Land Rights: A Handbook,* ed. Nicolas Peterson, 168-220. Canberra: Australian Institute of Aboriginal Studies, 1981.

Finlayson, Jock, Bruce Rigsby, and Hilary Bek, eds. *Connections in Native Title: Genealogies, Kinship, and Groups.* CAEPR Research Monograph No. 13. Canberra: Centre for Aboriginal Economic Policy Research, Australian National University, 1999.

Firth, Raymond. *Primitive Polynesian Economy.* London: G. Routledge, 1939.

Fisher, Douglas. *Water Law.* Prymont, NSW: LBC Information Services, 2000.

Fisher, Robin. *Contact and Conflict: Indian-European Relations in British Columbia, 1774-1890.* Vancouver: UBC Press, 1977.

Forbes, John R.S. "*Mabo* and the Miners – ad infinitum?" In *Mabo: The Native Title Legislation. A Legislative Response to the High Court's Decision,* ed. Margaret A. Stephenson, 49-70. St. Lucia: University of Queensland Press, 1995.

Forde, Cyril Daryll. *Habitat, Economy, and Society: A Geographical Introduction to Ethnology.* London: Methuen, [1934].

Foster, Hamar. "Indian Administration from the Royal Proclamation of 1763 to Constitutionally Entrenched Aboriginal Rights." In *Indigenous Peoples' Rights in Australia, Canada, and New Zealand,* ed. Paul Havemann, 354-61. Oxford: Oxford University Press, 1999.

Foster, Hamar, Heather Raven, and Jeremy Webber, eds. *Let Right Be Done: Aboriginal Title, the* Calder *Case, and the Future of Indigenous Rights.* Vancouver: UBC Press, 2007.

Foster, John. "Wintering, the Outsider Adult Male, and the Ethnogenesis of the Western Plains Métis." In *From Rupert's Land to Canada,* ed. Theodore Binnema, Gerhard Ens, and Roderick C. Macleod. Edmonton: University of Alberta Press, 2001.

Foster, Robert, Rick Hosking, and Amanda Nettelbeck. *Fatal Collisions: The South Australian Frontier and the Violence of Memory.* Kent Town: Wakefield Press, 2001.

Fustel de Coulanges, N.D. *The Ancient City: A Study on the Religion, Laws, and Institutions of Greece and Rome.* 1864; reprint, Garden City, NY: Doubleday Anchor Books, 1956.

Gaustad, Edwin S. *Liberty of Conscience: Roger Williams in America.* Grand Rapids: Eerdmans, 1991.

Gautney, Heather. "The Globalization of Violence in the 21st Century: Israel, Palestine, and the War on Terror." In *Implicating Empire: Globalization and Resistance in the 21st Century World Order,* ed. Stanley Aronowitz and Heather Gautney, 65-82. New York: Basic Books.

Gessner, Volkmar. "Law as an Instrument of Social Change." In *International Encyclopaedia of the Social and Behavioral Sciences,* ed. Neil J. Smelser and Paul B. Baltes, vol. 12, 8492-96. Amsterdam: Elsevier, 2001.

Giddens, Anthony. *Sociology.* 2nd ed. Cambridge, UK: Polity Press, 1993.

Gifford, Donald. *Statutory Interpretation.* Sydney: Law Book, 1990.

Gilbert, Jerémie. *Indigenous Peoples' Land Rights under International Law: From Victims to Actors.* Ardsley, NY: Transnational Publishers, 2006.

Gilbert, Margaret. "Norm." In *The Blackwell Dictionary of Twentieth-Century Social Thought,* ed. William Outhwaite and Tom Bottomore, 425-27. Oxford: Blackwell, 1993.

–. *On Social Facts.* London: Routledge, 1989.

Giokas, John. "Domestic Recognition in the United States and Canada." In *Who Are Canada's Aboriginal Peoples? Recognition, Definition, and Jurisdiction,* ed. Paul L.A.H. Chartrand. Saskatoon: Purich Publishing, 2002.

Giokas, John, and Paul L.A.H. Chartrand. "Who Are the Métis in Section 35? A Review of the Law and Policy Relating to Métis and 'Mixed Blood' People in Canada." In *Who Are Canada's Aboriginal Peoples? Recognition, Definition, and Jurisdiction,* ed. Paul L.A.H. Chartrand. Saskatoon: Purich Publishing, 2002.

Giokas, John, and Robert Groves. "Collective and Individual Recognition in Canada." In *Who Are Canada's Aboriginal Peoples? Recognition, Definition, and Jurisdiction,* ed. Paul L.A.H. Chartrand. Saskatoon: Purich Publishing, 2002.

Glover, Jeffrey. "Wunnaumwayean: Roger Williams, English Credibility, and the Colonial Market." *Early American Literature* 41 (2006): 429-53.

Godlewski, Christina, and Jeremy Webber. "The *Calder* Decision, Aboriginal Title, Treaties, and the Nisga'a." In *Let Right Be Done: Aboriginal Title, the Calder Case, and the Future of Indigenous Rights,* ed. Hamar Foster, Heather Raven, and Jeremy Webber, 1-33. Vancouver: UBC Press, 2007.

Goldberg, Carole. "Descent into Race." *UCLA Law Review* 49 (2002): 1373-94.

Goldman, Irving. "The Alkatcho Carrier: Historical Background of Crest Prerogatives." *American Anthropologist* 43 (1941): 396-418.

Goodall, Heather. *Invasion to Embassy: Land in Aboriginal Politics in New South Wales, 1770-1972.* Sydney: Allen and Unwin, 1996.

Goodenough, Ward H. *Culture, Language, and Society.* 2nd ed. Menlo Park, CA: Benjamin; Cummings Publishing, 1981.

Grattan, Scott, and Luke McNamara. "The Common Law Construct of Native Title: A 'Re-Feudalisation' of Australian Land Law." *Griffith Law Review* 8 (1999): 50-85.

Gray, Charles Montgomery. *Copyhold, Equity, and the Common Law.* Cambridge, MA: Harvard University Press, 1963.

Grimshaw, Patricia, Robert Reynolds, and Shurlee Swain. "The Paradox of 'Ultra-Democratic' Government: Indigenous Peoples' Civil Rights in Nineteenth-Century New Zealand, Canada, and Australia." In *Law, History, Colonialism: The Reach of Empire,* ed. Diane Kirkby and Catherine Coleborne. Manchester: Manchester University Press, 2001.

Hafner, Carole D. "Legal Reasoning Models." In *International Encyclopaedia of the Social and Behavioral Sciences,* vol. 13, ed. Neil J. Smelser and Paul B. Baltes, 8675-77. Amsterdam: Elsevier, 2001.

Hagen, Rod. "Lumpers, Splitters, and the Middle Range: Groups, Local and Otherwise, in the Mid-Murray Region." In *Connections in Native Title: Genealogies, Kinship, and Groups,* CAEPR Research Monograph No. 13, ed. Jock Finlayson, Bruce Rigsby, and Hilary Bek, 73-84. Canberra: Centre for Aboriginal Economic Policy Research, Australian National University, 1999.

Hall, Anthony J. *The American Empire and the Fourth World.* Vol. 1 of *The Bowl with One Spoon.* Montreal/Kingston: McGill-Queen's University Press, 2003.

–. "Confronting the Hard Realities of North America's Ongoing Indian War." *The Radical* 3, 5 (2001).

–. *Earth into Property: Aboriginal History and the Making of Global Capitalism.* Vol. 2 of *The Bowl with One Spoon.* Montreal/Kingston: McGill-Queen's University Press, 2007.

Hallowell, Alfred Irving. "The Nature and Function of Property as a Social Institution." In *Culture and Experience,* Alfred Irving Hallowell, 236-49 1943; reprint, Philadelphia: University of Pennsylvania Press, 1955.

Hanke, Lewis. *All Mankind Is One.* De Kalb: Northern Illinois University Press, 1974.

–. *The Spanish Struggle for Justice in the Conquest of America.* Philadelphia: American Historical Association, 1949.

Hann, Christopher M. *Property Relations: Renewing the Anthropological Tradition.* Cambridge, UK: Cambridge University Press, 1998.

Harmon, Alexandra, ed. *The Power of Promises: Perspectives on Treaties with Native Peoples of the Pacific Northwest.* Seattle: University of Washington Press, 2008.

Harring, Sidney L. "Crazy Snake and the Creek Struggle for Sovereignty: The Native American Legal Culture and American Law." *American Journal for Legal History* 34, 4 (1990): 365-80.

–. "'There Seemed to Be No Recognized Law': Canadian Law and the Prairie First Nations." In *Laws and Societies in the Canadian Prairie West, 1670-1940,* ed. Louis A. Knafla and Jonathan Swainger, 92-126. Vancouver: UBC Press, 2005.

Harris, Cheryl I. "Whiteness as Property." *Harvard Law Review* 106 (1992-93): 1707-91.

Harris, Douglas C. *Fish, Law, and Colonialism.* Toronto: University of Toronto Press, 2001.

Harris, James W. *Property and Justice.* Oxford: Clarendon Press, 1996.

Hart, H.L.A. *The Concept of Law.* 2nd ed. Oxford: Oxford University Press, 1994.

Havemann, Paul, ed. *Indigenous Peoples' Rights in Australia, Canada, and New Zealand.* Melbourne: Oxford University Press, 1991.

Haviland, William A. *Cultural Anthropology.* 9th ed. Fort Worth, TX: Harcourt Brace, 1999.

Hawkins, William E. *Electrifying Calgary: A Century of Public and Private Power.* Calgary: University of Calgary Press, 1987.

Haycox, Stephen. "Then Fight for It: William Lewis Paul and Alaska Native Land Claims." In *Let Right Be Done: Aboriginal Title, the* Calder *Case, and the Future of Indigenous Rights,* ed. Hamar Foster, Heather Raven, and Jeremy Webber, 85-97. Vancouver: UBC Press, 2007.

Hayes, Selwyn. "Defining *Kaitiakitanga* and the *Resource Management Act* 1991." *Auckland University Law Review* 8 (1998): 893-99.

Hechter, Michael, and Karl-Dieter Opp, eds. *Social Norms.* New York: Russell Sage, 2001.

Heidenreich, Conrad E. *Huronia: A History and Geography of the Huron Indians.* Toronto: McClelland and Stewart, 1971.

Henderson, James Youngblood. *First Nations Jurisprudence and Aboriginal Rights: Defining the Just Society.* Saskatoon: Native Law Centre, University of Saskatchewan, 2006.

Hickerson, Harold. *The Chippewa and Their Neighbors: A Study in Ethnohistory.* New York: Holt, Rinehart, and Winston, 1970.

–. "The Genesis of a Trading Post Band: The Pembina Chippewa." *Ethnohistory* 3 (1956): 289-345.

–. "The Virginia Deer and Intertribal Buffer Zones in the Upper Mississippi Valley." In *Man, Culture, and Animals: The Role of Animals in Human Ecological Adjustments,* ed. Anthony Leeds and Andrew Vayda, 43-66. Washington, DC: American Association for the Advancement of Science, 1965.

Highland, Howard L. "The Mote in the Common Law's Eye: Dislodging Europocentric Barriers to Just Recognition of Native Title in the Wake of *Yorta Yorta.*" *Washington and Lee Journal of Civil Rights and Social Justice* 13 (2007): 349-87.

Hill, Ernestine. *Water into Gold.* Melbourne: Robertson and Mullens, 1937.

Hodgins, Bruce W., and Jamie B. Benidickson. *The Temagami Experience: Recreation, Resources, and Aboriginal Rights in the Northern Ontario Wilderness.* Toronto: University of Toronto Press, 1989.

Hoebel, E. Adamson. "Fundamental Legal Concepts as Applied in the Study of Primitive Law." *Yale Law Journal* 51 (1946): 951-66.

–. *The Law of Primitive Man: A Study in Comparative Legal Dynamics.* Cambridge, MA: Harvard University Press, 1954.

–. *The Political Organization and Law-Ways of the Comanche Indians.* Vol. 54 of *Memoirs of the American Anthropological Association.* Menasha, WI: American Anthropological Association, 1940.

Hohfeld, Wesley Newcomb. *Fundamental Legal Conceptions as Applied in Judicial Reasoning.* Classical Jurisprudence Series. Aldershot: Ashgate Dartmouth, 2001.

Homans, George Casper. *Social Behavior: Its Elementary Forms.* New York: Harcourt, Brace, and World, 1974.

Horton, David, ed. *The Encyclopaedia of Aboriginal Australia: Aboriginal and Torres Strait Islander History, Society, and Culture.* Vol. 1, *A-L,* and vol. 2, *M-Z.* Canberra: Aboriginal Studies Press, 1994.

Howard, Bradley Reed. *Indigenous Peoples and the State: The Struggle for Native Rights.* Dekalb: Northern Illinois University Press, 2003.

Howard, Michael. *The Lessons of History.* Oxford: Clarendon Press, 1991.

Huddleston, Rodney, and Geoffrey K. Pullum. *The Cambridge Grammar of the English Language.* Cambridge, UK: Cambridge University Press, 2002.

Hughes, Thomas. *History of the Society of Jesus in North America, Colonial and Federal: Documents, Volume I (1605-1838), Part I.* London: Longmans, Green, 1907.

Hundley, Norris Jr. "The Dark and Bloody Ground of Indian Water Rights: Confusion Elevated to Principle." *Western Historical Quarterly* 9 (1978): 454-82.

–. *Water and the West.* Berkeley: University of California Press, 1975.

–. "The 'Winters' Decision and Indian Water Rights: A Mystery Reexamined." *Western Historical Quarterly* 13, 1 (1982): 17-42.

Hunt, Robert C., and Antonio Gilman. *Property in Economic Context*. Monographs in Economic Anthropology No. 14. Lanham, NY: University Press of America, 1998.

Hunter, Louis C. *A History of Industrial Power in the United States, 1780-1930*. Charlottesville: University Press of Virginia, 1979.

Hunter, Rosemary. "Aboriginal Histories, Australian Histories, and the Law." In *The Age of Mabo: History, Aborigines, and Australia,* ed. Bain Attwood, 1-16. Sydney: Allen and Unwin, 1996.

Hutchins, Peter W. "'Cede, Release, and Surrender': Treaty-Making, the Aboriginal Perspective, and the Great Juridical Oxymoron or Let's Face It – It Didn't Happen Here." In *Aboriginal Law since* Delgamuuk: *The Face of the Future*, ed. Maria Morellato, 431-64. Toronto: Canada Law Book, 2009. Chap. 16.

Hutchins, Peter W., and Anjali Choksi. "From *Calder* to *Mitchell*: Should the Courts Patrol Cultural Borders?" *Supreme Court Law Review* (2d), 16 (2002): 241-83.

Hutchins, Peter W., and Franklin S. Gertler. "The Marriage of History and Law in *R. v. Sioui*." *Native Studies Review* 6, 2 (1990): 115-30.

Ignatieff, Michael. *The Rights Revolution*. Toronto: Anansi Press, 2007.

International Work Group for Indigenous Affairs. *The Indigenous World 2004*. Copenhagen: IWGIA, 2005.

Irish University Press Series of British Parliamentary Papers. Colonies: Canada, 33 vols. Shannon: Irish University Press, 1968-71.

Ivison, Duncan. *Postcolonial Liberalism*. Cambridge, UK: Cambridge University Press, 2002.

Jackson, John, John Burtniak, and Gregory P. Stein. *The Mighty Niagara: One River – Two Frontiers*. Amherst, NY: Prometheus Books, 2003.

Jefferson, Thomas. *A Summary of the Rights of British America*. Williamsburg: Clementinarind, 1774; reprinted in *The Papers of Thomas Jefferson,* ed. Julian P. Boyd. Princeton: Princeton University Press, 1950.

Jenkins, Richard. "Ethnicity: Anthropological Aspects." In *International Encyclopaedia of the Social and Behavioral Sciences*, vol. 7, ed. Neil J. Smelser and Paul B. Baltes, 4824-28. Amsterdam: Elsevier, 2001.

–. *Social Identity*. London : Routledge, 1996.

Jenness, Diamond. *The Indians of Canada*. National Museums of Canada, Bulletin 65, Anthropology Series No. 15. Ottawa: National Museums of Canada, 1932.

Johns, Gary, ed. *Waking Up to Dreamtime: The Illusion of Aboriginal Self-Determination*. Singapore: Media Masters, 2001.

Johnson, Llewellyn, and Dominique Legros. *Journal of Occurrences at the Forks of the Lewes and Pelly Rivers, May 1848 to September 1852*. Occasional Papers in Yukon History No. 2. Whitehorse: Government of Yukon, 2000.

Kauffman, Paul. *Water and Fishing: Aboriginal Rights in Australia and Canada*. Woden, ACT: Aboriginal and Torres Strait Islander Commission, 2004.

Keal, Paul. *European Conquest and the Rights of Indigenous Peoples: The Moral Backwardness of International Society*. Cambridge, UK: Cambridge University Press, 2003.

Keesing, Roger. *Cultural Anthropology: A Contemporary Perspective*. 2nd ed. New York: Holt, Rinehart, and Winston, 1981.

Keon-Cohen, Bryan, ed. *Native Title in the New Millennium*. Canberra: Aboriginal Studies Press, 2001.

Kercher, Bruce. *Debt, Seduction, and Other Disasters: The Birth of Civil Law in Convict New South Wales*. Sydney: Federation Press, 1996.

–. "Native Title in the Shadows: The Origins of the Myth of *Terra Nullius* in Early New South Wales Courts." In *Colonialism and the Modern World: Selected Studies*, ed. Gregory Blue, Martin Bunton, and Ralph Croizier, 100-19. Armonk, NY: M.E. Sharpe, 2002.

–. "*R v. Ballard, R v. Murrell,* and *R v. Bonjon*." *Australian Indigenous Law Reporter* 3 (1998): 410-25.

–. "The Recognition of Aboriginal Status and Laws in the Supreme Court of New South Wales under Forbes CJ, 1824-1836." In *Land and Freedom: Law, Property Rights, and the*

British Diaspora, ed. Andreas Richard Buck, John McLaren, and Nancy E. Wright, 83-102. Aldershot: Ashgate, 2001.

–. "Recognition of Indigenous Legal Autonomy in Nineteenth Century New South Wales." *Indigenous Law Bulletin* 4, 13 (1997): 7-9.

Kingsbury, Benedict. "Competing Conceptual Approaches to Indigenous Group Issues in New Zealand Law." *University of Toronto Law Journal* 52, 1 (2002): 101-34.

Kirkby, Diane, and Catherine Coleborne, eds. *Law, History, Colonialism: The Reach of Empire.* Manchester: Manchester University Press, 2001.

Klein, Ulrich. "Belief-Views on Nature: Western Environmental Ethics and Maori World Views." *New Zealand Journal of Environmental Law* 4 (2000): 81-119.

Knafla, Louis A. "Introduction: Laws and Societies in the Anglo-Canadian North-West Frontier and Prairie Provinces, 1670-1940." In *Laws and Societies in the Canadian Prairie West, 1670-1940,* ed. Louis A. Knafla and Jonathan Swainger, 1-54. Vancouver: UBC Press, 2005.

Knafla, Louis A., and Susan W.S. Binnie, eds. *Law, Society, and the State: Essays in Modern Legal History.* Toronto: University of Toronto Press, 1995.

Knafla, Louis A., and Jonathan Swainger, eds. *Laws and Societies in the Canadian Prairie West, 1670-1940.* Vancouver: UBC Press, 2005.

Kobrinski, Vernon. "The Tsimshianization of the Carrier Indians." In *Problems in the Prehistory of the North/American Subarctic: The Athabaskan Question,* ed. J.W. Helmer, S. Van Dyke, and S. Kense, 201-10. Calgary: University of Calgary Press, 1977.

Kroeber, Alfred L. *Anthropology: Race, Language, Culture, Psychology, Pre-History.* New York: Harcourt Brace, 1948.

–. *Cultural and Natural Areas of Native North America.* Berkeley: University of California Press, 1939.

–. *Handbook of the Indians of California.* Bureau of American Ethnology Bulletin No. 78. Washington: Bureau of American Ethnology, 1925.

Kukutai, Tahu. "The Problem of Defining an Ethnic Group for Public Policy: Who Is Maori and Why Does It Matter?" *Social Policy Journal of New Zealand* 23 (2004): 86-108.

Kupperman, Karen Ordahl. *Indians and English: Facing Off in Early America.* Ithaca: Cornell University Press, 2000.

La Forest, Gérard V. "Reminiscences of Aboriginal Rights at the Time of the *Calder* Case and Its Aftermath." In *Let Right Be Done: Aboriginal Title, the* Calder *Case, and the Future of Indigenous Rights,* ed. Hamar Foster, Heather Raven, and Jeremy Webber, 54-58. Vancouver: UBC Press, 2007.

Lajoie, Andrée. "Introduction: Which Way Out of Colonialism?" In *Indigenous Legal Traditions,* Law Commission of Canada, 3-11. Vancouver: UBC Press, 2006.

Langlois, Simon. "Identity Movements." In *International Encyclopedia of the Social and Behavioral Sciences,* vol. 11, ed. Neil J. Smelser and Paul B. Baltes, 7163-66. Amsterdam: Elsevier, 2001.

Law Commission of Canada. *Indigenous Legal Traditions.* Vancouver: UBC Press, 2006.

–. *Justice Within: Indigenous Legal Traditions.* Ottawa: Law Commission of Canada, 2006.

Lester, Geoffrey S.. *Inuit Territorial Rights in the Canadian Northwest Territories.* Ottawa: Tungavik Federation of Nunavut, 1984.

Linton, Ralph. *Acculturation in Seven American Indian Tribes.* Gloucester, MA: P. Smith, 1963 (c. 1940).

–. *The Study of Man: An Introduction.* New York: D. Appleton-Century, 1936.

Llewellyn, Karl N., and E. Adamson Hoebel. *The Cheyenne Way: Conflict and Case Law in Primitive Jurisprudence.* Norman: University of Oklahoma Press, 1941.

Locke, John. *Two Treatises of Government.* Ed. Peter Laslett. New York: New American Library, 1965.

Low, Hickling Arthurs. *Social and Economic Review of the Impact of Land Survey and Registration Systems on Canada Lands.* Ottawa: Legal Surveys Division of Natural Resources Canada, 2001.

Lucy, John A. *Language Diversity and Thought: A Reformulation of the Linguistic Relativity Hypothesis.* Cambridge, UK: Cambridge University Press, 1992.

Luhrmann, Tanya M. "Identity in Anthropology." In *International Encyclopaedia of the Social and Behavioral Sciences,* vol. 11, ed. Neil J. Smelser and Paul B. Baltes, 7154-59. Amsterdam: Elsevier, 2001.

Lurie, Nancy. Interview with Arthur J. Ray, Milwaukee Public Museum, October 2002.

Maaka, Roger, and Augie Fleras. *The Politics of Indigeneity: Challenging the State in Canada and Aotearoa New Zealand.* Dunedin: University of Otago Press, 2005.

MacEwan, Grant. *Tatanga Mani: Walking Buffalo of the Stonies.* Edmonton: Hurtig Publishers, 1969.

MacIntyre, Alasdair. *Whose Justice? Which Rationality?* Notre Dame: University of Notre Dame Press, 1988.

Macklem, Patrick. "Distributing Sovereignty: Indian Nations and Equality of Peoples." *Stanford Law Review* 45, 5 (1993): 1311-67.

–. *Indigenous Difference and the Constitution of Canada.* Toronto: University of Toronto Press, 2001.

MacLean, D. "Rights." In *International Encyclopaedia of the Social and Behavioral Sciences,* vol. 20, ed. Neil J. Smelser and Paul B. Baltes, 13334-38. Amsterdam: Elsevier, 2001.

Maddock, Kenneth. *The Australian Aborigines: A Portrait of Their Society.* 2nd ed. Ringwood, Victoria: Penguin Books, 1982.

–. "Involved Anthropologists." In *We Are Here: Politics of Aboriginal Land Tenure,* ed. Edwin N. Wilmsen, 155-76. Berkeley: University of California Press, 1989.

–. *Your Land Is Our Land: Aboriginal Land Rights.* Ringwood, Victoria: Penguin Books Australia, 1983.

Magnet, Joseph Eliot. *Litigating Aboriginal Culture.* Edmonton: Juriliber, 2005.

Maine, Sir Henry Sumner. *Ancient Law: Its Connection with the Early History of Society and Its Relation to Modern Ideas.* London: Humphrey Milford; Oxford University Press, 1931.

Mainville, Robert. *An Overview of Aboriginal and Treaty Rights and Compensation for Their Breach.* Saskatoon: Purich Publishing, 2001.

Mantzaris, Christos, and David Martin. *Native Title Corporations: A Legal and Anthropological Analysis.* Sydney: Federation Press, 2000.

Matsui, Kenichi. *Native Peoples and Water Rights: Irrigation, Dams, and the Law in Western Canada.* Montreal/Kingston: McGill-Queen's University Press, 2009.

–. "'White Man Has No Right to Take Any of It': Secwepemc Water Rights Struggle in British Columbia." *Wicazo Sa Review* 20, 2 (2005): 75-101.

–. "The Winters Doctrine and Federal Indian Policies." In *Law and Power in the Margins: Voices from beyond the Centres,* ed. Douglas Harris et al., 1-11. Vancouver: Faculty of Law, University of British Columbia, 1997.

Matthiessen, Peter. *In the Spirit of Crazy Horse.* New York: Viking Press, 1983.

McCann, Michael, and Stuart Scheingold. "Rights: Legal Aspects." In *International Encyclopaedia of the Social and Behavioral Sciences,* vol. 20, ed. Neil J. Smelser and Paul B. Baltes, 13339-44. Amsterdam: Elsevier, 2001.

McClennen, E.F., and Susan Shapiro. "Rule-guided Behavior." In *The New Palgrave Dictionary of Economics and the Law,* vol. 3, ed. Peter Newman, 363-69. London: Macmillan, 1998.

–. "Rule-Guided Behaviour." In *The New Palgrave Dictionary of Economics and the Law,* vol. 3, ed. Peter Newman, 363-69. London: Macmillan Reference, 1998.

McCullough, David. *John Adams.* New York: Simon and Schuster, 2001.

McHugh, Paul G. *Aboriginal Societies and the Common Law: A History of Sovereignty, Status, and Self-Determination.* Oxford: Oxford University Press, 2004.

–. "Aboriginal Title in New Zealand: A Retrospect and Prospect." *New Zealand Journal of Public and International Law* 2 (2004): 139-202.

–. "From Sovereignty Talk to Settlement Time: The Constitutional Setting of Maori Claims in the 1990s." In *Indigenous Peoples' Rights in Australia, Canada, and New Zealand,* ed. Paul Havemann, 447-67. Melbourne: Oxford University Press, 1991.

–. "A History of Crown Sovereignty in New Zealand." In *Power and Loss: Uses of the Past – a New Zealand Commentary,* ed. Andrew Sharp and Paul McHugh, 189-211. Wellington: Bridget Williams Books, 2001.

McNeil, Kent. "Aboriginal Rights in Canada: From Title to Land to Territorial Sovereignty." *Tulsa Journal of Comparative and International Law* 5 (1998): 253-98.

–. "Aboriginal Title and the Supreme Court: What's Happening?" *Saskatchewan Law Review* 69 (2006): 283-308.

–. *Common Law Aboriginal Title.* Oxford: Clarendon Press, 1989.

–. "Continuity of Aboriginal Rights." In *Advancing Aboriginal Claims: Visions/Strategies/ Directions,* ed. Kerry Wilkins, 127-50. Saskatoon: Purich Publishing, 2004.

–. *Emerging Justice? Essays on Indigenous Rights in Canada and Australia.* Saskatoon: Native Law Centre, University of Saskatchewan, 2001.

–. "Judicial Approaches to Self-Government since *Calder:* Searching for Doctrinal Coherence." In *Let Right Be Done: Aboriginal Title, the Calder Case, and the Future of Indigenous Rights,* ed. Hamar Foster, Heather Raven, and Jeremy Webber, 129-52. Vancouver: UBC Press, 2007.

–. "Legal Rights and Legislative Wrongs: Māori Claims to the Foreshore and Seabed." In *Māori Property in the Foreshore and Seabed: The Last Frontier,* ed. Andrew Erueti and Claire Charters, 83-118. Wellington: Victoria University Press, 2007.

–. "The Meaning of Aboriginal Title." In *Aboriginal and Treaty Rights in Canada,* ed. Michael Asch, 135-54. Vancouver: UBC Press, 1997.

–. "Negotiated Sovereignty: Indian Treaties and the Acquisition of American and Canadian Territorial Rights in the Pacific Northwest." In *The Power of Promises: Perspectives on Treaties with Native Peoples of the Pacific Northwest,* ed. Alexandra Harmon, 35-55. Seattle: University of Washington Press, 2008.

–. "The Onus of Proof of Aboriginal Title." *Osgoode Hall Law Journal* 37 (1999): 775-803.

–. "Racial Discrimination and Unilateral Extinguishment of Native Title." *Australian Indigenous Law Reporter* 1 (1996): 181-221.

–. "Self-Government and the Inalienability of Aboriginal Title." *McGill Law Journal* 47 (2002): 473-510.

–. "Sovereignty and the Aboriginal Nations of Rupert's Land." *Manitoba History* 37 (1999): 2-8.

–. "The Vulnerability of Indigenous Land Rights in Australia and Canada." *Osgoode Hall Law Journal* 42 (2004): 271-301.

McNeil, Kent, and David Yarrow. "Has Constitutional Recognition of Aboriginal Rights Adversely Affected Their Definition?" *Supreme Court Law Review* 37 (2007): 177-212.

McRae, Heather, Garth Nettheim, Laura Beacroft, and Luke McNamara. *Indigenous Legal Issues: Commentary and Materials.* 3rd ed. Sydney: Lawbook, 2003.

Mead, Elwood. *Irrigation Institutions.* London: Macmillan, 1907.

Mead, George Herbert. *Mind, Self, and Society.* Chicago: University of Chicago Press, 1934.

Merlan, Francesca. "Assessment of von Doussa on Anthropology [in *Chapman v. Luminis Pty Ltd*]." In *The Hindmarsh Island Federal Court Decision: Implications for Anthropological and Legal Practice,* 1-12. Centre for Aboriginal Economic and Policy Research, Australian National University, 2001. http://www.aas.asn.au/Hindmarsconf/Merlan.pdf.

Miller, J.R. *Compact, Contract, Covenant: Aboriginal Treaty-Making in Canada.* Toronto: University of Toronto Press, 2009.

–. *Skyscrapers Hide the Heavens: A History of Indian-White Relations in Canada.* 3rd ed. Toronto: University of Toronto Press, 2000.

Miller, Mark Edwin. *Forgotten Tribes: Unrecognized Indians and the Federal Acknowledgement Process.* Lincoln: University of Nebraska Press, 2004.

Miller, Matthew. "An Australian Nunavut? A Comparison of Inuit and Aboriginal Rights Movements in Canada and Australia." *Emory International Law Review* 12 (1998).

Mingay, Gordon Edmund. *Parliamentary Enclosure in England: An Introduction to Its Causes, Incidence, and Impact, 1750-1850.* New York: Longman, 1997.

Moeke-Pickering, Taima. *Maori Identity within Whanau: A Review of Literature.* Hamilton, NZ: University of Waikato, 1996.

Montagu, Ashley. *Man's Most Dangerous Myth: The Fallacy of Race.* New York: Columbia University Press, 1942.

Moore, Bette. "The Victorian Aboriginal Land Council." In *Aborigines, Land, and Land Rights,* ed. Nicolas Peterson and Marcia Langton, 241-49. Canberra: Australian Institute of Aboriginal Studies, 1983.

Morgan, Lewis Henry. *Ancient Society.* 1877; reprint, New York: Holt, 1907.

Morris, Alexander. *The Treaties of Canada with the Indians of Manitoba and the North-West Territories Including the Negotiations on Which They Were Based and Other Information Relating Thereto.* Toronto: Bedfords, Clarke, 1880 [1991 rpt.]

Morton, John. "I-Witnessing I the Witness: A Response to Ken Maddock on Courtly Truth and Native Title Anthropology." *Asia Pacific Journal of Anthropology* 3 (2002): 89-97.

Munzer, Stephen R. *A Theory of Property.* Cambridge, UK: Cambridge University Press, 1990.

Napoleon, Val. "Extinction by Number: Colonialism Made Easy." *Canadian Journal of Law and Society* 16, 1 (2001).

Neeson, Jeannette M. *Commoners: Common Right, Enclosure, and Social Change in England, 1700-1820.* New York: Cambridge University Press, 1993.

Nettelbeck, Amanda, and Robert Foster. *In the Name of the Law: William Willshire and the Policing of the Australian Frontier.* Kent Town, SA: Wakefield Press, 2007.

Nettheim, Garth. "The Influence of Canadian and International Law on the Evolution of Australian Aboriginal Title." In *Let Right Be Done: Aboriginal Title, the Calder Case, and the Future of Indigenous Rights,* ed. Hamar Foster, Heather Raven, and Jeremy Webber, 177-97. Vancouver: UBC Press, 2007.

New Zealand Law Commission. *Maori Custom and Values in New Zealand Law.* Study Paper 9. Wellington: New Zealand Law Commission, 2001.

Newman, Peter, ed. *The New Palgrave Dictionary of Economics and the Law.* London: Macmillan Reference, 1998.

Niezen, Ronald. *The Origins of Indigenism: Human Rights and the Politics of Identity.* Berkeley: University of California Press, 2003.

Nigol, Paul N. "Discipline and Discretion in the Mid-Eighteenth-Century Hudson's Bay Company Private Justice System." In *Laws and Societies in the Canadian Prairie West, 1670-1940,* ed. Louis A. Knafla and Jonathan Swainger, 150-82. Vancouver: UBC Press, 2005.

Nygh, Peter E., and Peter Butt, eds. *Butterworths Australian Legal Dictionary.* Sydney: Butterworths, 1997.

O'Connell, Daniel Patrick. *State Succession in Municipal Law and International Law.* Vol. 1. Cambridge, UK: Cambridge University Press, 1967.

Odawi, Porter Robert, ed. *Sovereignty, Colonialism, and the Indigenous Nations: A Reader.* Durham: Carolina Academic Press, 2005.

Odgers, Stephen. "Criminal Cases in the High Court of Australia." *Criminal Law Journal* 19 (1995): 95-99.

Oliver, Edmund Henry, ed. *The Canadian North-West: Its Early Development and Legislative Records.* Vol. 1. Ottawa: Government Printing Bureau, 1915.

Opp, Karl-Dieter. "Norms." In *International Encyclopaedia of the Social and Behavioral Sciences,* vol. 16, ed. Neil J. Smelser and Paul B. Baltes, 10714-20. Amsterdam: Elsevier, 2001.

Otis, Ghislain. "Territoriality, Personality, and the Promotion of Aboriginal Legal Traditions in Canada." In *Indigenous Legal Traditions,* Law Commission of Canada, 136-68. Vancouver: UBC Press, 2006.

Otter, Albert Andy den. *Irrigation in Southern Alberta, 1882-1901.* Lethbridge: Historical Society of Alberta, 1975.

Outhwaite, William, and Tom Bottomore, eds. *The Blackwell Dictionary of Twentieth-Century Social Thought.* Oxford: Blackwell, 1993.

Pagden, Anthony. "Dispossessing the Barbarian: The Language of Spanish Thomism and the Debate over the Property Rights of the American Indians." In *The Language of Political Theory in Early Modern Europe,* ed. Anthony Pagden, 79-98. Cambridge: Cambridge University Press, 1987.

Palmer, K. "Forensic Anthropology." In *Expert Evidence,* ed. Ian Freckleton and Hugh Selby, 931-38. Sydney: Law Book Company, 1993.

Parkman, Francis. *The California and Oregon Trail; Being Sketches of Prairie and Rocky Mountain Life,* ed. Charles H.J. Douglas. 1910; reprint, New York: Macmillan 1949.

Parsonson, Ann. "The Fate of Maori Land Rights in Early Colonial New Zealand: The Limits of the Treaty of Waitangi and the Doctrine of Aboriginal Title." In *Law, History, Colonialism: The Reach of Empire,* ed. Diane Kirkby and Catherine Coleborne, 173-89. Manchester: Manchester University Press, 2001.

Pearce, Dennis C., and Robert S. Geddes. *Statutory Interpretation in Australia.* 3rd ed. Sydney: Butterworths, 1988.

Pearson, Noel. "The Concept of Native Title at Common Law." In *Our Land Is Our Life: Land Rights – Past, Present, and Future,* ed. Galarrwuy Yunupingu, 150-62. St. Lucia: University of Queensland Press, 1997.

–. "The High Court's Abandonment of 'the Time-Honoured Methodology of the Common Law' in Its Interpretation of Native Title in *Mirriuwong Gajerrong* and *Yorta Yorta.*" Sir Ninian Stephen Annual Lecture, Law School, University of Newcastle, 17 March 2003. http://www.capeyorkpartnerships.com.

–. "Native Title's Days in the Sun Are Over." In *The Age* [Melbourne], 28 August 2002. http://www.capeyorkpartnerships.com.

–. "Principles of Communal Native Title." *Indigenous Law Bulletin* 5, 3 (2000): 4-7.

–. "Where We've Come from and Where We're at with the Opportunity that Is Koiki Mabo's Legacy to Australia." 2003 Mabo Lecture, Native Title Representative Bodies Conference, Alice Springs, 3 June 2003. http://www.capeyorkpartnerships.com.

Penner, J.E. "The Analysis of Rights." *Ratio Juris* 10 (1997): 300-15.

–. "The 'Bundle of Rights' Picture of Property." *UCLA Law Review* 43 (1996): 711-820.

–. *The Idea of Property in Law.* Oxford: Clarendon Press, 1997.

Perry, Melissa, and Stephen Lloyd. *Australian Native Title Law.* Sydney: Lawbook, 2003.

Persky, Stan, ed. *Delgamuukw: The Supreme Court of Canada Decision on Aboriginal Title.* Vancouver: Greystone Books, 1998.

Peterson, Jaqueline, and Jennifer S.H. Brown, eds. *The New Peoples: Being and Becoming Métis in North America.* Winnipeg: University of Manitoba Press, 1985.

Peterson, Nicolas. *Aboriginal Land Rights: A Handbook.* Canberra: Australian Institute of Aboriginal Studies, 1981.

–. "Reeves in the Context of the History of Land Rights Legislation: Anthropological Aspects." In *Land Rights at Risk? Evaluations of the* Reeves Report, ed. Jon Altman, F. Morphy, and T. Rowse, 25-31. Canberra: Centre for Aboriginal Economic Policy Research, 1999.

Peterson, Nicolas, and Will Sanders, eds. *Citizenship and Indigenous Australians.* Cambridge, UK: Cambridge University Press, 1998.

Pevar, Stephen L. *The Rights of Indians and Tribes.* 3rd ed. Carbondale: Southern Illinois University Press, 2002.

Pilling, Arnold R., and Richard A. Waterman, eds. *Diprotodon to Detribalization: Studies of Change among Australian Aborigines.* East Lansing: Michigan State University Press, 1970.

Pisani, Donald J. *To Reclaim a Divided West: Water, Law, and Public Policy, 1848-1902.* Albuquerque: University of New Mexico Press, 1992.

Pollock, Frederick, and Frederic William Maitland. *The History of English Law before the Time of Edward I.* 2nd ed. Cambridge, UK: Cambridge University Press, 1968.

Pollock, Frederick, and Robert Samuel Wright. *An Essay on Possession in the Common Law.* Oxford: Clarendon Press, 1888.

Posner, Richard A. *Overcoming Law.* Cambridge, MA: Harvard University Press, 1995.

Povinelli, Elizabeth. *The Cunning of Recognition: Indigenous Alterities and the Making of Australian Multiculturalism.* Durham: Duke University Press, 2002.

Proulx, Craig. *Reclaiming Aboriginal Justice, Identity, and Community.* Saskatoon: Purich Publishing, 2003.

Prucha, Francis Paul. *American Indian Treaties: The History of a Political Anomaly.* Berkeley: University of California Press, 1994.

Radcliffe-Brown, Alfred Reginald. "Patrilineal and Matrilineal Succession." *Iowa Law Review* 20 (1935): 286-303.

Ray, Arthur J. "Anthropology, History, and Aboriginal Rights: Politics and the Rise of Ethnohistory in North America in the 1950s." In *Pedagogies of the Global,* ed. Arif Dirlik, 89-112. Boulder: Paradigm Publishers, 2006.

–. "Constructing and Reconstructing Native History: A Comparative Look at the Impact of Aboriginal and Treaty Rights Claims in North America and Australia." *Native Studies Review* 16 (2005): 15-38.

–. "Creating the Image of the Savage." Special Issue, *Native Studies Review* 6 (2), 13-28.

–. "The Early Economic History of the Gitksan and Wet'suwet'en-Babine Tribal Territories: 1822-30." Unpublished paper, 1985.

–. "Fur Trade History of Gitxzan and Wet'suet'en Territory." *Delgamuukw* Proceedings at Trial, Supreme Court of British Columbia, Smithers Registry No. 0843, 20 March 1989, Exhibit Number 963.

–. *Indians in the Fur Trade: Their Roles as Trappers, Hunters, and Middlemen in the Lands Southwest of Hudson Bay, 1660-1870.* Toronto: University of Toronto Press, 1974.

–. "Kroeber and the California Claims: Historical Particularism and Cultural Ecology in Court." In *Central Sites, Peripheral Visions: Cultural and Institutional Crossings in the History of Anthropology.* Vol. 11 of *History of Anthropology,* ed. Richard Handler, 248-74. Madison: University of Wisconsin Press, 2006.

Ray, Arthur J., and D.B. Freeman. *"Give Us Good Measure": An Economic Analysis of Relations between the Indians and the Hudson's Bay Company before 1763.* Toronto: University of Toronto Press, 1978.

Ray, Arthur J., J.R. Miller, and Frank Tough. *Bounty and Benevolence: A History of Saskatchewan Treaties.* 3rd ed. Montreal/Kingston: McGill-Queen's University Press, 2000.

Raz, Joseph. *The Concept of a Legal System: An Introduction to the Theory of Legal System.* Oxford: Clarendon Press, 1970.

Reeves, John. *Building on Land Rights for the Next Generation: Report of the Review of the Aboriginal Land Rights (Northern Territory) Act 1976.* Canberra: Australian Government Publishing Service, 1998.

Reisner, Marc. *Cadillac Desert: The American West and Its Disappearing Water.* New York: Penguin Books, 1986.

Reynolds, Henry. *The Law of the Land.* 2nd ed. Harmondsworth: Penguin Books, 1992.

Richardson, Benjamin, Shin Imai, and Kent McNeil, eds. *Indigenous Peoples and the Law: Comparative and Critical Perspectives.* Oxford: Hart Publishers, 2009.

Rigsby, Bruce. "Aboriginal People, Land Tenure, and National Parks." *Proceedings of the Royal Society of Queensland* 106 (1996): 11-15.

–. "Aboriginal People, Spirituality, and the Traditional Ownership of Land." *International Journal of Social Economics* 26 (1999): 963-73.

–. "Anthropologists, Indian Title, and the Indian Claims Commission: The California and Great Basin Cases." In *Fighting Over Country: Anthropological Perspectives,* ed. D.E. Smith and J. Finlayson, 15-45. Centre for Aboriginal Economic Policy Research Monograph 12. Canberra: Centre for Aboriginal Economic Policy Research, Australian National University, 1997.

–. "Indigenous Language Shift and Maintenance in Fourth World Settings." *Multilingua: Journal of Cross-Cultural and Interlanguage Communication* 6, 4 (1987): 359-78.

–. "Law and Custom as Anthropological and Legal Terms." In *Heritage and Native Title: Anthropological and Legal Perspectives,* ed. J. Finlayson and A. Jackson-Nakano, 230-52. Canberra: Native Title Research Unit, Australian Institute of Aboriginal and Torres Strait Islander Studies, 1996.

–. "'Race' in Contemporary Anthropology." *Proceedings of the Royal Society of Queensland* 107 (1998): 57-61.

–. "A Survey of Property Theory and Tenure Types." In *Customary Marine Tenure in Australia,* ed. N. Peterson and B. Rigsby, 22-46. Oceania Monograph 48. Sydney: University of Sydney, 1998.

Roberts, Mere, W. Norman, N. Minhinnick, D. Wihongi, and C. Kirkwood. "*Kaitiakitanga*: Mäori Perspectives on Conservation." *Pacific Conservation Biology* 2 (1995): 7-20.

Robertson, Lindsay G. *Conquest by Law: How the Discovery of America Dispossessed Indigenous Peoples of Their Lands.* Oxford: Oxford University Press, 2005.

Robinson, Sheila. "Protohistoric Developments in Gitksan and Wet-suet'en Territories." Unpublished report, 12 May 1987.

Ronaasen, Sheree, Richard O. Clemmer, and Mary Elizabeth Rudden. "Rethinking Cultural Ecology, Multilinear Evolution, and Expert Witnesses: Julian Steward and the Indian Claims Commission Proceedings." In *Julian Steward and the Great Basin: The Making of an Anthropologist,* ed. Richard O. Clemmer, L. Daniel Myers, and Mary Elizabeth Rudden, 170-202. Salt Lake City: University of Utah Press, 1999.

Ross, Monique. "The Dene Tha' Consultation Pilot Project." *Resources: The Newsletter of the Canadian Institute of Resources Law* 76 (2001): 1-4.

Ross, Norman A. *Index to the Expert Testimony before the Indian Claims Commission: The Written Reports.* New York: Clearwater Publisher, 1973.

Rowley, Charles. *The Remote Aborigines.* Canberra: Australian National University Press, 1971.

Rowse, Tim. *Obliged to Be Difficult: Nugget Coombs' Legacy in Indigenous Affairs.* Cambridge, UK: Cambridge University Press, 2000.

Rummery, Ione. "The Role of the Anthropologist as Expert Witness." In *Native Title: Emerging Issues for Research, Policy, and Practice,* ed. J. Finlayson and D.E. Smith, 39-57. Research Monograph No. 10. Canberra: Centre for Aboriginal Economic Policy Research, Australian National University, 1995.

Ruru, Jacinta. "A Politically Fuelled Tsunami: The Foreshore/Seabed Controversy in Aotearoa me te Wai Pounamu/New Zealand." *Journal of Polynesian Society* 113 (2004): 57-72.

–. "What Could Have Been: The Common Law Doctrine of Native Title in Land under Salt Water in Australia and Aotearoa/New Zealand." *Monash University Law Review* 32 (2006): 116-44.

Russell, Peter H. *Recognizing Aboriginal Title: The* Mabo *Case and Indigenous Resistance to English-Settler Colonialism.* Toronto: University of Toronto Press, 2005.

Sanders, Will. *Towards an Indigenous Order of Australian Government.* Discussion Paper No. 230. Canberra: Centre for Aboriginal Economic Policy Research, Australian National University, 2002.

Sapir, Edward. *Culture, Language, and Personality,* ed. David G. Mandelbaum. Los Angeles: University of California Press, 1949.

Schmaltz, Peter S. *The Ojibwa of Southern Ontario.* Toronto: University of Toronto Press, 1991.

Schroder, Mark B. "On the Crest of a Wave: Indigenous Title and Claims to the Water Resource." *New Zealand Journal of Environmental Law* 8 (2004): 1-54.

Seed, Patricia. *Ceremonies of Possession in Europe's Conquest of the New World, 1492-1640.* Cambridge, UK: Cambridge University Press, 1995.

Shurts, John. *Indian Reserved Water Rights: The Winters Doctrine in Its Social and Legal Context, 1880s-1930s.* Norman: University of Oklahoma Press, 2000.

Simmonds, Nigel E. "Introduction." In *Fundamental Legal Conceptions as Applied in Judicial Reasoning,* ed. David Campbell and Philip A. Thomas, ix-xxix. Aldershot: Ashgate Dartmouth, 1995.

Simpson, Alfred William Brian. "English Common Law." In *The New Palgrave Dictionary of Economics and the Law,* ed. Peter Newman, vol. 2, 57-60. New York: Stockton Press, 1998.

Simpson, S. Rowton. *Land Law and Registration.* Book 1. London: Her Majesty's Stationery Office, 1976.

Slattery, Brian. "Aboriginal Sovereignty and Imperial Claims." *Osgoode Hall Law Journal* 29 (1991): 681-703.

–. *Ancestral Lands, Alien Laws: Judicial Perspectives on Aboriginal Title.* Saskatoon: Native Law Centre, University of Saskatchewan, 1983.

–. "Making Sense of Aboriginal and Treaty Rights." *Canadian Bar Review* 79 (2000): 196-224.

–. "A Taxonomy of Aboriginal Rights." In *Let Right Be Done: Aboriginal Title, the* Calder *Case, and the Future of Indigenous Rights,* ed. Hamar Foster, Heather Raven, and Jeremy Webber, 111-28. Vancouver: UBC Press, 2007.

Smandych, Russell. "Contemplating the Testimony of 'Others': James Stephen and the Colonial Office, and the Fate of Australian Aboriginal Evidence Acts, *circa* 1839-1849." *Australian Journal of Legal History* 8 (2004): 237-83.

Smelser, Neil J., and Paul B. Baltes, eds. *International Encyclopaedia of the Social and Behavioral Sciences*. Amsterdam: Elsevier, 2001.

Smith, Benjamin R. "'All Been Washed Away Now': Tradition, Change, and Indigenous Knowledge in a Queensland Land Claim." In *Negotiating Local Knowledge: Power and Identity in Development*, ed. Johan Pottier, Alan Bicker, and Paul Sillitoe, 121-54. London: Pluto Press, 2003.

–. *Between Places: Aboriginal Decentralization, Mobility, and Territoriality in the Region of Coen, Cape York Peninsula (Queensland, Australia)*. London: University of London Press, 2001.

Smith, Clay, and Hardy Myers. "Indian Status and the Fifth Amendment Due Process Clause." In *American Indian Law Deskbook: Conference of Western Attorneys General*, 3rd ed., ed. Clay Smith and Hardy Myers. Boulder: University Press of Colorado, 2004.

Sollors, Werner. "Ethnic Groups/Ethnicity: Historical Aspects." In *International Encyclopaedia of the Social and Behavioral Sciences*, vol. 7, ed. Neil J. Smelser and Paul B. Baltes, 4813-17. Amsterdam: Elsevier, 2001.

Sommer, Bruce A. "Kunjen: Kinship and Communication." MA thesis, Northern Territory University [Darwin], 1998.

Sosin, Jack M. *Whitehall and the Wilderness: The Middle West in British Colonial Policy, 1760-1775*. Lincoln: University of Nebraska Press, 1961.

Splitting the Sky and She Keeps the Door. *From Attica to Gustafsen Lake*. Chase, BC: John Pasquale Boncore, 2001.

St. Germain, Jill. *Indian Treaty-Making Policy in the United States and Canada, 1867-1877*. Lincoln: University of Nebraska Press, 2001.

Stein, Peter. *The Character and Influence of the Roman Civil Law: Historical Essays*. London: Hambledon Press, 1988.

Steward, Julian H. "Carrier Acculturation: The Direct Historical Approach." In *Culture in History: Essays in Honor of Paul Rabin*, ed. Stanley Diamond, 732-44. New York: Columbia University Press, 1961.

–. "Recording Culture Changes among the Carrier Indians of British Columbia." In *Exploration and Field Work of the Smithsonian Institution in 1940*, 83-90. Washington, DC: Smithsonian Institution, 1941.

–. *Theory of Culture Change: The Methodology of Multilinear Evolution*. Urbana: University of Illinois Press, 1955.

–. "Theory and Practice in a Social Science." *Ethnohistory* 4 (1955): 292-93.

Stocking, George W. *Delimiting Anthropology: Occasional Essays and Reflections*. Madison: University of Wisconsin Press, 2001.

Stoeckel, Kate. "Case Note: *Western Australia v. Ward*." *Sydney Law Review* 25 (2003): 255-75.

Strack, Mick. "Customary Title over the Foreshore and Seabed of Aotearoa: A Property Rights Perspective." *Trans Tasman Surveyor* 6 (2004): 44-51.

Strelein, Lisa. *Compromised Jurisprudence: Native Title Cases since Mabo*. Canberra: Aboriginal Studies Press, 2006.

Sullivan, Ruth. *Driedger on the Construction of Statutes*. 3rd ed. Toronto: Butterworths, 1994.

Supiot, Alain. *Homo Juridicus: On the Anthropological Function of the Law*. London: Verso, 2007.

Sutton, Imre, ed. *Irredeemable America: The Indians' Estate and Land Claims*. Albuquerque: University of New Mexico Press, 1985.

Sutton, Peter. *Aboriginal Country Groups and the "Community of Native Title Holders."* National Native Title Tribunal Occasional Papers Series No. 1/2001. Perth: National Native Title Tribunal, 2001. http://www.nntt.gov.au.

–. *Dreamings: The Art of Aboriginal Australia*. Ringwood, Victoria: Viking Penguin Books Australia, 1988.

–. *Kinds of Rights in Country: Recognising Customary Rights as Incidents of Native Title*. National Native Title Tribunal Occasional Papers Series No. 2/2001. Perth: National Native Title Tribunal, 2001. http://www.nntt.gov.au.

–. *Native Title in Australia: An Ethnographic Perspective*. Cambridge, UK: Cambridge University Press, 2003.

–. *Native Title and the Descent of Rights.* Perth: National Native Title Tribunal, 1998.
–. "The Robustness of Aboriginal Land Tenure Systems: Underlying and Proximate Customary Titles." *Oceania* 67 (1996): 7-29.
Tanner, Adrian. "The New Hunting Territory Debate: An Introduction to Some Unresolved Issues." *Anthropologica* 28 (1986): 19-36.
Taylor, Alan John Percival. *Beaverbrook.* New York: Simon and Schuster, 1972.
Tindale, Norman B. *Aboriginal Tribes of Australia: Their Terrain, Environmental Controls, Distribution, Limits, and Proper Names.* Berkeley: University of California Press, 1974.
Tomas, Nin. "Implementing *Kaitiakitanga* under the RMA." *New Zealand Environmental Law Reporter* 1, 2 (1992): 39-42.
–. "Key Concepts of Tikanga Maori (Maori Custom Law) and Their Use as Regulators of Human Relationships to Natural Resources in Tai Tokerau, Past and Present." PhD diss., University of Auckland, 2006.
Tomas, Nin, and Kerensa Johnston. "Ask That Taniwha Who Owns the Foreshore and Seabed of Aotearoa." *Te Tai Haruru/Journal of Maori Legal Writing* 1 (2004): 10-52.
Toussaint, Sandy, ed. *Crossing Boundaries: Cultural, Legal, Historical, and Practice in Native Title.* Melbourne: Melbourne University Press, 2004.
Trigger, Bruce G. *The Children of Aataensic: A History of the Huron People to 1600.* Montreal/Kingston: McGill-Queen's University Press, 1976.
Tsosie, Rebecca. "Introduction: Symposium on Cultural Sovereignty." *Arizona State Law Journal* 34, 1 (2002): 1-14.
–. "Tribalism, Constitutionalism, and Cultural Pluralism: Where Do Indigenous People Fit within Civil Society?" *University of Pennsylvania Journal of Constitutional Law* 5 (2003): 357.
Tully, James. "Aboriginal Property and Western Theory: Recovering a Middle Ground." *Social Philosophy and Policy* 11, 2 (1994): 153-80.
United States Justice Department to Erminie Wheeler-Voegelin, 29 August 1956. Wheeler-Voegelin Papers, Indiana University, box 1/3.
Van Drunen, David. *Law and Custom: The Thought of Thomas Aquinas and the Future of the Common Law.* New York: Peter Lang, 2003.
Van Meijl, Toon, and Franz von Benda-Beckmann, eds. *Property Rights and Economic Development: Land and Natural Resources in Southeast Asia and Oceania.* London: Kegan Paul International, 1999.
Vattel, Emmerich de. *The Law of Nations.* Trans. Joseph Chitty. Philadelphia: T. and J.W. Johnson, 1863.
Von Savigny's Treatise on Possession, or, The Jus Possessionis *of the Civil Law* [1803], trans. Sir Erskine Perry (London: S. Sweet, 1848).
Waitangi Tribunal. *Report on the Crown's Foreshore and Seabed Policy.* Wellington: Wai 1071, 2004. http://www.waitangi-tribunal.govt.nz.
–. *Te Whanganui a Tara Me Ona Takiwa: Report on the Wellington District.* Wellington: Wai 145, 2003.
Waldron, J. *The Right to Private Property.* Oxford: Clarendon Press, 1988.
Wallace, Anthony F.C. "Political Organization and Land Tenure among the Northeastern Indians, 1600-1830." *Southwestern Journal of Anthropology* 13 (1957): 301-21.
Walters, Mark. "British Imperial Constitutional Law and Aboriginal Rights: A Comment on *Delgamuukw v. British Columbia." Queen's Law Journal* 17 (1992): 350-413.
–. "The Extension of Colonial Criminal Jurisdiction over the Aboriginal Peoples of Upper Canada: Reconsidering the *Shawanakiskie* Case (1822-26)." *University of Toronto Law Journal* 46 (1996): 273-310.
–. "The 'Golden Thread' of Continuity: Aboriginal Customs at Common Law and under the *Constitution Act, 1982." McGill Law Journal* 44 (1999): 711-52.
–. "*Mohegan Indians v. Connecticut* (1705-1773) and the Legal Status of Aboriginal Customary Laws and Government in British North America." *Osgoode Hall Law Journal* 33 (1995): 785-92.
–. "Towards a 'Taxonomy' for the Common Law: Legal History and the Recognition of Aboriginal Customary Law." In *Law, History, Colonialism: The Reach of Empire,* ed. Diane Kirkby and Catherine Coleborne, 125-39. Manchester: Manchester University Press, 2001.

Wand, Paul, and Chris Athanasiou. *Review of the Native Title Claims Process in Western Australia: Report to the Government of Western Australia.* Perth: Western Australian Government, 2001.

Weinberg, Albert K. *Manifest Destiny: A Study of Nationalist Expansion in American History.* Chicago: Quadrangle Books, 1963.

Weiner, James F. "Diaspora, Materialism, Tradition: Anthropological Issues in the Recent High Court Appeal of the Yorta Yorta." *Land, Rights, Laws: Issues of Native Title* 2, 18 (2002): 1-12.

Wheen, Nicola R. "A Natural Flow: A History of Water Law in New Zealand." *Otago Law Review* 9, 1 (1997): 71-110.

Whorf, Benjamin Lee. *Language, Thought, and Reality.* Ed. John B. Carroll. Cambridge, MA: MIT Press, 1956.

Wilkins, David E., and K. Tsianina Lomawaima, eds. *Uneven Ground: American Indian Sovereignty and Federal Law.* Norman: Oklahoma University Press, 2001.

Wilkinson, Charles F. *Crossing the Next Meridian: Land, Water, and the Future of the West.* Washington, DC: Island Press, 1992.

Williams, David V. "Customary Rights and Crown Claims: *Calder* and Aboriginal Title in Aotearoa New Zealand." In *Let Right Be Done: Aboriginal Title, the Calder Case, and the Future of Indigenous Rights,* ed. Hamar Foster, Heather Raven, and Jeremy Webber, 155-76. Vancouver: UBC Press, 2007.

Williams, Nancy M. *The Yolngu and Their Land: A System of Land Tenure and the Fight for Its Recognition.* Canberra: Australian Institute of Aboriginal Studies, 1986.

Williams, Robert A. Jr. *The American Indian in Western Legal Discourse.* New York: Oxford University Press, 1991.

Wilmer, Franke. *The Indigenous Voice in World Politics: Since Time Immemorial.* Newbury Park: Sage Publications, 1993.

Woodward, Justice. *Aboriginal Land Rights Commission: Second Report April 1974.* Canberra: Government Printer, 1974.

Woolford, Andrew. *Between Justice and Certainty: Treaty Making in British Columbia.* Vancouver: UBC Press, 2005.

Worster, Donald. *Rivers of Empire: Water, Aridity, and the Growth of the American West.* New York: Oxford University Press, 1985.

Wright, Lisa. *Themes Emerging from the High Court's Recent Native Title Decisions.* Perth: Legal Services Section, National Native Title Tribunal, 2003.

Wrong, Dennis H. "The Oversocialized Conception of Man in Modern Sociology." *American Journal of Sociology* 26 (1961): 183-93.

Wunder, John R. *Native American Law and Colonialism.* New York: Garland Publishing, 1996.

–. "No More Treaties: The Resolution of 1871 and the Alteration of the Indian Rights to Their Homelands." In *The Range: Essays on the History of Western Land Management and the Environment,* ed. John Wunder. Westport, CT: Greenwood Press, 1985.

Wurm, Stephen A. "Aboriginal Languages and the Law." *University of Western Australia Law Review* 6 (1963-64): 1-10.

–. "Native Criminal Jurisdiction after *Mabo*." *Current Issues in Criminal Justice* 6 (1994): 9-26.

Young, Simon. *The Trouble with Tradition: Native Title and Cultural Change.* Leichhardt, NSW: Federation Press, 2008.

Zavala, Silvio. "Fray Alonso de la Veracruz, iniciador del derecho agrario en México." In Mauricio Beuchot et al., *Homenaje a fray Alonso de la Veracruz en el cuarto centenario de su muerte (1584-1984),* 54-66. México: Universidad Nácional Autónoma de México, Instituto de Investigaciones Jurídicas, 1986, available at bibliojuridica.org/libros.

Zlotkin, Norman K. "Judicial Recognition of Aboriginal Customary Law in Canada: Selected Marriage and Adoption Cases." *Canadian Native Law Reporter* 4 (1984): 1-17.

Contributors

Brian Ballantyne is a lawyer who serves as Advisor to the Surveyor General and International Boundary Commissioner, within the Surveyor General Branch, Natural Resources Canada. He has degrees in surveying, geography, environmental ethics, and law; has published widely; and has lectured at universities in New Zealand and Canada. He has been retained as an expert to provide opinions on parcel boundaries, riparian issues, and survey law on thirteen litigation and negotiation files, by five land-surveying associations, and as a consultant in Canada, New Zealand, Brazil, Russia, and Ethiopia.

Paul L.A.H. Chartrand, IPC, Indigenous Peoples Counsel of the Canadian Indigenous Bar Association and formerly Professor of Law at the University of Saskatchewan, has held university appointments in Canada, Australia, New Zealand, and the United States and has been an advisor to Indigenous organizations on domestic and international matters. His professional work, interests, and numerous publications are mainly in the areas of law and policy relating to Indigenous peoples. He was the first President and CEO of the Institute on Indigenous Government founded by the Union of B.C. Indian Chiefs in 1996-97 and Head of Native Studies at the University of Manitoba in the period 1983-91. His public service includes appointments as a commissioner on the Royal Commission on Aboriginal Peoples (1991-95), on the Manitoba Aboriginal Justice Implementation Commission (1999-2001), and as a founding director on the board of the Aboriginal Healing Foundation (1998-99).

Peter W. Hutchins holds an LLL from Laval University and an LLM in international law from the London School of Economics, University of London. During his 38 years of practice devoted exclusively to Aboriginal peoples, Mr. Hutchins has been involved extensively in treaty negotiation, as well as trial and appellate litigation including numerous appearances before the Supreme Court of Canada, the United Nations Human Rights Committee, and the Inter-American Commission on Human Rights. Acting as counsel for First Nations and Inuit across Canada, he advises on historic and contemporary treaties, Aboriginal rights and title, human rights, environmental, constitutional, economic development, governance, and international law issues. He is a founding member and past-chair of the CBA National Aboriginal Law Section, and he has acted as Special Advisor on Aboriginal Self-Government to the Canadian Minister of Indian Affairs. Currently, he sits on the Rules Committee of the Federal Courts of Canada and its Expert Witness Sub-Committee and focuses on procedural reforms required for Aboriginal litigation. He has taught, written, and spoken extensively on Aboriginal law issues.

Louis Knafla is Professor Emeritus of History, and Director of Socio-Legal Studies, at the University of Calgary. He is a legal historian, and his major research and writing have been in the history of English and Canadian law. He was the editor of the international journal *Criminal Justice History* from 1984 to 2004, and his work on Natives has focused on the interaction of Native customary law with English common law on the Canadian Prairies. Initial thoughts are contained in his introduction to *Laws and Societies in the Canadian Prairie West, 1670-1940* (2005). He is currently part of a joint comparative research project with scholars at the Universities of Adelaide and Manitoba on Policing the Canadian and Australian Frontiers of Settlement, a collaboration to examine patterns of settlement and Native conflict, in comparative and transnational terms, that created "national memories" and a "truth" of the national past.

Kenichi Matsui is a new historian of Native rights and issues. A graduate of the University of British Columbia, Vancouver, he wrote his doctoral dissertation on "Reclaiming Indian Waters: Dams, Irrigation, and Indian Water Rights in Western Canada, 1858-1930," and his MA thesis at Arizona State University was on "Americanizing Indian Water: Agrarianism and Irrigation Projects at Navajo, Salt River, and Fort McDowell." A rising expert on Natives, irrigation, and water rights, he has a number of publications in this area ranging from the US southwest to Alberta and British Columbia, including "White Man Has No Right to Take Any of It" (2005) and *Native Peoples and Water Rights* (McGill-Queen's University Press, 2009). He is assistant professor in sustainable environmental studies at the University of Tsukuba, Japan.

Kent McNeil is a Distinguished Research Professor, Osgoode Hall Law School, York University, Toronto. He held a Killam Research Fellowship in 2007-8. His research focuses on the rights of indigenous peoples in Canada, Australia, the United States, and New Zealand. He has also acted as a consultant to First Nations on Aboriginal and treaty rights in the contexts of hydroelectric development, land claims, and self-government. He has published widely on indigenous issues, and his work has been relied on in leading judicial decisions on indigenous land rights in Canada and Australia, including *Delgamuukw* and *Mabo*. He has written two books, *Common Law Aboriginal Title* (1989) and *Emerging Justice? Essays on Indigenous Rights in Canada and Australia* (2001), and recently co-edited a collection of essays by leading indigenous and non-indigenous scholars entitled *Indigenous Peoples and the Law: Comparative and Critical Perspectives* (2009). He is currently examining the factual and legal bases for European assertions of sovereignty in North America, and the implications of these assertions for self-government.

Nicolas Peterson is professor in Anthropology in the School of Archaeology and Anthropology, Australian National University. He was awarded the Lucy Mair Medal for Applied Anthropology from the Royal Anthropological Institute of Great Britain and Ireland for contributing to "facilitating the recognition of Aboriginal rights in Australia, supported by rigorous anthropological scholarship." He has participated in nine major land claim and Native title fieldwork-based anthropological reports documenting the systems of tenure from the Torres Strait to southern Australia. A collaborator in several works with Bruce Rigsby, another author in this book, he has written most recently articles titled "The Modernising of the Indigenous Domestic Moral Economy" (2004) and "The Myth of the 'Walkabout'" (2004).

Arthur J. Ray, FRSC, is Professor Emeritus of History, University of British Columbia, Vancouver. He has held consultancies for Aboriginal land claims in Ontario, Saskatchewan, Alberta, and British Columbia, and he has served as an expert witness in several Native cases, including *Delgamuukw*. He held a Canada Council National Killam Research Fellowship in 2000-2, a Woodrow Wilson International Fellowship and a Bora Laskin National Fellowship in Human Rights in 2005-6, and his book *I Have Lived Here Since the World Began* (2002 [1996]) has won several honours. After an earlier career that focused on the Hudson's Bay Company and the fur trade, where he contributed some of the path-breaking historiography, and then on ethnohistory, genealogies, and kinship, he now focuses on Aboriginal title and treaty rights research in Australia, Canada, New Zealand, and the United States and on the problems of expert witness testimony.

Bruce Rigsby is Professor Emeritus of Anthropology, School of Social Science, University of Queensland, Australia. He has written reports for tribal councils and given expert opinion in the *Delgamuukw* case. He has written on Aboriginal people with regard to spirituality, land ownership, and title and on the role of anthropologists in land claims in Australia, Canada, and the United States. He is deeply concerned with the problem of objectivity in anthropological and historical research and with how it relates to testimony, oral and written, in cases tried before the courts, as reflected in his papers on "Aboriginal People, Spirituality, and the Traditional Ownership of Land" (1999) and "Representations of Culture" (2001).

Jacinta Ruru is Senior Lecturer in Law at the University of Otago, Dunedin, New Zealand. She received her LLB at Otago in 1999 and her LLM "with distinction" in 2002. Her LLM thesis was entitled "Te Tiriti o Waitangi and the Management of National Parks in New Zealand," which received the Inaugural Māori Academic Excellence Award for Law. The recipient of a Fulbright Travel Award for travel through the United States in 2002 talking on indigenous rights issues, she is a director on the Ngai Tahu Māori Law Centre Board and a New Zealand Law Society Māori women's representative. Her recent research and writing have focused on legislation for managing private land for public (and Aboriginal) benefit, the implications of current environmental management for the Māori, and the rights and obligations of their trustees and beneficiaries. She has published two chapters in Māori in the award-winning book *Relationship Property on Death* (2004).

Haijo Jan Westra is Professor of Greek and Roman Studies, University of Calgary. A keen student of Aboriginal problems from the Greco-Roman world to the colonial era of European contact in North America, he is currently studying the contacts of European missionaries with Native peoples in North America from Mexico to Canada. He has made some surprising discoveries regarding missionary-Native contact by taking a fresh look at the Latin writings of the early Jesuit missionaries and has recently published a paper on the influence of classical and biblical sources on missionary views of Native peoples, "The Sources of the Earliest Latin Descriptions of Canada and First Nations by the Jesuits," with Milo Nikolic and Alison Mercer, in *Fons Luminis* 1 (2009): 61-82. His article entitled "Références classiques implicites et explicites dans les écrits des Jésuites sur la Nouvelle-France" is forthcoming.

David Yarrow is a young scholar who has a LLB (1995) and LLM (1997) from the University of Queensland, Brisbane, Australia, and a MSc (1999) from Griffith University, Brisbane. Currently Lecturer in the Faculty of Law, Monash University, he has focused his research and writing on government policy and legislation in Native title grants, the impacts of public and private ownership of natural resources on Native title, and the problem of including Native participation in negotiating impact assessments in Australia and North America. He has been concerned with the use and abuse of the law in Native title litigation on both continents and with the problem of language in this litigation – translation and biculturality.

General Index

Index of Cases

Index of Statutes, Treaties, and Agreements

Patrick James
Constitutional Politics in Canada after the Charter: Liberalism, Communitarianism, and Systemism (2010)

Janet Mosher and Joan Brockman (eds.)
Constructing Crime: Contemporary Processes of Criminalization (2010)

Stephen Clarkson and Stepan Wood
A Perilous Imbalance: The Globalization of Canadian Law and Governance (2009)

Amanda Glasbeek
Feminized Justice: The Toronto Women's Court, 1913-34 (2009)

Kimberley Brooks (ed.)
Justice Bertha Wilson: One Woman's Difference (2009)

Wayne V. McIntosh and Cynthia L. Cates
Multi-Party Litigation: The Strategic Context (2009)

Renisa Mawani
Colonial Proximities: Crossracial Encounters and Juridical Truths in British Columbia, 1871-1921 (2009)

James B. Kelly and Christopher P. Manfredi (eds.)
Contested Constitutionalism: Reflections on the Canadian Charter of Rights and Freedoms (2009)

Catherine E. Bell and Robert K. Paterson (eds.)
Protection of First Nations Cultural Heritage: Laws, Policy, and Reform (2008)

Hamar Foster, Benjamin L. Berger, and A.R. Buck (eds.)
The Grand Experiment: Law and Legal Culture in British Settler Societies (2008)

Richard J. Moon (ed.)
Law and Religious Pluralism in Canada (2008)

Catherine E. Bell and Val Napoleon (eds.)
First Nations Cultural Heritage and Law: Case Studies, Voices, and Perspectives (2008)

Douglas C. Harris
Landing Native Fisheries: Indian Reserves and Fishing Rights in British Columbia, 1849-1925 (2008)

Peggy J. Blair
Lament for a First Nation: The Williams Treaties in Southern Ontario (2008)

Lori G. Beaman
Defining Harm: Religious Freedom and the Limits of the Law (2007)

Stephen Tierney (ed.)
Multiculturalism and the Canadian Constitution (2007)

Julie Macfarlane
The New Lawyer: How Settlement Is Transforming the Practice of Law (2007)

Kimberley White
Negotiating Responsibility: Law, Murder, and States of Mind (2007)

Dawn Moore
Criminal Artefacts: Governing Drugs and Users (2007)

Hamar Foster, Heather Raven, and Jeremy Webber (eds.)
Let Right Be Done: Aboriginal Title, the Calder Case, and the Future of Indigenous Rights (2007)

Dorothy E. Chunn, Susan B. Boyd, and Hester Lessard (eds.)
Reaction and Resistance: Feminism, Law, and Social Change (2007)

Margot Young, Susan B. Boyd, Gwen Brodsky, and Shelagh Day (eds.)
Poverty: Rights, Social Citizenship, and Legal Activism (2007)

Rosanna L. Langer
Defining Rights and Wrongs: Bureaucracy, Human Rights, and Public Accountability (2007)

C.L. Ostberg and Matthew E. Wetstein
Attitudinal Decision Making in the Supreme Court of Canada (2007)

Chris Clarkson
Domestic Reforms: Political Visions and Family Regulation in British Columbia, 1862-1940 (2007)

Jean McKenzie Leiper
Bar Codes: Women in the Legal Profession (2006)

Gerald Baier
Courts and Federalism: Judicial Doctrine in the United States, Australia, and Canada (2006)

Avigail Eisenberg (ed.)
Diversity and Equality: The Changing Framework of Freedom in Canada (2006)

Randy K. Lippert
Sanctuary, Sovereignty, Sacrifice: Canadian Sanctuary Incidents, Power, and Law (2005)

James B. Kelly
Governing with the Charter: Legislative and Judicial Activism and Framers' Intent (2005)

Dianne Pothier and Richard Devlin (eds.)
Critical Disability Theory: Essays in Philosophy, Politics, Policy, and Law (2005)

Susan G. Drummond
Mapping Marriage Law in Spanish Gitano Communities (2005)

Louis A. Knafla and Jonathan Swainger (eds.)
Laws and Societies in the Canadian Prairie West, 1670-1940 (2005)

Ikechi Mgbeoji
Global Biopiracy: Patents, Plants, and Indigenous Knowledge (2005)

Florian Sauvageau, David Schneiderman, and David Taras, with Ruth Klinkhammer and Pierre Trudel
The Last Word: Media Coverage of the Supreme Court of Canada (2005)

Gerald Kernerman
Multicultural Nationalism: Civilizing Difference, Constituting Community (2005)

Pamela A. Jordan
Defending Rights in Russia: Lawyers, the State, and Legal Reform in the Post-Soviet Era (2005)

Anna Pratt
Securing Borders: Detention and Deportation in Canada (2005)

Kirsten Johnson Kramar
Unwilling Mothers, Unwanted Babies: Infanticide in Canada (2005)

W.A. Bogart
Good Government? Good Citizens? Courts, Politics, and Markets in a Changing Canada (2005)

Catherine Dauvergne
Humanitarianism, Identity, and Nation: Migration Laws in Canada and Australia (2005)

Michael Lee Ross
First Nations Sacred Sites in Canada's Courts (2005)

Andrew Woolford

Between Justice and Certainty: Treaty Making in British Columbia (2005)

John McLaren, Andrew Buck, and Nancy Wright (eds.)
Despotic Dominion: Property Rights in British Settler Societies (2004)

Georges Campeau
From UI to EI: Waging War on the Welfare State (2004)

Alvin J. Esau
The Courts and the Colonies: The Litigation of Hutterite Church Disputes (2004)

Christopher N. Kendall
Gay Male Pornography: An Issue of Sex Discrimination (2004)

Roy B. Flemming
Tournament of Appeals: Granting Judicial Review in Canada (2004)

Constance Backhouse and Nancy L. Backhouse
The Heiress vs the Establishment: Mrs. Campbell's Campaign for Legal Justice (2004)

Christopher P. Manfredi
Feminist Activism in the Supreme Court: Legal Mobilization and the Women's Legal Education and Action Fund (2004)

Annalise Acorn
Compulsory Compassion: A Critique of Restorative Justice (2004)

Jonathan Swainger and Constance Backhouse (eds.)
People and Place: Historical Influences on Legal Culture (2003)

Jim Phillips and Rosemary Gartner
Murdering Holiness: The Trials of Franz Creffield and George Mitchell (2003)

David R. Boyd
Unnatural Law: Rethinking Canadian Environmental Law and Policy (2003)

Ikechi Mgbeoji
Collective Insecurity: The Liberian Crisis, Unilateralism, and Global Order (2003)

Rebecca Johnson
Taxing Choices: The Intersection of Class, Gender, Parenthood, and the Law (2002)

John McLaren, Robert Menzies, and Dorothy E. Chunn (eds.)
Regulating Lives: Historical Essays on the State, Society, the Individual, and the Law (2002)

Joan Brockman
Gender in the Legal Profession: Fitting or Breaking the Mould (2001)

Printed and bound in Canada by Friesens

Set in Stone by Artegraphica Design Co. Ltd.

Copy editor: Dallas Harrison

Proofreader: Jean Wilson